SOUL OF CP/M®

(How to Use the Hidden Power of Your CP/M® System)

by

Mitchell Waite and Robert Lafore

Howard W. Sams & Co., Inc.
4300 WEST 62ND ST. INDIANAPOLIS, INDIANA 46268 USA

FIRST EDITION
SECOND PRINTING—1984

International Standard Book Number: 0-672-22030-X
Library of Congress Catalog Card Number: 83-61059

Edited by: *Frank N. Speights*
Illustrated by: *Kevin Caddell*

Printed in the United States of America.

Preface

* Have you ever wanted to know how the CP/M® operating system *really* works?
* Would you like to use CP/M's hidden power in your own BASIC or assembly language programs?
* Are you a BASIC programmer who would like to learn assembly language, but have been told that it's too complicated?
* Do you need to modify CP/M to work with a particular printer or some other I/O device?
* Do you want to write programs that will work with *any* version of CP/M?

If the answer to any of these questions is yes, then this book, with its unique approach to teaching both CP/M systems calls and 8080 assembly language programming, is for you. Starting with simple three- and four-line programs, we ease you into the "soul" of CP/M: the universal system calls that make CP/M the world's most popular microcomputer operating system. Gradually and easily, you'll learn how to write programs to control all your I/O devices, including the disk system, and, also, perform a variety of other functions.

Remember, you don't need to know how to program in assembly language to understand this book! We'll teach you all the 8080 assembly language that you will need to know and, since you'll be learning the system calls at the same time, your programs will be able to perform powerful functions from the very beginning.

You'll also learn how to use these powerful system calls in your BASIC programs, how CP/M manages disk files, and how to modify CP/M's "BIOS" (Basic Input/Output System) to work with different I/O devices, so that you can customize CP/M for a particular printer or other device.

All in all, if you want to do more with your CP/M system than simply run applications programs, then this book is for you!

MITCHELL WAITE
AND ROBERT LAFORE

Acknowledgments

The authors would like to thank Mark Berger, Phil Chapnick, and Scott Kamins for their many helpful comments, criticisms, and suggestions. Their pioneering journey on the road followed by this book has resulted in removing many obstacles from the path of future readers.

Dedication by Robert Lafore
This book is dedicated to my parents.

Contents

APPENDIX F

APPENDIX G

Introduction

SOUL OF CP/M®

What do we mean by the "Soul" of CP/M? One of CP/M's most pleasant features is its ease of use. The loading of applications programs, the use of such CP/M functions as DIR, STAT, and PIP, and the use of higher-level languages such as BASIC or FORTRAN, are all simple and straightforward

in the CP/M environment. In fact, this efficient facade is all that many users will ever know about CP/M. And yet, below this smooth and easy-going surface, CP/M has a whole different level; a powerful inner structure that is easily used if you know how, which can control your computer's input and output devices, including the disk drives, with a precision and a versatility that is impossible to obtain from a higher-level language. We call this deeper and more powerful level the "Soul" of CP/M and, in this book, you will learn all about it.

WHO IS THIS BOOK FOR?

This book is aimed primarily at BASIC or other high-level language programmers who are working with a CP/M system and need to do more than they can with their higher-level language. If you need to write custom I/O routines, handle disk records in a way not accessible to your high-level language, or use an assembly language routine to add more power or speed to your programs, this book will teach you how to do it.

This book is also aimed at the assembly language programmer who is either not familiar with 8080 assembly language, or who needs to know more about how to program in the CP/M environment.

WHAT THIS BOOK WILL TEACH YOU

First, this book teaches how to use CP/M's built-in system calls. These system calls are the key to programming in a CP/M system, since they allow your program to communicate with a wide variety of I/O devices, using a universal format that works on any CP/M system. Once you've learned how to use these calls, you are freed of the restraints imposed by BASIC or whatever other high-level language you are using. You can *directly* access the video screen, the keyboard, the disk system, and other I/O devices, so that they respond the way *you* want them to, not the way the designers of your particular language decided they should.

Second, you will learn all about the CP/M disk system. You will learn how it is organized, and how you can take control of it for use in your own programs.

Third, you will learn how to "customize" CP/M to work with different I/O devices. Since there is no universally accepted format for the communication between I/O devices and computers, it is almost always necessary to write a special program called a "driver" in order to make your computer work with a new I/O device. CP/M's solid, well-organized, I/O system makes this easy, and we teach you how to do it.

Fourth, and this is thrown in as a sort of fringe benefit, you will learn 8080 assembly language. (If you already know it, that's fine too. We've placed all the descriptive text about assembly language in distinctive boxes, which are easy to skip over if you wish.) As you learn assembly language, you will also be learning the use of the CP/M programs DDT, LOAD, and ASM.

8080, 8080A, 8085, Z-80: WHAT'S THE DIFFERENCE?

A "chip" is the tiny slice of silicon which contains the thousands of transistors that make up a microprocessor. The exact design of this chip determines the "instruction set" of the computer; that is, it determines what commands you have to give it to make it work. Different chips are given different names. One of the most famous is the "8080" chip manufactured by Intel Corporation. After this chip had been in production for a time, Intel improved it by coming out with a faster version called the 8080A. Later, Intel added the 8085 chip, which is very similar to the 8080 and 8080A, except for some improvements in the way that it handles interrupts.

Throughout this book, when we refer to the "8080" microprocessor chip, we are also referring to the 8080A and the 8085. The differences are relatively minor and, in any case, only apply to the interrupt system which we will not be concerned with.

Also, this family of chips is "upward compatible." This means that any program written for an earlier chip (the 8080, say) will run on any later chips (the 8080A and the 8085). Thus, even if we used the interrupt system, by programming for the 8080, we ensure that our programs will run not only on the 8080 but, also, on the 8080A and the 8085 as well.

The Z-80 is a chip manufactured by Zilog. Although it is also upward compatible with the 8080, it has a considerably enlarged instruction set. Generally speaking, programs written for the 8080 will run on the Z-80 as well, although there are exceptions.

What it comes down to is this. The programs that you learn to write for the 8080 microprocessor will also run on the 8080A, the 8085, and (usually) on the Z-80. So, no matter which of these chips is used in your CP/M system, this book will tell you what you need to know to write working programs.

WHAT YOU NEED TO KNOW TO GET THE MOST OUT OF THIS BOOK

Before you start this book, you should have some minimal experience with a CP/M system, including the use of DIR, PIP, and STAT. (If you need to learn CP/M from the ground up, consult *CP/M Primer*, by Stephen Murtha and Mitchell Waite, and *CP/M Bible*, by Mitchell Waite and John Angermeyer.) You should also have at least a nodding acquaintance with a text-editor of some sort, either the ED program that comes with CP/M or another of the many popular text-editors, such as WordStar®.

Also, of course, you need access to a CP/M system, with the programs ASM, DDT, LOAD, and your word-processing program.

This book will not teach you all of the bells and whistles of 8080 assembly language programming. Since our emphasis is on CP/M, we will teach you only enough assembly language to handle the examples in the book. Although this is actually a fairly large chunk of assembly language, if you want to go on and write your own complex applications programs, you should read a good 8080 assembly language primer, such as *8080A–8085 Assembly Language Programming,* by Lance A. Leventhal.

You should probably also have some experience with some programming language, such as BASIC, FORTRAN, or Pascal, before you start this book, so that you are familiar with fundamental programming concepts.

HOW THIS BOOK IS ORGANIZED

Chapter 1 is an introduction to CP/M's organization. You'll learn why CP/M can run on many different computers and why many different programs can run on CP/M. The way CP/M fits into memory will also be explained. Also, we'll talk a little about how 8080 assembly language works, and how DDT can be used to write simple programs.

In Chapter 2, we'll start by writing some very short routines to access the simplest of the systems calls, starting with outputting a single character to the video screen. At the end of the chapter, we'll write an actual program which can be executed directly from CP/M, like any other program. Every step of everything you need to do will be explained in detail, so that no matter how new all this is to you, you can't go wrong!

WordStar is the registered trademark of MicroPro™ International Corp., San Rafael, CA 94901

Chapter 3 will advance further into the realm of system calls and you'll learn how to handle strings of text, both for input from the keyboard and output to the screen. Throughout Chapters 2 and 3, you'll also be learning the rudiments of assembly language, using DDT as a fast and easy way to try out the small programs needed for the examples.

In Chapter 4, we'll introduce you to ASM, the CP/M assembler, which simplifies the writing of larger assembly language programs. You'll also write and operate a useful program–one which translates hexadecimal numbers (the kind the computer uses) to decimal numbers (the kind humans use) and makes use of the system calls you've been learning. (In case you're not familiar with the hexadecimal numbering system, it's described in detail in Appendix A.)

Chapters 5 and 6 cover the disk system. You'll learn about the fundamental building blocks of disk storage: records and files, and how to manage them. You'll also write a variety of programs making use of the disk system calls. These programs will be used to write files and retrieve them from the disk in both sequential and random format, and there will even be a program to count the number of lines and pages in a file. As a bonus, we'll delve into the mysterious world of CP/M file directories and you'll learn how to "rescue" a file which has been mistakenly erased!

Chapter 7 covers a larger program in detail. This is "WORDS", which counts the number of words in a text file. This program will make use of "wildcards" (the use of * and ? in a program name to represent unknown characters). It will also introduce the idea of "stack management," so that you can avoid a variety of pitfalls in your programming.

Chapter 8 deals with how to use system calls and assembly language from BASIC. You'll learn how to "call" assembly language routines from BASIC, how to pass numbers back and forth between BASIC and your assembly language routine, and where to put all these routines in memory. As examples, we'll use routines that allow you to use hexadecimal numbers in BASIC and allow you to convert BASIC string variables from lowercase to uppercase letters. Although BASIC is used as the example language here, many of the techniques described are applicable to other high-level languages as well.

In Chapter 9, we explain how to go about modifying your CP/M to use different I/O devices. A specific example–writing a driver for a particular printer–will be described in detail.

Finally, a number of appendices are given that cover hexadecimal notation and provide summaries of all CP/M system calls, 8080 instructions, and DDT commands. They also include some useful and entertaining programs which make use of the material covered in the book.

HOW TO ENJOY THIS BOOK

This book starts out easily and teaches you more and more as it goes along. For this reason, don't try to understand it by starting in the middle somewhere (unless you're already a hot 8080 and CP/M programmer). Start at the beginning, take it easy, and before you know it, you'll be doing things with your computer that you never dreamed were possible!

CHAPTER 1

The Big Picture

How CP/M Is Organized

In this chapter, we're going to talk, in very general terms, about CP/M itself—how it does what it does and why it's such a popular operating system. Then, we'll present a few fundamental facts about how the 8080 microprocessor works to prepare you for the introduction to 8080 instructions in the next

chapter. And, finally, we'll briefly discuss DDT, a program that lets you write short assembly language programs quickly and easily.

The idea of this chapter is to provide you with a sort of aerial view of the terrain we're going to cover. Don't worry about specific details yet. What we're interested in here is concepts: what an operating system is, how it does what it does, how the computer itself operates, and why we need a program like DDT. In the next chapter, we'll get down to specific examples and, then, the broad outlines described in this chapter will become clearer.

WHAT IS AN OPERATING SYSTEM, ANYWAY?

If you are using a small microcomputer with only a cassette system to store your programs, you probably don't even need an operating system. Generally speaking, a language like BASIC is built into these small computers, and by using BASIC's CSAVE AND CLOAD commands or their equivalent, you can save and load programs from cassettes in much the same way that you would record and play back a musical selection on a tape recorder.

However, when you add a disk system to your computer, things get a little more complicated. Now you can have dozens or even hundreds of programs sitting on a diskette, and you need a way to load a particular one, or list what they all are, or delete one, or rename it. Operating systems were originally devised to handle these kinds of housekeeping chores, and that is all many operating systems do. CP/M, however, goes beyond these simple tasks.

WHAT'S SO GREAT ABOUT CP/M?

CP/M is by far the most popular operating system ever devised for microcomputers. Why is this? One of the main reasons can be summed up in a single word: transportability. "Transportability" means that something can be moved somewhere else and still work in the same way. CP/M has two kinds of transportability, both of which contribute to its popularity.

Program Transportability

An analogy may make clearer what we mean by "program transportability." Imagine an international chain of hotels, scattered across the globe in the major cities of the world. In order that the typical American traveler will feel at home in all of these hotels, they are all constructed and operated so as to be as similar to one another as possible. Thus, the furnishings, the interior decorations, and the food are the same in any city.

For example, if you're staying at one of these hotels in Hong Kong and you order a chicken sandwich, you get a chicken sandwich that is identical, as far as you can tell, to the one you would get if you ordered it in San Francisco, or Madrid, or Bangkok. Of course, even though the sandwich is the same, the way that it is made may vary a great deal from one city to the next. In San Francisco, the hotel employees get their chicken from a restaurant supply house. In Madrid, they get it from a man who drives up to the hotel with a truck full of chickens. And, in some cities, the hotel employees have to run out into the street and *catch* a chicken to make the sandwich.

We can think of these hotels as having two levels: the guest's level, where a chicken sandwich is always the same, and the hotel employee's level, where the making of the sandwich may be very different, depending on the location of the hotel.

A program running on a CP/M system is like a guest staying at one of our hotels. The program "thinks" that it is operating in the same environment, even though it may be runnning one day on one computer and the next day on a very different computer. It's the job of the operating system, as it is the job of the hotel employees, to make the program "feel at home" (that is, operate correctly), wherever it is. One way that CP/M does this is through the use of "system calls."

System Calls

The "system call" is the connection between a program operating in a CP/M environment and the I/O devices that the program wants to use. It is analogous to the hotel guest picking up his phone and calling room service. The system call is essentially a CALL instruction to a subroutine in the input/output section of the operating system. (CALL means "execute subroutine" and is similar to a GOSUB in BASIC.) Since these CALLs are all made in exactly the same way, no matter what machine a program happens to be operating on, the program thinks it is operating in the same environment and will work on many different computers. This is what we mean by program transportability.

System calls do such things as printing a single character on the screen, reading a character from the keyboard, and reading and writing records to disks. In fact, system calls can handle all the input and output in the CP/M system. Since these calls must be made using instructions in 8080 assembly language, they are usually used in assembly language programs, but they can also be used from BASIC or other higher-level language programs if you know how. (We'll cover the use of system calls from BASIC in Chapter 8.)

Machine Transportability

The subroutine that a particular program calls will be different, depending on the actual physical characteristics of the I/O device the program wants to use, just as the hotel employees and their particular method of obtaining a chicken will be different in different cities. This brings us to the second kind of transportability that makcs CP/M so versatile: machine transportability.

The only part of the CP/M operating system that actually interracts with physical input/output devices is called the BIOS, for "Basic Input/Output System." It consists of a number of short separate subroutines, each of which performs an input or output operation on a specific device. These subroutines are easy to modify if a particular piece of I/O equipment (such as a printer or video display) is changed. Thus, it is easy to reconfigure CP/M to make it work with different equipment and on different computers. We'll talk more about the BIOS later.

The diagram shown in Fig. 1-1 illustrates symbolically the relationship of CP/M to its programs and to its operating environment.

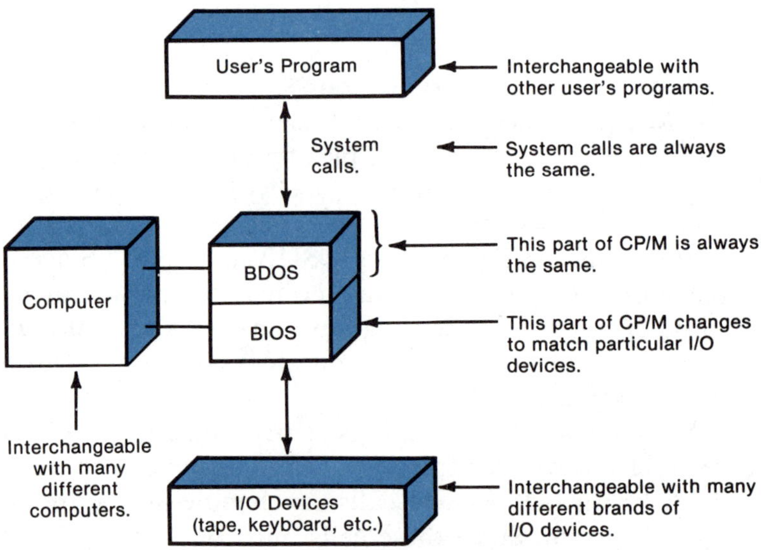

Fig. 1-1. How CP/M is organized.

CP/M's Golden Rule

The preceding ideas can be summarized in what is sometimes called CP/M's Golden Rule: "A call to BDOS on one machine is a call to BDOS on all machines." Or, using our hotel analogy, "A chicken sandwich in one city is a chicken sandwich in all cities." (We'll explain what "BDOS" means in the next section.)

THE PARTS OF CP/M

The CP/M operating system is divided into several parts, each of which occupies a different area of memory. In this section, we'll briefly review these different parts, what they do, and where they're located in memory. The diagram in Fig. 1-2 shows the various parts of the software of a CP/M system, and where they fit in the computer's memory.

First, let's talk about the TPA, or transient program area. This is the part of memory where the user's program goes. This program could be a language interpreter, like BASIC, or it could be an assembly language program written by a user, or it could be one of the utility programs that are part of the CP/M system, like PIP or STAT.

On most CP/M machines, the TPA starts at location 100H, meaning 100 in hexadecimal notation, which is 256 in decimal. (If you don't know any-

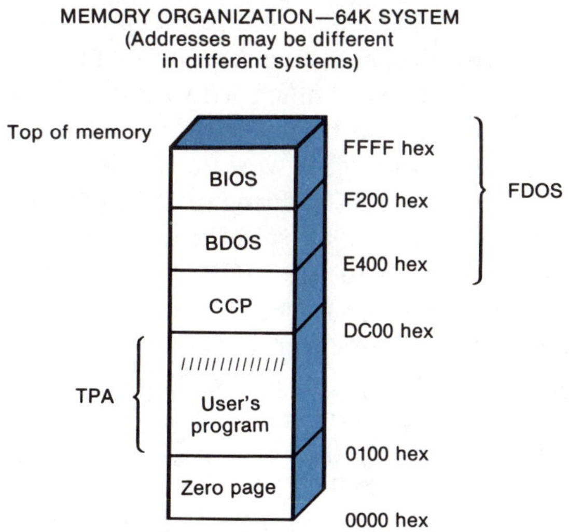

Fig. 1-2. The parts of CP/M.

thing about the hexadecimal numbering system, now is the time to become familiar with it by reading Appendix A.) The size of the TPA is dependent on how much memory your machine has. In a 64K system (the maximum for most systems running CP/M), the TPA will be about 56,000 (decimal) bytes long. (It will probably be a day or two until you are writing programs that large!)

The next part of the CP/M system is called the CCP, for Console Command Processor. This does just what the name says. It deals with commands typed in by the user from the console keyboard. Thus, every time you see the "A>" prompt, it is the CCP that printed it and the CCP is waiting for you to type something in on the keyboard. When you do type something in, the CCP will either deal with your command itself, if it is a "resident command" like DIR or TYPE, or it will call another program if it is a "transient command" like STAT or PIP. The CCP might start at around DC00 hex, in a 64K system, and will occupy about 2000 (decimal) bytes.

Although the CCP must listen to your commands that are typed at the keyboard, read and write files to the disk system, and send messages to the screen, it doesn't carry out these actual input/output operations itself. For that, it must call on the next part of the CP/M operating system, the BDOS.

The BDOS, for "Basic Disk Operating System," is located just above the CCP in memory. BDOS handles all requests for input and output made by your program. This includes the reading and writing of information from and to disks, the maintaining of a directory of disk files, and the allocation of the space that these files occupy on the disk.

BDOS also acts as a sort of intermediary for system calls that you make to nondisk devices such as the keyboard and the video console. Sometimes BDOS does not do very much with these calls itself, but merely passes them along to the BIOS portion of CP/M (which we'll describe next). Other times, it needs to do considerable work to prepare data for the BIOS. For instance, if you tell BDOS to print a string of characters on the video screen (the "Print String" system call), BDOS will break the string up into individual characters before sending it on to the BIOS, since the BIOS driver routine only deals with one character at a time.

Like the CCP, BDOS is entirely independent of the particular computer or disk-system it is being run on, so it does not have to be changed when it is moved to a different system.

Finally, we come to the part of CP/M which actually communicates with the outside world: the BIOS (for Basic Input/Output System). The BIOS, as we've mentioned before, contains the subroutines that actually communicate with I/O devices like the disk drives and the console and the printer. It is these subroutines which must be modified when the hardware is changed in a particular system. BIOS reaches all the way to the top of memory: FFFF (hex), or 65535 (decimal), in a 64K system.

Since the BIOS is the only part of the CP/M system that communicates with the physical devices in the outside world, it's the only part that has to be changed if the devices are changed. The systems calls, by which a program communicates with BDOS, are always the same, no matter how BIOS must be rewritten to accommodate some strange new printer or disk drive.

BDOS and BIOS together are sometimes called "FDOS." This stands for "Full Disk Operating System." When you do a "cold boot"—by hitting the reset switch on your computer, for example—both the CCP and FDOS are loaded into the computer's memory from the disk. When you do a "warm boot"—by hitting the control–c key—only the CCP is loaded in.

These various parts of CP/M can also be thought of as being arranged in layers, like an onion (Fig. 1-3). On the outside is the user, who communicates with the CCP. Or, there is the user's program. Either the CCP or the user's program communicates with the BDOS. BDOS, in turn, communicates with BIOS. And the BIOS, finally, communicates with the actual I/O devices, like the disk drives and the console.

There is another section of memory which, although small, is very important in the operation of the CP/M. This is the so-called "page zero", or those addresses from 0 to FF (hex) that are located just below the start of the TPA. The CP/M uses this area mainly for passing information of various kinds back and forth between the CP/M system and the user's program. For instance, locations 6 and 7 contain the lowest address used by the CCP. This lets a program figure out just how much room it has for itself in memory.

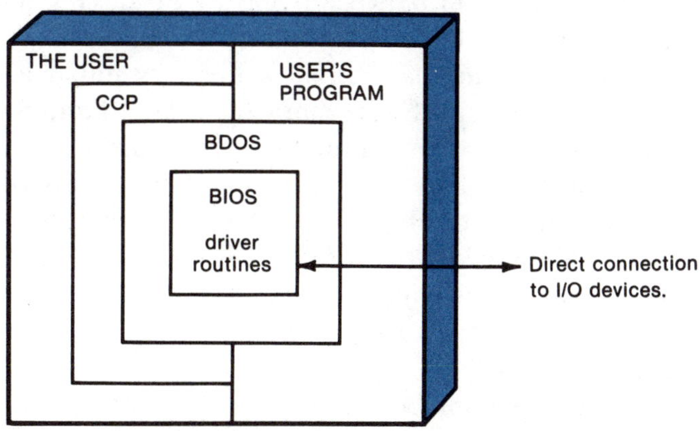

Fig. 1-3. CP/M is like an onion.

(For example, BASIC can look at these locations and determine how large a user program it can accept). We'll cover other uses of page zero as we explore the workings of the disk system.

8080 ARCHITECTURE

In this section, we're going to describe a few fundamentals about how computers work on the assembly language level. (If you're already familiar with assembly language, you can skip to the next section.)

For a programmer, a computer can be thought of as consisting of two parts: the memory and the CPU. The CPU, or Central Processing Unit, contains a number of *registers*. We'll talk about memory first and, then, describe what registers are and what they do.

Memory

As you already know, a computer's memory consists of a large number of things called "bytes" (65,536 of them in a 64K system). On the kind of computers that we will be talking about (those that run standard CP/M), each of these bytes consists of 8 bits, where each bit is represented by either a binary digit 1 or 0. All computer programs, and much of the data they operate on, are stored in memory; that is, they occupy a number of these memory locations. You can think of these memory locations as little boxes, each with an "address" (a number between 0 and FFFF hex) to identify it, that are capable of holding one 8-bit byte.

Fig. 1-4 shows how a section of memory might look if the word "CAT" was stored in it in ASCII characters. This section of memory may look "upside down" to you, with the low numbers above the high numbers. Unfortunately, there are two more or less standard ways of showing memory. Big blocks of memory are shown with the high numbers on top, as in the diagram of BIOS, TPA, etc., that is given in Fig. 1-2. But when small sections of memory are shown, the small numbers are at the top because that's the way they appear on program listings (the same as do the line numbers in a BASIC program).

What do the numbers 43, 41, and 54, stored in the memory locations, mean? If you look at the table of ASCII values given in the Appendix D, you'll see that 43 hex is the ASCII value for "C," 41 is the value for "A," and

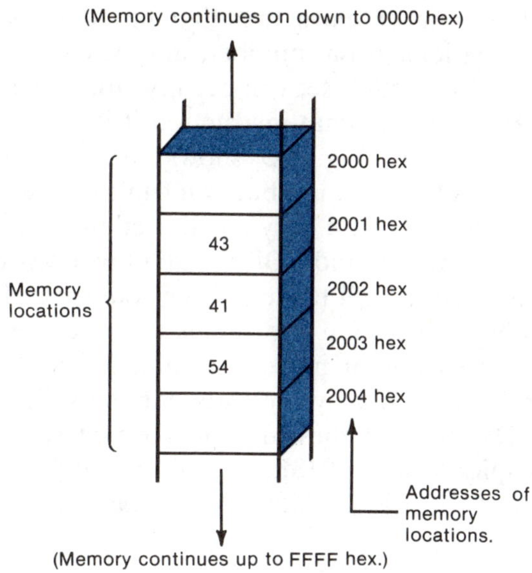

Fig.1-4. Memory.

54 is the value for "T." The ASCII code is simply the way that the computer stores characters. (It stands for "American Standard Code for Information Interchange.") Since the computer must always think in terms of numbers, it translates all characters (letters, punctuation, etc.) into two-digit hex numbers.

Numbers that aren't ASCII characters can also be stored in memory. One byte (one memory location) can hold a number between 0 and 255 decimal (0 to FF hexadecimal). Two bytes (two memory locations) used together can hold numbers from 0 to 65535 decimal (0 to FFFF hex.)

One of the important differences between assembly language (we'll abbreviate it A-L from now on) and a high-level language, such as BASIC, is that when you program in the higher-level language, you don't need to know exactly *where* in memory a particular program or variable is stored. The language processing program (such as the BASIC interpreter) takes care of deciding where to put the program and its variables. In A-L, on the other hand, the programmer must decide himself where to put everything—this instruction will go in this memory location, that variable will go in that memory location, and so on. For this reason, all the addresses (which is the same as saying memory locations) are numbered, starting at 0 and going up to FFFF (hex).

The program, which consists of a list of instructions, each of which is represented by one or more two-digit hexadecimal numbers, goes in specific memory locations just as numbers and ASCII characters do. The instructions in the 8080 instruction set will occupy either one, two, or three memory locations, depending on what instruction it is.

The drawing in Fig. 1-5 shows three instructions stored in memory. They're part of a program, but you can't see the rest of the program because we're only looking at a very small section of memory. The instructions are MOV E,A, CALL 5, and POP D. Don't worry if they don't mean anything to you at this point; we'll be describing some actual instructions in detail in the next chapter. There are two things to notice here. First, each instruction is represented by one or more hex numbers (MOV E,A is represented by the number 5F, CALL 5 by the three numbers CD, 05, 00, and POP D by the number D1). Second, these numbers occupy specific places in memory; MOV E,A occupies location 018E, and so on. MOV E,A and POP D each occupy one memory location, while CALL 5 occupies three locations.

Registers

There is another place a program can store data; it is in special hardware devices called "registers." A register is something like a memory location, but it is part of the microprocessor "chip," and can therefore be operated on

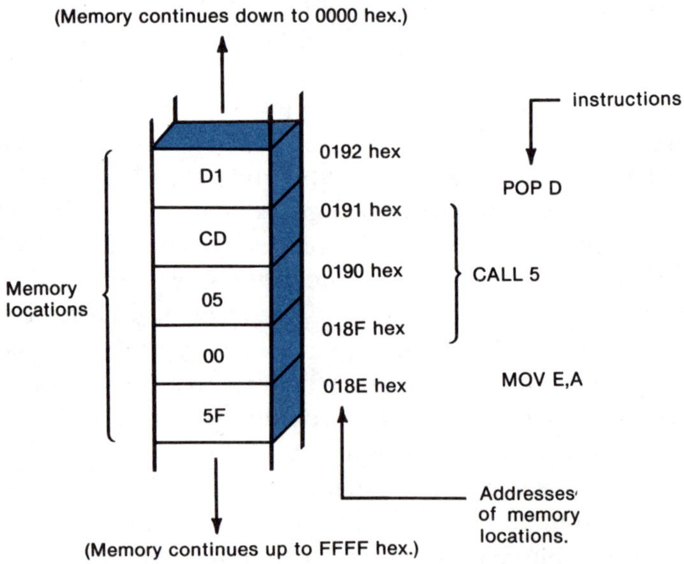

Fig. 1-5. Three instructions stored in memory.

faster than a memory location, which is on a separate memory chip located some distance from the microprocessor. A register also usually has some special attributes that memory locations don't have.

A microprocessor "chip," such as an 8080, consists mainly of registers and the instruction-decoding circuits that let the chip know what we want to do when we execute a specific instruction.

You can think of registers as the work areas where data are processed. Data are stored in the memory, and the instructions for handling the data—the program—are also stored in the memory. We execute the instructions in the program one after the other, like items on a list. Suppose we want, for example, to add together two numbers that are stored in memory. Our program will contain an instruction that will take the first number out of memory and will put it in one of the registers. The next instruction will take the second number from memory and add it to the contents of the register. The third instruction in our program might cause the result of the addition to be put back into yet another memory location or, perhaps, it might send it to an output device like the video screen. The point is that the addition operation was carried out in a register, not in memory.

In the 8080 chip, there are 7 main registers for handling data. (There are a few others, but we'll ignore them for the moment.) These 7 registers are called the A, B, C, D, E, H, and L registers.

Of these, the most important is the A-register. The "A" stands for "accumulator." In the early days of computing, many computers had only one register. This was used to hold the results of all arithmetic calculations, in the same way that your pocket calculator keeps its arithmetic results in a single register (whose contents you can see in the little window). Since this register "accumulates" the results of previous arithmetic calculations, it was called the accumulator. The A-register in the 8080 still handles all of the 8-bit arithmetic (that is, numbers up to FF hex or 255 decimal), such as addition and subtraction, as well as logical ANDs, ORs, shifts, and the like.

Bytes of data can be moved from the A-register to memory and back, and also between the A-register and the other 8-bit registers.

The other registers, B, C, D, E, H, and L, can function as temporary storage places for 8-bit (one byte) quantities. They can also be used in a different way—as register *pairs* to hold 16-bit (two-byte) data quantities. When used in this way, the B and C registers are placed together to form the BC register, the D and E registers are placed together to form the DE register, and the H and L registers are placed together to form the HL register. The 16-bit data, which are numbers from 0 up to FFFF hex (65535 decimal), can be transferred between these register pairs, or between specific register pairs and pairs of memory locations. The diagram given in Fig. 1-6 shows the principle 8080 registers.

Don't worry if all this talk about registers seems a bit obscure at this point. In the next chapter, we'll introduce you to some specific operations with registers and their uses will become clearer. For a more complete picture of the registers, look in Appendix C for a "Summary of 8080 Instructions."

To summarize, the principal parts of the 8080 microprocessor are seven registers and a large number (up to 65536) of memory locations. This is shown in Fig. 1-7.

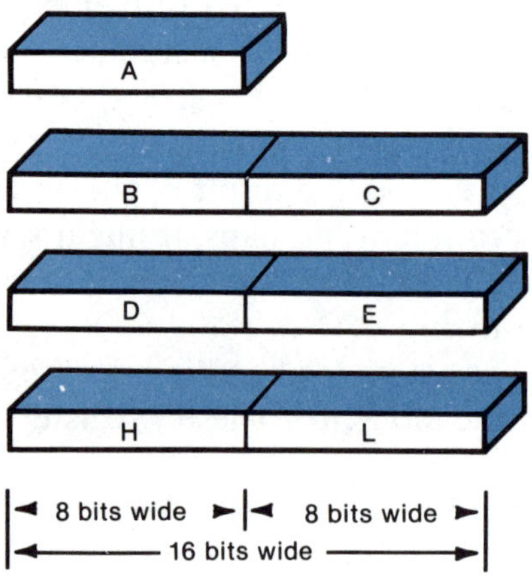

Fig. 1-6. The principal 8080 registers.

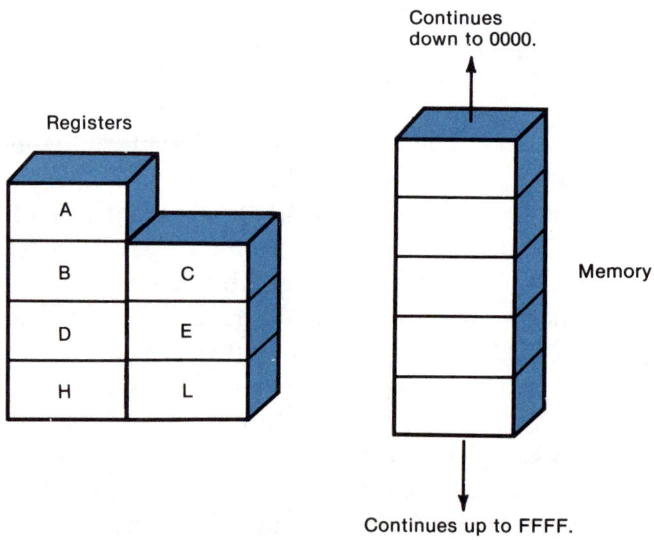

Fig. 1-7. The principal parts of the 8080 microprocessor.

DDT—THE PROGRAMMER'S X RAY AND PROBE

All right, you say, I've got this computer sitting on my desk, and you tell me there are things called registers inside it. And, something called memory. Well, I can't see them and I can't touch them. How am I supposed to do anything with them? How can I find out how they work?

Good questions. What we need are a set of tools. We need the programmer's equivalent of an x-ray machine and of some long probes, so we can examine the registers and the memory and also manipulate them; so we can change their contents. Fortunately, the kind folks at Digital Research (the makers of CP/M) have provided just such a set of tools; it's a program called DDT. (They also make a similar program called SID. You can use that too, if you like, but our discussion is geared to DDT.)

DDT (for "Dynamic Debugging Program") is one of the "transient commands" (programs not built into CP/M but provided with it as a separate program). This program was devised to make it easier to work with the computer on a very fundamental level. DDT is able to examine and modify the contents of both particular memory locations and of the various registers in the 8080.

For example, if you are using DDT and you type "d100", DDT will print out the contents of all the memory locations from 100 (hex) to 1FF (hex) (or 256 locations). You can change the contents of a memory location by typing, say, "s100" to alter the contents of location 100. And, you can examine and modify the contents of registers; typing "xa" will permit you to examine and modify the contents of the A-register.

DDT has another important ability—one which we will make use of extensively in this book. That is, you can type in a program in symbolic assembly language and DDT will assemble the symbolic instructions into a program which can be executed directly.

Here's why we need this ability to handle symbolic programs. The instructions for the 8080, like those for all computers, take the form of lots of binary numbers when they are in the machine. (Of course, these aren't abstract binary numbers, but groups of transistors being set to either the "on" or "off" states. For our purposes, it amounts to the same thing.) Again, read Appendix A on hexadecimal notation if you are not familiar with binary numbers or their relationship to hexadecimal numbers.

As an example, the instruction to subtract the contents of the C-register from the contents of the A-register is the binary number 10010001. Now binary numbers are hard to read and to remember, so we usually write the instruction in its hexadecimal form of 91. (See the table of binary to hexadecimal conversions in Appendix A.) However, even this is hard to remember. What the "symbolic assembler" function of DDT lets us do is write this number as "sub c". It's much easier to see that this means "subtract the contents of the C-register from the contents of the A-register" than it does when you look at the number "91."

It wouldn't hurt at this point to look over the DDT commands in Appendix F, or even the section on DDT in the CP/M documentation provided with your computer, just to get a rough idea of everything that DDT is capable of. Don't worry if you don't understand every detail; we'll explain how it all works as we go along.

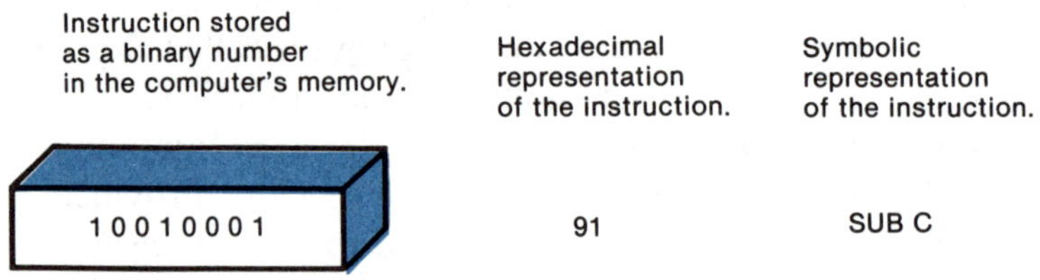

Fig. 1-8. Number conversion.

BACK DOWN TO EARTH

Now that you've gotten a fast aerial overview of the various major aspects of the terrain, it's time to land and take a close-up look at a specific area. We'll do this in the next chapter, on Console System Calls. If you feel you're not quite sure of what's happening and where all these concepts are leading, read on. The specific examples that we'll cover next should help to pull everything together.

CHAPTER 2

One Toe in the Water

Console System Calls

In this chapter, you're going to begin your journey into the mysterious and exciting world of CP/M system calls. System calls, as we mentioned in the last chapter, are links between your program and BDOS, CP/M's Basic Disk Operating System. BDOS examines your system call and then uses one of the

routines in BIOS (the Basic Input/Output section of CP/M) to communicate with a specific device, such as the video screen, keyboard, or disk drive. Understanding how to use these calls is the key to programming in the CP/M environment, since by using the calls, you can create programs that are efficient to write and are easily transportable from one computer to another. There is a complete list of system calls in Appendix E. You might want to glance over these calls at this point, just to get an idea of the kinds of things they do.

Our first programs will be very short, and will introduce the simplest of system calls at the same time that you're learning just enough assembly language to use the call. For simplicity and ease of operation, we'll use DDT to create the examples. By the end of the chapter, you'll be well on your way to understanding both system calls and 8080 assembly language.

We'll introduce each system call with a box containing the important facts about how to use it. Don't worry if you don't understand what we mean by "REG C = 2", and so on, in the following explanation box; we'll get to that soon.

CONSOLE OUTPUT SYSTEM CALL

CONSOLE OUTPUT FUNCTION 2 (dec) = 2 (hex)

Enter with: REG C = 2
REG E = ASCII character to be displayed

The first system call that we'll learn is a simple one called "Console Output." This call is nothing more than a way to send a single character from your program to the CP/M display screen. It's like a one-character-at-a-time version of the PRINT statement in BASIC. We'll describe how the call is used, then write a program that makes use of the call, and, finally, show you how to type the program into the computer's memory and execute it using DDT.

In order to execute this system call, your assembly language program must do three things:

1. Put the number 2 in the C-register.
2. Put the ASCII character you want to print in the E-register.
3. Execute a CALL instruction to memory location 5.

That's all there is to it! If you do these three things, a character will be printed on the screen. You don't need to understand anything about the actual instructions that CP/M uses to send the character to a particular kind of terminal or crt screen, since the routine in BIOS takes care of that for you.

Briefly, here's what each step does. First, the number "2" is the number of the system call in hex. CP/M uses the C-register as the "mail-box" for a program to tell CP/M what systems call it wants to use. Second, the ASCII code for any character can be looked up in Appendix D found at the back of this book. In this system call, CP/M gets the ASCII value of the character that is to be displayed from the E-register. And, finally, *all* system calls, no matter what they are, use a CALL to location 5 in order to enter BDOS, where the BIOS and BDOS routines will do whatever input or output function has been requested; in this case, printing a character on the screen.

Your First Program

All right, you ask, how do I actually go about writing down these steps in a form that the computer can understand? Let's look at a program that does just what we want:

```
mvi c,2
mvi e,48
call 5
```

Well, it's short enough, but what does it all mean? Easy. The first instruction puts the number 2 in the C-register. The second instruction puts the number 48 in the E-register. And the third instruction causes the program to "call" or jump to the entry point of BDOS, which is at memory location 0005.

All the numbers used in programs in this chapter are in hexadecimal, so the 2, the 48, and the 5 are all hexadecimal numbers. (The 2 and 5 are the same as their decimal equivalents, but the 48 is equal to 72 decimal.)

Statement "Fields"

Each of the three lines in the preceding program is called a "statement." As you can see, each of these statements consists of two parts separated by a space. These parts are called "fields."

The first field shown is the "operation" field. The instruction, or *what you're going to do* goes in this field; "mvi" and "call" are instructions. (To confuse the issue, the word "instruction" is also used to refer to the entire statement.)

Following the space (which could be several spaces, or a tab) comes the "operand" field. This field contains *the thing you're going to do it to.* Thus, in the first line, "mvi" is the instruction or operand. It operates on the operand field, which contains "c,2", and causes the number 2 to be placed in the C-register. In the third line, CALL is the instruction, and it operates on the operand 5, causing the program to jump to location 5. Later, we'll learn about other fields in the instruction line, but for the time being these two will keep us busy.

Something to notice here is that the order in which things are written in the operand field may seem backwards. In the example, "MVI C,2", it's the 2 that is placed into the C-register, not the other way around. It's like the statement "LET C=2" in BASIC, where the variable C is given the value 2.

The MVI Instruction

"MVI" is an instruction that means "move immediate." The word "immediate" means that the data to be moved *immediately* follows the instruction in memory. (Later, we'll look at instructions that can take a constant from other places in memory and put it in a register.)

As we mentioned before, the memory locations in these drawings start at the top and go downward. This may seem strange at first, but you'll get used to it.

The number to be moved using MVI can be any 1-byte number–that is, any number from 0 to FF hex (0 to 255 decimal). Also, the register that the number is moved to can be any of the seven main registers: A, B, C, D, E, H, or L. In the diagram of Fig. 2-1, the number is moved to the C-register. The second time that the MVI instruction is used in our example program, the number 48 is moved to the E-register.

The use of a constant as *part of an instruction* can be confusing. Some computers require that constants be stored in a different part of memory from the program. However, in the "immediate" instructions used in the 8080 microprocessor, constants actually become a closely connected part of some instructions, such as MVI. Notice how the instruction occupies two bytes of memory. The first byte, at location 100, is the code that tells what the instruction is going to be: 0E. This means the instruction is going to transfer a constant into the C-register; in other words, it's the code for the "MVI C"

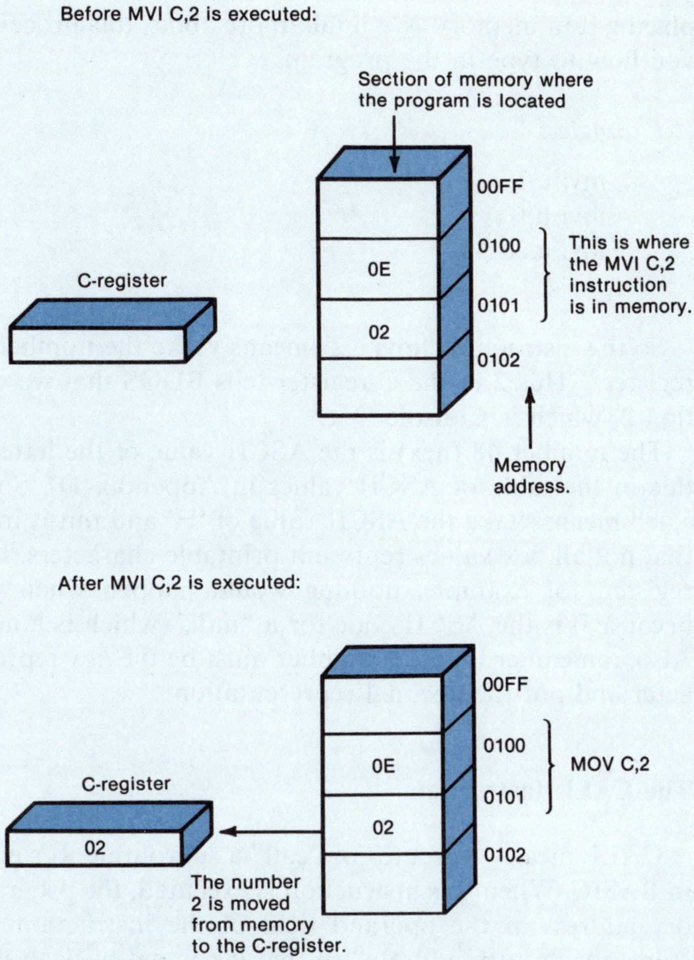

Fig. 2-1. The MVI instruction.

part of the instruction. This number will vary, depending on which of the seven registers the constant is to be placed in. The constant itself is given in the second byte of the instruction, at location 101; it's the hexadecimal number 02.

We're not going to be too concerned with the exact hexadecimal codes for the instructions we learn, but it's important to understand the relationship of the codes to the symbolic instructions that we'll be typing in using DDT. We'll type in a symbolic instruction, like "mvi c,2", and DDT will take care of the dirty work of figuring out the corresponding hexadecimal code and placing it in memory. We'll talk more about this process later, when we show you how to type in the program.

Examples:

```
mvi c,2
mvi h,ff
mvi e,20
```

So the instruction "mvi c,2" means "take the number 2 and put it in the C register." This 2 in the C-register tells BDOS that we want to execute Function 2, which is Console Out.

The number 48 (hex) is the ASCII value of the letter "H" (you can check this in the table of ASCII values in Appendix D). So the instruction "mvi e,48" means "take the ASCII value of 'H' and put it in the E register." Note that not all hex values represent printable characters. If you put a 0 in the E register, for example, nothing would happen when you tried to print it, because 0 is the ASCII code for a "null," which is a nonprintable character. Also, remember that this number must be the *hex* representation of the character and not the decimal representation.

The CALL Instruction

CALL means "execute" or "call" a subroutine. It's equivalent to a GOSUB in BASIC. When this instruction is executed, the program jumps to the memory address in the operand field of the instruction. Also, the instruction stores the "return address" so that it can get back to the proper place in the calling program when the subroutine is completed. The place that the program wants to return to in the program—the return address—is simply the location following the CALL instruction. The place where the CALL instruction saves the return address is called the "stack." We'll learn more about the stack later. For now, think of it as a handy place for the program to save an address until it's needed again.

Fig. 2-2 is a diagram of how CALL operates. In this case, when the call instruction is executed, program control will go to location 02C0, and location 107 will be stored on the stack. When the subroutine, which starts at location 02C0, is completed, program control will resume at location 107. (This is done using the RET instruction, which we'll cover later in this chapter.)

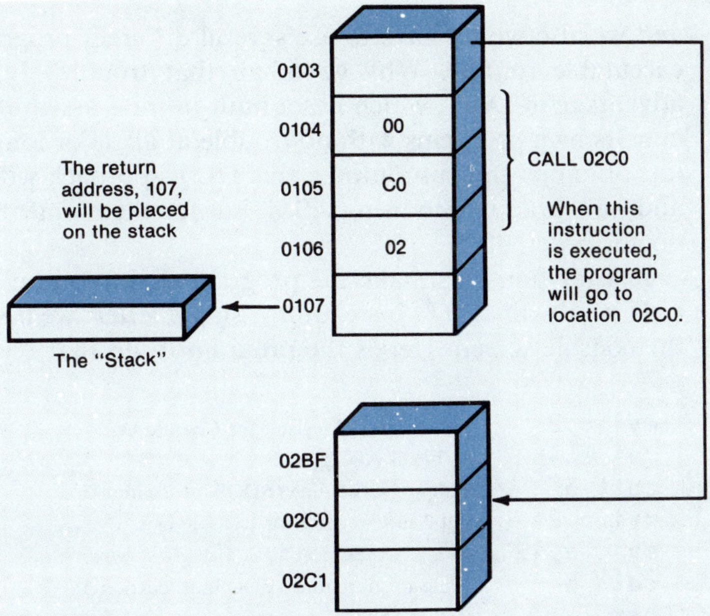

Fig. 2-2. Operation of the CALL instruction.

Examples:

```
call 5
call 100
call bf00
```

So, in our little program, the "call 5" means "execute the subroutine at memory location 5 hex" and 5 hex turns out to be the entry point for all system calls. What really happens is that locations 5, 6, and 7 contain a jump instruction to the actual BDOS entry point in high memory. We'll talk more about that later in the book. But for now, all you need to know is that in order to do a system call, you execute a CALL 5 instruction.

So there it is, your first CP/M system call, a simple 3-instruction program, written in assembly language. But, how do we get it to do what it's supposed to do–put a character on the screen? In other words, how do we put the program into the computer's memory and execute it?

We could actually write the program in "official" assembly language, using the ASM assembler program that comes with CP/M, and, then, execute it as a COM file (the same way systems programs are executed). But if we did that, we would have to add other instructions to the program to make it work and we also would have to use several different programs to convert it to an executable routine. Why go to all that trouble? Instead, we simply take advantage of DDT, which has a built-in mini-assembler, and which can execute its own programs with no trouble at all. (For longer programs involving lots of jumps and subroutines, this DDT approach will begin to hold us back and we'll graduate to using ASM, but for the moment, DDT is just what the doctor ordered.)

Just for fun, let's make the program slightly more complicated before we type it in with DDT. Instead of a single letter, we'll send the word "HI" to the console screen. Here's the program to do that:

```
mvi c,2       Put 2 in the C-register for Console Out.
mvi e,48      48 hex is ASCII "H".
call 5        Jump-to-subroutine (BDOS) at location 5.
mvi c,2       Put 2 in C-register for Console Out.
mvi  e,49     49 hex is ASCII "I".
call 5        Jump-to-subroutine (BDOS) at location 5.
rst 7         Return to DDT.
```

This program is very much like the last one, except that we print two letters instead of one. In other words, we use the Console Out system call twice, once with "H" and once with "I."

Something to note here is that we have to restore the "2" in the C-register (as well as putting the new character in the E-register) before we can "call 5" the second time. This is because the system call itself trashes the contents of the C-register. ("Trash" is a programmer's word meaning to change something, usually with disastrous results.)

Also, we've added comments to each line, to make the program clearer (although you can't actually type in such comments in DDT). And, there is a final addition to the program—the "rst 7" instruction at the end.

The RST Instruction

This instruction was actually designed to be used with the interrupt system of the 8080 chip. Since this book does not cover the interrupt system, we won't say anything further about RST, except to note that, since DDT uses the interrupt system, this instruction must be used to terminate programs when they are being executed under DDT. When used in DDT, RST returns control from the program to the DDT monitor. It's a little like the STOP or END instruction in BASIC. Without the rst 7, the computer would just keep on executing all the instructions in memory that happened to follow the end of the program.

Example:

rst 7

Typing in the Program Using DDT

The first step in writing our program is to load and get into DDT. (Notice that our typed input will be in lowercase letters, while CP/M's output is in uppercase letters. Don't worry about this. CP/M is good at translating the lowercase input to uppercase.) After you load DDT by typing "ddt" following the "A>" prompt, DDT will print a "sign-on" message and then print a dash ("-") and will wait for your command. (The dash "-" is the DDT prompt character.)

```
A>ddt              Call up DDT.
DDT VERS 2.2       DDT sign-on message.
-                  DDT's prompt character.
```

You can now type "a100", which means "start assemblying a program at location 100 (hex)." DDT will respond to this command by printing 100, which is the location where the next instruction will go in memory. Each time that we type in an instruction and hit the carriage return, DDT will reply with the next available memory location. Here's how our program will look when typed in using DDT:

```
A>ddt
DDT VERS 2.2
-a100 <---------------- Assemble code at 100 hex. (Type each instruction, followed by a
0100  mvi c,2             return.)
0102  mvi e,48
0104  call 5
0107  mvi c,2
0109  mvi e,49
010B  call 5
010E  rst 7
010F <----------------- Press return to end assembly.
-
^      ^
|      |_______________ You type the program in this column.
|
|______________________ DDT types these addresses.
```

We began at 100 hex because that's the standard beginning address for all CP/M programs and that is where the SAVE utility looks for code to save. (We'll talk about that later.) Notice how different instructions take up different amounts of memory: mvi takes two bytes, call takes 3, and rst only needs 1. When we've typed the last instruction, we type a carriage return instead of another instruction to let DDT know that we're done.

Let's make sure the code is set up right by using the "l" (lowercase "L") list command. The "l" command prints out or "lists" a program in the same format that we typed it in.

(This is a lowercase "L".)

(This is the number 100.)

```
-l100                List the code to see that it's all right.
0100  MVI   C,02
0102  MVI   E,48
0104  CALL  0005
0107  MVI   C,02
0109  MVI   E,49
010B  CALL  0005
010E  RST   07
```

Looks great. If you made any errors in entering your code, use the "A" (assemble) command again to reenter the correct code. For example, if you mistakenly typed CALL 6 at line 104, you would change it by typing: "a104" (return). The address 0104 would appear. Then, you would simply type "call 5", hit return twice, and you're finished:

```
-l100
0100  MVI   C,02
0102  MVI   E,48
0104  CALL  0006     Woops—typed the wrong thing.
0107  MVI   C,02
0109  MVI   E,49
010B  CALL  0005
010E  RST   07
-
-a104                Start at the offending instruction. Type the right thing,
0104  call 5           another carriage return, and it's fixed!
0107
-
```

Now that our little program is entered into the computer's memory, it's time to actually execute it, using DDT. We use the "go do it" command "g", followed by the address where our program starts (100 hex).

`-g100` Run the program at address 100 hex.

`HI*010E` Program prints HI and the last address preceded by a "*".

Wow! It actually printed what it was supposed to! The asterisk tells us that the program is finished, and the 010E tells us that the last instruction to be executed was a "rst 7" at location 010E. The HI, of course, stands for "Highly Ingenious."

To reward yourself for successfully writing and executing your first CP/M program, why not take the rest of the day off? Or, at least treat yourself to a beer!

Saving the Program

Now that you've written the program, you will want to be able to save it onto disk so that you can use it later. Here's how to do it:

1. Type "g0" to take you out of DDT and back into CP/M.
2. Following the "A>" prompt, type "save 1 test.ddt".

(This is the number "zero," not the letter "Oh".)

`-g0` Leave DDT.
`A>` Get the A> prompt back.

`A>save 1 test.ddt` Save the program.

Since 0 is where the computer automatically goes to do a warm boot, typing "g0" from DDT takes you back to CP/M. (It actually loads the CCP back into memory and executes it. You could also have typed a control–c, which has the same effect.) "SAVE" is a "resident command" that automatically writes to the disk the program that is occupying the TPA, starting at 100 hex. It saves the program using the name that you type in; in this case, "test.ddt". The "1" tells SAVE how many 256-byte "pages" of memory we want to save; in this case, just one page, since our program is less than 256 bytes long.

If you want to reload the program, you can do it at the same time that you're loading DDT:

```
A>ddt test.ddt
```

Then, to execute the program, type:

```
-g100
```

Don't try to execute the program directly from CP/M by typing A>test.ddt. For one thing, only files with an extension of "COM" can be executed this way and, for another, the fact that the program ends with "rst 7" (instead of "ret") will cause problems if you do change the extension to COM and try to execute it. This is because RST takes you to an address that DDT is able to deal with but which CP/M is not expecting at all. Later, we'll learn how to execute programs directly from CP/M.

Using the "Control–S" Feature

There is more you should know about the way CP/M handles the Console Output function. As we mentioned earlier, BDOS does not simply pass the request for output along to the input/output routine in BIOS–it does some interpretation of its own. This gives it the opportunity to add some useful features to the input/output routines that can be used by any program running in the CP/M environment.

For example, when you use the Console Output system call, BDOS checks to see if you've typed a "control–s", which has the effect of starting and stopping the scrolling of material displayed on the screen. (Control–s is the character generated when you hold down the "control" or "alt" key, and type "s". You've probably used it in such CP/M utilities as "TYPE".) So if you press control–s as the program is running, CP/M will freeze your output on the screen–that is, stop running–until you press another control–s.

Want to see control–s work on our sample program? Unfortunately, the program prints "HI" and returns to DDT so fast that you don't have time to type anything. The solution to this is to replace the "return to DDT" instruction–"rst 7"–with a jump to the beginning of the program, so that we have an endless loop printing the word HI. Then, you can try the control–s and verify that it freezes the program, and restarts it as well.

The JMP Instruction

A JMP instruction is just like a GOTO in BASIC. When the program executes it, control goes to the address specified in the operand field of the instruction. Of course, in assembly language, the address is an actual memory location, not a line number as in BASIC. JMP differs from a CALL instruction in that no return address is stored; the program doesn't remember where you were before you executed the jump.

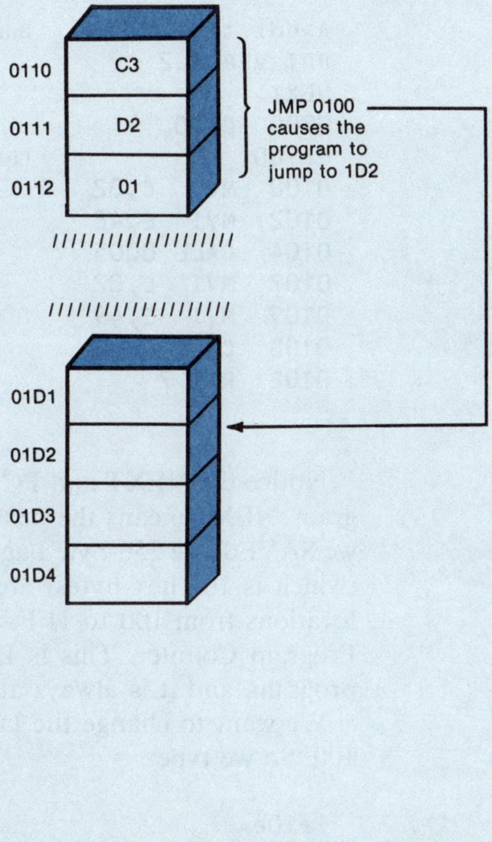

Fig. 2-3. The JMP instruction.

Examples:

jmp 100
jmp bf00

Which Half Comes First?

You may have noticed something a little strange if you've been examining the diagrams of the programs carefully. Whenever there's an address in a program listing or diagram, it seems to be backwards. An address consists of two bytes. For instance, 01D2 is stored in the computer's memory as the two bytes 01 and D2. However, the makers of the 8080 (and the 8085, Z-80, and so forth), for reasons best known to themselves, chose to put the least-significant byte first, followed by the most-significant byte. That is, if you have the instruction "JMP 01D2" in a program, the JMP will come first (represented by the number C3), then the D2, and then the 01. This makes listings and diagrams confusing to read, until you get used to the procedure. Of course, you can simply ignore the hexadecimal values that the "a" function of DDT puts in memory and just look at the symbolic instructions.

To check the control–s feature, type the following:

```
A>ddt test.ddt          Bring up DDT and our previous program.
DDT VER 2.2
NEXT   PC
0200  0100
-l100                   List the code to see that it's all right.
0100  MVI  C,02
0102  MVI  E,48
0104  CALL 0005
0107  MVI  C,02
0109  MVI  E,49
010B  CALL 0005
010E  RST 7
-
```

Notice the NEXT and PC headings that DDT prints when you load a program. NEXT means the next memory location after the one loaded in. Since we SAVEd one 256-byte page when we saved our program, 256 decimal bytes (which is 100 hex bytes) are loaded in along with DDT. This fills memory locations from 100 to 1FF, so the next available one is 200 hex. PC means Program Counter. This is DDT's way of keeping track of where it is in a program, and it is always at 100 when a program is first loaded.

We want to change the last instruction in the program, RST 7, to a JMP 100. So we type:

```
-a10e                   Change the rst 7 to a JMP 100.
010E  JMP 100
0110 <-----------       Carriage return.

-g0                     Now return to the CCP.

A>save 1 test1.ddt      Save the program as TEST1.
```

`A>ddt test1.ddt`	Go back to DDT.
`-g100`	Execute the program.

```
HIHIHIHIHIHIHIHIHIHIHIHIHIHIHIHIHIHIHIHI------etc.
```

A huge amount of HIs are sent to the screen, quickly filling it up. The program will continue to send HIs until the control–s key is pressed; at which point, the display will freeze. Pressing another control–s will allow it to restart.

But how do you stop the entire program, so you can get back to DDT or CP/M? Unfortunately, you're in big trouble in this regard. The only way to regain control of the computer is to hit the reset button. That will cause a "cold boot," and you'll be back in CP/M. The moral of this is to avoid writing assembly language programs with loops that never terminate. In BASIC you can always hit the Break key but, in assembly language, you need to write an escape route into your program. In the next section, we'll show you how to modify your program so that it can be interrupted from the keyboard.

So, you're now an expert on the CP/M function call "Console Output." The nice thing about this is, as we mentioned earlier, that what you've learned is applicable to any machine running CP/M, whether it has an 8080 chip, an 8085, a Z-80, or whatever. It's also applicable to any sort of display terminal, whether it's from TeleVideo, IBM, Amdek, or any of the dozens of other manufacturers.

There are many other nondisk CP/M system calls, some of which are more powerful than this one, and some of which are pretty mundane. Understanding them all will help you discover how CP/M works and how to write programs that make use of CP/M's full capabilities.

The next CP/M function call that we will study is a simple but important one that is used by almost all of the CP/M utilities.

GET CONSOLE STATUS

GET CONSOLE STATUS	FUNCTION 11 (dec), 0B (hex)
Enter with:	REG C = 0B
On return:	REG A = 0 if no key pressed
	REG A = non-0 if key is pressed

Get Console Status (sometimes called Interrogate Console Ready) is used mainly for signaling to your program that the user has pressed a key. It doesn't tell *what* character was typed, only that some key was pressed. What good is that? Well, remember the last program example of sending continuous HIs to the screen? We had to press the reset button on the computer to stop the display. The program was locked into a tight loop, continuously using the "Console Out" routine, and there was no way we could stop it.

Let's fix this problem. We'll change our program so that every time we print "HI" on the screen, we also use "Get Console Status" to check if the user has pressed a key. If he has, we'll have the program end itself and return to DDT.

First, bring in the old test1.ddt program with DDT:

```
A>ddt test1.ddt
NEXT PC
0200 0100
-l100                   List the code to see if it's all right.
0100  MVI   C,02
0102  MVI   E,48
0104  CALL  0005
0107  MVI   C,02
```

```
0109  MVI   E,49
010B  CALL  0005
010E  JMP   0100
```

Looks fine—an endless loop that prints HI on the screen forever, or at least until RESET is pressed causing a cold boot of CP/M. Not the most elegant way to end the program.

Change your code as follows:

```
-a10e
010E mvi c,b      Put 0B hex in C register.
0110 call 5       Call BDOS.
0113 ora a        OR A with itself—to set zero flag.
0114 jz 100       Go do HI again if no key pressed.
0117 rst 7        Back to DDT if key is pressed.
0118
-
```

Now list the whole thing:

```
-l100
0100 MVI  C,02
0102 MVI  E,48
0104 CALL 0005
0107 MVI  C,02
0109 MVI  E,49
010B CALL 0005
010E MVI  C,0B
0110 CALL 0005
0113 ORA  A
0114 JZ 0100
0117 RST 7
0118
-
```

You can save this program as "test2.ddt" and then bring it back into memory with DDT in the usual way:

```
-g0

A>save 1 test2.ddt

A>ddt test2.ddt
```

What do these new instructions do? Let's explain. What's basically changed here is that, in line 10E, we don't simply jump back and repeat the loop. Instead, we put 0B hex in C-register to set up the Get Console Status system call. Then, we do a call to BDOS with CALL 5. This will make CP/M go and check the keyboard to see if a key has been pressed.

This system call is a little different from the last one, in that our program is trying to *find out* something from CP/M (namely whether a key was pressed) rather than trying to tell CP/M something. Thus, we don't need to put anything in the E-register before we do our "call 5." But we do want to know what CP/M has to tell us, so after the "call 5" is executed, we want to find out if the A-register contains a 0 (which would mean that no key was pressed) or if it contains something else (which would mean that a key *was* pressed). To do this, we need to use something called the "zero flag."

The Zero Flag

We've already mentioned that arithmetic and logical operations involving 8-bit quantities are always carried out in the A-register. Often, after performing such an operation, our program needs to know what the results of the operation were. For instance, if we do an addition, we might like to know if the result is zero. The 8080 does this through what's called the "zero flag," which is simply a switch in the CPU that is set to "1" whenever the results of an arithmetic or logical operation are zero, and set to "0" when they're not. (This might seem backwards, setting the flag to 0 when the result is nonzero, but remember, it's called the "zero flag." It gets *set*, meaning "set to 1," when the result is 0.)

Once this "zero flag" switch is set, it can be used to affect the results of other instructions, such as jumps, in much the same way that a BASIC statement, such as "IF A=0 THEN GOTO 1000", is used.

When we use the "Get Console Status" system call, the A-register comes back with an 8-bit quantity in it, and we want to find out if it's zero or not. The way to do this is to test the zero flag, but (remember this!) *the zero flag is not set until we perform an arithmetic operation.* So we need to do some arithmetic on the A-register which will set the zero flag if the A-register is zero. An old programming trick here is to OR the A-register with itself.

The "ORA" Instruction

"OR" means to take the bits in the A-register and OR them with the corresponding bits in some other register. This is illustrated in Fig. 2-4. Either the B, C, D, E, H, or L register will work fine. As you no doubt recall from BASIC:

0 ORed with 0 is 0
0 ORed with 1 is 1
1 ORed with 0 is 1
1 ORed with 1 is 1

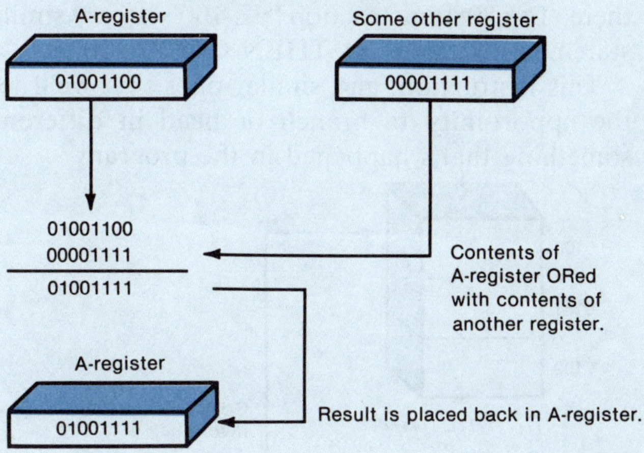

Fig. 2-4. The ORA instruction.

Examples:

ora b
ora h

In our particular program, instead of ORing the A-register with some other register (B or C, or whatever), we OR it with itself. And, as you can see from the above definition, if we OR anything with itself, all we'll get back is itself again! While this may sound like an exercise in futility, it's important because when we perform an OR operation, the *zero flag is set.* That's the only reason for the ORA instruction: to set the zero flag.

Following the "ora a" instruction, we know that the zero flag is *set* (= 1) if the A-register came back from the "Get Console Status" system call set to zero, and *cleared* (= 0) if the A-register came back with some nonzero quantity. How does our program make use of this information? The "jump-on-zero" (jz) instruction takes care of it nicely by doing just what its name implies.

The JZ Instruction

This instruction is a special case of a regular jump (JMP) instruction. If the zero flag is set, this instruction will act like a jump and go to the address given in the operand field of the instruction. However, if the zero flag is not set, nothing at all will happen. No jump will occur and the program will just go on to the instruction following the JZ just as if the JZ hadn't even been there. The 8080 instruction "JZ 100" is very similar in function to the BASIC statement of "IF Z=1 THEN GOTO 100".

This instruction, and similar ones that we'll learn later, give our program the opportunity to branch or head in different directions, depending on something that's happened in the program.

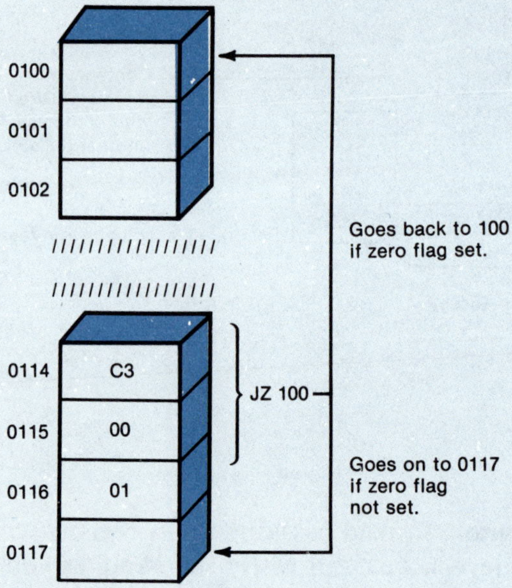

Fig. 2-5. The JZ instruction.

Examples:

jz 100
jz bf00

In our case, if the A-register returns with zero, it means no key was pressed, so the zero flag will be set to 1, the jz 100 instruction will cause program control to go back to 100, and the program will continue to print "HI" on the screen. However, if a key *is* pressed, the A-register will return with nonzero, the zero flag will be cleared (set to 0), and when we execute the jz 100 instruction, we won't jump at all but, instead, will go to the last instruction in the program (the "rst 7" instruction) which will return us to DDT.

So, does all this actually work?

```
-g100    Execute the program.

HIHIHIHIHIHIHIHIHIHIHIHIHIHIHIHIHIHIHIHIHIHIHIHIHIHIHIHIHIHIHI
HIHIHIHIHIHIH....etc.
```

Watch the "HI's" fill up the screen.

Try pressing control–s. The display should freeze. Press control–s again to unfreeze the display.

Now for the big test. Try pressing any key—for instance, the "z". The program should come back to DDT, like this:

```
....HIHIHIHIHIHIHIHIH*(0117)
-z
?
-
```

We pressed a key here and the program stopped.

Here we are, back in DDT! Lo and behold, our modified program works too! It's not perfect, because the letter we pressed gets passed along to DDT. That's the "z" you see printed out following the DDT prompt. If we type a carriage return, DDT will think the "z" is input and will output a question mark when it can't understand it. Aside from this minor glitch, the program is certainly very successful in getting us out of the endless loop.

Congratulations are again in order. You have just created your third CP/M program and learned a new system call! At this rate, you'll be writing programs for mass consumption within days!

BARBER-POLE DISPLAY PROGRAM

Here's a somewhat longer exercise that demonstrates the "Console Output" and "Get Console Status" functions while showing how to program a loop with a changing variable in 8080 code. The goal of the exercise is to write a program that will display the entire ASCII set on the console, over and over again. We'll use "Console Output" to send the characters to the screen and the "Get Console Status" to end the program if a key is pressed. (WARNING: Do not turn on your printer while running this program as it does not send a carriage return/linefeed to the screen, and it will, therefore, cause the printer to go to the right edge of the paper and just sit there, typing over and over on the same spot.) This program uses several new and interesting instructions and it introduces you to that useful but mysterious device, the "stack."

Again, get into DDT and enter this program with the A (assemble) command:

```
-a100
0100  mvi e,20    Set up E-register for first ASCII character.
0102  mvi c,2     Ready for output.
0104  push d      Save the DE register-pair (save E).
0105  call 5      Send character to the screen.
0108  pop d       Get the DE pair back (E is restored).
0109  inr e       Bump E by +1.
010A  mov a,e     Put the E-register in the A-register.
010B  cpi 7f      Is it the 127th character?
010D  jnz 102     If result not zero, then no, so loop.
0110  mvi c,b     Check console status.
0112  call 5      Call BDOS.
0115  ora a       Set zero flag based on contents of A.
0116  jz 100      If a=0, then no key pressed, so loop.
0119  rst 7       Return to DDT.
```

You can save the program as "barber" by exiting DDT and typing:

```
A>save 1 barber.ddt
```

The program can be executed in the usual way by loading it along with DDT:

```
A>ddt barber.ddt
```

And, typing:

```
-g100
```

But, before you do that, take a minute to understand just what's going on. There are a lot of new instructions in the program that you need to learn. (Too late, right? You already ran it. That's all right, we admire impetuous programmers.)

Fig. 2-6 gives a flowchart of the program's operation. You can refer to the flowchart as you read about the new instructions the program uses.

A flowchart is simply a pictorial representation of the operation of a program. Sometimes, certain conventions are followed in flowcharting. For instance, actions which result in the program making a choice between two different routes are placed in diamond-shaped boxes. Rectangular boxes show actions which don't result in a choice; there's only one way out of a rectangle. Circles show places where the program enters or leaves the chart.

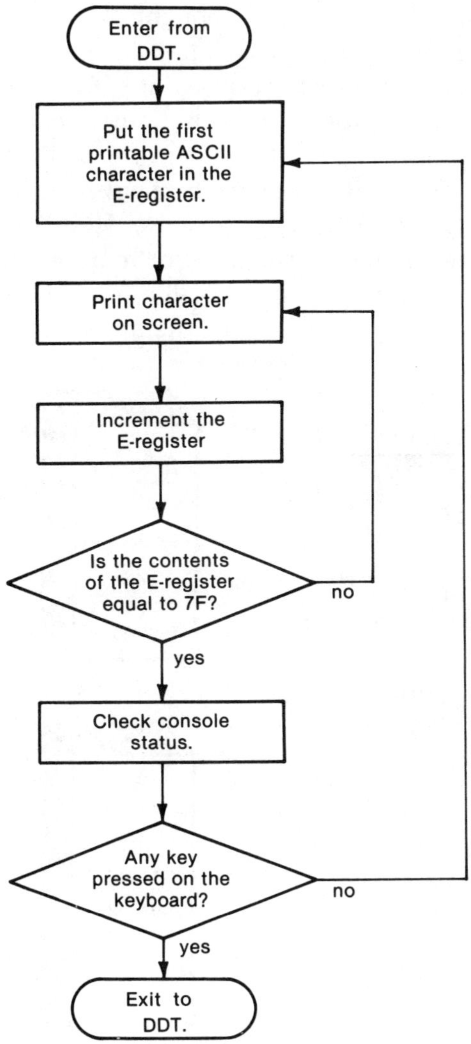

Fig. 2-6. Flowchart of the Barber-Pole Display program.

The Stack

The first unfamiliar instruction in the program is the "push d" at location 104. In order to understand this instruction and the one at location 108, "pop d", you need to know about a strange, wonderful, and, occasionally, infuriating thing called the stack.

We showed you earlier how the stack can be used as a convenient place to store the return address when we call a subroutine. But the stack can store more than one thing. It can be thought of as, well, a stack. A stack of dishes, for example. When you've washed a dish, you put it on the top of the stack for storage. If you need a dish, you take it off the top of the stack. (This kind of stack is called LIFO, for "last in, first out.") There is a stack in the memory of your CP/M computer and it works in the same way except, of course, that it doesn't store dishes, it stores *the contents of register pairs.* The contents of a register pair is two bytes long (which is 16 bits, or four hexadecimal digits).

There are two main instructions for manipulating the stack: PUSH (which puts something on the stack), and POP (which takes it off). The operation of these instructions is shown in the diagrams of Figs. 2-7 and 2-8. Notice that

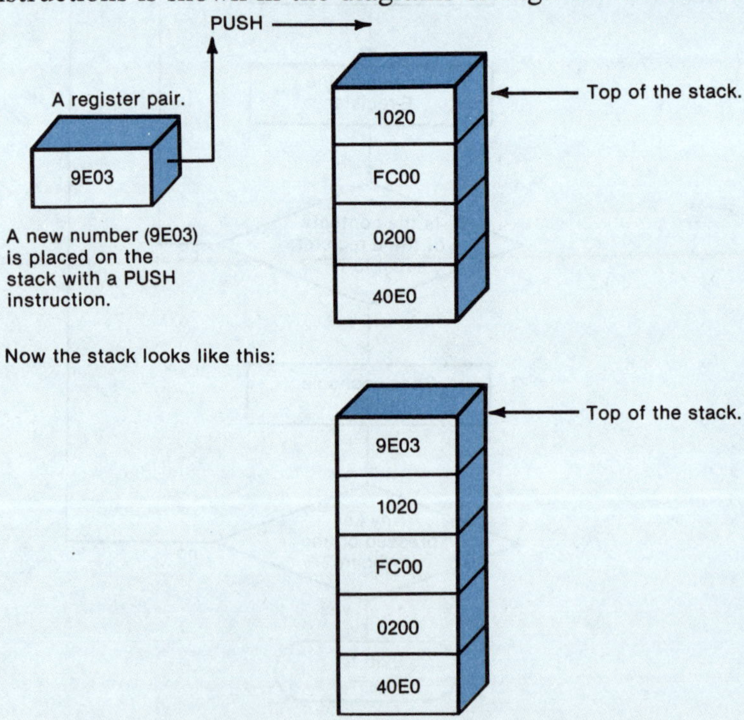

Fig. 2-7. Using the PUSH to manipulate the stack.

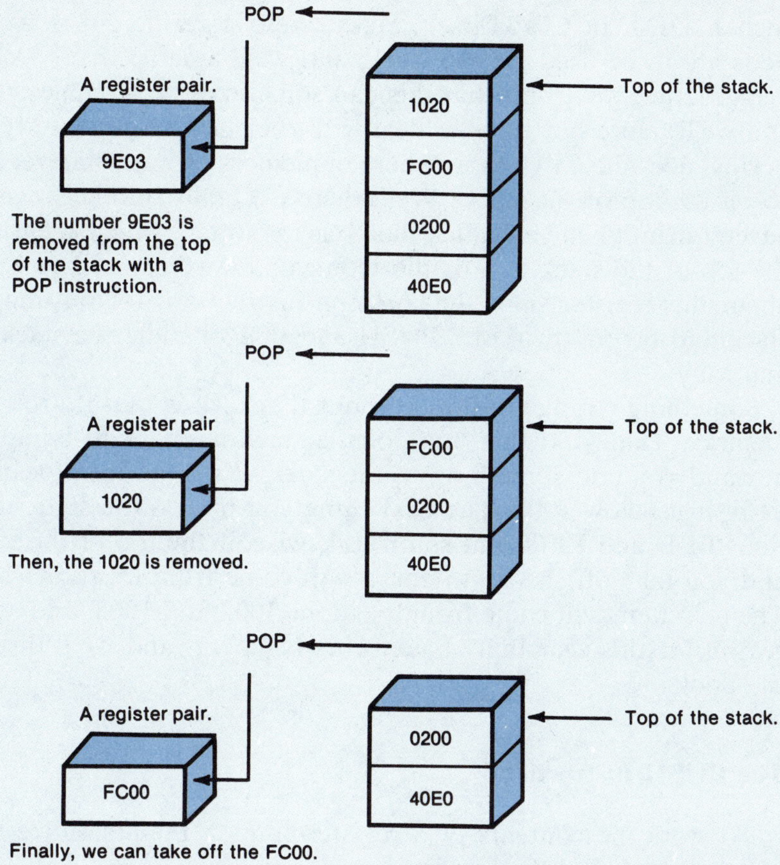

Fig. 2-8. Using the POP to manipulate the stack.

each box in the diagrams stands for *two* memory locations, since each is holding a two-byte quantity.

We can't take a number out of the middle of the stack. If we want the number FC00, for example, we must first remove the 9E03, then the 1020, and finally the FC00. This is illustrated in Fig. 2-8.

Remember how, in the last chapter, we mentioned that the B and C registers, the D and E registers, and the H and L registers could be put together to form the BC, DE, and HL register-pairs? It's the contents of these 16-bit register-pairs that are stored on our stack. Sometimes these 16-bit quantities are simply numbers that we want to save, other times they are addresses.

What does the stack consist of? It's just a series of memory locations, somewhere in your computer's memory. Often the program you're using, such as DDT, or CP/M itself, takes care of figuring out what memory locations are to be used for the stack, and we'll assume that's true for the time being. Later, we'll find that this can sometimes be a dangerous assumption, and we'll figure out ways to deal with the stack more directly.

How does the CPU know where in memory to put whatever is supposed to go on the top of the stack? Well, there's actually another register, which we haven't mentioned yet, called the "stack pointer," which keeps track of where the top of the stack is. For the moment, we won't need to know too much about this register since the common instructions for putting things on the stack and taking them off–PUSH and POP–handle the stack pointer automatically.

Something strange to notice about the stack is that it grows *downward* in memory. That is, if the "top" of the stack happens to be at location 1000 hex and you add something to the stack, it will go into locations FFF and FFE, just below 1000. The next thing you put on the stack will go in locations FFD and FFC, and so on. Likewise, if the top of the stack is at 1000 and you take off the first item, it will come from locations 1000 and 1001. The next item will come from locations 1002 and 1003, and so on. There's a reason for this seemingly backwards behavior, and we'll discuss it later in the book.

The PUSH Instruction

To store the contents of a register-pair on the stack, we use the PUSH instruction. It has the format:

```
push x
```

where the x can stand for either "b", "d", or "h". In this case, "b" stands for the BC-register, "d" stands for the DE-register, and "h" stands for the HL-register. When this instruction is executed, the 16-bit (two bytes, four hex digits) contents of the register-pair x are copied into the vacant memory location at the top of the stack.

This is the memory location pointed to by the stack pointer register. Once the quantity is written into this location, PUSH takes care of changing the stack pointer register so that it points to the new top of the stack–the next available place where a quantity can go.

Examples:

```
push b
push h
```

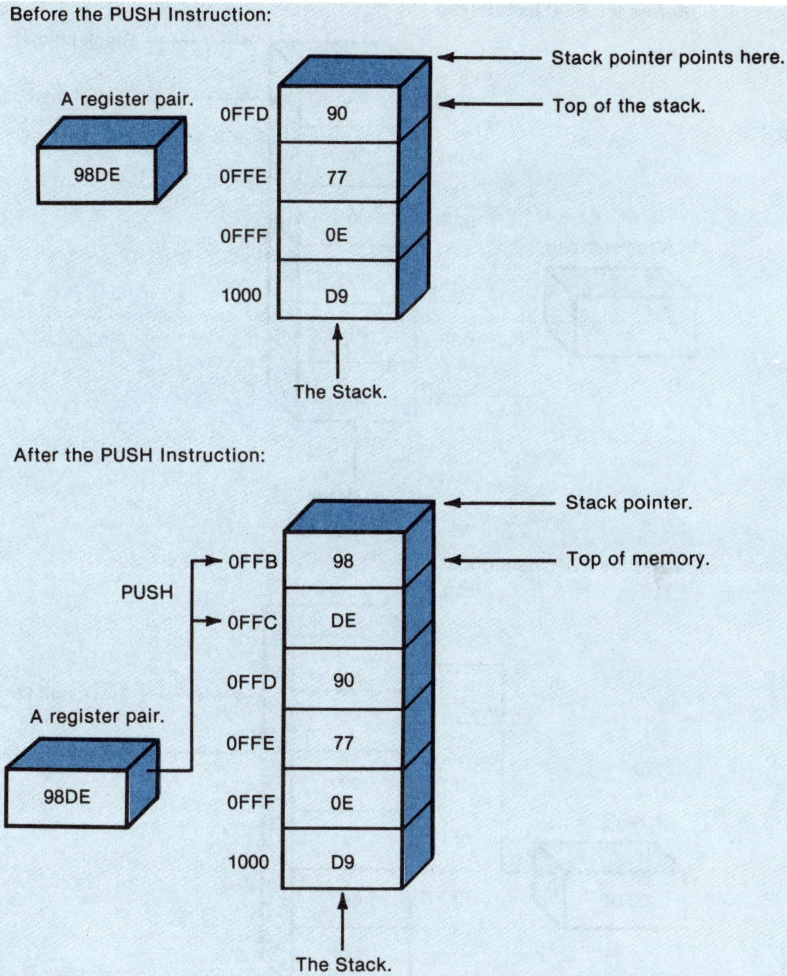

Fig. 2-9. The PUSH instruction.

The POP Instruction

POP is simply the opposite of PUSH. It takes things *off* the stack, from where PUSH put them *on* the stack. The 16-bit quantity removed from the stack is written into the register-pair specified in the operand field of the instruction:

```
pop x
```

where x can be either "b", "d", or "h" and stands for the BC, DE, or HL registers.

POP takes care of incrementing the stack pointer so that it points to the next free memory location.

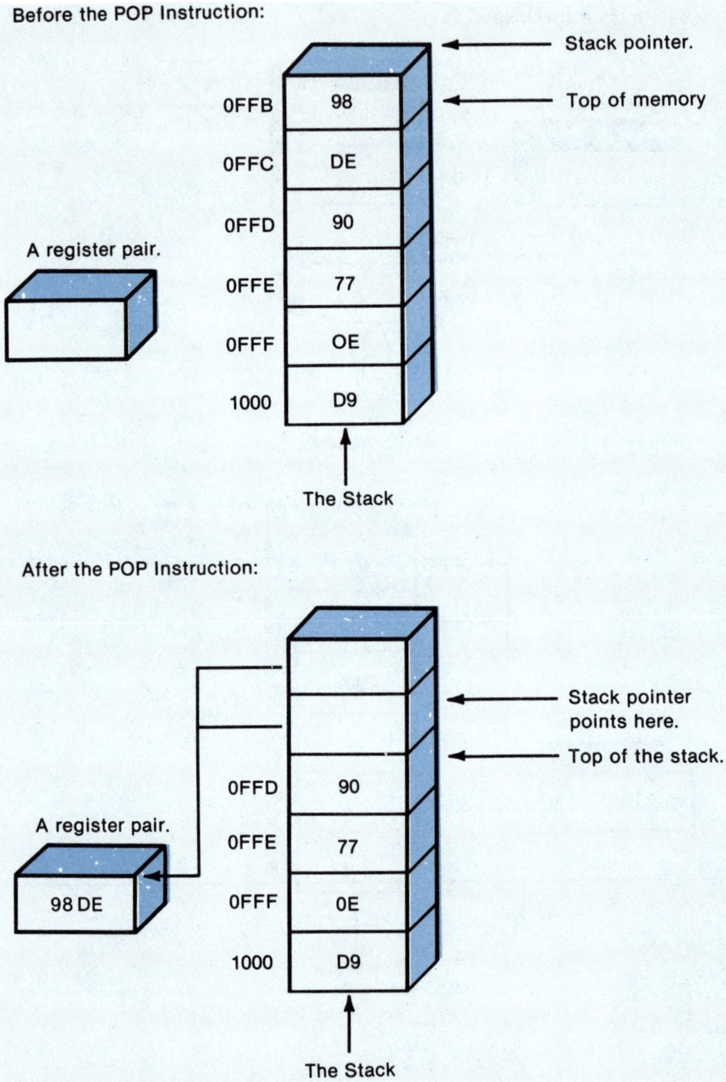

Fig. 2-10. The POP instruction.

Examples:

```
pop d
pop h
```

In our "barber-pole" program, we need to save the E-register each time that we call the "Console Output" routine. Why? Because we're going to use the E-register to hold the ASCII value of the character that we want to print.

And, every time we call the Console Out routine, we want to increase the ASCII value of the contents of the E-register by one, so as to print the next character. Unfortunately, however, the Console Out routine trashes (destroys) the contents of the E-register when it is called. To prevent this unfortunate occurrence, we save the E-register on the stack with a "push d" instruction before calling "Console Output," and restore it afterwards with a "pop d." Notice that, even though it's the E-register we want to save, we use "d" in the PUSH and POP instructions, because it is the first letter in the register-pair "DE." The instruction saves both the "D" and "E" registers but, in our case, the "D" register is just along for the ride.

We mentioned that we wanted to increment the ASCII value in the E-register each time that we call the Console Out routine, so that we will print all the ASCII characters in order. How do we go about incrementing (adding 1 to the contents) a register?

The INR Instruction

This instruction is simply a way to add the quantitiy 1 to the contents of a register (see Fig. 2-11). It works on any of the registers A, B, C, D, E, H, and L. (It doesn't work on register-pairs–there's another instruction for that, which we'll get to later.)

This instruction adds 1 to whatever is in the register. If the number in the register is FF, adding 1 will change it to 00, and the zero flag will be set. (This instruction will also set other flags, which we'll discuss later.)

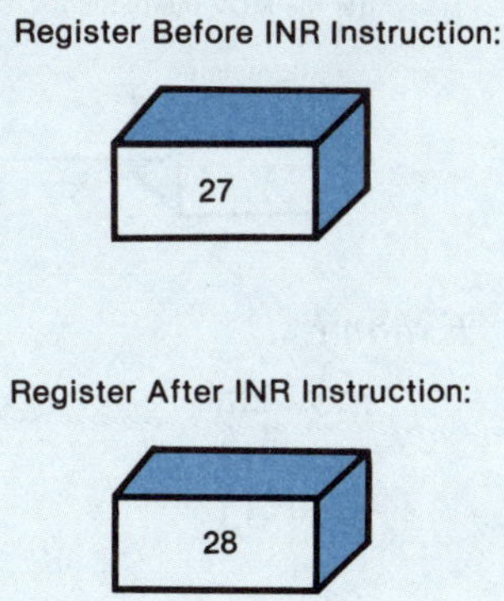

Fig. 2-11. The INR instruction.

Examples:

```
inr e
inr a
inr h
```

The MOV Instruction

You've already learned that the MVI instruction will take a fixed 8-bit number from *memory* (from the location immediately following the instruction) and put it in a register. The MOV instruction, on the other hand, takes the 8-bit contents of a *register* and puts it in another register. MOV can be used to MOVe data from any 8-bit register to any other 8-bit register. The format is:

```
mov x,y
```

where the contents of register "y" is moved into register "x." (As we mentioned before, this may seem backwards, or at least a little arbitrary, but you'll get used to it. Think of the data as going from *right to left* in the instruction. All the 8080 instructions do things from right to left in this way.)

In the diagram of Fig. 2-12, the contents of the B-register are copied into the E-register by the MOV instruction. The contents of the B-register are not changed.

This instruction does not cause any flags to be set. Thus, if you MOV zero into a register, the zero flag will not be set.

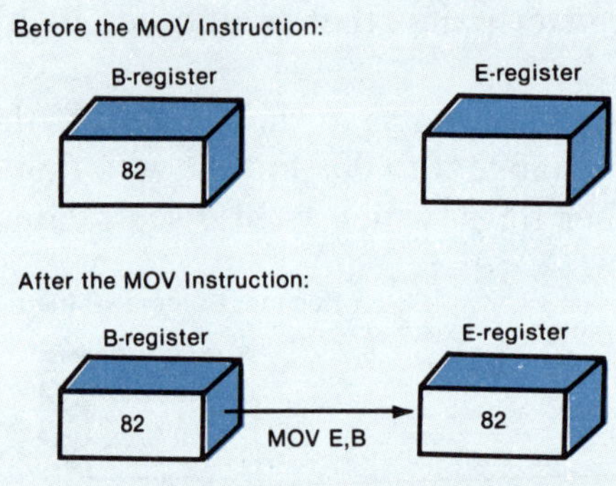

Fig. 2-12. The MOV instruction.

Examples:

```
mov e,a
mov h,l
mov d,b
```

We mentioned earlier that not all hex numbers are printable as ASCII codes. In fact, the printable ASCII codes run from 20 (hex), which is a space, to 7F (hex), which is the rubout. Sending numbers greater or less than these to your console device or printer is likely to cause strange and unpredictable results. Thus, we want to start our program by sending 20 (hex) to the console, and when we've sent 21, 22, and so on up to 7F, we want to start over again with 20. The first instruction in the program, "mvi e,20", starts us off with 20, but how will we know when we get to 7F?

The CPI Instruction

The answer is the CPI instruction, which stands for "Compare Immediate." CPI performs a comparison between the number in the A-register and the number in memory immediately following the CPI instruction. The result of the comparison is used to set the various flags, including the zero flag. How do we know what flags will be set? The idea here is to think of this instruction as a sort of "phantom" subtraction of a fixed 8-bit quantity from the A-register. Why isn't it a "real" subtraction? Because the quantity in the A-register is not actually changed; nothing is subtracted from it. However, the zero flag (and the various other flags that we will learn about later) *act as if* the subtraction had been carried out.

This is easy to understand in the case of the zero flag: *if the two numbers are equal, the zero flag is set.* Why? Because when you subtract a number from the same number, the result is zero.

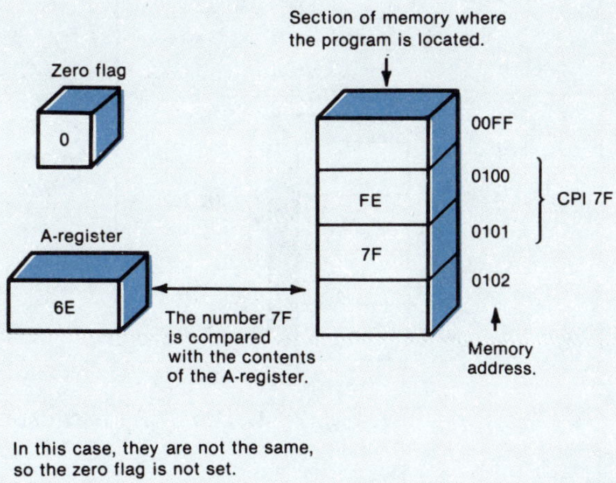

Fig. 2-13. The CPI instruction.

Examples:

```
cpi 7f
cpi 2
```

In our case, the "cpi 7f" instruction compares the contents of the A-register with 7F hex. The first time through the loop, the A-register will contain 20, because the E-register contains 20. So the result of the subtraction will NOT be zero. The next time, the A-register will contain 21, because the E-register contains 21, because we incremented it with the INR instruction. The next time it will contain 22, and so on, until we've counted up to 7F. When the A-register *is* 7F, the results of the comparison will be 0, and the zero flag will be set. What use will we make of the zero flag?

The JNZ (jump-on-not-zero) Instruction

As you can guess, this instruction is similar to the JZ instruction that you've already encountered, except that it jumps if the zero flag is NOT set. Otherwise, it goes on to the next instruction in the program.

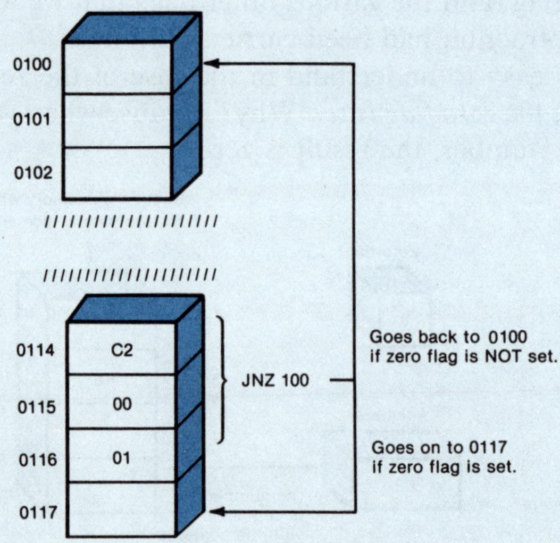

Fig. 2-14. The JNZ instruction.

Examples:

```
jnz 100
jnz bf00
```

In the case of our barber-pole program, the CPI instruction will result in the zero flag not being set until all the ASCII characters from 20 to 7F have been printed. So each time the JNZ instruction will take us back to the second instruction in the program—at location 102. When we've printed all the ASCII characters, the program will go on to location 110, where it will perform the "Get Console Status" system call to see if any key of the keyboard has been pressed. If not, it will start the program over. If so, it will return to DDT, as in the example shown in our previous program.

Running the Program

When you run the program, you should get something like this display:

```
A>ddt barber.ddt

-g100

!"#$%&$¦()*+'-./01234567890:;<=>?ABCDEFGHIJKLOMNOPQRSTUVWXYZ[
\]^_‘abcdefghijklmn opqrstuvwxyz{¦}~ !"#$%&¦()*+’-./01234567890
:;<=>?ABCDEFGHIJKLOMNOPQRSTUVWXYZ[\]^_‘abcdefghijklmn opqrstuvw
xyz{¦}~!'#$%&$¦()*+’-./01234567890:;<=>?ABCDEFGHIJKLOMNOPQRSTUVW
XYZ[¦]^_‘abcdefghijklmn opqrstuvwxyz{¦}~ !"#$%&$¦()*+’-./0123456
7890:;<=>?ABCDEFGHIJKLOMNOPQRSTUVWXYZ[\]^_‘abcdefghijklmn opqrs
tuvwxyz{¦}~......[etc. until you press any key]
```

This is a good program to keep in your wallet and memorize for when you're at a party or at a new friend's house and you want to impress them with your knowledge of CP/M and 8080 code.

CONSOLE INPUT

CONSOLE INPUT	FUNCTION 1 (dec) = 1 (hex)
Enter with:	REG C = 1
On return:	REG A = ASCII character from keyboard

Console Input is perhaps the most-often used CP/M function call. Its purpose is to get a character from the keyboard into your program. Console Input is used by almost all programs that run under CP/M which request user input from the keyboard. For example, all text editors for CP/M use the console input function to get an ASCII value from the keyboard. It works much like the GET statement in BASIC. When Console Input is called, it reads the next console character into the A-register of the 8080. It will "echo" your character to the screen as well. It will not echo control characters but will react to many of them. If no key is pressed, the function will hang, waiting until a key is pressed, and, thus, suspending execution if a character is not ready.

There are some special features of the Console Input function that you should be aware of. Most important is the way it responds to CP/M control characters. It does not respond to a warm boot (control–c), or to the printer stop/start toggle (control–p). This makes complete sense, as you often DON'T want the user to be able to warm-boot the system or turn on the printer from inside your program. When you DO wish the user to have such control, you can use another CP/M console function called "Read Console Buffer." This call, which we will describe shortly, is the one that comes with a complete set of editing commands, and is used by many of the CP/M utilities. You'll hear more about "Read Console Buffer" later.

Beep Program

Let's do a simple exercise program with the Console Input system call. This program will cause CP/M to echo everything typed in at the keyboard onto the screen, accompanied with a little beep that is provided by your console's "beep" or "bell" sound.

Bring up DDT and enter this short program.

```
-a100
0100 mvi c,2        Set up for console output.
0102 mvi e,7        ASCII 7 = bell.
0104 call 5
0107 mvi c,1        Set up for console input.
0109 call 5
010C jmp 100        Loop forever getting key and echoing it.
```

Save it with:

```
-g0
A>save 1 test3.ddt
```

Now, run it by typing:

```
A>ddt test3.ddt
```

and

```
-g100
```

Try it out. Each time you press a key, the console beeps and the character is printed on the screen. Neat. But if you try to press control–c to reboot, nothing happens. Great Scott, we're caught in a deadly endless loop . . . ; we'll have to press reset to escape. But first, while you have your program running, try a few of these keys and verify what happens on your system. All should cause a beep.

^C	Nothing happens and nothing gets displayed.
^P	Same as above.
^J	Causes a line feed to occur.
^M	Causes a carriage return to occur.
^S	Nothing happens (or seems to happen).
^G	Nothing happens.
^H	Backspaces the cursor.

What this tells us is that the Console Input function does not respond to all the normal CP/M control-key conventions. If you wanted it to respond, for instance, to the control–c key, you would have to write a special part of your program yourself, to do just that.

Also, you can see that our program has a "bug" in it, in that the only way we can turn it off is to do a cold boot by resetting the system. This, again, is less than elegant. Can you think of a way out of this problem? Could you rewrite the program so that it looks for the control–c and causes the program to end if it sees one? Yes, Watson, and here's how to do it!

Take our old code:

```
0100 mvi c,2     Set up for console output.
0102 mvi e,7     ASCII 7 = bell.
0104 call 5
0107 mvi c,1     Set up for console input.
0109 call 5
010C jmp 100     (Replaced with cpi 3.)
```

Enter this new code:

```
-a10C
010C cpi 3        Check if A=3.
010E jnz 100      If not, repeat loop.
0111 rst 7        Yes, it was a 3, so end.
```

You can save the program as "test4.ddt".

What do these new instructions do? The ASCII code for a control–c is 3 (hex), so we now check each character typed in to see if it has a value of 3, using the cpi instruction as in the previous example. If it does, we go back to DDT with the "rst 7" instruction. Otherwise, we keep looping.

Run the program from DDT with g100 and see if you can stop the program by pressing a control–c.

As an exercise, you could try modifying this program by having the captured character do something other than end the program. Perhaps it could cause a warm boot when a control–c is typed. The next function call (system reset) explains how that is done. But first, we need to learn how to execute programs directly from CP/M.

EXECUTING PROGRAMS FROM CP/M

So far we have executed all our programs from DDT by typing g100. This is fine for short exercises, but many times we want to be able to execute a program directly from CP/M without calling up DDT at all, simply by typing the name of the program following the CP/M prompt A>.

In theory, this is simple. We write the program in DDT, then SAVE it as a COM file, and, then, execute it directly from CP/M. However, in practice, there's a problem, and it's this: if our program contains a "rst 7" instruction, and we attempt to execute it directly from CP/M, we'll probably "crash the system" (cause error messages followed by a cold boot), because CP/M does not respond to "rst 7" the same way that DDT does. "rst 7" can be used only to return to DDT. To return to CP/M, we use another instruction—"ret".

The RET Instruction

RET is usually used in connection with the CALL instruction. CALL takes you from your main program to a subroutine, and RET takes you back again. Remember how, in the CALL instruction, the address immediately following the CALL was placed on the stack? Well, the RET instruction takes this address off the stack and transfers control back to this address in the main program.

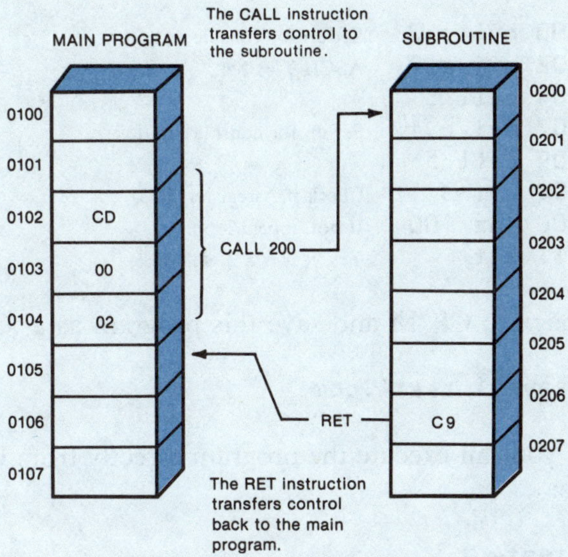

Fig. 2-15. The RET instruction.

Example:

ret

RET is ordinarily used to return us to the calling program from a subroutine. Now, the way CP/M is set up, applications programs–that is, programs we want to execute directly from CP/M–are treated as subroutines by the CP/M operating system. This makes it easy to leave a program and go back to CP/M. All we have to do is execute a RET instruction and, presto, we're back in the monitor with the A> prompt.

However, if we attempt to execute a program directly in CP/M that *doesn't* use RET to return to the monitor, then we can be in big trouble. Specifically, if we attempt to execute a program in CP/M that ends with RST 7, disaster will probably result.

So, before we can use any of the programs we've written so far in a direct CP/M mode, we need to go through them and change any "rst 7" instructions we find to "ret" instructions. Let's do that on the last example, which beeped when we typed in characters, but which went back to DDT when we typed a control–c. Simply change the last instruction in the program, rst 7, to ret. Here's the resulting code:

```
0100 mvi c,2     Set up for console output.
0102 mvi e,7     ASCII 7 = bell.
0104 call 5
0107 mvi c,1     Set up for console input.
0109 call 5
010C cpi 3       Check if A-register = 3.
010E jnz 100     If not, repeat loop.
0111 ret         Yes, it was a 3, so end.
```

Go back to CP/M and save this program as a .COM file by typing:

```
A>save 1 test4.com
```

Now you can execute the program directly from CP/M, simply by typing its name:

```
A>test4
```

Type in some stuff. Listen to the beeps. What happens when you type a control–c? You're back in CP/M again! This is just how programs are executed in the big leagues.

SYSTEM RESET–A WARM BOOT

SYSTEM RESET	FUNCTION 0 (dec) = 0 (hex)
Enter with: REG C = 0	

The System Reset system call is used for causing a warm boot from your program. The warm boot, as you recall, causes the CCP part of the CP/M operating system to be reloaded. Also, several locations in FDOS (BDOS plus BIOS) are reset to their initial values.

The reason that you need to know how to do a warm boot is simple. Sometimes you will need as much memory space in the TPA as you can get. As you know, BIOS, BDOS, and CCP take up room in the top of RAM. It turns out that you can remove the entire CCP from RAM and still use all of the system calls, provided you don't wipe out FDOS. When you want to return to CP/M, you do a "System Reset" and the CCP will be reloaded and FDOS reinitialized. System reset works just as if you pressed control–c from the keyboard. You'll hear the disk click as the CCP is read off the disk into memory.

Here's a little program that will cause a warm boot (system reset). But, look out! You can't test it from DDT because it will wipe itself out in the process of resetting the system, thus, resulting in error messages and trouble!

```
-a100
0100 mvi c,0      Set up for system reset.
0102 call 5       Call BDOS.
0105 ret          Return to CP/M.

-g0
```

Enter the program from DDT, exit DDT with a g0 (which also causes a warm boot and replaces DDT with the CCP), and do a:

```
A>save 1 test5.com
```

Now, you can execute the program directly from CP/M:

```
A>test5     Test the program.
A>          Hear disk click, new prompt.
```

Now you know how to make your program go back and reinitialize CP/M whenever you want. That means that you can run programs that use the memory space usually occupied by the CCP and can be assured that you can reinitialize the system later.

SO LONG, CHAPTER 2, IT'S BEEN GOOD TO KNOW YOU

By this time, you know more about CP/M and 8080 programming than you ever expected to. You've learned the Console Out, Get Console Status, Console Input, and System Reset systems calls. And, you've learned a whole batch of 8080 instructions: MVI, CALL, RST, JMP, ORA, JZ, PUSH, POP, INR, MOV, CPI, JNZ, and RET.

That's enough 8080 instructions to write some pretty complicated code. And, since you now know how to do input and output to your video screen and keyboard, there's really no limit to the programs you can write. However, there are other, more powerful, systems calls that will give you greater flexibility and will simplify your programming. We'll cover them in the next chapter, so hang onto your hats!

CHAPTER 3

Getting in Deeper

Advanced Console System Calls

In this chapter, we'll look at some console input/output system calls that operate on whole groups of characters, rather than on one character at a time as did the system calls in the last chapter. Then, we'll introduce you to an unusual display program which will act as a review of what you've learned so

far. We'll describe "Direct Console I/O," which lets you interact much more directly with the screen and the keyboard than have our previous system calls. Finally, to wrap up our study of nondisk system calls, we'll cover a number of functions which deal with nonstandard I/O equipment.

PRINT STRING

PRINT STRING	FUNCTION 9 (dec) = 9 (hex)
Enter with:	REG C = 9 hex
	REGs DE = starting address of string
Comments:	String must end in a "$" (24 hex)

Here's the way to send complete words or even sentences to the screen from inside CP/M. In the programming world, as you know, a series of characters like a word or a sentence is called a "string" (it's just a collection of strung-out characters). In CP/M, a string may goeth and a string may cometh, meaning that we can send strings to the screen and we can accept strings from the keyboard. The Print String function is for making your string goeth to the console display screen. It's an advanced version of the Console Out system call in the the last chapter, which only sent one character to the screen at a time. Print String is sort of like the PRINT statement in BASIC, except it is a bit more indirect to use, as you will see.

Print String expects that you have stored the string you want to send to the screen in a continuous area of memory as a sequence of ASCII bytes. (We'll show you how to do this presently.) You must end the string with hex 24, the ASCII value for the "$" symbol. Then, to print the string, you put the address where the string starts in the DE register-pair, put a 9 in your C REG and do a BONSAI TO BDOS (a very excited call 5).

Of course, manually typing in and looking up the ASCII equivalents for all of the characters in the message that you want to display can certainly be a tedious process. Be patient! In the next chapter, we are going to show you how to use ASM, the CP/M assembler, to simplify this process. When using an assembler (as opposed to a miniassembler like that in DDT), you can simply enter the letters for the string into the source listing directly from the keyboard. So take heart, we'll eventually learn to do Print String the easy way. In the meantime, using DDT will be a bit tedious, but it will give us a better idea of what's really going on.

Typing in a Message With DDT

First use the DDT Set command "s" to put the hex values for the letters "A B C D E" into memory starting at location 010A hex. The set command first displays the current contents of the memory location that you are about to type in to. In this case, these numbers are of no interest to us. Each time you type a two-digit (one byte) value and hit the carriage return, your number is stored in the memory location shown, overwriting the old value.

```
                These are the old values.

                You type numbers in this column.
-s10a
010A 53 41      DDT displays 010A 53 and you typed 41 (hit return after every value
                  you type in).
010B 49 42
010C 47 43
010D 48 44
010E 54 45
010F 20 24 <--- This is the $ to end the string.
0110 28 .  <--- Type a period to end the Set command.
-
```

Now you can check that you have entered the string correctly, using the D command:

```
-d10a,10f
010A 41 42 43 44 45 24          ABCDE$
```

As you can see, the numbers are just as we entered them, with the ASCII letters that they represent shown in the right-hand display column. Now we are ready to enter the program that will actually print the string:

```
-a100
0100 mvi c,9       Set up for Print String.
0102 lxi d,10a     We start our string at 10A hex.
0105 call 5        Our famous BDOS call.
0108 rst 7         Return to DDT.
```

Save it as test5.ddt.

The LXI Instruction

As you recall from the last chapter, the mvi instruction took a one-byte constant and placed it into the register indicated in the instruction. LXI is similar, except that it puts a *two*-byte constant into the indicated register-pair. This two-byte constant is stored in the program in the two bytes immediately following the lxi instruction in memory.

As in the MVI instruction, the "I" in LXI means that the constant to be stored *immediately* follows the instruction in memory (as shown in the diagram of Fig. 3-1). The "X" means that the instruction operates on a register

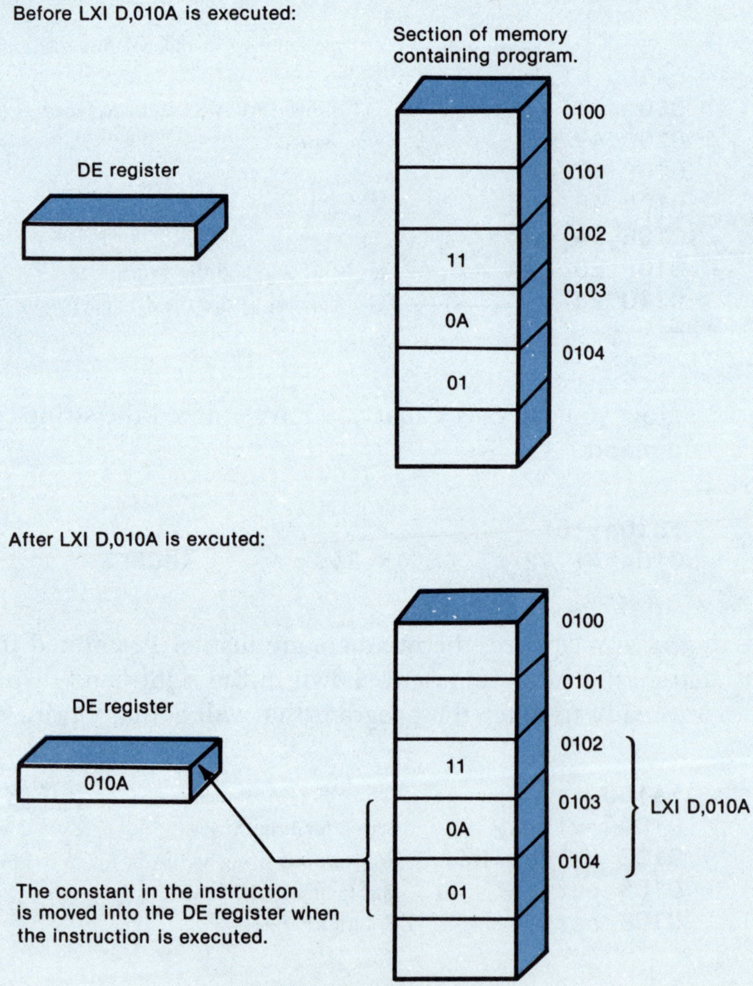

Fig. 3-1. The LXI instruction.

pair and not on a single 8-bit register. These are both conventions which make it slightly easier to remember the mnemonics (abbreviations) for the instructions.

Don't forget when using LXI that you need to type in *four* hexadecimal digits, not two as with MVI.

Examples

```
lxi d,1234
lxi h,01ff
lxi b,bf00
```

Now try executing the "test5.ddt" program:

```
-g100
ABCDE*0108        Worked perfectly! ABCDE got printed.
-
```

There is almost no limit to the size of the string you can print. To see this, use the "fill" command in DDT to put a large number of the same ASCII letter after the ABCDE string. To use "fill," type f, followed by the address where you want to start filling, the address where you want to stop filling, and the constant you want to fill in. For instance,

-f10f,400,41

will fill memory from 10f to 400 with ASCII "A's". *Don't forget to put the 24 hex at the end of the string,* using the "s" function.

```
-s401
401 FD 24        This is the ASCII for "$".
402 D0 .         Period used to terminate "s".
```

Now try your program on this new string. The screen will simply fill with the letter "A" continually until it reaches the end. DON'T TURN ON YOUR PRINTER. There are no carriage returns at the end of every 80th character of the string, so the printhead may go to the right side of the carriage and bang itself to death there.

READ CONSOLE BUFFER

READ CONSOLE BUFFER	FUNCTION 10 (dec) = 0A (hex)
Enter with:	REG C = 0A hex REG DE = Buffer address DE+0 = Maximum number of characters
On return:	DE+1 = Number of characters typed DE+2, etc. = Typed characters in buffer
Comments:	Max length string = 255 characters Responds to all CP/M line editing commands

Read Console Buffer is one of CP/M's most useful functions. Its purpose is to accept a string of characters typed in at the console device (usually the keyboard) and put them in a "buffer" area in memory so your program can use them. Read Console Buffer is similar to the Console Input function we covered earlier in that it accepts information typed at the keyboard. However, the similarity stops there, for the read buffer function allows the user to type a complete string of up to 255 characters. It's also a little more complicated to set up than Console Input. We'll explain how to do it, and what "DE+1" and similar notations mean, in a minute.

CP/M's Built-in Editing Commands

One feature that makes Read Console Buffer especially useful is that it responds to the set of CP/M control-character commands and, thus, permits editing while you're typing in the string. Perhaps the most important of these commands is control-c. If this is typed at the beginning of the string, CP/M does a warm boot. Thus, by using Read Console Buffer, you allow your program user the opportunity to reboot the program during input. This may be desirable or not, depending on the type of program being used. Read Console Buffer offers a host of other useful line editing features. The commands available to the lucky user of this function are (press CONTROL with all these letters):

H backspaces one character position.

X backspaces to the beginning of the line and erases all characters (start over, erase).

U moves cursor down to beginning of next line and IGNORES previous typed line (start over, still view old line).

R retypes the current line after the new line. Useful when you overused the DEL key and can't figure out what the line means.

E causes "physical end of line," meaning the cursor returns to the left margin, one line down.

J is a line-feed character, and terminates input line (as if a carriage return was typed).

M is a carriage return, terminates input line.

DEL removes and echos the last character typed. An old-fashioned way to remove characters, left over from the old days of hardcopy-only teletypewriter machines.

C does a warm boot.

We don't want to go too far off on a tangent at this point by getting too involved in these editing features. You can practice them on the string that we will be using in the next exercise. For now, here is a short way to remember the most important commands:

H Hard left one space, no Hurt.
X X out the whole line, start over.
U yUck, start over next line.
R Retype line, down one line.
E End this line, go down a line.

You can copy this out and stick it up near your computer, or on the forehead of a passing co-worker.

How to Set Up Read Console Buffer

The Read Console Buffer system call "reads" a line of edited console input into a buffer addressed by the contents of register-pair DE. You must set up the buffer address in the DE-register before making the call. The LXI instruction is used to do this, just as in the Print String function. In addition, you must set up a number in the beginning of the buffer which represents the maximum number of characters you want to accept. If you put a hex 20, for example, in the buffer, then as soon as the user types more than 32 characters (decimal), the function will terminate. We call this "ending by OVERFLOW." The user can also terminate the string by typing a RETURN (or a control–J or -M).

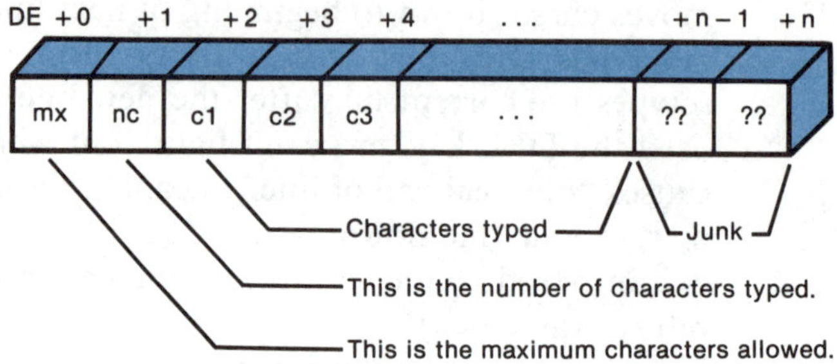

Fig. 3-2. Buffer address in the DE register.

The buffer that we set up looks like the diagram in Fig. 3-2.

This is what it means. "DE+0" is simply shorthand for *the address sent to the function in the DE-register.* DE+1 is the next address after this, and so on. Thus, if you put 400 in the DE-register when you call this function, DE+1 will be at 401, DE+2 will be at 402, and so on up to DE+n, which will depend on the length of your message.

The "mx" indicates the maximum number of characters that the function will allow to be typed into the buffer, a number from 1 to FF hex (1 to 255 decimal). Your program must put this value in the first position in the buffer. The "nc" is the number of characters actually typed by the user and this is set by FDOS when the function returns to your program. This number is useful for determining how long the input string actually is. It is found at DE+1. Following "nc" are the actual characters read from the keyboard. If the number of characters actually typed by the user is less than the number set by mx (nc < mx), then the remaining positions in the buffer are whatever they were before the function was called and have no meaning. These are marked as ?? in Fig. 3-2.

Note that some control characters typed into the print buffer will get stored in their proper ASCII codes. Tabs, for example, appear as 09 hex. A control–c in the middle of a line will appear as a 03 hex.

Our Read Console Buffer example is really quite simple. Let's assume that we're going to start our buffer at 200 hex. Type the following in DDT:

```
-a100
0100 mvi a,20      Set max characters to 32 (dec)
0102 sta 200         and put in first buffer position.
0105 mvi c,a       Set up REG C for Read Console Buffer.
0107 lxi d,200     Load DE with location of buffer start.
010A call 5        Finally, call BDOS.
010D rst 7         Back to DDT.
```

You can store this program as "test6.ddt".

As you can see, there's a new instruction listed: STA. Let's see what it's all about.

The STA Instruction

This instruction will take the 8-bit value in the A-register and store it anyplace in memory. Where this value will be stored is determined by the address in the operand field of the instruction. For instance:

```
sta 2000
```

will take the 8-bit value in the A-register, which might be anything from 00 to FF, and store it in memory location 2000.

In DDT, this address is represented by a four-digit hexadecimal number. In the next chapter, when you learn how to use the assembler, you will find that this address can also be represented by a name.

Notice the difference between this instruction and others that we've learned about earlier. For instance, MOV B,A takes an 8-bit value from the A-register and stores it, not in memory as STA does, but in a register: the B-register. An instruction like MVI A,7F is different from STA in two ways. First, it's loading an 8-bit value from memory into the A-register, not storing it from the A-register into memory as STA does. Second, MVI A,7F refers to a constant at a place in memory immediately following the MVI instruction, while STA refers to a location in memory that can be located far away from the STA instruction itself. For this reason, STA uses an *address* in the operand field, while MVI uses the actual 8-bit value.

Examples

```
sta 2010
sta 0100
sta bf00
```

Our example program first puts a 20 (hex) into the A-register and stores it at the beginning of our buffer at 200 (hex). This is "mx," the maximum number of characters. The program then calls Read Console Buffer, using the address 200 as the start of the buffer. It then waits for you to type something in.

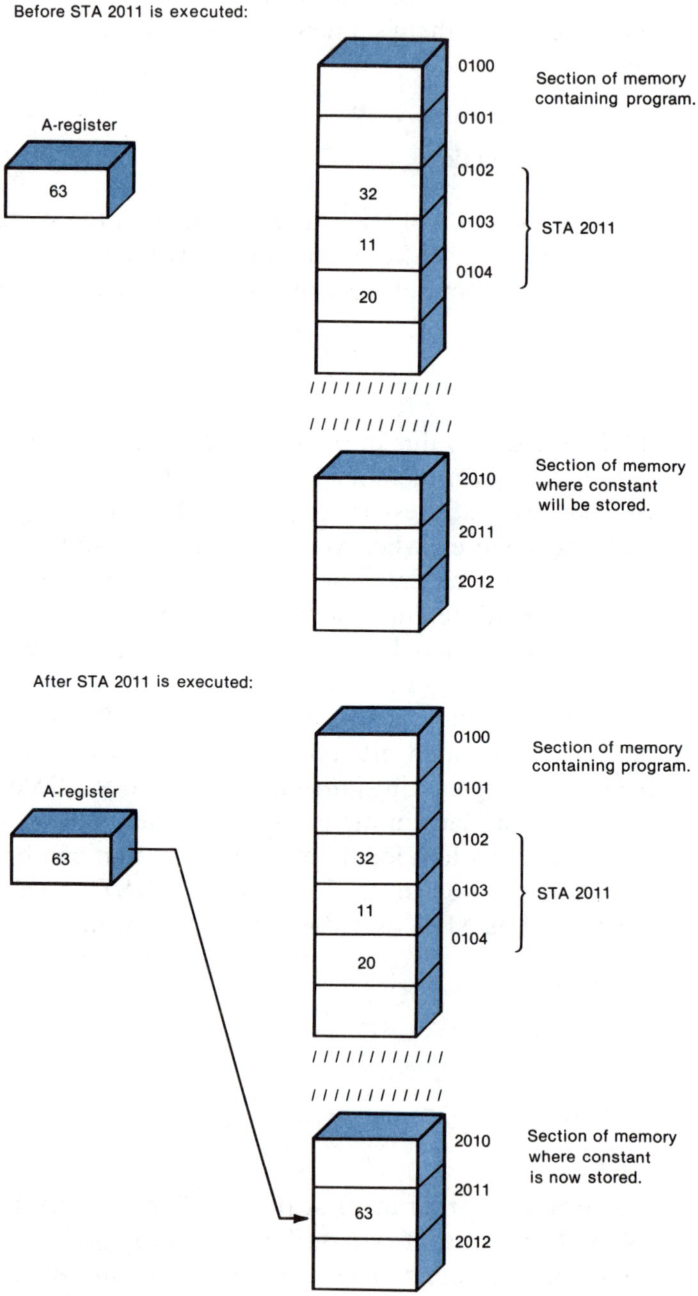

Fig. 3-3. The STA instruction.

```
-g100                   <——— Start the program.
Now is the time. <——— Type this in.
*010D                   <——— This will actually overwrite the first part of the input.
```

There is a small glitch in that the "*010D", which DDT prints when the program is over, overwrites part of the line that we typed in. This would be easy to fix, as we'll see in the next example, but for the time being we'll live with it.

Now you can dump (display) the buffer at 200 (hex) to see if what you were supposed to put there has actually arrived.

```
-d200,21f

0200 20 10 4E 6F 77 20 69 73 20 74 68 65 20 74 69 6D  .Now is the tim
0210 65 2E CD 05 00 F5 79 CD 8F 06 F1 C9 FE 20 C8 FE e.....y...... ..
```

There it is! The 20 at location 200 is the maximum number of characters "mx," which you put there with the STA instruction. The 10 in location 201 is the actual number of characters typed in (10 hex is 16 decimal). The rest of the buffer from 212 on is still filled with whatever junk was in it before.

Let's see what happens if we type in more characters than are specified by "mx."

```
-g100

Now is the time for all good men <——— Type this in, keep typing.
*010D                             └——— At this point, the function took
-                                        over and returned us to DDT.
```

Dump the buffer again and there's our input, safely stored away. This time the number of characters that were actually typed in is the same as the maximum "mx."

```
-d200,22f

0200 20 20 4E 6F 77 20 69 73 20 74 68 65 20 74 69 6D   Now is the tim
0210 65 20 66 6F 72 20 61 6C 6C 20 67 6F 6F 64 20 6D e for all good m
0220 65 6E FE 2C C8 FE 0D C8 FE 7F CA 24 05 C9 0E 0D en.,.......$....
```

There it is again, just as you typed it. Later we'll see how a program can make use of this function to accomplish all sorts of useful and exciting things.

ECHO PROGRAM

Let's put together the two string-handling system calls that you've just learned–Print String and Read Console Buffer–into a single short program.

```
-a100
0100  mvi a,20      Put max characters at start of buffer.
0102  sta 1fe
0105  mvi c,0a      Call Read Console Buffer.
0107  lxi d,1fe
010A  call 5
010D  mvi c,2       Use Console Out to print linefeed.
010F  mvi e,0a
0111  call 5
0114  mvi c,9       Print String.
0116  lxi d,200
0119  call 5
011C  rst 7         Back to DDT.
011D
```

You can save this as "test7.ddt".

This program will accept the input that you type, store it in a buffer, and then print it out on the screen, echoing what you typed in. There are several things to notice. First, we had to add a section to the program to print a linefeed. This keeps the Print String function from printing right over the string that you typed in. To do this, we use the Console Output function to print a 0A ASCII character, which is the linefeed.

The next thing to notice is that we tell the Read Console Buffer and the Print String functions different addresses for the start of the buffer. Read Console Buffer is told to start at 1FE, while Print String is told to start at 200. This is because Read Console Buffer needs two extra bytes at the start of the buffer to enter the maximum number of characters "mx" and the number of characters actually typed "nc." These will go in 1FE and 1FF, respectively, so that the actual typed characters will start at 200.

Try typing in some input. But, BE CAREFUL! Since Print String requires that the string it prints be terminated with a dollar-sign character, you *must type a "$" at the end of your string.* Otherwise, as we noted earlier, Print String won't know when to stop, and may end up printing a lot of weird characters that will do strange things to your terminal. For this reason, you must also make sure you don't type any more than 32 decimal (20 hex) characters. If you do, Read Console Buffer will terminate itself before you have time to type the dollar-sign character.

```
-g100                          ┌── Don't forget the $.
                               ↓
Now is the time.$      ←── You type this.
Now is the time.*011C  ←── Program types this.
-
```

NAME DISPLAY PROGRAM

The next program also makes use of the Read Console Buffer and Print String functions. It's a little more ambitious–which is to say longer and more complicated–and is really included just to give you something a little frivolous and amusing to play with. So don't worry if every nuance of the program's operation isn't clear to you. However, in addition to Print String and Read Console Buffer, it also makes use of the Console Output and Get Console Status system calls and it uses most of the 8080 instructions we've covered so far. So it can serve as a review of what you've learned up to this point. It also introduces the loop-within-a-loop, a concept that is good to get used to, as we'll be seeing it again later.

What exactly does the program do? Well, that's a little hard to explain. You start off by typing your name and the program then uses your name to make some rather surprising patterns on the video screen. One picture, they say, is worth a thousand words, so why not type in the program (very carefully) and see what happens?

```
-a100
0100  mvi   a,20     Put max characters at start of buffer.
0102  sta   o1fe
0105  mvi   c,0a     Set up to get input string,
0107  lxi   d,1fe      store it at 1fe.
0108  call  5          Call "Read Console Buffer."
010D  mvi   b,30     Set initial B-register value to 30
010F  push  b          and save on stack.
0110  pop   b        Get B from stack,
0111  inr   b          increment it,
0112  mov   c,b        store it in C,
0113  mov   a,b        and in A,
0114  push  b          and put it back on stack.
0115  cpi   50       Is the B-register = 50 yet?
```

```
0117   jz     108      Yes, so go reset it.
011A   mvi    c,2      Set up to print a space,
011C   mvi    e,20       (20 hex is a space),
011E   call   5          call "Console Output."
0121   pop    b        Get BC, to decrement C.
0122   dcr    c          Decrement C,
0123   push   b          save BC.
0124   jnz    115      If C-register not 0, go print space.
0127   mvi    c,9      Print the string;
0129   lxi    d,200      starts 2 bytes past 1fe.
012C   call   5          Call "Print String."
012F   mvi    c,b      Keyboard character typed?
0131   call   5          Call "Get Console Status."
0134   ora    a          Is A-register still = 0?
0135   jz     10B        Yes, so do another line.
0138   rst    7        Back to DDT.
```

You can save this program as "namedisp.ddt". Be careful while typing in the code. One disadvantage of using the microassembler in DDT is that if you make a mistake in your input, sometimes it's not easy to go back and change it. This is because different instructions have different lengths, and if you put a two-byte instruction in a place where you meant to put a three-byte instruction, and then you want to go back and try to change it to the 3-byter, it won't fit. Using the assembler will eliminate this problem, as we will see in the next chapter.

Here's how this program works. When you first start it, you type in your name. As in the last example, BE CAREFUL! *You must terminate your name with a dollar-sign character!*

```
-g100                  <------ Start the program.

Alfred E. Newman$      <------ Type your name (press return).

                       <------ Watch what happens!
```

Unfortunately, we can't reproduce in this book a picture showing the motion that the program displays. However, we can describe how the program works. After you've typed in your name, the program prints a string of spaces, then your name, then a string of spaces (which is one space longer than the first string of spaces), then your name, then a string of spaces which is two spaces longer than the first one, then your name, and so on. The result is a pattern of shifting parabolas which seems far too complicated to have come from such a simple program.

The constants in the program, 30 hex and 50 hex, are set up to work on an 80-column screen. If your screen is a different size, the program may not produce the desired results. Try changing the 30 in line 108 and the 50 in line 110 to different values. Experiment a little.

Two registers are used to hold the variables that the program needs to remember what it's doing. The B-register holds the number of spaces to be printed on the current line. This number starts at 30 hex and goes up to 50 hex. (These values were determined by trial and error.) The C-register counts how many of these spaces have already been printed. That is, if the number in the B-register is 40, then the C-register will start off at 40 and count downward to 0, printing a space each time. When all these spaces have been printed, the program will go back, increment B by one, and start over printing the new number of spaces.

There's one new instruction used in this program; it's called DCR.

The DCR Instruction

This instruction is the opposite of the INR instruction that you learned about earlier. Where INR incremented (added 1 to) the one-byte register specified in the instruction, DCR decrements (subtracts 1 from) the register. Any 8-bit register (A, B, C, D, E, H, or L) may be used in the operand field.

Note that this instruction also sets the appropriate flags. That is, if decrementing the register causes it to become 0, the zero flag will be set; otherwise, it will be cleared. (Some other flags may be set as well.)

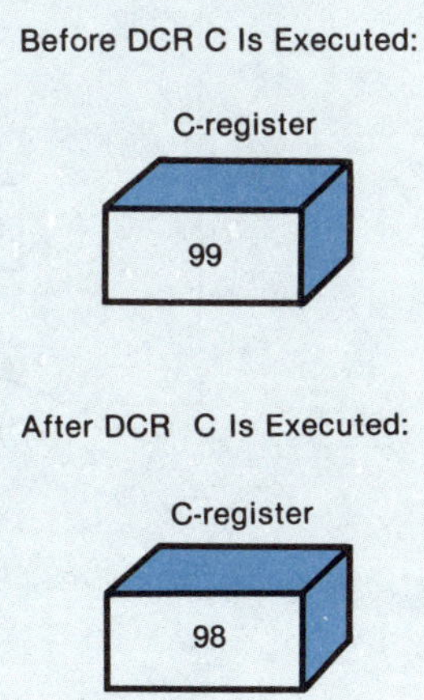

Fig. 3-4. The DCR instruction.

Examples:

dcr b
dcr h

Fig. 3-5 is a flowchart that details the operation of the program. The memory locations where the different parts of the code occur are shown on the side.

By studying the flowchart along with the program listing, you should begin to understand how the program works. The heart of the program is the print-

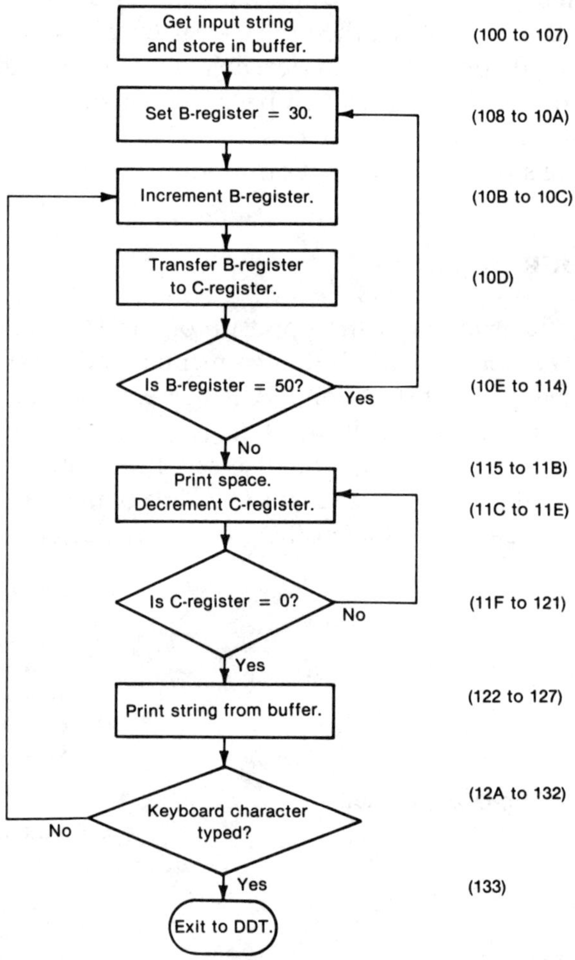

Fig. 3-5. Flowchart for the DCR instruction.

ing of a string of spaces, in lines 115 to 119. Register C is set at the beginning of this section to the number of spaces to be printed and is decremented each time until it is zero. Then, the user's name is printed and the program checks to see if a keyboard character was typed to halt the program. After this, the program returns to 10B to increment the B-register, which started off with 30 and will end at 50. The B-register holds the value that is given to the C-register in line 10D so that the correct number of spaces will be printed each time through.

Again, don't worry if every detail isn't crystal clear. The point really is just to understand how a number of systems calls can work together in a single program.

DIRECT CONSOLE I/O

DIRECT CONSOLE I/O	FUNCTION 6 (dec) = 6 (hex)
Enter with:	REG C = 06 hex REG E = FF hex *on input* REG E = ASCII character *on output*
On return:	REG A = ASCII character, or 00 (no character) *on input.*
Comments:	A dual-purpose function call, for input and output. No echo, bypasses all CP/M line-editing commands.

Direct Console I/O provides the serious programmer with a means of getting characters from the keyboard and displaying characters on the screen *without* echo and *without* the previously described built-in control-character functions, which it does not acknowledge. This is useful in those special circumstances where you want to do something nonstandard with the user's input or the screen output. For instance, you might be writing a word-processing program, and you might want to use control-c to cause the cursor to move to another part of the document, rather than causing a warm boot as it normally does. Or, you might want to define a special function for control-s, instead of having it halt the display.

The use of Direct Console I/O lets you define control characters as you wish and, thus, gives you a great deal of flexibility and control over your input and output. However, you sacrifice all the capabilities that CP/M

offers for free, such as, freeze the display, warm boot, retype line, backspace, printer on/off, etc. If you want these functions in Direct Console I/O, you must build them into your program yourself.

Since using the control characters in a nonstandard way can lead to confusion if you're not careful, the makers of CP/M (Digital Research, Inc.) recommend that you not use Direct Console I/O. Of course, many programmers use it anyway.

Direct Console I/O is unusual in another way. It's actually two functions, accessed with the same system call.

On input, put ff (hex) into the E-register. The function will immediately return with a 0 in the A-register, and will continue to return 0 until something is typed on the keyboard. Then, it will return the ASCII value of the character typed, but nothing will appear on the screen. This function is unlike both the Console Input and Read Console Buffer system calls in that it *does not wait* until the user types something before it returns to the calling program. (In this way, it's like the INKEY$ function in some versions of BASIC.) Thus, you must continually check to see if the A-register is zero, and do the call again if it is.

On output, put the ASCII character you want to send to the screen into the E-register. The function will print it, without checking to see if it is a control character.

A Short Example

Here's a very short DDT program demonstrating how the calls are made to both the input and output functions of Direct Console I/O. All this program does is echo on the screen whatever is typed on the keyboard.

```
-a100
0100  mvi   c,6      Get keyboard character;
0102  mvi   e,ff       ff indicates input.
0104  call  5
0107  ora   a        Is A-register = 0?
0108  jz    100        Yes, go try again.
010B  mvi   c,6      Got character, so print it;
010D  mov   e,a        put it in E-register.
010E  call  5
0111  jmp   100      Go wait for next character.
```

Save the program as "test8.ddt" and then try it out. Notice how none of the editing control keys has any effect. Also, the backspace doesn't work. And, most inconvenient of all, there is no way to stop the program since control–c is inoperative. If you needed to use Direct Console I/O, you'd have to build all these features into your program.

Password Program

Have you ever used an automated bank teller that required you to type in an account number? Or a time-sharing computer that requested a password before giving you access to the system? In both these cases, what you type in is often not echoed to the screen. This is a security precaution. It keeps anyone who happens to look over your shoulder from learning your number or password. Our next example is a short program that shows how the Direct Console I/O system call might be used to implement such a function.

Type in the following program and save it as "test9.ddt:"

```
-a100
0100  lxi   h,200    Put buffer address in HL;
0103  push  h          save it on stack.
0104  mvi   c,6      Set up Direct Console I/O;
0106  mvi   e,ff       specify "input."
0108  call  5
010B  ora   a        Anything typed yet?
010C  jz    0104       Not yet.
```

```
010F   pop   h        Yes. Restore address in HL.
0110   mov   m,a      Store character in buffer.
0111   inx   h        Increment address.
0112   cpi   24       Was character a "$"?
0114   jnz   0103       No, go get next character.
0117   mvi   c,9      Yes. Print string in buffer;
0119   lxi   d,200      set buffer address.
011C   call  5
011F   rst   7        Back to DDT.
```

This program lets you type in a string of characters, without echoing them to the keyboard, just as a real "password" program would do. To terminate the input string, you type a dollar sign ($). Then, to ensure that everything is working the way we expect, the program prints out the complete phrase. (It wouldn't do this, of course, in a real password application.)

The Phantom "M" Register

You may have noticed something new going on in this program. It is the letter "m" in the "mov m,a" instruction at location 0110. What is this? We've never mentioned an "M" register before. Well, as it turns out, there *isn't* any such register. "M" is nothing more than a handy abbreviation for *the memory address pointed to by the HL-register.* This usage is possible because the designers of the 8080 gave the HL register the useful ability to *indirectly* address a memory location. That is, other 8-bit instructions, such as MVI and MOV, can "pretend" there is an "M" register, but what they really do (when we write an "m" following the instruction) is to first look at HL to get the address it holds and then operate on the memory location pointed to by that address, as if the memory location were a register. This is a useful concept when we want to store a series of data items in sequential memory locations, as we do here with the characters that are read in using the Direct Console I/O routine. This is illustrated by the diagram shown in Fig. 3-6.

Here's how it works. We start off by putting the address of the first memory location where we want to store our series of characters—in the HL register. In this case, we put 200 into HL (line 100). Now that we've done this, we know that every time we refer to the "M" register, we're really referring to memory location 200 (until we change the contents of HL). So—the first time it is executed, anyway—the "mov m,a" instruction in line 110 has the effect of taking the character in the A-register and putting it in location 200. But we don't want to put *all* the characters in location 200—we want the second char-

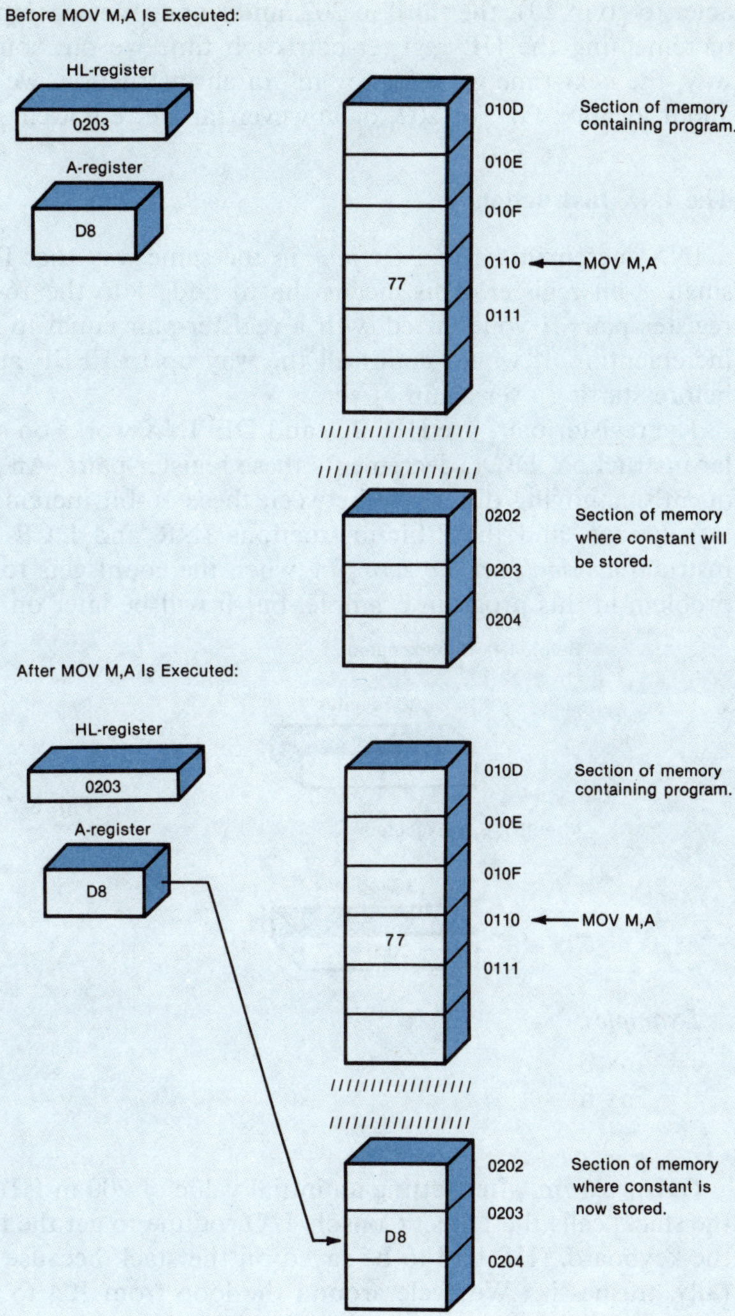

Fig. 3-6. The phantom "M" register.

acter to go in 201, the third in 202, and so on. We accomplish this by simply incrementing the HL register-pair each time we put something in it. That way, the next time we refer to "m" in an instruction, we'll really be talking about location 201, or 202, or however far we've gotten.

The INX Instruction

INX increments a register *pair* in the same way that INR incremented a single 8-bit register. This means that it adds 1 to the 16-bit number in the register pair. If you started with a register-pair equal to zero and just kept incrementing, it would count all the way up to FFFF hex (65535 decimal) before starting over again at zero.

The register pairs are HL, BC, and DE. INX works on all of them. A similar instruction, DCX, decrements these register-pairs. An important and frequently annoying difference between these 16-bit increment and decrement instructions, and the 8-bit instructions INR and DCR, is that the 16-bit instructions *don't set the zero flag* when the count gets to zero. That's not a problem in this program example, but it will be later on.

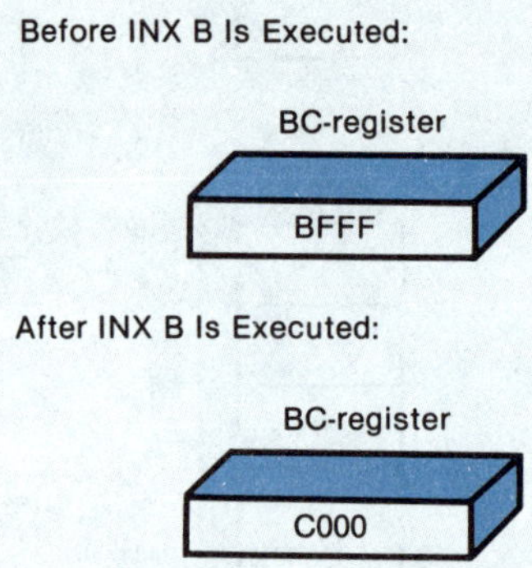

Fig. 3-7. The INX instruction.

Examples:

```
inx b
inx h
```

Our program, after setting an initial value of 200 in HL and saving HL on the stack, calls the Direct Console I/O routine to get the first character from the keyboard. (HL had to be saved on the stack because this routine, naturally, trashes it.) We cycle around the loop from 104 to 10C, waiting tor a nonzero value in the A-register to indicate that a character was typed. Once we get the character in A, we do several things: we get HL back from the stack (line 10F), we store the character in the buffer (line 110), and we increment the HL-register (line 111) so it will point to the next sequential location in the buffer when we next call it.

To find out if the user has finished his message, we then check, with the "cpi 24" instruction, to see if the character typed was a dollar sign. If not, we jump up to 103, save HL again, and wait for a new character. If it was a dollar sign, we go on and print the contents of the buffer, starting at location 200, using our old friend the Print String system call. Since we required that the message be terminated with a dollar sign on input, we know that there will be one at the end of the buffer to end the message for Print String. Finally, we return to DDT.

LIST OUTPUT TO PRINTER

LIST OUTPUT (PRINTER) FUNCTION 5 (dec) = 5 (hex)

Enter with: REG C = 05 hex
REG E = ASCII character

Comments: Similar to Console Output, except character is sent to LIST device.

This system call lets you send a character to the LIST device, which is usually the printer, in the same way that Console Output lets you send a character to the console screen. Of course, there are some differences in the way the printer operates, as compared with a video screen, that must be taken into account.

First, the usual situation is that a printer will absorb a certain number of characters, such as one line, without doing anything; at least, anything you can see. The characters sent are stored in an internal buffer in the printer, until either (1) the printer's line length is exceeded, or (2) a carriage return or other terminating character is sent. At this point, the printer will print the entire line of characters. So, if your program wants to ensure that what it has sent is what gets printed out, it must send a carriage return as the last character.

Some printers automatically supply a linefeed when they receive a carriage-return character, others don't. If yours doesn't, then you need to send one following the linefeed, to keep the printer from overprinting the previous line.

Second, keep in mind that some characters look different on the screen than they do on the printer. Control characters, for example, may appear as characters preceded by a caret (^) on the screen but, instead, cause strange nonprinting actions to the printer, such as changing the printing pitch.

Program to Type to the Printer

This program will accept a line of input from the keyboard using the Read Console Buffer system call and then will output the string to the printer using List Output.

```
-a100
0100  mvi   a,50     Get input string. Max line length
0102  sta   01fe       into buffer.
0105  mvi   c,a        Read Console Buffer.
0107  lxi   d,1fe      Buffer address.
010A  call 5
010D  lxi   h,200    Set up HL and B. HL is buffer address.
0110  lda   01ff       Number of characters typed.
0113  mov   b,a        Goes in B.
0114  mvi   c,5      Send character to printer.
0116  mov   e,m        Get character from buffer.
0117  inx   h          Increment pointer.
0118  push h             save H.
0119  push b             save B.
011A  call 5           Do it!
011D  pop   b            restore B.
011E  pop   h            restore H.
011F  dcr   b        Check if done. Decrement count.
0120  jnz   114        Not done. Go print next character.
0123  mvi   c,5      Done. Print linefeed.
0125  mvi   e,a
0127  call 5
012A  mvi c,5        Print carriage return.
012C  mvi e,d
012E  call 5
0131  rst 7          Back to DDT.
```

You can save this program as "test10.ddt". A flowchart of the program is given in Fig. 3-8.

The program uses two different registers to keep track of two different things. The HL register-pair (16 bits) holds the address in the buffer of the

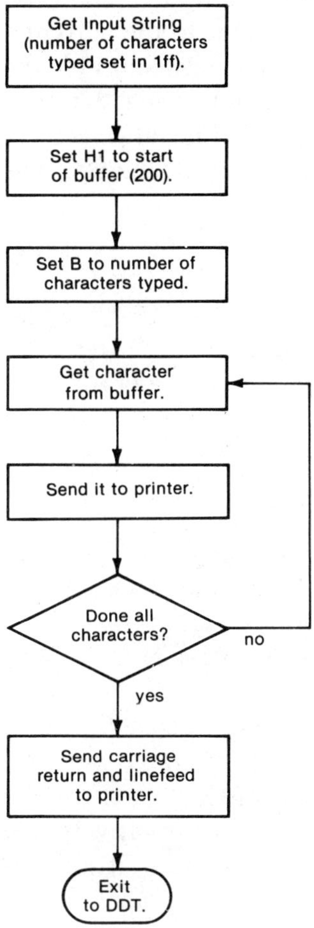

Fig. 3-8. Flowchart for outputting data to the printer.

character currently being processed—that is, it's a "pointer" to the current character in the buffer. The B-register (8 bits) holds the number of characters remaining to be printed in the buffer.

We'll put the actual typed characters into the buffer starting at memory address 200 hex. As is usual when using Read Console Buffer, the first location in the buffer (1fe hex) holds the maximum character count, which we set at 50 hex (80 decimal) to avoid getting more than one line of characters. The second address of the buffer (1ff hex) will be filled in with the number of characters actually typed and this quantity is put in the B-register, which then uses it as the count when sending the characters to the printer. The typed input will be stored in the buffer starting at 200 hex, so this is the address we put in the HL register-pair, which is the pointer to the current character.

The program loops between 114 and 120, getting a character from the buffer (line 116), incrementing the pointer to the next character (line 117), sending the character (line 11A, set up in line 114), and decrementing the count (line 11f) to see if all the characters have been sent.

The LDA Instruction

LDA is the opposite of the STA instruction that we described earlier in this chapter. It loads the A-register with an 8-bit value taken from the memory address specified in the operand field of the instruction. This is illustrated in Fig. 3-9.

Managing the Stack

Notice in the preceding printer program how we need to save *both* the HL and the B registers on the stack to keep them from being destroyed by the Read Console Buffer, which we call in line 11A. The important thing to notice here is that *the order in which we save the registers is the opposite of the order in which we restore them.* This is because the stack is "last in first out," so that the number we put on first will be "pushed down" into the second position from the top when we put the next number on.

It's easy to get confused when using the stack and pop things off into the wrong registers. This is a relatively simple example, but when the stack is used extensively in a program, it's important to pay close attention to its use. Program bugs involving the stack can cause more bizarre results than usual, and they always seem to be particularly hard to track down.

READER INPUT

READER INPUT FUNCTION 3 (dec) = 3 (hex)

Enter with: REG C = 03 hex

On return: REG A = ASCII character

Comments: Same as Console Input, except uses tape reader.

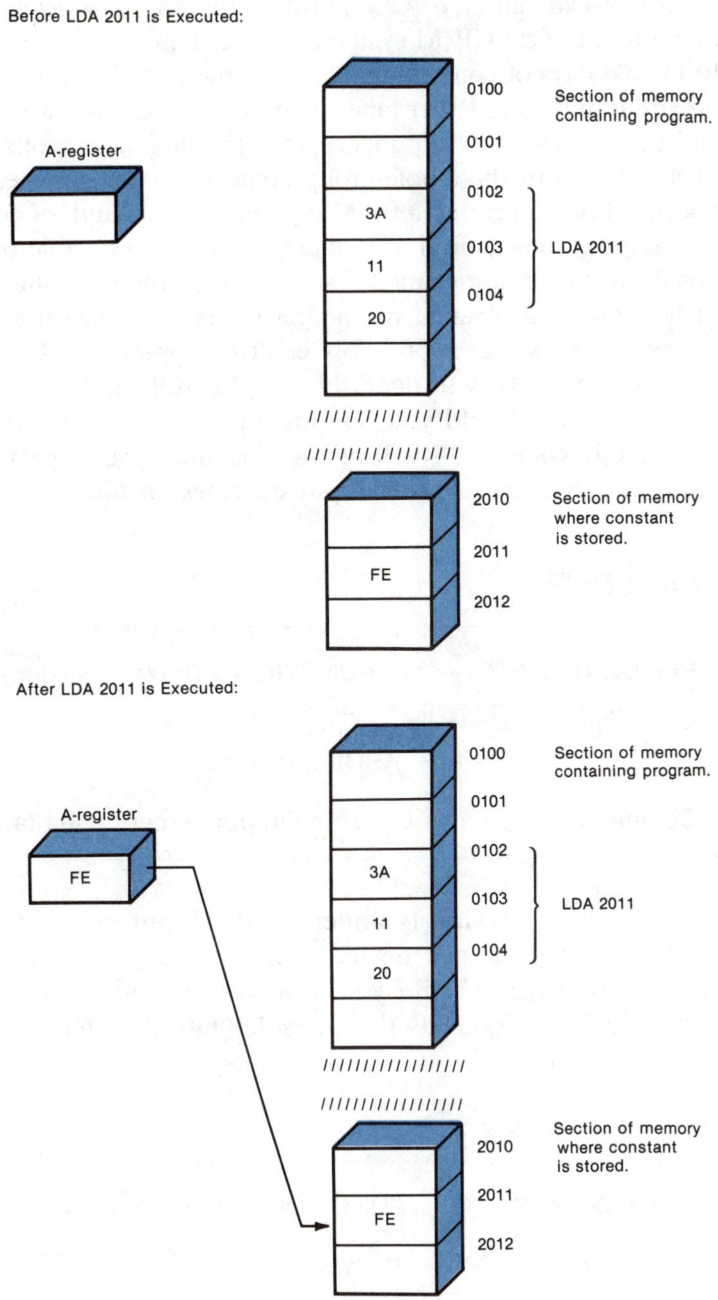

Fig. 3-9. The LDA instruction.

This system call, and the one following, apply to devices that are no longer found in a typical CP/M system: a paper-tape reader and a paper-tape punch. In the old days of computing, paper tape was an important medium for storing programs and data. Paper tape came in long rolls that were about an inch wide, and each character was punched into the tape as a group of 7 hole-positions. Each position in the 7-hole group could be either punched (indicating a 1) or not punched (indicating a 0). Many tape readers and, of course, all tape-punch devices, were mechanical and, therefore, not too reliable or fast. The introduction of magnetic storage media, such as magnetic tapes and floppy disks, caused such a dramatic change in the reliability and pleasure of using mini- and microcomputers that it probably can't be appreciated by anyone who has not struggled endlessly with fiendishly tangled rolls of paper tape.

In any case, should you be unfortunate enough to be using a paper-tape device, this system call will operate on the paper-tape reader in exactly the same way that the Console Input operates on the console device.

PUNCH OUTPUT

PUNCH OUTPUT FUNCTION 4 (hex) = 4 (dec)

Enter with: REG C = 04 hex
REG E = ASCII character

Comments: Same as Console Output, except uses tape punch.

As discussed previously under Reader Input, this function is usually used for a paper-tape punch device, which are no longer found in most CP/M systems. However, should you have occasion to use it, Punch Output functions exactly the same as the Console Output system call.

GET I/O BYTE

GET I/O BYTE FUNCTION 7 (hex) = 7 (dec)

Enter with: REG C = 07 hex

On return: REG A = I/O Byte Value

Logical and Physical I/O Devices

This system call, and the following one (Set I/O Byte), are not often used in the operation of a typical CP/M system. However, they can be very useful when nonstandard devices, such as a modem, are attached to the system. What these calls do is make possible the assignment of different physical I/O devices to the logical devices that the program thinks it is talking to.

What do we mean by "logical" and "physical" devices? "Physical" simply means the actual device itself, such as the keyboard, video screen, or printer. Now it's a strange and amazing fact that *in CP/M,* a systems call to, say, the keyboard (such as Console Output) *doesn't necessarily* have to go to the keyboard. By setting a group of four software switches, you can actually cause the character that you sent to the keyboard (with a Console Output call) to end up at the printer, or you can cause what you sent to the printer to end up on the console device. The actual device that receives the character is called the "physical" device, whereas, the device that the program *thinks* it is sending the character to is called the "logical" device.

All this is explained in general books on CP/M (such as *CP/M® Bible*, by John Angermeyer and Mitchell Waite) in the description of the STAT function. STAT can be used to do all the things the GET I/O Byte and Set I/O Byte system calls do, but they must be done by the user from the keyboard. What Get I/O BYTE and Set I/O BYTE do is let your *program* change the device assignments without human intervention.

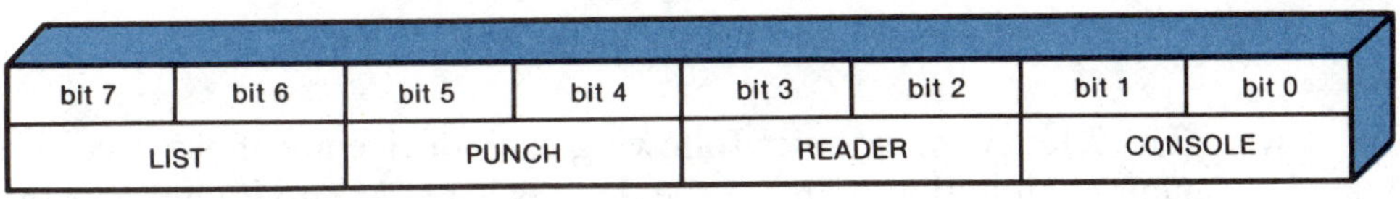

Fig. 3-10. Breakdown of the I/O Byte.

The I/O Byte

The byte referred to as the "I/O Byte" in these system calls has a memory location in a typical CP/M system of 0003 hex. The byte is broken up into four fields, each of which represents a *logical* I/O device. It is arranged as illustrated in Fig. 3-10.

Each of the four logical devices is assigned two bits: the console gets bits 0 and 1, the list device gets bits 6 and 7, and so on. Each of these 2-bit fields can represent four numbers (00=0, 01=1, 10=2, 11=3). Each of the resulting four numbers is assigned to a *physical* device, according to the following list:

CONSOLE FIELD (bits 0,1)

0–Printer device (TTY:)
1–Crt device (CRT:)
2–Batch mode: READER is CONSOLE input, LIST is CONSOLE output (BAT:)
3–User-defined device (UC1:)

READER FIELD (bits 2,3)

0–Teletypewriter device (TTY:)
1–High-speed reader device (RDR:)
2–User-defined reader device No. 1 (UR1:)
3–User-defined reader device No. 2 (UR2:)

PUNCH FIELD (bits 4,5)

0–Teletypewriter device (TTY:)
1–High-speed punch (PUN:)
2–User-defined punch No. 1 (UP1:)
3–User-defined punch No. 2 (UP2:)

LIST FIELD (bits 6,7)

0–Teletypewriter device (TTY:)
1–Crt device (CRT:)
2–Line printer device (LPT:)
3–User-defined list device (UL1:)

The 3-letter mnemonics following each device are those used in the STAT function. Note that many of the devices listed are no longer used in a typical CP/M system. Usually the CONSOLE is assigned to the "console printer device" which CP/M thinks of as the teletypewriter (TTY). Although your console uses a crt (cathode-ray tube), this device name (CRT:) is not usually used for the console.

How does all this look on a typical system? Bring up DDT and type -d0,f. This will cause the contents of the first 16 bytes of memory to be displayed. Look at the byte in location 3. It will typically have a value like 94 (hex). Let's decode this to see what's happening. Write down 94 in binary, like this:

10010100

Then, divide it into groups of two bits:

10,01,01,00

The first two bits, 10, show that the LIST function has been assigned to the line-printer device, as can be seen using the preceding list. The next two bits, 01, show that the PUNCH device has been assigned to the high-speed punch. The next two bits, 01, show that the READER device has been assigned to the high-speed reader, and the last two bits, 00, show that the CONSOLE device has been assigned to the console printer device.

That's how a human being can read the IOBYTE. How about a computer program? That's where the Get I/O Byte system call comes in. Try typing this program in using DDT:

```
-a100
0100  mvi  c,7     Call Get I/O Byte.
0102  call 5
0105  mvi  b,4     Set count of 4 in B-register.
0107  rlc          Rotate A-register.
0108  rlc            2 bits left.
0109  mov  c,a     Save result in C-register.
010A  ani  3       Mask off all but lower 2 bits.
010C  adi  30      Add ASCII value of 0.
010E  mov  e,a     Store result in E-register for printing.
010F  push b       Save BC register.
0110  mvi  c,2     Call Console Out.
0112  call 5
0115  pop  b       Get BC back.
0116  mov  a,c     Put number back in A-register.
0117  dcr  b       Done 4 digits yet?
0118  jnz  107       No.
011B  rst  7         Yes, back to DDT.
```

Save the program as "test11.ddt". What it does is simply display the contents of the IOBYTE. The first two instructions are the Get I/O Byte system call, which returns with the IOBYTE in the A-register. The problem then is how to take each of the four 2-bit numbers and display them separately on the screen as ASCII characters. We do this by *rotating* the contents of the A-register 2 bits to the left, printing the two bits that are now on the right-hand end of the IOBYTE (converting them to ASCII first), then rotating the contents again and printing again; doing this four times. To do all this, we need to introduce three new instructions.

The RLC (Rotate Left) Instruction

There are 8 bits in the A-register. Think of them as being 8 chairs placed in a line. Two kinds of people can sit in the chairs: zeros and ones. The chairs are numbered from 7 on the left down to 0 on the right. When the RLC instruction is executed, everyone stands up and moves over to the chair on his left. The person on the leftmost chair (number 7) has no chair to his left, so he runs all the way around to the right and sits on the rightmost chair (number 0). This is what "rotate" means in computer instructions; the bits rotate around the A-register.

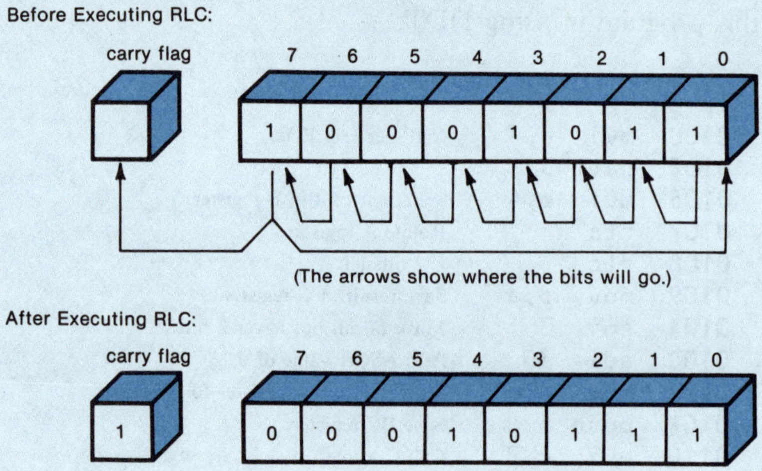

Fig. 3-11. The RLC instruction.

Another detail, although we won't be concerned with it in this example, is that the value of the bit in position 7 is not only copied into position 0, but also into a special 1-byte register called the "carry flag." This can be useful in many circumstances, such as when you want to rotate 16-bit numbers. Later, there will be an example of that.

The ANI Instruction

This instruction means "AND Immediate." Immediate means that the value to be ANDed with the A-register is part of the instruction (rather than being stored someplace else in memory). The logical AND operation is somewhat like OR, except that when you AND two numbers together, *both* bits in the corresponding locations in the operands must be set in order for the result to be set, as the following listing shows:

0 AND 0 = 0
0 AND 1 = 0
1 AND 0 = 0
1 AND 1 = 1

The following is an example of two 8-bit numbers being ANDed together:

```
  0 1 1 0 1 0 0 1
  1 0 1 1 0 0 1 0
-----------------
  0 0 1 0 0 0 0 0
```

One useful application of the ANI instruction is to "mask off" unwanted bits in a particular byte. How does this work? When we AND a bit with 0, it doesn't matter whether that bit was 1 or 0, the result is always 0. So, if we want to get rid of some bits in a particular quantity, we AND them with 0. In the diagram of Fig. 3-12, we've ANDed 66 with 0F. This has the effect of masking off, or setting to zero, the left four bits of the 66.

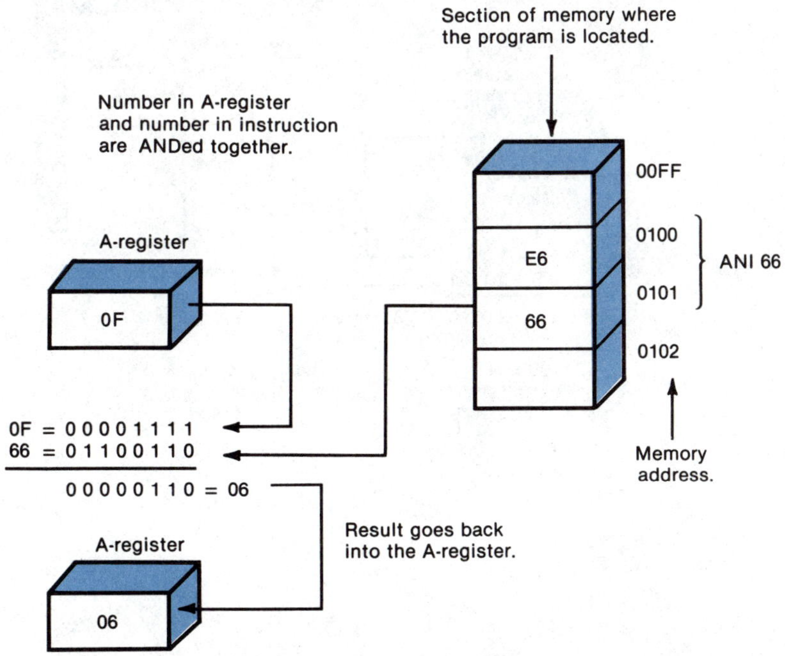

Fig 3-12. The ANI instruction.

In our program, we want to get rid of all the bits in the A-register except the two on the right (positions 1 and 0). So we "AND Immediate" a 3, which is the number with the two rightmost bits set: 00000011. All the bits in the A-register that match up with a 0 will be set to 0, and all the bits that match up with a 1 will be preserved—that is, set to 1 if they are a 1 already, and cleared to 0 if they are a 0.

The ADI (Add Immediate) Instruction

This instruction is similar to the preceding ANI instruction, except that the contents of the A-register are *added* to the number following the instruction. This is a simple arithmetic addition of two hexadecimal numbers. If there is a carry (that is, if the the resulting sum is greater than FF hex, 255 decimal), the carry flag is set. The other flags are also set. In particular, if the result of the addition is zero, the zero flag will be set; otherwise, it will be cleared.

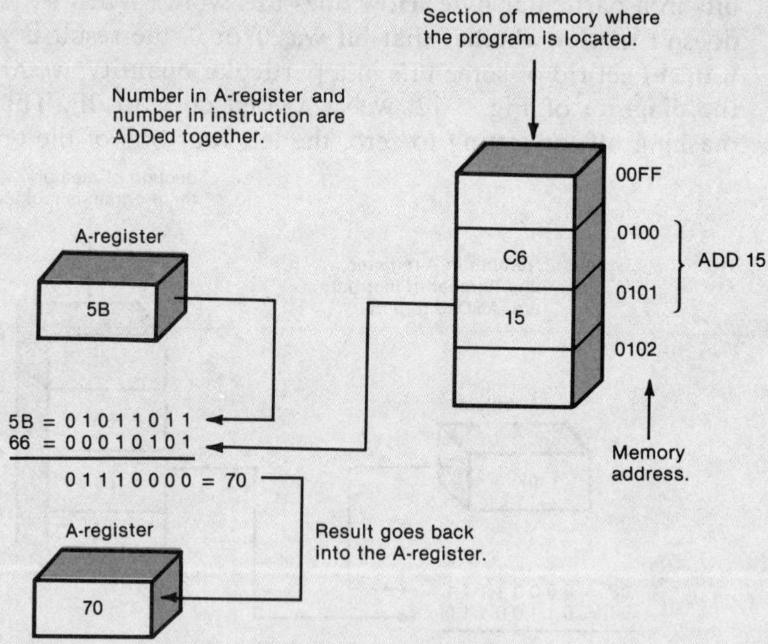

Fig. 3-13. The ADI instruction.

Examples:

adi 30
adi 7f

In the preceding program example, we want a 2-bit value of 0 (00) to print out as an ASCII "0," a 2-bit value of 1 (01) to print out as an ASCII "1," and so on. However, the ASCII code for "0" is 30 hex (not 0), "1" is 31 hex, 2 is 32 hex, and 3 is 33 hex; so we need to add 30 hex to each of our little 2-bit numbers before printing them out. The ADI instruction does it nicely.

The program uses the B-register to hold the count of how many 2-bit numbers remain to be printed. This starts at 4 (set in line 105) and counts down to 0, at which point the program returns to DDT (lines 117 to 11B). The C-register is used to keep all eight bits of the IOBYTE (rotated either two, four, six, or eight times) as the program progresses. Since the B and C registers can both be saved on the stack with the "push b" instruction (line 10F), we can save both the count and the current rotated state of the I/O byte at the same time, and, similarly, can restore them with a "pop b" in line 115. We need to save them because the Console Out system call that we use to print out the 2-bit numbers destroys both the B and C registers when it's called.

Try running the program. It should give you the same value for the IOBYTE that you found by using the "d" function in DDT.

SET I/O BYTE

SET I/O BYTE FUNCTION 8 (dec) = 8 (hex)

Enter with: REG C = 08 hex
REG E = new I/O byte

This is a straightforward system call whose purpose is to set the IOBYTE described in the last section to a new value. In fact, unless you have some unusual I/O devices on your CP/M system, there's not really too much you can do that's interesting by changing the values of the IOBYTE. Here's a little experiment you can do, however, to see if everything is working as advertised.

Write the following program in DDT:

```
-a100
0100  mvi c,8     Set I/O Byte system call.
0102  mvi e,14    New IOBYTE makes LIST the Console.
0104  call 5
0107  rst 7       Back to DDT.
```

This program simply changes the IOBYTE from the 94 (hex) that we found in the last section to 14 (hex). What does this do? Hex 94 is 10010100, while hex 14 is 00010100. Thus, we changed the leftmost two bits from 10 to 00, which (looking back at the diagram of the IOBYTE and the list of device assignments in the last section) means that we've changed the destination device of the LIST device from the lineprinter to the "console printer device" (TTY:). How do we know that's what's happened? Read on!

Turn on the printer with a control–p. Now type something. It doesn't matter what it is, *it will get printed twice on the screen!* Why is that? It gets sent once because the screen is simply echoing the keyboard as it normally does. It gets printed the second time because we've turned on the printer echo with a control–p, but the characters which would normally go to the printer have been re-routed to the console device because we put a 0 in the LIST field of the IOBYTE, instead of a 2.

GOODBYE, NONDISK SYSTEM CALLS

We've now covered all 12 of the nondisk system calls. You've learned a lot about how CP/M works, and even more about how to program in 8080 assembly language.

This might be a good time to review what you've learned so far. Go back and look at the various example programs. Experiment a little with them, changing a line here and a line there, to see what happens. You should feel comfortable assemblying and running short programs with DDT, and you should understand the operation of the 8080 instructions covered so far.

In the next chapter, we're going to explain how the CP/M assembler ASM works. Using ASM will save a lot of time, trouble, and agony, as compared with typing long programs in directly using DDT. It has a lot of other great features too, and you may find it almost too luxurious–but we figured that you deserved a break.

CHAPTER 4

Using the Assembler

Until now, you've been writing programs using the built-in miniassembler in DDT. This is fine for short routines, but its disadvantages begin to be apparent on longer programs. The most obvious problem is that once the program is written you can't go back and insert a new instruction in the middle. This is because each instruction is converted into machine code, and the appropriate memory space is assigned to it as you type it in.

A true assembler such as ASM, on the other hand, doesn't convert any of the instructions into machine language until the entire program has been typed in. This makes modifications to the program much easier and also permits the use of various other wonderful features, such as symbolic labels to refer to memory addresses rather than hex numbers.

In this chapter, we'll explain how an assembler works, show you how to use the CP/M assembler ASM, and cover the use of the LOAD program, which converts the output of ASM into a form that can be executed directly from CP/M. We'll start off by assemblying "TEST1" (one of the first programs from Chapter 2) and then move along to a routine ("DECIBIN") that accepts decimal numbers from the keyboard and converts them into binary for the computer to read. This routine makes up part of our next program, "DECIHEX," which is used to convert decimal numbers typed in at the keyboard into hex numbers on the screen. DECIHEX is a useful utility program, as well as providing a testing ground for the use of the assembler. Finally we'll describe how to simplify the assemblying process through the use of the CP/M utility, SUBMIT.

WHAT'S AN ASSEMBLER DO, ANYWAY?

The purpose of an assembler is to take instructions that are written in a form which is more or less understandable to a human and convert them into the binary numbers that a computer can read. When you typed "mvi c,2" in the DDT microassembler, for instance, DDT automatically converted this into the two bytes 0E, 02. The 0E is the code for the "mvi c" part of the instruction, and the 02 byte is the number that you want to put in register C. Similarly, a "call 5" instruction is converted into three bytes: CD, 05, 00. The CD is the code for "call," and the 05, 00 is the address 0005. (As we mentioned earlier, in 8080 machine language, the low-order or least-significant byte *precedes* the high-order or most-significant byte.) You might not even have been aware that these numbers were being generated when you used DDT's microassembler if you didn't look into the TPA (where the program was stored, at 100 hex), using the "d" command.

Let's try that now. Bring up DDT and a simple program such as test1.ddt:

```
-ddt test1.ddt
```

Then list it to see how it looks in symbolic form:

```
-l100
0100  MVI   C,02
0102  MVI   E,48
0104  CALL  0005
0107  MVI   C,02
0109  MVI   E,49
010B  CALL  0005
010E  JMP   0100
```

Now, dump the contents of the memory locations occupied by the program, using "d":

```
-d100,110
```

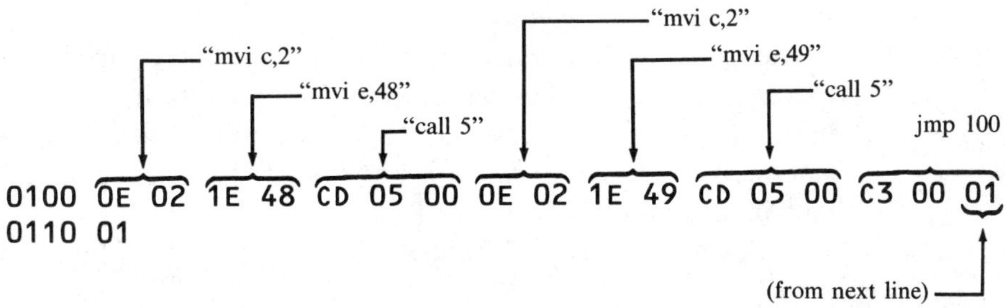

Notice how the mvi instructions have different codes depending on what register they're addressing: 0E for the C-register and 1E for the E-register. In general, instructions that include an 8-bit byte (like the 02 in "mvi c,2") are two-bytes long, and those that include a 16-bit address, like the "call" and "jmp" instructions, are three-bytes long.

The hexadecimal numbers revealed by the "d" function are representations of the binary numbers that the computer actually operates on when it is executing a program. The microassembler in DDT has taken symbolic instructions, such as "mvi c,2", and converted them into these binary numbers (which DDT translates into hexadecimal, so we can read them more easily). This is essentially what all assemblers do, but true assemblers do it much more elegantly than the DDT microassembler.

WHAT ASM DOES

In DDT, you typed symbolic instructions using the "a" function, and DDT assembled them one at a time as you typed them in. In ASM, the process is quite different and is somewhat more involved. You first type your symbolic input into a *text* file, using a word-processing program, just as if you were writing a letter. This text file, which is called an ASM file (and must have a file extention of ASM), is then stored on the disk, like any other text file. You then call up the assembler program ASM, which performs the actual assembly process: that is, figuring out what binary numbers should stand for each symbolic instruction. ASM generates two files: (1) the HEX file, which consists of the binary numbers, but in a special format which is not yet directly executable, and (2) the PRN (for "print") file, which is the same as the original ASM file, but with the hexadecimal addresses and instructions included alongside the original symbolic instructions so that you can see how they all fit together.

Finally, the LOAD program is used on the HEX file to generate a COM file, which can be executed directly by CP/M.

Alternatively, the HEX file can be executed, inspected, and modified directly from DDT. This is useful if the program has a bug in it (a topic we'll discuss later), or if access to the 8080 registers is necessary while the program is being used, as is the case in the "DECIBIN" routine that will be described later in this chapter.

The diagram in Fig. 4-1 shows the relationship of these files and programs.

Using the Word Processor

As we indicated in the introduction, we assume that your system includes a word processor or text-editor program. ED is included as a basic part of all CP/M systems, and most people who use CP/M also run one of the popular word-processing programs, such as WordStar, Spellbinder, Select, or Magic Wand. (For a complete description and comparison of these and other word-processing programs, see *Word Processing Primer* by Mitchell Waite and Julie Arca.) Since there are so many different word-processing programs, we will not attempt here to describe how they work. We will simply assume that you have one running on your system and that you know how to use it.

Our first project will be to use ASM to assemble the program that we have just investigated using DDT. To begin assembling the program, use your word processor to open a file which has a file extension of ASM and the file name TEST1. (Some word processors have a special "nondocument" mode for writing program listings: it suppresses page breaks and word wrap-around. If your word processor has such a feature, now is the time to turn it on.)

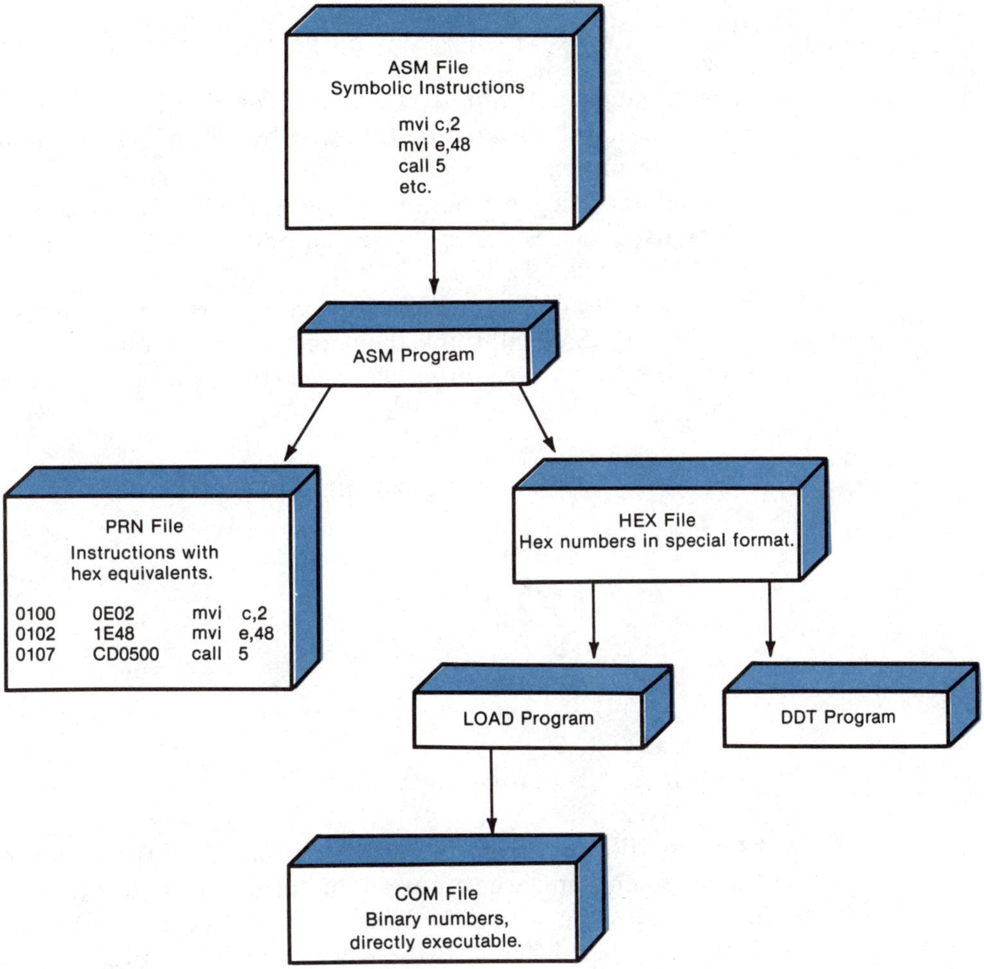

Fig. 4-1. Assemblying using ASM.

Format Differences Between DDT and ASM

There are several differences in the way that you type in programs using DDT and the way you type them using ASM.

1. Programs in ASM must start with an ORG (for "ORiGin") directive to tell ASM where the program is to go in memory. (DDT assumed that the program would go at 100 hex.) We'll explain more about "directives" later in the chapter. Since the LOAD program (we'll get to that later too) requires programs to begin at 100 hex, the ORG directive

must be followed by 100h, as shown in the first line of the following program.

2. ASM assumes that numbers are in *decimal* unless it is told otherwise. Thus, hex numbers must be followed by an "h." (DDT assumed numbers were in hex.)
3. The fields of the instruction are separated from each other by tabs. (DDT used spaces.) Also, there is a new field to the left of the operation field for labels.
4. Hexadecimal numbers which start with a letter must be preceded by a zero (0), or ASM will think they are symbolic names rather than numbers. *This is very easy to forget, so remember it!* Don't write ffh, write 0ffh.

Let's try typing in a program, keeping these rules in mind:

```
        org     100h
start   mvi     c,2
        mvi     e,48h
        call    5
        mvi     c,2
        mvi     e,49h
        call    5
        jmp     start
```

That's not *so* different from the DDT version, is it? We've started off with the ORG statement, and we've put an "h" after all the hex numbers (except those that are the same in both hex and decimal, like 2 and 5). You've probably noticed one other difference: the word "start" that precedes the first mvi c,2 instruction and, also, follows the jmp instruction. What's this all about?

Symbolic Labels

One of the really nice things about using an assembler is that it relieves you of the responsibility of figuring out what memory address a particular instruction or data item occupies. In DDT, it was necessary, when we wrote the jmp instruction at the end of the program, to look up at the place at the beginning of the program where we wanted to jump to, and then write that same number following the "jmp"; in this case, "jmp 100." Of course, that's not a problem in this particular example, but in longer programs, especially those where you want to jump *down* (that is to an instruction you haven't yet written), the use of symbolic labels is invaluable. Also, as you will see in the next few programs, the labels given to subroutines can visually help to break the program into separate and more understandable sections.

You can use a label to refer to any particular address. A label can be any group of letters and numbers, but it must start with a letter, and it should not be longer than 8 characters or it will cause formatting problems when you try to type it in, and when ASM generates the PRN file. (Although, actually, ASM can accept up to 16 characters.) This label is placed in the "label field" in the program: that is, the first column of the listing. The instruction itself (as we learned earlier) then goes in the next column, which is called the "operation field." The third column is called the "operand field" since it contains the thing that the instruction is going to *operate on*—the operand. This operand can contain either register names and constants, as is the case with the mvi instructions, or it can be a symbolic label, as in the case of the jmp instruction. There is another column, the "comment" field, which we'll explore later. The fields are separated from each other either by tabs or by any number of spaces, but using the tab key makes for neater listings.

```
| label      | operation  | operand   | comment
|            |            |           |
|decibin     |lxi         |h,0        |;set HL to zero
|            |            |           |
```

In using symbolic labels, writing "jmp start" is equivalent to writing "jmp 100," providing that we have already defined "start" as representing the address 100 by putting it in the label field at the appropriate place.

Assemblying the Program

Once you've written the program and checked it over for errors, save it on your disk using the appropriate command from your word-processor program. Don't forget that it must have an ASM file extension. If it doesn't, the ASM program won't function correctly.

Now, return to CP/M and call up ASM, followed by the name of the program you want to assemble. But *don't type any file extension following the name of your program.* Just type the program name and a carriage return—don't even type a period. This is because ASM interprets the letters, which appear in the place usually occupied by the file extension, in an entirely different way. For the time being, we won't worry about this, so leave the letters out.

```
A>asm test1                     Assumes "test1.asm" exists.
CP/M ASSEMBLER - VER 2.0        Sign-on message.
0111                            Address following program.
000H USE FACTOR                 % of symbol table used.
END OF ASSEMBLY
```

ASM introduces itself with a sign-on message that gives its version number, and then proceeds to assemble the program. When it is done, it prints the address following the last address used in the program; 0111 in this case. The "USE FACTOR" has to do with the amount of space used by symbolic labels. There is only a certain amount of space for storing these labels in ASM; if you use too many labels, you're in trouble. The USE FACTOR tells you the percentage of available space used in your program. The programs used in this book seldom have a USE FACTOR of more than 3%. In the present case, with only one label in the program ("start"), the USE FACTOR doesn't even get up to 1%.

If you have made any errors in typing your program, ASM will print them out during the assembly process. The error messages are single letters incorporated into the offending program line and can be rather obscure; usually, a glance at the line will show you where you went wrong.

Finally ASM tells you END OF ASSEMBLY, and returns you to CP/M. If you now use "dir", you will see that two new files have been generated: TEST1.HEX and TEST1.PRN. To see what ASM has been up to, display the PRN file:

```
A>type test1.prn


 0100                      org     100h
 0100 0E02        start    mvi     c,2
 0102 1E48                 mvi     e,48h
 0104 CD0500               call    5
 0107 0E02                 mvi     c,2
 0109 1E49                 mvi     e,49h
 010B CD0500               call    5
 010E C30001               jmp     start
```

You've got to admit that's pretty slick. Everything is all neatly printed out, you can see at a glance what hex values go with what symbolic instructions, and the program has even figured out that "jmp start" means "jmp 100." About the only inconvenience is having to remember to reverse the order of the address bytes; thus, at line 104, the CD0500 means "call 0005," not "call 0500."

Using the LOAD Program

You can't actually execute (run) the HEX file from CP/M: it's not in quite the right format. You'll need to put the program into the correct format for execution, using the LOAD program. To do this, simply type "load" followed by the name of the program, *again without a file extension.* LOAD assumes that it will be operating on a file with an extension of HEX, so typing the extension can cause trouble. LOAD also assumes it will be operating on a program that starts at 100 hex, so don't forget the "org 100h" directive at the start of your program.

```
A>load test1                  Assumes test1.hex exists.
FIRST ADDRESS 0100            Must start at 100 hex.
LAST  ADDRESS 0110
BYTES READ    0011
RECORDS WRITTEN 01            Number of 128-byte records.
```

The messages generated by LOAD are largely self-explanatory. When LOAD returns you to CP/M, use DIR to see what's happened. You'll find a new file has been created: "TEST1.COM". This file can be directly executed from CP/M, so type:

```
A>test1     (No extension necessary for COM files)
```

The program will start and the screen will fill up with the word "HI", just as it did under DDT. Another pat on the back is in order. You've just assembled and executed your first program using ASM. You are now a real programmer! All that stands between you and fame and fortune is a little more practice, some of which we're about to give you.

Source Code and Object Code

Some nomenclature might be in order here. The ASM file that you type in is often called the "source file." The COM file that you actually execute is called the "object file." Individual lines of the source file are called "source code," and individual lines of the object file are called "object code." These terms won't make you a better programmer, but they'll make you *sound* like a real pro if you drop them into your conversation from time to time. (As in, "A head crash trashed my object file, so I had to reassemble.")

THE "DECIBIN" ROUTINE–READS DECIMAL FROM KEYBOARD

The routine that we're about to describe takes a decimal number that you type in at the keyboard and converts it into binary form, but leaves it in the HL-register where other routines (which we will write later) can have access to it. In order to verify that the correct binary number has indeed turned up in the HL-register at the end of the program, we're going to execute the program in DDT. This will give us a chance to use the "x" function of DDT, which permits us to examine the contents of any of the 8080 registers.

Decimal to Binary Conversion

Before we describe how our DECIBIN routine works, you should make sure that you understand the distinction between binary and hexadecimal numbers. If necessary, read Appendix A. Essentially, *binary* is the way that the computer stores numbers, while *hexadecimal* is a convenient way for human beings to talk about binary numbers. A computer program can take the binary numbers stored in the computer and print them out on the screen in hexadecimal notation. (It could also print them out in binary notation, but that wouldn't be so easy for a human to read.)

Frequently, when we talk about numbers in the computer, the distinction between binary and hexadecimal becomes a little fuzzy. The number in the computer is in binary, but when we print it out so that we can see it, as we might do with DDT, we'll look at it as a hexadecimal number. It's really always a binary number, but when it reveals itself to us on our computer screen, we see it as hexadecimal.

The DECIBIN routine that we're about to discuss reads in a decimal number from the keyboard and changes it to a binary number and stores it in the HL-register. At least, it's a binary number when it's safely in the computer. If we wanted to see what the number was, we would print out the contents of the HL-register using DDT, and the number will appear in hexadecimal form.

The program uses a different strategy to convert from decimal to binary than a human might. (For a human approach to decimal-to-binary conversion, see Appendix A on Hexadecimal Notation.) Here's how the program does it. It uses the HL-register to store the binary number. At the beginning of the program, it sets HL to 0. Then, each time the user types in a decimal digit, the program performs the following steps:

1. It converts the new digit from decimal to binary.
2. It multiplies the old number in HL by 10 (decimal).
3. It adds the new digit to the old value in HL.

Thus, if the user types "432," the program first sees the 4, and converts it to binary (which we'll refer to as 4 hex). The old value in HL was 0, so when it multiplies this by 10 it's still 0. Then, when it adds the new digit, the result is 4 hex. Next, the user types the 3. The program converts this to 3 hex, multiplies the old 4 hex by 10 decimal (which makes it 28 hex), and adds the 3; thus, obtaining 2B hex. If the user at this point typed a return, signaling that he was finished typing in the number, the correct binary translation of 43 decimal would be in the HL-register: 2B hex. However, the user now types a 2, little realizing how hard he's making the program work.

The program converts the 2 to 2 hex and, then, proceeds to multiply the old 2B hex by 10 decimal, which makes it 1AE hex. (2B hex is 43 decimal, times 10 is 430 decimal, which is 1AE hex.) Adding the 2 to 1AE makes it 1B0 hex, and that's what remains in the HL-register if the user now types a return. Whew! All that trouble just to go from decimal to hex notation.

Hex number in HL-register				
H		*L*		
0	0	0	0	
				←—— User types "4", program multiplies 0 by 10
0	0	0	0	
				←—— and adds the 4.
0	0	0	4	
				←—— User types "3", program multiplies 4 by 10
0	0	2	8	
				←—— and adds the 3.
0	0	2	B	
				←—— User types "2", program multiplies 2B by 10
0	1	A	E	
				←—— and adds the 2.
0	1	B	0	
				←—— User types "return", 1B0 hex is 432 decimal.

Why do it this way, rather than dividing by 4096, then by 256, and then by 16, as shown in Appendix A? Because it's easier for the computer to multiply by 10 than it is to divide by all those other numbers. Next question: how does the computer multiply by 10 when there are no multiplication instructions in the 8080? Well, the computer can easily double a number simply by adding it to itself.

Can you figure out how to multiply a quantity by 10 simply by using the doubling operation? Here's how the program does it. It takes the original number in HL and copies it into the DE-register. Then it adds HL to itself, which doubles the number. If, for example, we started with 1, we now have 2. The result is in the HL-register. It adds HL to HL once more, which again doubles the number giving us a 4 in HL, with a 1 still left in the DE-register. It adds DE to HL which gives a 5, and, finally, it adds HL to HL again which doubles the result, giving us 10. Clever, no?

Decibin Routine Listing

Listing 4-1 shows the DECIBIN routine. We have used the PRN file so that it will be easy to refer to the particular program lines by their memory addresses.

You'll notice that the program is liberally sprinkled with comments. This is made possible by the semicolon (;). Anything following a semicolon is a comment and is ignored by ASM (in the sense that it won't try to turn it into binary instructions). The semicolon can occur any place in a program line, but the usual place to put it is at the beginning of a line (when you want the entire line to be a comment) or at the beginning of the comment field (the one on the right). It's always a good idea when you write a program to use even more comments than may seem necessary, since a program listing is never as clear when you look at it some time after you've written it as it is when you're writing it. And, in assembly language, there is no penalty for comments, as there is in interpreted languages such as BASIC (where comments occupy memory space when the program is running and, also, slow down execution speed). In assembly language, the comments exist only in the ASM and PRN files–they disappear completely when the program is rendered down into binary in the HEX and COM files.

Something else to notice about the listing is that we have added an "end" statement to the end of the program. Although the ASM assembler does not require this statement, many other assemblers do and it is good practice to include it. The "end" statement has another use in ASM and that is to specify where a program will start; that is, what instruction will be *executed* first.

Listing 4-1. The DECIBIN Subroutine

```
             ;*****************************************************
             ;DECIBIN-reads decimal number from keyboard,
             ;        converts to binary in HL-register
             ;
             ;
0100                 org  100h
             ;
             ;
             ;calling program-to call routine and return to DDT
             ;
0100 CD0401          call decibin ;call routine
0103 FF              rst  7       ;back to DDT
             ;
             ;decibin subroutine
             ;
0104 210000 decibin lxi  h,0      ;set hl to 0
0107 E5     newdig  push h        ;save hl (Con Input uses it)
0108 0E01           mvi  c,1      ;get character
010A CD0500         call 5
010D E1             pop  h        ;restore hl
010E D630           sui  30h      ;convert from ASCII to binary
0110 F8             rm            ;return if it was < 0
0111 FE0A           cpi  10d      ;is it > 9 ?
0113 F0             rp            ;if so, return
             ;
             ;multiply contents of hl by 10 (dec), then add new digit
             ;
0114 E5             push h        ;put hl in de
0115 D1             pop  d
0116 29             dad  h        ;add hl to hl (double it)
0117 29             dad  h        ;double it again
0118 19             dad  d        ;add de (original number) to hl
0119 29             dad  h        ;double result
011A 16             mvi  d,0      ;zero in d
011B 5F             mov  e,a      ;new digit in e
011C 19             dad  d        ;add digit to number
             ;
             ;result is now in hl
             ;
011D C30701         jmp  newdig   ;go look for next digit
             ;
0120                end
```

(Note that this is not the same as the first instruction in the program, nor where the program starts in memory.)

If, for example, the last statement in your program is

```
end   100h
```

then, the first instruction to be executed will be at 100 hex. (This information is included by ASM in the HEX file.) This is useful if you have a program that you want to start executing in the middle. Only HEX files will be given an arbitrary address this way; COM files are assumed to start at 100 hex.

Subroutines

We have used the "call" instruction many times before when executing a system call to BDOS ("call 5"). As we pointed out, "call" is like a "GOSUB" in BASIC. It can be used to call any sort of subroutine, not just BDOS. A subroutine is simply a section of code that performs some function, that has a beginning (which is the address one uses to "call" the subroutine), and which ends with a "ret" instruction (which returns control to the calling program). If you're hazy on what CALL does, you might want to review the description of it at the beginning of Chapter 2.

In our DECIBIN routine, note that lines 100 and 103 are actually the "program." All these lines do is call the DECIBIN subroutine (which starts at 104) and, then, return to DDT with a "rst 7" instruction. Why make DECIBIN a subroutine? Because later, we're going to use DECIBIN in a larger program where it will need to operate along with other subroutines and, also, because we can simplify the coding of the program if we can use instructions such as RM and RP, instead of RST 7.

The RM and RP Instructions, and the Sign Flag

The RM instruction means "return on minus," while RP means "return on plus." They are both very much like the RET instruction, except that they will only cause the return to the calling program if certain conditions are met. These conditions have to do with the state of something called the "sign flag." You've already learned about the zero flag, which is set if the result of an arithmetic operation or a comparison turns out to be zero. The sign flag is similar, but it is set to "m" for minus or "p" for plus depending on the result of an arithmetic operation. Thus, if you subtract 5 from 3, the sign flag will be set to minus, but if you subtract 5 from 10, it will be set to plus.

The RP instruction will cause a return (the same as a ret instruction) if the result of a preceding arithmetic operation has set the sign flag to plus. If the sign flag is minus and this instruction is executed, control will simply continue on to the next instruction after the RP. The RM instruction will cause a return if the sign flag is minus; if it is plus, control will go on to the following instruction.

The RP instruction functions in the same way, except that it causes a return to the calling program if the sign flag is set to plus.

Examples:

rm
rp

The SUI Instruction

This instruction is similar to the ADI instruction covered before, except that the number included in the instruction is *subtracted* from the contents of

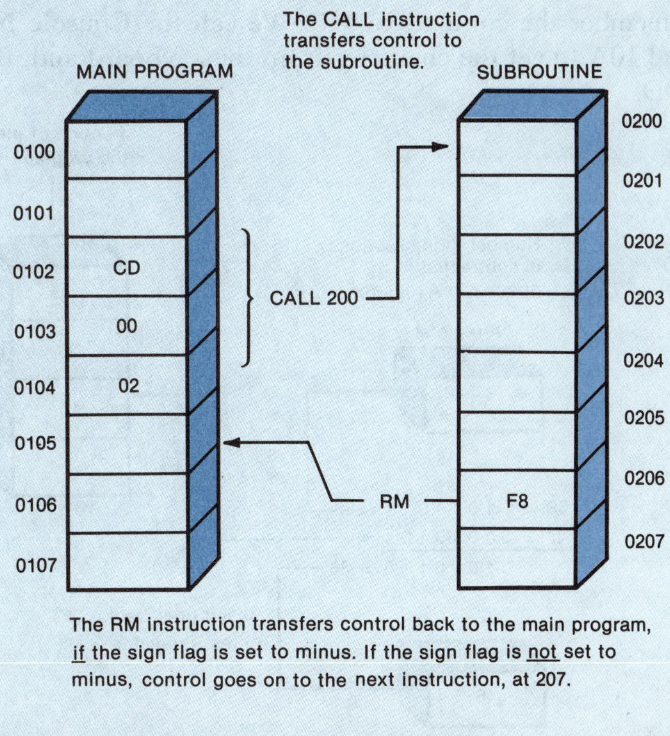

Fig. 4-2. The RM instruction.

the A-register, rather than being added. Thus, "sui 2" means "subtract 2 from the contents of the A-register." This instruction, like other 8-bit arithmetic instructions, sets the zero flag and, also, the sign flag.

Examples:

sui 30
sui 7f

In the DECIBIN routine, the first half of the program, from locations 104 to 113, is concerned with figuring out if the character that the user has typed in is a decimal digit or not. If it is, it's converted to binary. If not—that is, if the user types any character other than a decimal digit—the subroutine is terminated and control returns to line 103 and, thus, back to DDT.

Let's look at this in detail. The lxi h,0 instruction clears the HL register, which we need to do at the beginning of the program to get ready to add the digits to it. Then we save HL with a "pop h" instruction, since the Console In system call, as we've learned before, trashes all the registers and we need to remember the contents of HL. We call the Console In routine in lines 108 and 10A to get the character from the keyboard and, then, we restore HL in 10D.

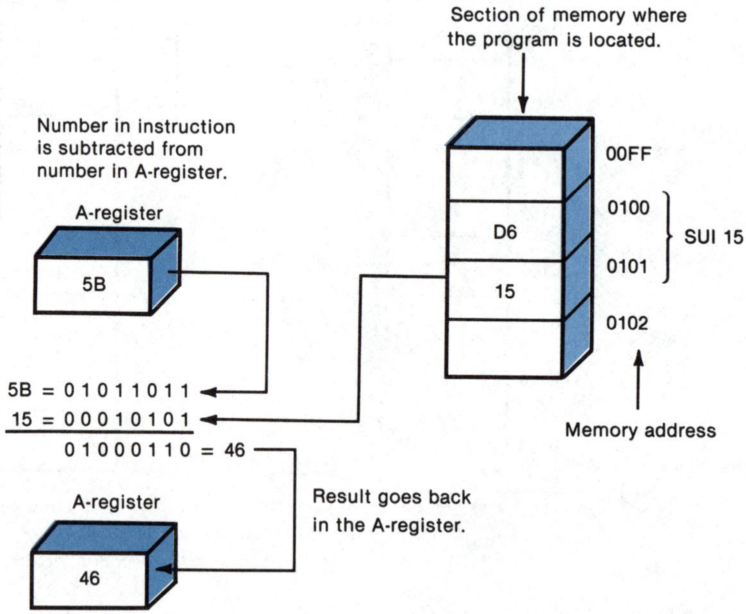

Fig. 4-3. The SUI instruction.

Now comes the interesting part. We have the character in the A-register. Is it a decimal digit? To find out, and at the same time to convert it from ASCII to binary, we subtract 30 hex in line 10E. (Recall that 30 hex = "0" in ASCII, 31 hex = "1," and so on up to 39 hex = "9.") If, when we subtract 30 hex, the result is negative, then we know that the character typed in must have had an ASCII value less than 30 and, therefore, it could not have been a decimal digit. If the result is positive, then it *may be* a decimal number, provided it isn't too big. Since we've changed it to a binary number, we now need to see if it is greater than 9, so we do a "cpi 10d" which performs a "phantom" subtraction of 10 decimal from the contents of the A-register, and sets the flags accordingly. If the result is positive (or 0, which is considered to be positive by the sign flag), then it must have been greater than 9, and is therefore not a decimal digit. The "rp" instruction will, therefore, cause a return to 103 and back to DDT.

The DAD Instruction

The DAD instruction adds the contents of a register-pair to the contents of the HL-register.

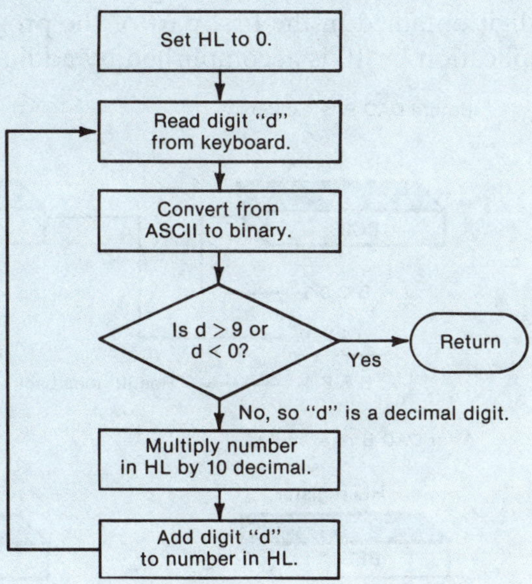

Fig. 4-4. Flowchart of DECIBIN subroutine.

There are not nearly so many arithmetic instructions for 16-bit quantities in the 8080 as there are for 8-bit quantities. In fact, except for incrementing and decrementing, which are rather limited arithmetic operations, DAD is the only one! It was probably included in the 8080 instruction set to provide a way to calculate addresses but it is, of course, useful for other 16-bit quantities as well. Any of the 16-bit register-pairs—BC, DE, or HL—can be added to the contents of the HL register-pair. The result is always left in HL.

As in other register-pair instructions, only the first letter of the register-pair name is used in the operand field. Thus, "dad d" means "add the contents of the DE register-pair to the contents of HL"; "dad h" means "add the contents of HL to itself."

Note that *DAD does not set either the zero flag or the sign flag.* It does, however, set the carry flag.

Examples:

```
dad d
dad b
dad h
```

The second part of the subroutine, from 114 to 11C, is concerned with multiplying the contents of the HL-register by 10 and then (line 11C) adding the new digit obtained in the first part of the program. As described earlier, the multiplication by 10 is accomplished by adding the contents HL to itself

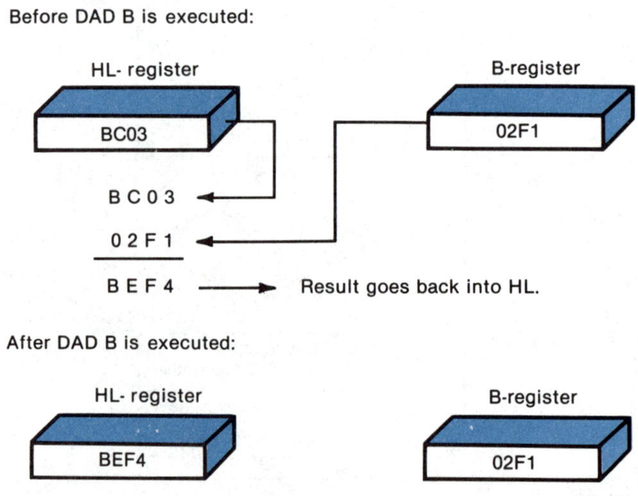

Fig. 4-5. The DAD instruction.

twice (lines 116 and 117), then (in line 118) adding the original number (stored for that purpose in the DE-register in lines 114 and 115), and, finally, adding HL to itself again in line 119.

Notice, in lines 114 and 115, how easy it is to copy the 16-bit number from HL into DE. We simply do a PUSH H to write the number from HL into the stack and, then, a POP D to read it back into the DE-register. As long as we make sure to follow a PUSH with a POP, the stack is left unchanged.

The new digit is then added to the result in HL by placing it in the DE register-pair and adding DE to HL in line 11C. Notice how the D-register is first cleared and then the new digit is transferred from the A-register to the E-register (lines 11A and 11B), since it takes two 8-bit transfers to fill up a 16-bit register. After this, we go back to get another character with the "jmp newdig" in line 11D.

Assembling and Executing the DECIBIN Routine

Type the program using your word-processing program, assign it the name "decibin.asm", and then assemble it with ASM. Look at the resulting PRN file. It should look just like the one just shown. If ASM tells you there are errors, then you've probably made a typo somewhere. Fix it up until you have an error-free assembly.

Since we need to look at the HL register-pair after we execute this routine to see if it has done its job, we'll run the program using DDT. DDT (unlike CP/M) can load HEX files directly, so we'll use the HEX file version of our program. When you start the program, it will just sit there waiting for you to type a decimal number. When you've finished typing the number and hit return, it will return to DDT and print the asterisk and the ending address. When it does this, DDT will overprint your original number, but that's all right; the program has already read it.

Now you want to examine the contents of the HL-register, so you type "x" for eXamine, followed by "h" for the HL-register, and return. DDT will print out the contents of HL, and then wait for you to type a number to *enter* into HL; but that's not necessary here, so hit return to get back to DDT.

```
A>ddt decibin.hex
-g100               Start the program.
4096                Type decimal number (then return).
*0103               (Actually prints over above line.)
-xh                 Type this to look at HL.
H=1000              DDT prints out contents (in hex).
```

Since 1000 hex is the equivalent of 4096 decimal, you know the program is working correctly. You can try it with other decimal numbers.

```
-g100
10          Decimal number.
*0103
-xh
H=000A      Hex equivalent.
-g100
32767       Decimal number.
*103
-xh
H=7FFF      Hex equivalent.
-
```

And so forth. Notice that you can't input a number greater than 65535, because that's the largest number that can be represented by 16 bits (four hex digits).

DECIHEX PROGRAM–CONVERTS DECIMAL TO HEX, ON SCREEN

Hold on to your hats. For the first time, we're going to write a program that is actually useful! By adding a routine which prints a hex number on the screen to the DECIBIN routine already described, we're going to create a program that will convert a decimal number that you type in, to a hex number, right before your very eyes! The program will be a COM file so you can run it directly from CP/M, thus amazing your friends and teaching you the hexadecimal numbering system at the same time. Fig. 4-6 shows how the routines fit together.

BINIHEX–BINARY TO DECIMAL CONVERSION ROUTINE

Let's talk about the new subroutine we're going to add, which prints a binary number out on the screen. We'll call it BINIHEX. It turns out that it's surprisingly difficult to convert a four-digit hex number (really a 16-bit binary number) into four individual ASCII digits. This is because two of the digits are in one register (H) and two are in another (L), and two are on the left side of their respective registers while two are on the right. We'll make the project somewhat simpler by always printing four digits, even if they are leading zeros. Fig. 4-7 shows how it will look.

Digit 1, the most-significant digit, will be printed first, and so on, down to digit 4. To print the digits on the left-hand sides of the registers (1 and 3), we will have to shift them over to the right-hand side of the A-register so that they can have 30 (hex) added to them to make them into an ASCII code. (The digits on the right-hand sides, 2 and 4, don't need to be shifted.)

Another problem is that the hex digits, A to F, need to be converted to ASCII in a slightly different way than the digits 0 to 9. This is because the letters A, B, C, etc., don't immediately follow the numbers 7, 8, 9 in the ASCII coding system. (An unfortunate situation that results from the fact

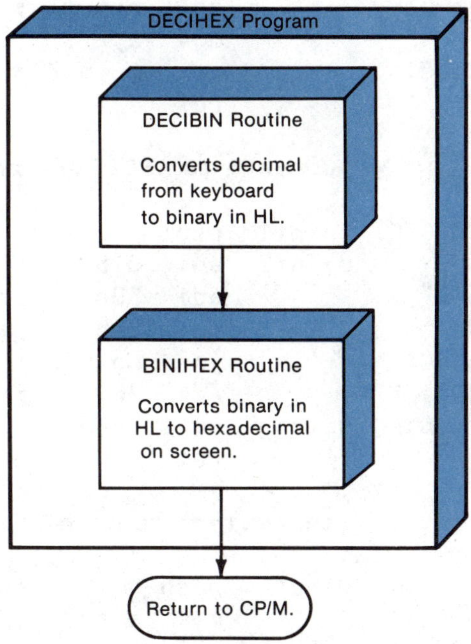

Fig. 4-6. The DECIHEX program.

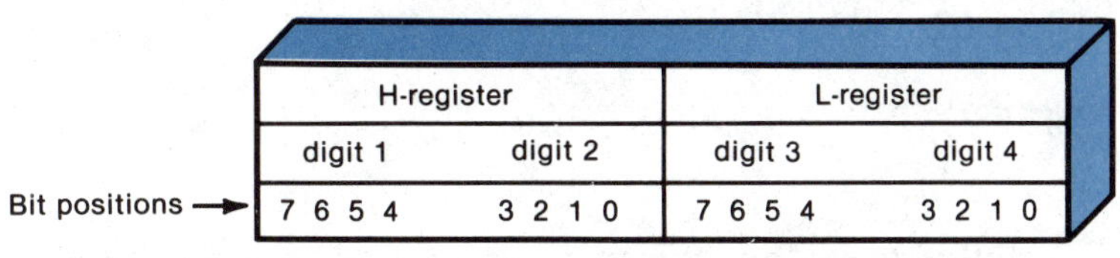

Fig. 4-7. BINIHEX subroutine.

that ASCII was invented before hexadecimal notation became popular.) Listing 4-2 shows the BINIHEX subroutine.

Listing 4-2. The BINIHEX Subroutine

```
                 ;binihex-subroutine to print binary number in
                 ;        hl out on screen in hex
                 ;
0128 7C          binihex mov   a,h      ;put h in a (first digit)
0129 CD3901              call  print1   ; print left-hand digit
012C 7C                  mov   a,h      ;put h in a (second digit)
012D CD3D01              call  print2   ; print right-hand digit
0130 7D                  mov   a,l      ;put l in a (third digit)
0131 CD3901              call  print1   ; print left-hand digit
0134 7D                  mov   a,l      ;put l in a (fourth digit)
0135 CD3D01              call  print2   ; print right-hand digit
0138 C9                  ret            ;exit binihex
                 ;
                 ;convert to ASCII and print
                 ;
0139 07070707    print1  rlc! rlc! rlc! rlc   ;move high 4 bits to low
013D E60F        print2  ani   0fh      ;get rid of high 4 bits
013F C630                adi   30h      ;change hex to ASCII
0141 FE3A                cpi   3ah      ;if more than 9
0143 FA4801              jm    notbig   ; (it's not)
0146 C607                adi   7h       ; then add bias (10=A, etc)
0148 CD4C01      notbig  call  pchar    ;print digit
014B C9                  ret
                 ;
                 ;subroutine to print char in a-reg out on screen
                 ;
014C E5          pchar   push  h        ;save hl (conout uses it)
014D 5F                  mov   e,a      ;print hex digit
014E 0E02                mvi   c,2
0150 CD0500              call  5
0153 E1                  pop   h        ;get hl back
0154 C9                  ret
                 ;
0155                     end
```

Notice first, that this is a subroutine, not an executable program. That's why the memory locations don't start at 100. What we've done is simply showing this subroutine by itself for clarity, even though it forms part of a larger program (as you can see by looking ahead a few pages).

BINIHEX consists of three parts. PCHAR is a subroutine whose only function is to print a character on the screen. It is entered with the character in the A-register, and before it calls the Console Out routine (lines 14E and 150), it saves the HL-register because this is where the 16-bit binary number that we're going to print out is stored.

PRINT1 and PRINT2 are two different entry points for the subroutine that prints out, in ASCII, the 4-bit hexadecimal digit that is in the A-register when the routine is entered. If you want to print the hex digit on the left side of the A-register, you call PRINT1; if you want to print the hex digit on the right, you call PRINT2. This is because entering at PRINT1 causes four additional instructions to be executed. The instructions are written in a somewhat unusual way.

The Exclamation Point (!)

If you want to write a number of instructions on the same line, rather than on separate lines as we have done so far, all you need to do is separate the instructions by exclamation points. This is useful when a group of similar instructions that perform the same task can be grouped together. In this case, we need to rotate the A-register 4 bits to the left so that the leftmost 4 bits will end up on the right. Since each RLC instruction rotates the contents of the A-register 1 bit, we'll do four instructions to move it the required 4 bits, and we'll separate the instructions with exclamation points for clarity. (Of course, we could also have written each RLC instruction on a separate line—the assembled binary program would have been just the same.)

So, whether the A-register must be rotated or not, when we get to line 13D we know that the hex digit we want to print is on the right side of the A-register. Our next step is to "mask off" the upper 4 bits, which are meaningless. We do this with the "ani 0fh" instruction. The number "0f hex" is 00001111 in binary, so when we AND it with our 8-bit number, only the rightmost 4 bits will be left. Then, we add 30 (hex), to change the digit from binary into ASCII (since 30 hex is the ASCII code for 0).

Now we have to figure out if the resulting 4-bit ASCII digit is in the range from 0 to 9 or in the range from A to F. To determine this, we do a "compare immediate" with 3ah, since 3a (hex) is the ASCII code for 10. If the result is minus, we know that the number is less than 10 (decimal), so we jump over the next instruction and go to "notbig." On the other hand, if the result is plus, we know that our ASCII digit is more than 9, so it must be in the range from A (hex) to F (hex). If you look at the table of ASCII values in Appendix D, you'll see that "A" is 41 hex, while "9" is 39 hex. If "A" immediately followed "9" in the ASCII table, it would be at 3A hex, so there are seven characters between where "A" actually is in the ASCII table and where it should be. To make up for this difference we need to add an extra "7" to any ASCII character representing the hex numbers from A to F. We do this in line 146. Finally, in line 148, we call the PCHAR subroutine, already described, to print the ASCII digit on the screen.

Now, we can look at the main part of the BINIHEX routine, from line 128 to line 138. These lines are responsible for making sure that the four digits that get printed come from the right place. The first two lines print the left side of the H-register. This is done by putting the H-register into the A-register and then calling PRINT1 which, as we have seen, prints the left-hand digit (4 bits) of whatever is in the A-register. The next two lines print the right side of the H-register. Finally, the last four lines repeat the process with the L-register, and then returns to the main program.

The Complete DECIHEX Program

Now we can put together the DECIBIN and BINIHEX routines into a complete program. The combined DECIHEX program is given in Listing 4-3.

Listing 4-3. The DECIHEX Program

```
                ;*************************************************
                ;DECIHEX-converts decimal input from keyboard
                ;        to hex on screen
                ;
                ;
0001 =          conin   equ  1h
0002 =          conout  equ  2h
0005 =          bdos    equ  5h
000A =          lf      equ  0ah
                ;
0100                    org  100h
                ;
                ;main program-links subroutines together
                ;
```

```
0100 CD0C01          call decibin  ;get decimal, convert to binary
0103 3E0A            mvi  a,lf     ;print linefeed
0105 CD4C01          call pchar
0108 CD2801          call binihex  ;convert binary to hex and print
010B C9              ret
             ;
             ;decibin-reads decimal number from keyboard,
             ;         converts to binary
             ;
010C 210000  decibin lxi  h,0      ;set hl to 0
010F E5      newdig  push h        ;save hl (conin uses it)
0110 0E01            mvi  c,conin  ;get character
0112 CD0500          call bdos
0115 E1              pop  h        ;restore hl
0116 D630            sui  30h      ;convert from ASCII to binary
0118 F8              rm            ;return if it was < 0
0119 FE0A            cpi  10d      ;is it > 9 ?
011B F0              rp            ;if so, return
             ;
             ;multiply contents of hl by 10 (dec), then add new digit
             ;
011C E5              push h        ;put hl in de
011D D1              pop  d
011E 29              dad  h        ;add hl to hl (double it)
011F 29              dad  h        ;double it again
0120 19              dad  d        ;add de (original number) to hl
0121 29              dad  h        ;double result
0122 50              mov  d,0      ;zero in d
0123 5F              mov  e,a      ;new digit in e
0124 19              dad  d        ;add digit to number
             ;
             ;result is now in hl
             ;
0125 C30F01          jmp  newdig   ;go look for next digit
             ;
             ;
             ;binihex-program to print binary number in hl
             ;         out on screen in hex
             ;
0128 7C      binihex mov  a,h      ;put h in a (first digit)
0129 CD3901          call print1   ; print left-hand digit
012C 7C              mov  a,h      ;put h in a (second digit)
012D CD3D01          call print2   ; print right-hand digit
```

```
0130 7D                 mov  a,l       ;put l in a (third digit)
0131 CD3901             call print1    ; print left-hand digit
0134 7D                 mov  a,l       ;put l in a (fourth digit)
0135 CD3D01             call print2    ; print right-hand digit
0138 C9                 ret            ;exit binihex
               ;
               ;convert to ASCII and print
               ;
0139 07070707  print1   rlc! rlc! rlc! rlc  ;move high 4 bits to low
013D E60F      print2   ani  0fh       ;get rid of high 4 bits
013F C630               adi  30h       ;change hex to ASCII
0141 FE3A               cpi  3ah       ;if more than 9
0143 FA4801             jm   notbig    ; (it's not)
0146 C607               adi  7h        ; then add bias (10=A, etc)
0148 CD4C01    notbig   call pchar     ;print digit
014B C9                 ret
               ;
               ;subroutine to print character in a-reg out on screen
               ;
014C E5        pchar    push h         ;save hl (conout uses it)
014D 5F                 mov  e,a       ;print hex digit
014E 0E02               mvi  c,conout
0150 CD0500             call bdos
0153 E1                 pop  h         ;get hl back
0154 C9                 ret
               ;
0155                    end
```

The EQU Directive

You've already learned about ORG and END. They're instructions to the *assembler program*, rather than to the 8080 itself, like most instructions in an assembly listing. Digital Research, who wrote ASM, refers to such entities as "directives," so we'll do that too, although many other assembler writers call them "pseudo-ops," meaning that they aren't quite like real 8080 op codes.

Anyway, you will by now have noticed, unless you have fallen asleep at the wheel, that our DECIHEX program starts off with a number of statements containing "equ", like "conin equ 5h". EQU is another directive. What's it for? The idea with these statements is to make the program listing clearer by using *names* for things instead of *numbers*. We know, for instance, that to call the Console In system call, we need to do an "mvi c,1" instruction. That's fine, but the number "1" is not really very descriptive of what the instruction is trying to do. It's much clearer to be able to use an illustrative sort of name in the instruction, like "mvi c,conin", which is exactly what we do in line 110. But how will the assembler program know what we mean when it sees "conin" used in this way? It won't, unless we tell it, and that's what the EQU directive is for. Using EQU, we can tell the assembler that every time it sees a certain name, it is to substitute the number given in the equ statement.

As another example, in line 103, we say "mvi a,lf". (These are the lower-case letters "LF," for "Linefeed.") What we're doing here is loading the ASCII code for a linefeed into the A-register, where this value has already been defined in the statement "lf equ 0ah" at the beginning of the program. We could have said "mvi a,0ah" in line 103, but unless we happened to remember that 0a hex is the hex code for linefeed, we wouldn't have known what the instruction meant.

When to use an EQU directive and when to simply use a regular hex or decimal number in an instruction is largely a matter of style. Many programmers follow the convention that instructions that refer to memory locations *outside of the program*, such as the entry point to BDOS at 5 hex, *must* be given a symbolic name with an EQU directive. This convention makes it easier to go back and change the program if, for example, you wanted it to work on a CP/M system where BDOS started at a location other than 5 hex. Otherwise, EQU is used when it will make the program easier to read. By convention, EQU statements are all grouped at the beginning of a program where they are easier to find.

Since we already know all about the DECIBIN and BINIHEX subroutines in this program, there isn't too much more to say about the program. The first four lines, from 100 to 10B, link the subroutines together. First, we call DECIBIN, to get the decimal number that the user will type in on the keyboard. The number is placed in the HL-register where it will remain when we return to the main program in line 103. Then, we print a linefeed, so that when we print the hex number, it won't print on top of the decimal number that was just typed in. To print the linefeed, we make use of the PCHAR subroutine that is already a part of the BINIHEX routine. We put the ASCII code for a linefeed in the A-register and call PCHAR. To print the hex version of the number, we then call BINIHEX, in line 108, and our job is done!

Assembling and Using DECIHEX

Type in the entire DECIHEX program using your word-processor program and give it a file name and an extension of "decihex.asm". Then, assemble it in the usual way:

```
A>asm decihex
CP/M ASSEMBLER - 2.0
0155
000 USE FACTOR
END OF ASSEMBLY
```

Now, since we want to run this program directly from CP/M (rather than DDT), we'll convert the HEX file to a COM file with the LOAD program:

```
A>load decihex

FIRST ADDRESS 0100
LAST ADDRESS  0154
BYTES READ    0055
RECORDS WRITTEN 01
```

And now, lo and behold, we can actually execute the program and see if it works. Type the program name (no extension needed to execute a COM file), and when the program is loaded and waiting, type any decimal number between 0 and 65535:

```
A>decihex
65535
FFFF
A>
```

Wow! It did it! FFFF is the hex equivalent of 65535, so we're really in business. Try it with other numbers and, then, file it away on a disk for the next time when you need to do decimal-to-hex conversions. DECIHEX is a lot faster than thumbing through some greasy table.

USING CP/M's SUBMIT UTILITY

You've probably noticed that if you do a lot of assemblying, it gets a little tedious going through all the steps to assemble, load, and execute the program. Also, when the process is finished, you're left with a lot of files for each program: ASM, BAK, HEX, PRN, and COM. (You may not have a BAK file if your word processor doesn't create one.) Of these, you only need to store the ASM and COM files, since you can generate the others from the ASM file whenever you want to. Wouldn't it be nice if there were a way to start with the ASM file and end up with just the ASM and COM files without having to go through all the steps of creating and, then, erasing the intermediate files? The CP/M utility program SUBMIT permits us to do just that.

If you haven't used SUBMIT before, here's a brief description of how it works. The idea is to take a string of CP/M commands (the kind you type following the A> prompt) and put them together in a text file. Then, if you run the SUBMIT program, these commands will be executed one after the other.

Let's try it out. Use your word processor to create the following file, and give it the name "quick.sub":

```
 ┌──Type this in.        ┌──These are just comments; don't type them in.
 ↓                       ↓
era $1.bak          Erase the "bak" file.
asm $1              Assemble the program.
era $1.prn          Erase the "prn" file.
load $1             Load the program.
era $1.hex          Erase the "hex" file.
$1                  Execute the program.
```

Now, let's assume that you have the following files on your disk in drive A:

1. "quick.sub" (which you just made above).
2. "decihex.asm" (which you typed in on your word processor).
3. "decihex.bak" (which your word processor created).
4. "submit.com".

Type the following:

```
A>submit quick decihex
```

My goodness, what a clicking and whirring of the disk drive there is now! It's hard to believe that one little phrase could cause so much activity. CP/M is erasing the "decihex.bak" file, assemblying the "decihex.asm" file with ASM, erasing the "decihex.prn" file, LOADing the "decihex.hex" file and then erasing it, and, finally, it executes the "decihex.com" file.

How does all this happen? SUBMIT looks first for the file with an extension of SUB whose name was typed in following SUBMIT: in this case,

QUICK. It then proceeds to "execute" the lines of this file as if they were a program written in "CP/M language," which, in a way, they are. When SUBMIT sees the "era $1.bak" statement, for example, it looks for the file name that was typed in following the name of the submit file QUICK; in this case, DECIHEX. Then, wherever there is a $1, SUBMIT will fill in the name of the file: DECIHEX. So, the first line is translated into "era decihex.bak". The second line is translated into "asm decihex", and so on. (Actually, more than one file name can be dealt with in this way, by using $2, $3, and so on, but we don't need to get into that here.)

Amusing, no? And also a great time saver. You can customize this little QUICK file to suit your needs. For instance, if you want to retain the BAK file for safety's sake, leave out "era $1.bak". And, if you don't want to execute the program right away, leave out the last line: "$1".

GRADUATION TIME

You now know almost as much about 8080 assembly language as anyone. Oh, sure, there are some more instructions in the 8080 repertoire, but the ones you've already learned are used in 95% of all programming situations. In fact, you could probably write any program you wanted to by just using only the instructions you've learned so far. We'll pick up a few more along the way, but they won't be too different from what you know already.

Also, you've learned to use the sophisticated (at least when compared with DDT) ASM assembler to assemble your program. Now you can write programs of almost unlimited length (subject to the limitations of your computer's memory, of course) with the assurance that you'll be able to turn them into object code. So, how about a round of champagne? You've graduated from 8080 school!

CHAPTER 5

Disk System Calls

You can do some interesting things with the system calls you've learned so far, especially those that deal with the keyboard, the video screen, and the printer. However, most serious application programs deal with *data* in some form or other, and data in a CP/M system are usually stored on a disk. If you're writing a word-processing program, the text files are stored on the disk. If you're writing a spreadsheet program like Visicalc, the data you put in the spreadsheet are stored on the disk. If you're writing an improved CP/M file directory program, the data you want to look at (the disk directory) are stored on the disk. In short, understanding the CP/M disk system is indispensable if you want to write programs that make use of the full capability of your CP/M system.

The CP/M disk system calls are amazingly powerful. Remember our analogy in the introduction about ordering a chicken sandwich in hotels in different cities? The idea was that no matter what city you were in, you could always get the same chicken sandwich, even if the hotel employees, depending on whether they were in Calcutta or Istanbul, had to engage in very different practices to prepare the sandwich.

Let's extend this analogy a little. If using the system calls for the console (keyboard and video) is like ordering a chicken sandwich, then using them for the disk drives is like ordering duck á l'orange with a magnum of Lafite Rothschild '63. When you used the console system calls, you were dealing with single characters or character strings. With disk system calls, you can handle whole records and files at a time, all without having to worry about how CP/M and your computer actually go about reading and writing information to the disk. And, of course, your programs will read and write files on any computer or disk system, as long as it is running CP/M.

Learning how to use these disk system calls is the purpose of this chapter. You'll find out about the "mailbox" system that CP/M programs use to tell CP/M what files to read or write, and you'll explore several short system calls which will be all you need to have to read any file into your program. By the end of this chapter, you'll be able to reproduce the CP/M "type" command and also write a program that counts the number of lines in a text file. (We'll save *writing* to the disk until the next chapter.)

If this sounds complicated, relax. Thanks to the transportability features of CP/M, learning how to input and output information to the disk is scarcely more complicated than it is for the console. Well, maybe a little more complicated, but it'll be fun. Trust us!

RECORDS, FILES, TRACKS, SECTORS, ALLOCATION UNITS, EXTENTS, AND GOODNESS KNOWS WHAT ELSE

One of the truly wonderful things about CP/M is that you can write programs in 8080 assembly language, which will do almost anything you want with the disk drives, *without knowing anything about most of the terms,* such as those listed in the heading of this section. All you really need to understand are records and files. We won't talk (too much) about the other terms until Chapter 7, when we get to such mysterious topics as the file directory and saving erased files.

Files

From the user's viewpoint, the fundamental unit of information on a disk is a *file.* You're already familiar with files and how they are named ("test1.com" and so on). A file is simply a whole lot of bytes stored on the disk. Files in CP/M can be almost as small or as large as the person generating them wants them to be. The minimum size is 256 bytes (which is 256 characters, if the file consists of text), and the maximum size is *more than 8 million bytes.* Now, that's really big. Because CP/M can handle such large files, it needs to be able to break them down into smaller sections. Why is this? Mostly because the memory of the computer is much smaller than this maximum file size and, also, smaller than the space on a typical 8-inch floppy disk. The memory of a typical CP/M computer is 65,536 bytes (some of which are used by CP/M itself). When you add the user's program, there may not be more than a few thousand (or even a few hundred) bytes left for storing data on the disk. On the other hand, an 8-inch disk will hold from about 75,000 bytes to upwards of more than one million bytes. Clearly, if you have a file that occupies most of a disk (or more than one disk), you can't cram it all into memory at the same time. So a file is broken down into smaller units called *records,* only one of which is loaded into memory at any one time.

Records

The designers of CP/M had to determine what size records they wanted to break a file into. If they made the records too large, the records would take up too much memory when they were read in, but if they were too small, the disk drives would have to work too hard to transfer a file into memory, since each record requires a separate disk access. They chose a fairly small record: 128 bytes. Remember this number–you'll be seeing it again. Use your DECIHEX conversion program to find out what 128 decimal is in hex.

TALKING TO BDOS

When it is reading or writing information to the disk, the Basic Disk Operating System (BDOS) uses two areas of memory to communicate with the program calling it. These are the DMA buffer and the File Control Block (FCB). Understanding the DMA and the FCB and how they're used is the key to understanding the CP/M disk system calls.

Fig. 5-1 shows where the DMA buffer and the FCB are located in memory. They're both in the "zero page," the portion of memory from 0000 hex to 00FF hex.

The DMA Buffer

When you want to read a file from the disk into memory, the process goes like this. You set aside a place in memory that is 128 bytes long. This space is called the "DMA buffer." (DMA stands for "Direct Memory Access" and is actually a term better used with large mainframe computers that can transfer a block of data without the intervention of the a program—but that's another story. The name got started and here it is.) The DMA buffer is usually located at memory address 80 (hex), which is called the "DMA Address," although you can change it to any address you want, as we will soon see.

Once the DMA buffer is set up, you read the first record of the file into this space. When your program has done whatever it's going to do with this record (printing it out on the screen, doing arithmetic on data in the record, or whatever), it then reads in the next 128-byte record, processes it, and so on—until the end of the file is reached.

The File Control Block (FCB)

How can your program tell CP/M what file to read? We need a way to pass *file names* from your program to CP/M, so that BDOS can take care of all the tedious details of looking for the file on the disk, finding the record we want and reading it off the disk, and putting it in memory in the DMA buffer. To pass these file names, we set up a sort of "mailbox" in memory,

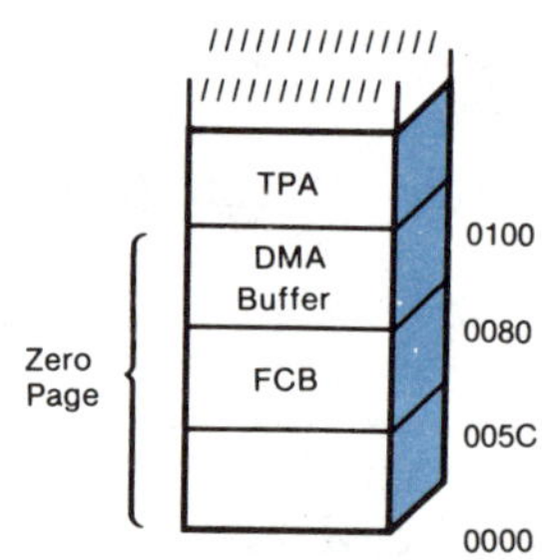

Fig. 5-1. The memory location of the DMA buffer and the FCB.

which we call the FCB, for File Control Block. This is simply a section of memory, 36 (decimal) bytes long, where we can put the file name. CP/M also uses the FCB to store information about where the file is located and some other things, but we don't need to worry about that now. The FCB is usually located at memory address 5C (hex), just below the DMA address.

The following listing shows the various sections of the file control block (FCB). For the time being, we are only interested in the place where the file name and extension go. (The mnemonics shown in parentheses are the designations given the various bits by Digital Research.)

Byte number (decimal)	Location (hex)	Contents	
0	5C	0	Drive number (dr).
1	5D	T	File name (8 bytes) (f1 to f8).
2	5E	E	
3	5F	S	
4	60	T	
5	61	1	
6	62	0	
7	63	0	
8	64		
9	65	T	File extension (3 bytes) (t1 to t3).
10	66	X	
11	67	T	
12	68	00	Current extent (ex).
13	69	00	Used internally by CP/M (s1).
14	6A	00	(User should set to zero) (s2).
15	6B	02	Nbr of records in current extent (rc).
16	6C	54	Allocation units (d0 to d10).
17	6D	00	
18	6E	00	
19	6F	00	
20	70	00	
21	71	00	
22	72	00	
23	73	00	
24	74	00	
25	75	00	
26	76	00	

27	77	00	Allocation units (d11 to d15).
28	78	00	
29	79	00	
30	7A	00	
31	7B	00	
32	7C	01	Current record (cr).
33	7D	00	Random record number (r0, r1, r2).
34	7E	00	
35	7F	00	

Now that you know about the DMA buffer and the FCB, we're ready to plunge on into our first system call.

OPEN FILE

OPEN FILE	FUNCTION 15 (dec) =0F (hex)		
Enter with:	REG C	=	0F (hex)
	REGs DE	=	FCB Address
On return:	REG A	=	directory code.
Comments:	Directory Code	=	0,1,2, or 3 if file found.
	Directory Code	=	FF (hex) if file not found.

What does it mean to "open" a file? Before a program can do any reading or writing to a file, BDOS has to figure out where the file is on the disk. It is alerted to do this with the "Open File" system call. When this call is executed, BDOS finds the addresses of the various parts of the file (they're called "allocation units") and records them in the FCB for later reference. Since there is only one FCB, there can only be one file open at any one time. (Actually, there can be several FCBs operating at once, but we're not going to get into that now.)

Here's a little program to open a file using this system call:

```
mvi   c,f      Put f in C-register for Open File.
lxi   d,5c     Put address of FCB in DE-register.
call  5        Call BDOS.
rst   7        Back to DDT.
```

Type in this program using DDT, save it as "test100.ddt", and then execute it by typing -g100. You should hear your disk drive click and DDT will print out the usual star and ending address:

```
-g100
*0108      (Click!!)
-
```

Wow–what a powerful program–it made the disk drive click! What's the click mean? You've told BDOS to open the file whose name is in the FCB. What name is in there? We don't really know, since we haven't put anything in the FCB ourselves. Maybe there's an old file name left over from a previous operation, maybe not. Whatever is in there, even if it's a string of blanks or zeros, BDOS will try to find a file with that name. If it finds it, BDOS will "open" the file by recording the numbers of its allocation units in the FCB. If it doesn't find the file, it will still make the disk drive click by looking for the file in the disk directory. (We'll talk more about the directory in Chapter 7.)

It's not hard to see what's in the FCB. From DDT, simply type "d5c,7f". If there's nothing in the FCB but zeros, you'll get a printout like this:

```
-d5c,7f
005C 00 00 00 00 ....
0060 00 00 00 00 00 00 00 00 00 00 00 00 00 00 00 00 ................
0070 00 00 00 00 00 00 00 00 00 00 00 00 00 00 00 00 ................
```

The first line shows the memory locations from 5C to 5F, and the next lines, the locations from 60 to 7F. A name would be in here somewhere if there was one, but there isn't.

You can make sure a file name is placed in the FCB by simply calling up DDT with the name of another program. For instance, assuming you have saved the "test100.ddt" program described above, you can put its name in the FCB in the following way. First, exit from DDT with a -g0. Now, to get back into DDT, and at the same time, load the new program into the TPA at 100 hex *and leave the name of the program in the FCB,* type:

```
A>ddt test100.ddt
```

Now look at the FCB with "d":

```
-d5c,7f
005C 00 54 45 53 .TES
0060 54 31 30 30 20 44 44 54 00 00 00 00 00 00 00 00 T100 DDT......
0070 00 00 00 00 00 00 00 00 00 00 00 00 00 00 00 00 ..............
```

There's the name of the program! The name itself starts at location 5D, is 8 bytes long, and ends at location 64. The numerical ASCII values of the characters are shown on the left, and the actual characters on the right. Since "TEST100" is only seven characters long, the last space of this 8-space field is filled in with a blank (20 hex) at location 64. The file extension "DDT" occupies locations 65 to 67 hex.

If we now run our little program with a -g100, it will find an existing file, namely itself, in the FCB and open it.

Can we tell whether the Open File system call has been successful in finding the file whose name is in the FCB? Yes, by making use of what is called the "directory code," which is returned in the A-register following the call. To use this feature, we need to add a few lines to our program to print out the number returned in the A-register.

```
0100 mvi  c,f     Put f in C-register for Open File.
0102 lxi  d,5c    Put address of FCB in DE-register.
0105 call 5       Call BDOS.
0108 mvi  c,2     Set up Console Out.
010A adi  30      Add 30 hex to A-register to get ASCII.
010C mov  e,a     Put result in E-register.
010D call 5       Call BDOS.
0110 rst  7       Back to DDT.
```

Type this program in using the "a" option in DDT, save it with "A>save test101.ddt", call it back in with "A>ddt test101.ddt" and run it with a "g100". You should get the following on the screen:

```
-g100
3*0110
```

The "3" preceding the usual asterisk and ending address is the number printed out by our program, and is the number that was in the A-register on completion of the Open File system call. It might also be a 0, or a 1, or a 2. Any of these numbers mean that the file, whose name was in the FCB, was found by the Open File system call. (Whether the number is a 0, 1, 2, or 3 is determined by the place in the disk directory that is actually occupied by the file name—a topic we're going to avoid until the next chapter.)

The "i" Command in DDT

It would be more convenient if there were a way to place other file names into the FCB directly, without having to enter them when calling up DDT. This is the purpose of the "i" (for "Input") command.

Suppose you have a program on your disk called TESTPROG.TXT. If you're already in DDT, and you want to put this name into the FCB, all you need to do is type:

```
-itestprog.txt
```

Doesn't that seem easy? Let's try it out to see if it really works. First, we'll fill the FCB with "FF's" to make sure there's nothing in it, and then we'll use "i" to fill in a program name. Then, we'll check to see if it's there.

```
-f5c,7f,ff
-d5c,7f
005C FF FF FF FF ....
0060 FF FF FF FF FF FF FF FF FF FF FF FF FF FF FF FF ................
0070 FF FF FF FF FF FF FF FF FF FF FF FF FF FF FF FF ................

-itestprog.txt

-d5c,7f
005C 00 54 45 53 .TES
0060 54 50 52 4F 47 54 58 54 00 FF FF FF FF FF FF FF TPROG...........
0070 FF FF FF FF FF FF FF FF FF FF FF FF FF FF FF FF ................
```

The name is there, just as it was when we called it in with DDT. Notice also that byte 0 at location 5C and byte 12 at location 68, which are the drive number and "current extent," respectively, are also zeroed out by the "i" function. A "0" drive number stands for the "default drive," which is the one we're in unless otherwise specified, and the "current extent" is 0 unless we're reading from a file that is more than 16,384 bytes long. (More on that later.)

It is possible to do "by hand" what the "i" command does, if we translate the letters of the file name into ASCII values and put them into the correct locations using the "s" command in DDT; but, of course, the "i" command is far more convenient.

You can now check to see if your Open File program can find all sorts of different programs. Use "i" to insert the name of a program that *is* on the disk, and then run your program.

```
-itestprog.txt     Existing program name.
-g100
3*0110             "3" means it was found.
-
```

The program should print out a 0, 1, 2, or 3. Now try it with a program name that *isn't* on your disk.

```
-inotaprog.com     Nonexistent program.
-g100
/*0110             "/" means it wasn't found.
-
```

If the file isn't found, the A-register will contain FF when the program returns from the Open File system call. The program should then print out a slash (/), since this is the character with an ASCII value of 2F (30 plus FF), which we calcuated in line 010A of the program. (FF has the value −1 in 8-bit arithmetic, and 30 minus 1 is 2F.)

THE PROBLEM WITH WHERE THE DMA IS LOCATED

The next thing that we want to do after opening a file is to read it into memory so that our program can examine it, print it out, send it to the printer, or whatever. We also want to be able to do this from DDT, because the "i" command makes it so easy to set up the FCB for a particular record. *Unfortunately,* there is a small problem with using DDT at the same time that we're using the DMA in its normal location from 80 to FF (Fig. 5-2). The problem is that DDT uses this area for its stack (the place where the contents of registers go when you "push" them). These two areas can't occupy the same space at the same time without causing error messages. What to do?

There are two solutions to this problem: an easy one and a good one. We'll explore the easy one first.

The Easy Solution to the DMA Dilemma

The easy solution is to read only very short records into the DMA. Since DDT's stack grows down from the address FF, and records are read into the DMA buffer at 80 and moving upward toward FF, if the records are short, we can avoid conflict. We'll try this just because it makes for a nice easy

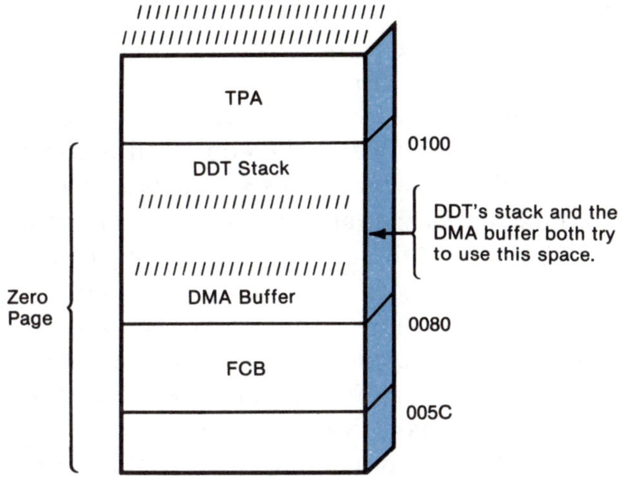

Fig. 5-2. The conflict between DMA and DDT.

program, even though it has a built-in potential for disaster if we try to read too long a record.

The first thing to do is to create a very short record. Call up your word-processing program and type in some characters, but make sure you don't type more than a line (80 decimal characters). End your line with a "return." Save this as a file called "short.txt". Since this file is so short, it is a 1-record file. (It will show up as a 2K file in the directory, but only one 128-byte record will be used.)

Now the only thing that stands between us and writing a program to read this record into the DMA is learning the Read Sequential system call.

READ SEQUENTIAL SYSTEM CALL

READ SEQUENTIAL RECORD FUNCTION 20 (dec) = 14 (hex)

Enter with:	REG C	= 14 (hex)
	REGs DE	= FCB address
On return:	REG A	= directory code.
Comments:	Directory Code = 0 if read was successful.	
	Directory Code = nonzero if end-of-file.	

This system call looks a good bit like the Open File call, but note that it reads a *record*, where the Open File call opened a whole *file*. What does "sequential" mean? It means that the call will start off reading the first 128-byte record in a file, will read the second one the next time it is called, the third one the next time, and so on, until it comes to the end of the file.

How does it know when it's at the end of a file? In either of two possible ways. First, it can find an "end-of-file" mark in the file. This is only possible if the file is a text file, so that one of the characters can be set to the ASCII character for "end-of-file," which is a 1A hex.

Secondly (and more important), since CP/M keeps track of how many records are in a file and stores this information in the FCB when the file is opened, all the Read Sequential system call has to do is keep track of how many records it has already read to know if it has read the last record. The total number of records in a file is stored in byte 15 (decimal) of the FCB, and the number of the next record to be read is stored in byte 32. By comparing these two numbers, the Read Sequential call knows when it's finished an entire file.

If the Read Sequential system call does find an end-of-file marker, it sets the A-register to a nonzero value on its return. Otherwise, the A-register is set to 0, which indicates that the read was successful.

Reading a Record

Here's the routine to read into the DMA the record that we created earlier: "short.txt". (Don't try to read anything longer, or bad trouble and error messages will result.) Call this program "test102.ddt".

```
-a100
0100  mvi   c,f     Open file.
0102  lxi   d,5c      Set FCB address.
0105  call  5         Call BDOS.
0108  mvi   c,14    Read record.
010A  lxi   d,5c      Set FCB address.
010D  call  5         Call BDOS.
0110  rst   7       Back to DDT.
```

Before running this program, you need to be sure that (1) your short file "short.txt" is on your disk, and (2) that you have put the name of this file into the FCB by typing "ishort.txt" from DDT. Now, run it with a "-g100". What happens? The disk drive should click. Big deal—no better than the last program? No. This time there's a tangible result.

Use "d" to look at the DMA buffer. Assuming that your "short.txt" file consisted of the line "Now is the time for all good men to come to the aid of their country," you should see the following when you dump the buffer:

```
-d80,ff
0080 4E 6F 77 20 69 73 20 74 68 65 20 74 69 6D 65 20 Now is the time
0090 66 6F 72 20 61 6C 6C 20 67 6F 6F 64 20 6D 65 6E for all good men
00A0 20 74 6F 20 63 6F 6D 65 20 74 6F 20 74 68 65 20 to come to the
00B0 61 69 64 20 6F 66 20 74 68 65 69 72 20 63 6F 75 aid of their cou
00C0 6E 74 72 79 2E 0D 0A 00 00 00 00 00 00 00 00 00 ntry............
00D0 00 00 00 00 00 00 00 00 00 00 00 00 00 00 00 00 ................
00E0 00 00 00 00 00 00 00 00 00 00 00 00 00 00 00 00 ................
00F0 00 00 00 00 00 00 00 00 C1 D6 9B D4 42 d4 44 00 ................
```

These numbers inserted by DDT stack process.

The record ends with the codes for carriage return and linefeed: 0D, 0A. The zeros after that could be any junk that happened to be in the buffer before the record was read in, although you could guarantee they were zeros by using "f" to fill the buffer before executing the program.

So, there's the record, sitting safe and sound in the DMA buffer, just where it should be. And the program to read it in is only 7 lines long! That's even easier than reading a record in BASIC! However, as you're aware, we're restricted to very short records with this program. What we need now is a way to avoid the conflict that results when the DMA buffer and the DDT stack try to share the same space.

The Good Solution to the DMA Dilemma

Fortunately CP/M offers an easy solution to this problem; we can move the DMA buffer using the "Set DMA Address" system call.

SET DMA ADDRESS

SET DMA ADDRESS	FUNCTION 26 (dec) = 1A (hex)
Enter with: REG C = 1A (hex)	
REGs DE = New DMA address	

This system call looks easy enough to use, and it is. All we need to say is:

```
mvi  c,1a     Set up for Set DMA Address.
lxi  d,400    Move DMA address to 400.
call 5        Call BDOS.
```

We chose 400 (hex) as the new DMA address simply because it's high enough in memory so that we know it isn't going to interfere with our program at 100 hex. Actually, you can put the DMA anywhere you want, as long as it doesn't interfere with your program or the CP/M operating system (or DDT, if you're using that).

Let's incorporate these program lines into our read record program:

```
0100 mvi  c,f      Open file.
0102 lxi  d,5c
0105 call 5
0108 mvi  c,1a     Set DMA address to 400.
010A lxi  d,400
010D call 5
0110 mvi  c,14     Read record.
0112 lxi  d,5c
0115 call 5
0118 rst  7        Back to DDT.
```

Save this program as "test103.ddt". Now, use it to read in the first record of any file you want, no matter how long it is. Here's how to do it:

1. Load the program with DDT with "A>ddt test103.ddt".
2. Put the file name of the program you want to look at in the FCB with "-iprogname.ext" (fill in the name of the file you want).
3. Run the program with "-g100".
4. Check the DMA buffer with "-d400" to see that whatever was in the record was read in correctly.

If you want to read the second record of a file that is longer than one record, simply repeat Steps 3 and 4. Each time you execute the program a new record will be read into the DMA buffer, where you can look at it with the "-d" command. You can examine any sort of record this way, whether it contains text, hex values, or whatever. This can be useful in investigating what's *really* going on, on the bit level, in a record on your disk.

For instance, some word-processing programs use the high-order bit (bit 7) of each character to indicate that there is something special about the character. A normal space is 20 hex, but the "soft" space used in some processors to justify text lines might be represented by A0 hex, since 20 hex is 0010,0000 in binary, and A0 hex is 1010,0000. They're the same, except that the high bit is turned on in A0.

Dumping a record using DDT this way immediately reveals the difference between hard and soft spaces, and a variety of other things as well. Read different kinds of files and look them over. You may be surprised at what you discover.

Fancy Read Record Program

We've left two things out of our program: (1) the check to see if the file we're trying to open really exists, and (2) the check to see if the record we've read is a valid record or an end-of-file. Let's modify the program so that it prints out the directory codes returned in the A-register twice; first when it returns from opening the file, and second, when it returns from reading the record. This way, we can tell if the file we are trying to read really exists, and if we have read a valid record in the file or an end-of-file. We'll call this program "test104.ddt".

```
-a100
0100  mvi   c,f          open file
0102  lxi   d,5c
0105  call  5
0108  mvi   c,2          print resulting directory code
010A  adi   30
010C  mov   e,a
010D  call  5
0110  mvi   c,1A         set DMA to 400
0112  lxi   d,400
0115  call  5
0118  mvi   c,14         read record
011A  lxi   d,5c
011D  call  5
0120  mvi c,2            print resulting directory code
0122  adi 30
0124  mov e,a
0125  call 5
0128  rst 7              back to DDT
```

Let's try out this program on the "short.txt" file that we created before. After saving the program, reload it with DDT. Then, set up the FCB with the "i" instruction and run the program.

```
-ishort.txt
-g100
30*0128
```

The "0" says that the record was read successfully.

The "3" (or 0, or 1, or 2) says that the file was found.

Now we can dump the contents of the DMA to see that the record is really there:

```
-d400,47f
0400 4E 6F 77 20 69 73 20 74 68 65 20 74 69 6D 65 20 Now is the time
0410 66 6F 72 20 61 6C 6C 20 67 6F 6F 64 20 6D 65 6E for all good men
0420 20 74 6F 20 63 6F 6D 65 20 74 6F 20 74 68 65 20 to come to the
0430 61 69 64 20 6F 66 20 74 68 65 69 72 20 63 6F 75 aid of their cou
0450 6E 74 72 79 2E 0D 0A 00 00 00 00 00 00 00 00 00 ntry............
0460 00 00 00 00 00 00 00 00 00 00 00 00 00 00 00 00 ................
0470 00 00 00 00 00 00 00 00 00 00 00 00 00 00 00 00 ................
```

But, now, if we try to read the next record of this file, we find that a directory code of 1 is returned, indicating an end-of-file:

```
-g100
31*0128
```

The "1" indicates that the record was *not* sucessfully read; it was an end-of-file.

The "3" means the file was found.

Continuing to attempt to read records from the file will yield the same result: a directory code of nonzero indicating end-of-file.

Try out this program on some more existent and some nonexistent files. Check the contents of the DMA with the "d" command both before and after reading a nonexistent file. They don't change since there's nothing in the file. Read a file with a fairly small number of records and see how the contents of the DMA change for each succeeding record. Watch the directory code printout change from 0 to a nonzero value when the last record is reached.

Using this program with the DDT dump function, you can explore how a variety of files are stored on the disk. You can find out what the contents of your files *really* are, rather than just what your applications programs tell you they are.

TYPE2 PROGRAM—IMITATES THE "TYPE" COMMAND

We're now going to put together some of the things we've learned in order to show how to perform a simple but useful function involving the disk system. In fact, this function is so useful that Digital Research has already incorporated it into CP/M. It's the "type" function, which simply prints out on the screen the contents of a text file.

Our program will operate in almost exactly the same way as "type," so we'll call it "type2.com". It will operate directly from CP/M as a COM file. To use it, you type:

```
A>type2 progname.ext
```

where "progname" is the name of the file you want to look at and "ext" is its file type. Executing the program in this way has the effect of putting the program name which *follows* "type2" into the FCB, just as it did when we called DDT and followed it with a program name. In fact, this is always true; when you type two program names in a row following the A> prompt, CP/M will load the first program into the TPA, and put the filename of the second into the FCB.

Look at the listing of TYPE2 in the following pages. The program starts by opening the file whose name is in the FCB and, then, checking to see if the file was found. If not, it prints the message "No such filename" and exits back to CP/M. Assuming that the file exists, it reads the first record from the file and checks to see if it is a valid record or an end-of-file (EOF). If it is the EOF, the program figures its job is done and exits to CP/M. Otherwise, it knows it has a valid record, which it prints out using the Console Out system call in the subroutine "pchar" (for "print character"). We could have used the Print String system call, but then we wouldn't have been able to print strings containing dollar signs, since these act as terminators to Print String.

Since this is a fairly long program which we don't want to run from DDT anyway, we'll assemble it using ASM. The program is given in Listing 5-1.

Listing 5-1. The TYPE2 Program

```
                ;**************************************************
                ;TYPE2-program to imitate CP/M "type" function
                ;
000F =          openf   equ     0fh         ;open file
0014 =          readr   equ     14h         ;read record
0009 =          prints  equ     9h          ;print string
0002 =          conout  equ     2h          ;console out
005C =          fcb     equ     5ch         ;file control block
0080 =          dma     equ     80h         ;start of dma buffer
0005 =          bdos    equ     5h          ;operating system entry
                ;
0100                    org     100h
                ;
                ;open file (name must already be in fcb)
0100 0E0F               mvi     c,openf
0102 115C00             lxi     d,fcb
0105 CD0500             call    bdos
0108 3C                 inr     a           ;if a was ff, now it's 0,
0109 CA2701             jz      nofi        ; so no such file name
                ;
                ;read record from file
                ;
010C 0E14       nextr   mvi     c,readr
010E 115C00             lxi     d,fcb
0111 CD0500             call    bdos
                ;
                ;if end-of-file, then exit to CP/M
0114 B7                 ora     a           ;is a=0?
0115 C0                 rnz                 ; no, so eof, back to CP/M
                ;
                ;display contents of dma buffer
0116 218000             lxi     h,dma       ;set pointer in hl
0119 0680               mvi     b,128d      ;set count in b
011B 5E         loop    mov     e,m         ;get char from buffer
011C CD3001             call    pchar       ;display it
011F 23                 inx     h           ;increment hl
0120 05                 dcr     b           ;decrement b-done?
0121 C21B01             jnz     loop        ; not yet
0124 C30C01             jmp     nextr       ;yes, go get next record
                ;
                ;no such file name: print message and exit
0127 0E09       nofi    mvi     c,prints
0129 113A01             lxi     d,nfmess
012C CD0500             call    bdos
012F C9                 ret                 ;back to CP/M
```

```
                  ;
                  ;subroutine to display one character on screen
0130 E5C5         pchar   push h!  push b!   ;save registers
0132 0E02                 mvi      c,conout  ;print character in e
0134 CD0500               call     bdos
0137 C1E1                 pop b!   pop h!    ;restore registers
0139 C9                   ret
                  ;
013A 4E6F207375nfmess db           'No such filename.$'
                  ;
014C                      end
```

Most of the programming tricks used in this program you've seen before. We've used a lot of EQU statements at the beginning of the program in an attempt to make the rest of the listing easier to read. A flowchart for the TYPE2 program is given in Fig. 5-3.

In lines 108 and 109, we check for EOF by incrementing the directory code in the A-register. If it was FF hex, indicating an EOF, incrementing it will cause it to become zero, and our "jz" (jump on zero) instruction will then be activated and will cause control to go to "nofi" (for "no file"), where the "No such filename" message is printed out using the Print String system call. You've used this system call before, but the way we type the message into the listing, using the "db" directive, may be new to you.

The "DB" Directive

As we pointed out earlier, it's tedious to convert long strings of characters into their ASCII values and then type them in by hand when a message is called for in a listing. ASM provides a way to simplify this task with the "db" directive, which stands for "define bytes." This directive is used whenever you want to put 1-byte values into your listing. These values can be represented by either numbers from 0 to 255 decimal (0 to FF hex), strings of characters (which ASM will translate into their ASCII values), or labels that refer to 1-byte numbers. Combinations of these things may be used, separated by commas. Strings of characters must be enclosed in single quotes. Thus, any of the following statements are valid:

```
max     db  12d                 ;single number
data    db  43h,41h,54h         ;group of numbers
mess    db  'speak to me!'      ;string of characters
mess2   db  'your name?'0D,0A   ;string plus numbers
mess3   db  'your name?'cr,lf   ;string plus labels
```

The hex values for carriage return and linefeed are 0D and 0A, respectively. Thus, mess2 and mess3 are equivalent, provided the labels "cr" and "lf" have been set to these values with EQU statements.

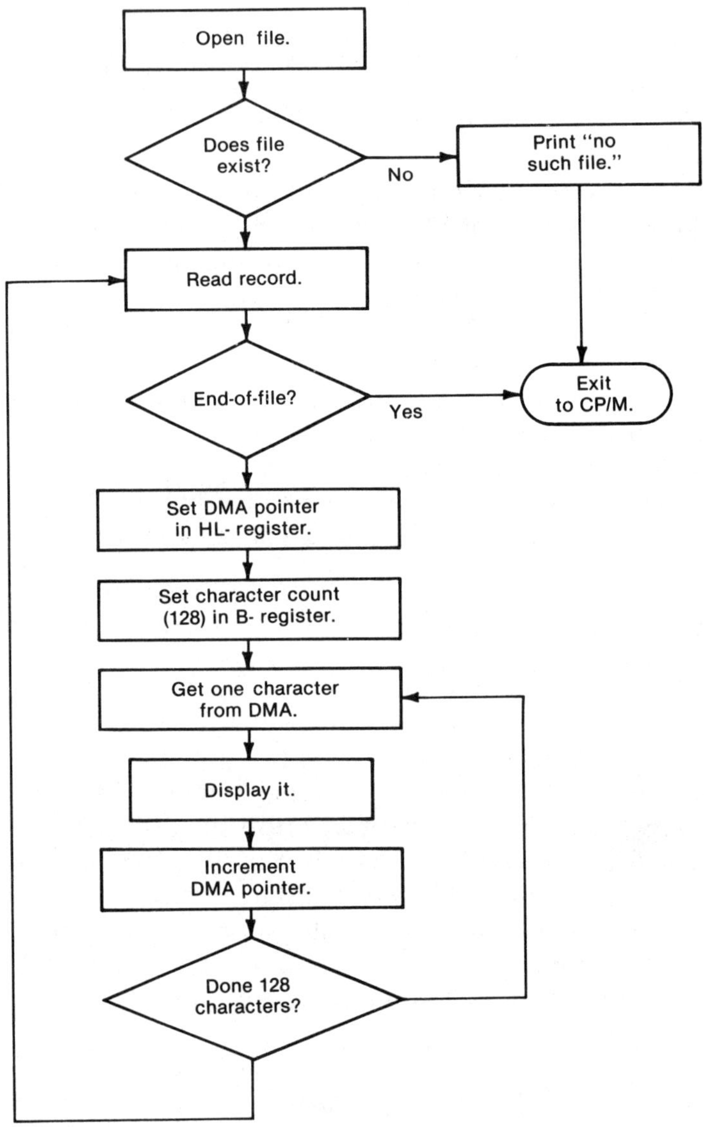

Fig. 5-3. Flowchart for the TYPE2 program.

After reading a record, TYPE2 checks for end-of-file by ORing the A-register with itself; if it's not zero, the program returns to CP/M. To display the contents of the DMA buffer on the screen, the program sets up a loop. The B-register holds the count of characters in the buffer (which is 128 decimal) and the HL-register holds the address of the particular characters in the buffer. We can then just put a character in the E-register with a "mov e,m" instruction and print it with a call to pchar. Next, we do a loop, incrementing the HL pointer, decrementing the B-register counter, and printing the characters, until the count is zero, at which time we go off to read another record.

Type the program in using your word processor, giving it a filename of "type2.asm". (Don't type the hex values on the left-hand side, of course.) Assemble it with ASM, load it with LOAD, and you're ready to execute it directly from CP/M. Type "type2" followed by the name of the program that you want printed out.

Terrific! It's just like CP/M's "type" command. You can even start and stop the scrolling with control–s, just as you can with "type." So look at you! Now you're writing CP/M system programs. In a few more pages, you'll be ready to apply for a job at Digital Research!

LINES PROGRAM–PRINTS NUMBER OF LINES IN TEXT FILE

For our next program, and the last one in this chapter, we've tackled something a little more ambitious. We're going to write a program that will read through a file and count the number of linefeeds it encounters, thus providing a line count of a document or listing.

Actually, the LINES program should look more or less familiar to you, since it consists of system calls and concepts you've looked at before–except for one section. So we're not going to go into detail on every part of the program. We'll talk about a few new things, and we'll cover the BINIDEC subroutine which converts a binary number in the HL-register into a decimal number and prints it out on the screen. This subroutine has a cute way of doing what it does, so we'll describe it briefly.

The BINIDEC Subroutine

The BINIDEC subroutine occupies locations 175 to 1B2 in the LINES program. Here, in Listing 5-2, is how it looks, separated from the rest of the listing.

Listing 5-2. The BINIDEC Subroutine

```
            ;binidec-converts binary number in hl to
            ;          decimal, prints result on screen.
            ;
            ;
0175 11F0D8 binidec lxi     d,-10000 ;print number of 10,000s
0178 CD9401         call    subcnt
017B 1118FC         lxi     d,-1000  ;print number of thousands
017E CD9401         call    subcnt
0181 119CFF         lxi     d,-100   ;print number of hundreds
0184 CD9401         call    subcnt
0187 11F6FF         lxi     d,-10    ;print number of tens
018A CD9401         call    subcnt
018D 11FFFF         lxi     d,-1     ;print number of ones
0190 CD9401         call    subcnt
0193 C9             ret              ;that's all
            ;
0194 0E2F   subcnt  mvi     c,'0'-1  ;c holds ASCII ver of count
0196 0C     sub2    inr     c        ;increment count
0197 22B301         shld    temp     ;save hl
019A 19             dad     d        ;add neg const from de to hl
019B FA9601         jm      sub2     ;loop til result in hl is neg
019E 2AB301         lhld    temp     ;get last pos value back in hl
01A1 79             mov     a,c
01A2 CDA601         call    pchar    ;print digit
01A5 C9             ret
            ;
            ;print character in a-register on screen
01A6 D5C5E5 pchar   push d ! push b ! push h     ;save registers
01A9 5F             mov     e,a      ;character in e
01AA 0E02           mvi     c,conout
01AC CD0500         call    bdos     ;call conout routine
01AF E1C1D1         pop h ! pop b ! pop d     ;get registers back
01B2 C9             ret
            ;
01B3 0100   temp    dw      0
```

The routine uses the following strategy to convert a binary to a decimal number. To start with, it knows that no 16-bit binary number can be larger than 65535 decimal (FFFF hex). The first thing it wants to do then is to find out how many ten thousands there are in the number. There could be as many as 6, there could be 0, or there could be some number in between. How can it find this out, working only in binary? Not so hard. It merely subtracts 10,000 decimal (2710 hex) from the number and checks to see if the result is negative. If not, it knows that the number is larger than 10,000, so it subtracts it again. If the result is still not negative, it knows that the number is larger than 20,000. It keeps subtracting until the result is negative, at which point it knows (since it's been counting) just how many 10,000's there are in the number. It prints this out, since it's the first digit of the decimal translation of the number. Then, it restores the original number to the value it had just before the subtraction that made it go negative; this is the number with the 10000's digit removed.

Let's say the number is 8000 hex, which we happen to know is 32768 decimal. When we subtract 2710 (hex) from B000, the result is not negative, as we can easily see by performing the arithmetic in decimal: 32768 minus 10000. So we do it again. We have to do it three times, so we print out 3 (which is right) and restore the number to 0AD0 hex, which is 2768 decimal: the number with the 10000's digit removed.

Now we have a new number that we know must be less than 10,000, so we can start subtracting 1,000 (*one* thousand) from it to see how many of them there are. And, so on, until we've printed out the hundreds, tens, and ones places. In 8080 assembly language, there isn't a subtraction instruction for 16-bit numbers, so we put negative numbers into the program when we assemble it and add them with a "dad" instruction. This subtraction process is similar for each of the five values that we need to subtract, so we put it in a subroutine that we will call each time with the value in the DE-register.

Another part of this routine is tricky. Look at line 194. What we want to do here is put the count of how many times we have had to subtract 10000 (or 1000, or 100, etc.). But, we want to be able to print this count out, so we want it in ASCII and we want to start at −1 instead of 0, because we *always* subtract the number the first time—that doesn't count. So the clever way of generating a −1 in ASCII is to specify '0' (that's zero, not oh) in single quotes, which gives us the ASCII code for zero, and then we subtract 1 from it: '0'−1.

Yes, you can write this kind of arithmetic statement in the operand field of an instruction. ASM will carry out the arithmetic operations for you, unless they get too complicated.

You may want to use the BINIDEC subroutine in other programs that you write. If so, just plug it in where it's appropriate. All you need to remember is to define "conout" and "bdos" at the start of your program, so it will know where they are.

We've actually used this subroutine in a program which is in the appendices: the HEXIDEC program which converts a hex number typed in at the keyboard into a decimal number on the screen. This is another useful utility program (like DECIHEX in the last chapter) if you work with hexadecimal numbers. Once you've typed BINIDEC in for the LINES program, you might as well juggle it around with your word processor so that you can use it in HEXIDEC too.

You'll notice a few other unfamiliar things in LINES: two new instructions and a new assembler directive.

The "SHLD" Instruction

This instruction is somewhat like the STA instruction, in that it stores the contents of a register directly into memory. However, STA stored the 8-bit contents of the A-register, while SHLD stores the 16-bit contents of the HL-register. Note that this means that *two* bytes of memory have to be set aside, whereas only one was needed for STA. To do this, see the DW directive described next. The place where the two bytes are to go can either be named with a hex address, or with a symbolic name, either of which are pointers to the first byte of the two-byte "word."

Examples:

```
shld 2011
shld penny
```

The "LHLD" Instruction

"LHLD" is the opposite of SHLD, as you may have guessed. It takes the 16-bit value from the referenced memory location and loads it back into the HL-register.

Examples:

```
lhld 2011
lhld whistle
```

The "DW" Directive

We've already discussed the directive DB which defined a byte or number of bytes to be specific 8-bit values. The DW directive is similar, except that it

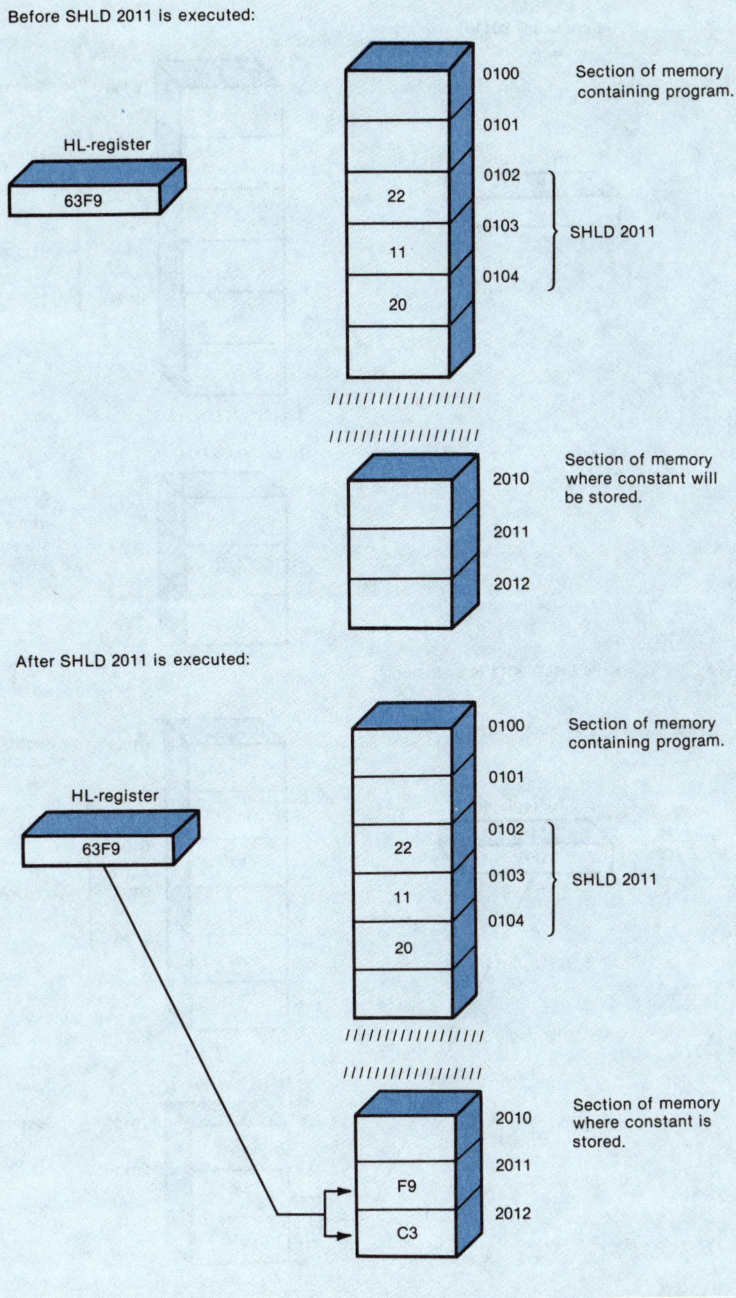

Fig. 5-4. The SHLD instruction.

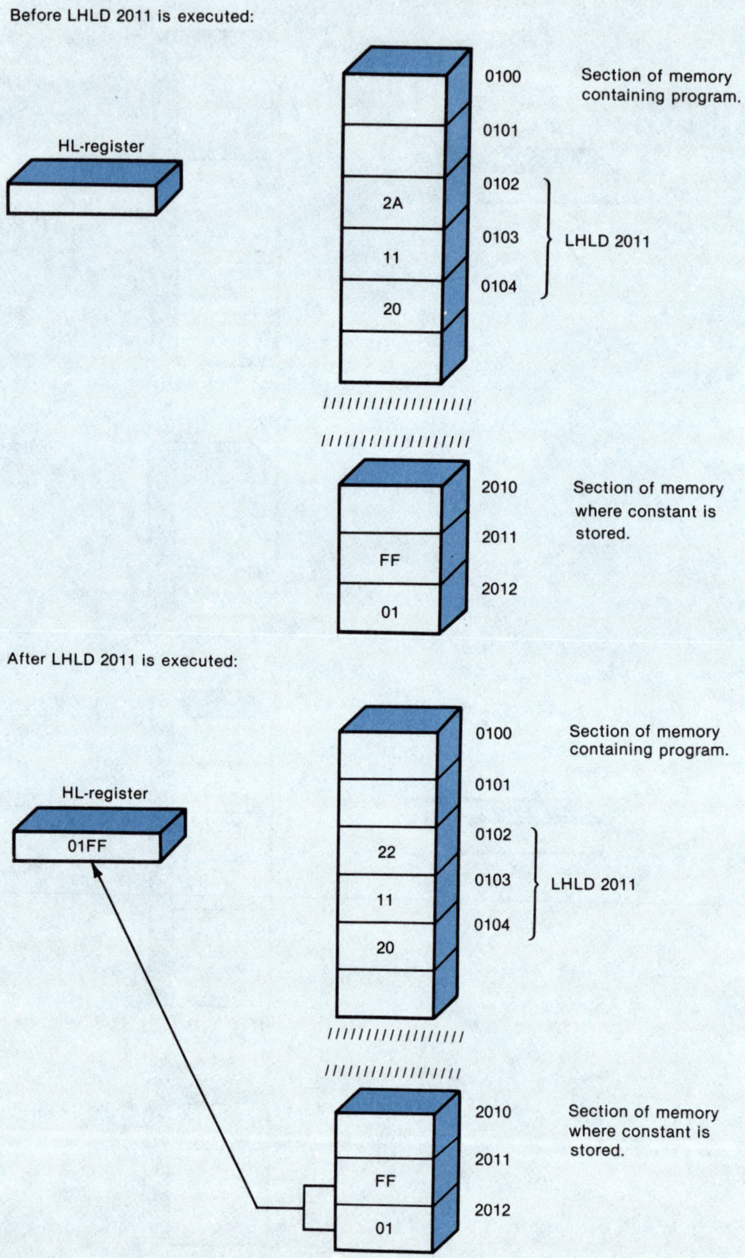

Fig. 5-5. The LHLD instruction.

defines a *word* (which is two bytes) to be a specific 16-bit value. In our program, we need two locations to store 16-bit values because all the registers are already used: "ctr" to store the number of linefeeds counted so far, and "temp," in BINIDEC, to store the original number in HL before we subtract from it each time. Both of these storage areas are reserved by using DW directives.

Like DB, DW can define either numerical or character constants. Several constants can be used together if they're separated by commas.

```
addrs   dw   0ff00h
crlf    dw   0D0Ah
abchar  dw   4142h
busy    dw   4142h,4344h
series  dw   1000,1001,1002,1003
```

Fig. 5-6 gives a flowchart showing the operation of LINES. Using this chart and the descriptions of the various sections of the program given earlier, you should be able to to figure out what the program is up to. The LINES program is given in Listing 5-3.

Listing 5-3. The LINES Program

```
                ;********************************************************
                ;LINES-program to print out number of lines in file
                ;
000F =          openf   equ     0fh     ;open file
0014 =          readr   equ     14h     ;read seq record
0009 =          prints  equ     9h      ;print string
0002 =          conout  equ     2h      ;console output
0005 =          bdos    equ     5h      ;BDOS entry
005C =          fcb     equ     5ch     ;file control block
0080 =          dma     equ     80h     ;DMA address
0080 =          recsiz  equ     128d    ;size of record in DMA
007F =          mask    equ     7fh     ;kills bit 7
001A =          eof     equ     1ah     ;end-of-file character
000A =          lf      equ     0ah     ;linefeed character
                ;
0100                    org     100h
                ;
                ;open file, initialize, read records
                ;
```

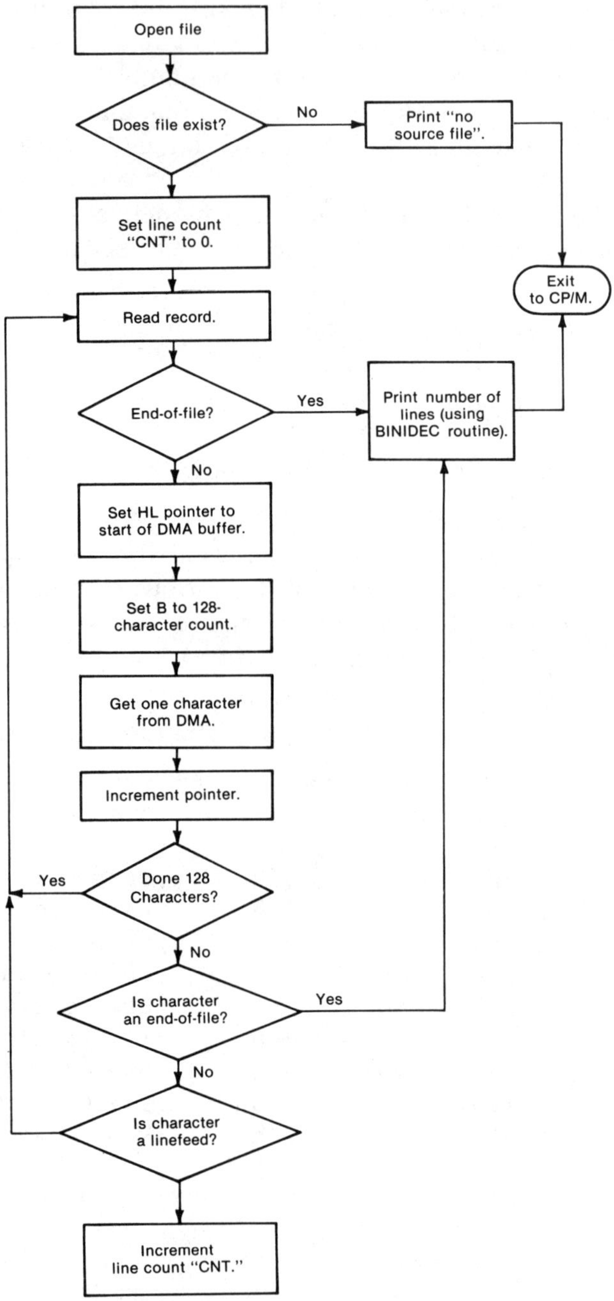

Fig. 5-6. Flowchart for the LINES program.

```
0100 0E0F               mvi     c,openf ;open file
0102 115C00             lxi     d,fcb   ; (addr of fcb in de)
0105 CD0500             call    bdos
0108 116501             lxi     d,nfmess;put "no file" mess in de
010B 3C                 inr     a       ;add 1 to a, if it was ff,
010C CA4D01             jz      nofile  ; now it's 0, so no such file
                ;
010F 210000             lxi     h,0     ;set hl to 0
0112 225301             shld    ctr     ;save for line counter
                ;
0115 0E14       newrec  mvi     c,readr ;read record
0117 115C00             lxi     d,fcb   ; into dma buffer
011A CD0500             call    bdos
011D B7                 ora     a       ;check a to see if eof
011E C24401             jnz     done    ;non-0 is eof
                ;
                ;count number of linefeeds in record stored in dma
                ;
0121 218000             lxi     h,dma   ;put dma addr in hl as pointer
0124 0680               mvi     b,recsiz;put record size in b as counter
                ;
0126 7E         newch   mov     a,m     ;get character from dma buffer
0127 E67F               ani     mask    ;mask off high bit
0129 23                 inx     h       ;increment pointer
012A 05                 dcr     b       ;decrement character counter
012B CA1501             jz      newrec  ;when count is 0, get new record
012E FE1A               cpi     eof     ;is the character an eof?
0130 CA4401             jz      done    ; yes
0133 FE0A               cpi     lf      ;is the character a linefeed?
0135 C22601             jnz     newch   ; no, get next character
0138 E5                 push    h       ;save address which is in hl
0139 2A5301             lhld    ctr     ;increment line count
013C 23                 inx     h       ; (using hl)
013D 225301             shld    ctr
0140 E1                 pop     h       ;get address back in hl
0141 C32601             jmp     newch   ;go get next character
                ;
                ;end-of-file, or no file, so print result and exit
                ;
0144 2A5301     done    lhld    ctr     ;get count in hl for binidec
0147 CD7501             call    binidec ;print number of lines in dec
014A 115501             lxi     d,lmess ;set up "lines" message
014D 0E09       nofile  mvi     c,prints;print message
```

```
014F CD0500                 call    bdos
0152 C9                     ret             ;back to CP/M
                 ;
0153             ctr        dw      0       ;linefeed counter
                 ;
0155 206C696E65lmess        db      ' lines in file.$'
0165 4E6F20736Fnfmess       db      'No source file.$'
                 ;
                 ;
                 ;binidec-converts binary number in hl to
                 ;          decimal, prints result on screen.
                 ;
                 ;
0175 11F0D8      binidec lxi        d,-10000;print number of 10,000s
0178 CD9401                 call    subcnt
017B 1118FC                 lxi     d,-1000 ;print number of thousands
017E CD9401                 call    subcnt
0181 119CFF                 lxi     d,-100  ;print number of hundreds
0184 CD9401                 call    subcnt
0187 11F6FF                 lxi     d,-10   ;print number of tens
018A CD9401                 call    subcnt
018D 11FFFF                 lxi     d,-1    ;print number of ones
0190 CD9401                 call    subcnt
0193 C9                     ret             ;that's all
                 ;
0194 0E2F        subcnt     mvi     c,'0'-1 ;c holds ASCII version of count
0196 0C          sub2       inr     c       ;increment count
0197 22B301                 shld    temp    ;save hl
019A 19                     dad     d       ;add neg const from de to hl
019B FA9601                 jm      sub2    ;loop til result in hl is neg
019E 2AB301                 lhld    temp    ;get last pos value back in hl
01A1 79                     mov     a,c
01A2 CDA601                 call    pchar   ;print digit
01A5 C9                     ret
                 ;
                 ;print character in a-register on screen
01A6 D5C5E5      pchar      push d ! push b ! push h    ;save registers
01A9 5F                     mov     e,a     ;character in e
01AA 0E02                   mvi     c,conout
01AC CD0500                 call    bdos    ;call conout routine
01AF E1C1D1                 pop h ! pop b ! pop d    ;get registers back
01B2 C9                     ret
                 ;
```

```
01B3 0100       temp    dw      0
                ;
01B5                    end
```

Try typing in LINES, assemblying it, and running it on some of your test files. Not bad, eh? Now when someone asks you how many lines are in some program that you've written, you can tell them exactly, in about three seconds.

LIFE ON THE FAST TRACK

In this chapter, you've learned the fundamentals of how your programs communicate with CP/M's disk operating system. Our examples have shown you how to read records and files from the disk. In the next chapter, you'll learn how to write to the disk. With this knowledge, we'll go on to write the STORE program, which will enable you to enter text files onto the disk. Then we'll learn how to delete files and, finally, go on to master the intricate Random Read and Random Write system calls.

CHAPTER 6

Writing to the Disk

In the last chapter, you learned how to *read* records from a disk file. In this chapter, we're going to move on to *writing* records and files to the disk. To write to the disk, you'll need to know the "Make File," "Write Sequential File," and "Close File" system calls. After explaining these calls, we'll illustrate their uses with an example program, STORE, which is a very simple word-processing program. We'll show you two versions of the program, one of which uses the "Delete File" system call.

The next area that we'll cover is that of "random" records. Random, in this case, doesn't mean that the records contain just any old random words and numbers, it means that it's possible to read or write to *any* record in a file, without starting at the beginning of the file and without reading all the records until you get to the one you want. Thus, "random"is the opposite of "sequential." We'll describe the "Random Read" and "Random Write" system calls, and then use them in a program (RANDYMOD) which will permit the modification of any record in a file.

WRITING A SEQUENTIAL RECORD

In this section, we're going to describe the three new system calls that are necessary for writing a sequential record: Make File, Write Sequential, and Close File. Since these calls are all necessary to do the writing operation, we're going to describe each of them before we go on to give an example program.

MAKE FILE

MAKE FILE	FUNCTION 22 (dec) = 16 (hex)
Enter with:	REG C = 16 (hex) REGs DE = FCB address
On return:	REG A = Directory Code
Comments:	Directory Code = 0, 1, 2, or 3 if file made successfully. Directory Code = FF (hex) if disk directory is full.

In the last chapter, you learned that to read a record from a file, you had to first "open" the file using the "Open File" system call. This was necessary, first to tell the BDOS routines of CP/M what file you wanted to read the record from (the file name passed in the FCB), and secondly, to tell BDOS to determine where the various records of the file were so that they could be easily accessed by subsequent Read system calls. BDOS then wrote the locations of the records in the FCB in the area called "allocation units."

When we want to *write* a new file, the procedure is somewhat different. Since the file does not yet exist, it cannot be "opened" but, instead, must be (as Digital Research puts it) "made." To do this, we use the "Make File" system call. This call records the new file name in the disk directory so that BDOS knows what to do with subsequent "Write Record" system calls. Using "Make File" assumes that the file whose name is being "made" doesn't already exist. If there's any chance that it might exist, then it is the programmer's responsibility to delete the file before trying to "make" it. We'll describe the "Delete File" system call later.

The Make File call is similar in format to Open File. The returned directory code is different, in that a value of FF hex (meaning "unsuccessful") is returned only if the directory is full—a rare occurrence. Otherwise, a 0, 1, 2, or 3 is returned as in Open File.

A code fragment for using this call might be:

```
mvi  c,16    Set up for Make File.
lxi  d,5c      Set FCB address.
call 5         Call BDOS.
```

We'll show how this code fragment is used when we get to the STORE program.

WRITE SEQUENTIAL RECORD

WRITE SEQUENTIAL RECORD		FUNCTION 21 (dec) = 15 (hex)
Enter with:	REG C = 15 (hex)	
	REGs DE = FCB address	
On return:	REG A = Directory Code	
Comments:	Directory Code = 0 if write is successful.	
	Directory Code = nonzero if disk is full.	

Before the "Write Sequential Record" call can be used, several conditions must be met:

1. The name of the file to be written must be in the FCB.

2. The file must have been initialized with a Make File system call. (It is also possible to use the Write Sequential call with an *existing* file that has been initialized with an "Open File" system call. This is described later in this chapter.)
3. The record to be written must be in the 128-byte (128 hex) DMA buffer. If the DMA buffer is not in the usual (or "default") position at 80 hex, a Set DMA system call must have been issued to put it in the appropriate place.

The format of the Write Sequential system call is similar to the Read Sequential Record call. The directory code returned in the A-register is different, in that a nonzero value indicates that the disk is full, a fairly rare occurrence and one we won't worry about with our small sample programs.

A typical section of code used to write a sequential record might be:

```
mvi  c,15    Set up for Write Sequential.
lxi  d,5c    Set FCB address.
call 5       Call BDOS.
```

Like the Read Sequential system call, Write Sequential writes to the first record of the file the first time that it is called, writes to the second record the second time it is called, and so on. (That's why it's called "sequential.") How does BDOS "remember" what record it's supposed to write to next when it executes this call? To understand this, we'll need to look somewhat more deeply into the workings of the FCB.

The "CR" Byte in the FCB

Look back at the diagram of the File Control Block in the last chapter (Fig. 5-1). The "cr" byte is number 32 in the FCB, and is located at memory location 7C (if the FCB is in its usual place). The purpose of this byte is to keep track of what record is currently being written to (or read) by a sequential write (or read) operation. Thus, when you execute a call to the Sequential Write system call, the record in the DMA buffer will be written to the record number that is in this cr byte. After either a write or a read operation, the number in cr is incremented so that the next record will be written to the next record in order.

This byte is typically set to zero by the user at the same time that the file is opened (or "made"), so that the first record will be written into record 0, the second into record 1, and so on.

Those of you who have caught on to the hexadecimal numbering system will now be wondering what happens if a file has more than 256 records, since that's all that can be described in a single byte. The answer is that when the cr byte "overflows" (that is, goes from 127 to 128 decimal, which is from 7F to 80 hex), then a new "extent" is automatically opened. Why doesn't this overflow take place at 255 records, instead of 127? The reason for this action has to do with allocation units, sectors, and the way records are stored on the disk, a topic which we'll cover later.

Extents

The next question is, "What's an *extent*?" An extent is 128 records. Extents are necessary because of the way CP/M keeps track of where the various records of a file are stored on the disk. In general, a programmer doesn't need to know too much about this process, since CP/M takes care of it more or less automatically. Again, we'll postpone further discussion of these topics until the next chapter, where we'll talk about the disk directory.

For the time being, just keep in mind that the cr byte in the FCB is incremented each time a record is read or written sequentially, until the value in cr reaches 127 decimal. At this point, a new extent is opened. This means that the value in cr is reset to 0 and another byte in the FCB is incremented. This is the "ex" or "current extent" byte, which is number 12 and is located at address 68 hex. This byte, too, is normally set to zero when a file is first made or opened for sequential operations.

CLOSE FILE SYSTEM CALL

CLOSE FILE	FUNCTION 16 (dec) = 10 (hex)	
Enter with:	REG C	= 10 (hex)
	REGs DE	= FCB address
On return:	REG A	= Directory Code
Comments:	Directory Code = 0,1,2,3 if file closed successfully.	
	Directory Code = FF (hex) if file name not in directory.	

After you have opened or "made" a file and started writing to it with Write Sequential system calls, CP/M's BDOS takes care of deciding where on the disk each record is going to be written. This information, which constitutes a *map* of the disk showing where the various records of a file are stored, is kept in memory as long as the file is "open"; that is, currently being written to. If, after writing a bunch of records, you just turned off your computer and walked away, this "mapping" information would be lost forever and, then, when you powered up again and tried to read the file from the disk, CP/M wouldn't know where to find it. It's the purpose of the Close File call to make sure this doesn't happen.

When the Close File call is executed, CP/M takes the mapping information, which is stored temporarily in memory, and writes it onto the disk in a region called the "disk directory." When you next try to read this file, BDOS will look for the file name in the directory on the disk and will write the information it finds there back into memory. This is done by the Open File system call.

The moral of all this is that after you have finished writing records to a file, you had better close it, or you will never be able to read it back in. You don't have to close a file after reading it, however, because the directory has not been changed. Thus, the directory information on the disk is still valid, even though the directory in memory may be destroyed.

The format of the Close File call is similar to that of an Open File. Here's a section of code used to close a file:

```
mvi  c,10    Set up Close File.
lxi  d,5c    Set FCB address.
call 5       Call BDOS.
```

PROGRAM TO WRITE A SEQUENTIAL RECORD

Now we're ready to put together the three system calls that we've just learned into a real program to write something to the disk. Here's the program:

```
-a100
0100  mvi  c,1a    Set DMA address to 400.
0102  lxi  d,400
0105  call 5
0108  mvi  c,16    Make file.
```

```
010A  lxi  d,5c
010D  call 5
0110  mvi  c,15      Write file.
0112  lxi  d,5c
0115  call 5
0118  mvi  c,10      Close file.
011A  lxi  d,5c
011D  call 5
0120  rst  7         Back to DDT.
```

Before we can execute this program *from* DDT, however, there are a number of things that we need to do.

First, make sure that there is no file on your disk with the name "newfile.txt". Next, we need to insert the name of the file that we're going to be creating into the FCB. We'll do this using the "i" operation. Thirdly, we need to put something into the DMA buffer so that we can write it onto the disk. This is a little cumbersome to do from DDT, but we'll try it just to get the feeling of what the routine is doing. For this, we'll use the "s" operation.

Type in the program in DDT, save it as "test105.ddt", and return to DDT with the program ("A>ddt test105.ddt"). Then, type in the following:

```
-inewfile.txt        Put name of file in FCB.

-s400                Fill stuff into DMA.
0400 08 41 ⎫
0401 DC 42 ⎪
0402 D3 43 ⎬         ASCII values for text: "ABCDE"
0403 01 44 ⎪
0404 67 45 ⎭
0405 3A 0A           Linefeed.
0406 00 0D           Carriage return.
0407 53 1A           End-of-file mark. Don't forget this!
0408 9F  ↑
     ↑   └────────── These are the numbers you type in.
     │
     └────────────── This is junk that was in the buffer already.
```

We won't fill in all 128 decimal bytes of the DMA, since that would take too long using the "s" operation. (Although you could fill the whole DMA buffer with the same character using the "f" option.)

We end our message with a carriage return and a linefeed so that when we print out the record it won't be overprinted by the next line. And, most importantly, the last character of our record is an end-of-file character: 1A hex. This is necessary to tell BDOS that the record is finished, when we go to read it back.

Now run the program and then exit to CP/M and see if the file is in the directory:

```
-g100
*0120
-g0
A>dir newfile.txt
A: NEWFILE.TXT
```

So far, so good. Now, let's see what's really in the record, using the CP/M built-in TYPE function. (We can't use TYPE2 here because it isn't sophisticated enough to see the end-of-file mark in the middle of the record and it will print out all the junk in the DMA buffer following the "ABCDE" message.)

```
A>type newfile.txt

ABCDE
A>
```

There it is! It may not be *War and Peace,* but it is the very first file that you've written to the disk with your own program.

There's another way to examine the contents of newfile.txt to see if it's really there. Call up DDT along with newfile.txt:

```
A>ddt newfile.txt
```

When DDT is loaded, dump the DMA buffer, which is where the first record of a file is loaded when the file is called in with DDT:

```
-d80,ff
0080 41 42 43 44 45 0A 0D 1A 51 01 CD 8C 00 C3 51 01 ABCDE...Q......Q.
```

First record of newfile.txt — ASCII version

There it is! This is a good way to examine files that have only one short record.

Now we're going to expand this little program into one that you can actually use as a mini word processor.

STORE PROGRAM–STORES TEXT IN FILE

The program we're about to describe accepts text typed in on the keyboard and puts it into a file. Since we'll assemble the program with ASM and store it on the disk as a COM file, you can execute it directly from CP/M.

```
A>store newfile.txt
This is the line that you type in, to be stored on disk.
Type another line into next record.

A>
```

Terminate lines with a "return".

Typing "return" at the beginning of a line ends the program.

When the program is executed, it first finds out if the file name you typed in following "store" exists or not. If it does, the program will read (without printing) to the end of the file, wait for you to type something in, and then write it at the end of the file. If the file doesn't exist, the program opens a new file with that name (using the Make File system call), waits for you to type something in, and then writes it at the beginning of the file.

We have made the restriction that you can only type in one line–no more than 80 characters–at a time. This avoids a lot of complexity about how to handle "returns" embedded in the text. At the end of your line, you must press "return" to tell the program that you've finished. It will then write the line to the disk as a single record. If you press "return" without writing anything, the program will assume that you've finished with the entire file and will close the file and exit to CP/M.

Listing 6-1. The STORE Program

```
                ;***********************************************
                ;store-Program to store text in a file.
                ;       Stores one line of text, terminated
                ;       by a return, per record. Type return
                ;       to exit.
                ;
                ;
000F =          openf   equ     0fh             ;open file
0016 =          makef   equ     16h             ;make file
000A =          reads   equ     0ah             ;read string
0015 =          writer  equ     15h             ;write sequential record
0014 =          readr   equ     14h             ;read sequential record
0009 =          prints  equ     9h              ;print string
0010 =          closef  equ     10h             ;close file
0002 =          conout  equ     2h              ;console out
0005 =          bdos    equ     5h              ;operating system
005C =          fcb     equ     5ch             ;file control block
0080 =          dma     equ     80h             ;dma buffer
00FF =          del     equ     0ffh            ;delete character
000A =          lf      equ     0ah             ;linefeed
000D =          cr      equ     0dh             ;carriage return
                ;
                ;
0100                    org     100h
                ;
                ;try to open file (name must already be in fcb)
0100 0E0F               mvi     c,openf ;open file
0102 115C00             lxi     d,fcb
0105 CD0500             call    bdos
0108 3C                 inr     a               ;if a was ff, now it's 0
0109 C25B01             jnz     alex            ; not 0, so file exists
                ;
                ;file does not already exist, so we'll create it
010C 0E16               mvi     c,makef
010E 115C00             lxi     d,fcb
0111 CD0500             call    bdos
                ;
                ;fill the dma buffer with delete marks
0114 218000     newrc   lxi     h,dma           ;put dma address in hl
0117 0680               mvi     b,128d          ;put count in b
0119 36FF       loop    mvi     m,del           ;store delete in memory
```

```
011B 23               inx  h         ;increment hl pointer
011C 05               dcr  b         ;decrement count
011D C21901           jnz  loop      ;not done yet
               ;
               ;print a linefeed
0120 0E02             mvi  c,conout
0122 1E0A             mvi  e,lf
0124 CD0500           call bdos
               ;
               ;read characters into buffer from keyboard
0127 3E50             mvi  a,80d     ;set count to screen width
0129 327E00           sta  dma-2     ; (string buffer starts 2
012C 0E0A             mvi  c,reads   ; bytes before dma
012E 117E00           lxi  d,dma-2   ; buffer, to leave room for
0131 CD0500           call bdos      ; max-count and count)
               ;
               ;find out if buffer is empty-if so, exit
0134 3A7F00           lda  dma-1     ;get number of char input
0137 B7               ora  a         ;is it 0?
0138 CA5201           jz   finito    ; yes
               ;
               ;insert cr and lf in buffer following text
013B 5F               mov  e,a       ;character count in de
013C 1600             mvi  d,0       ;
013E 218000           lxi  h,dma     ;dma address in hl
0141 19               dad  d         ;add count to addr, put in hl
0142 360D             mvi  m,cr      ;store carriage return
0144 23               inx  h         ;increment pointer
0145 360A             mvi  m,lf      ;store linefeed
               ;
               ;write record to disk
0147 0E15             mvi  c,writer  ;write it
0149 115C00           lxi  d,fcb
014C CD0500           call bdos
014F C31401           jmp  newrc     ;go read next record
               ;
               ;close file before exiting
0152 0E10      finito mvi  c,closef
0154 115C00           lxi  d,fcb
0157 CD0500           call bdos
015A C9               ret            ;back to CP/M
               ;
               ;file already exists, so read till EOF
```

```
015B 0E09       alex    mvi  c,prints ;print message
015D 117201             lxi  d,almess
0160 CD0500             call bdos
0163 0E14       read2   mvi  c,readr  ;read record
0165 115C00             lxi  d,fcb
0168 CD0500             call bdos
016B B7                 ora  a        ;end-of-file (a not 0) ?
016C CA6301             jz   read2    ;no, so read next record
016F C31401             jmp  newrc    ;yes, so go write new record
                ;
                ;
0172 5465787420almess db   'Text will be added to file.',cr,lf,'$'
                ;
0190                    end
```

Type the program in with your word processor, assemble it, and try it out, before you read the explanation of how it works. This will give you an idea what the program is supposed to do, which will be helpful in understanding the following comments. Fig. 6-1 is a flowchart of the program's operation.

We will first try to open the file. If it already exists, we jump down to the "alex" label at line 15B and print the following message to the user: "Text will be added to file." This will alert her to the fact that she's not writing into a new file. Then, we read the first record of the file and check to see if there's an EOF. If not, we read the next record and check again. If there is an EOF, we go back to line 114, where we would have started if the file had not existed in the first place.

Since our input lines are 80 character or less, and the records we're writing into are 128 characters, we're going to have left-over space in the record. We don't want these extra characters to appear on the screen, or cause the printer to do anything weird if we want to print out the file, so we want to ensure that the rest of the buffer after our typed-in line is filled with some harmless character. A good harmless character, and one that we can send to the printer without causing any action at all, is the "rubout" character, which is 7F hex (FF hex if we include the high-order bit). The section of code from 114 to 11D fills the entire DMA buffer with rubouts before any characters are typed in by the user, thus ensuring that there will be no printable garbage following the text.

We do a linefeed and, then, at line 127, read the characters from the keyboard into the DMA buffer. Since we're not using DDT, we can put the DMA buffer where it's supposed to go at 80 hex (its default address), which we tell the program about with an EQU directive. We use the Read String

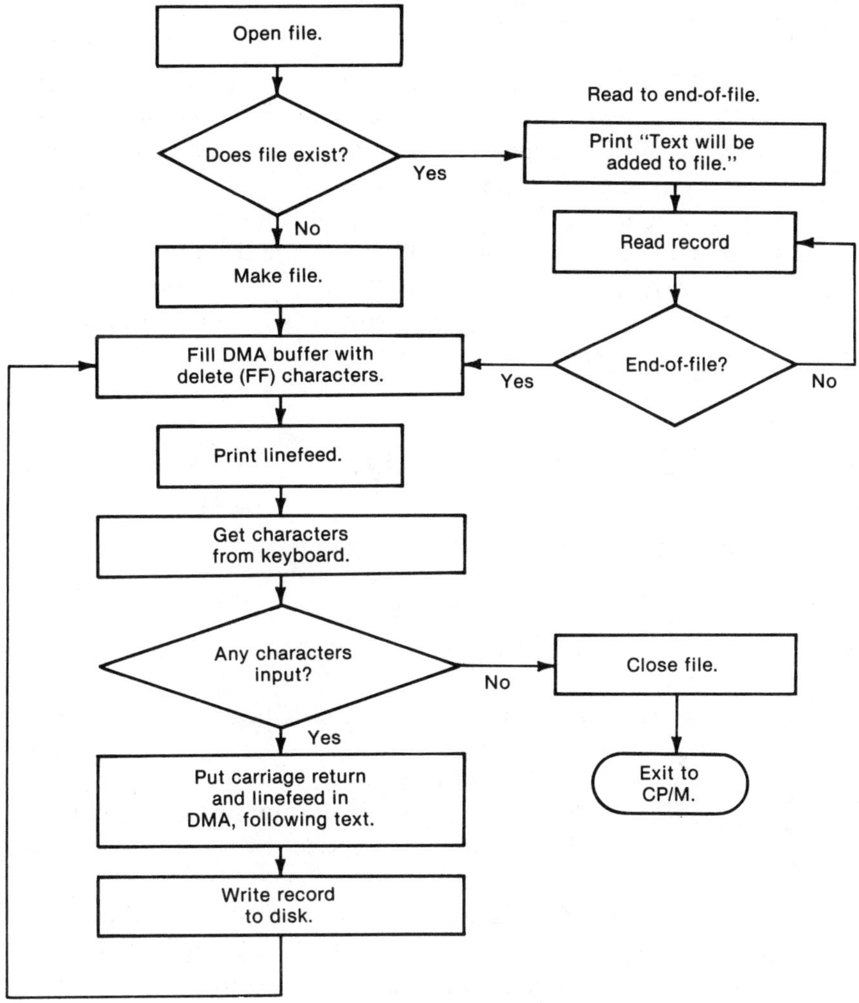

Fig. 6-1. Flowchart of the STORE program.

system call, which requires that the maximum count of words be set two addresses before the first character, and which fills in the number of characters that are actually read in from the keyboard at the address that is one byte before the first character.

If the buffer is empty after this call, we know the user is done and we close the file and exit to CP/M. Otherwise, we write a carriage return and linefeed into the buffer following the text, so that each record typed in doesn't overprint the one before it. Then, we write the record to the disk and go back up to "newrc" to get another record from the keyboard.

Your Own Text Editor

Now you can type in files using STORE and can read them out again using TYPE2. As text editors go, this may not be too fancy, but it does give you the satisfaction of having written it all yourself and, we hope, of understanding how the programs work.

Use STORE to create a file called "sample.txt", which contains 10 or 12 records, by typing in 10 or 12 lines one after the other (separated only by single carriage returns). Check that the whole record is there, using TYPE2. We'll use this file later to experiment with the Random Read and Random Write system calls.

DELETE FILE SYSTEM CALL

DELETE FILE	FUNCTION 19 (dec) = 13 (hex)	
Enter with:	REG C	= 13 (hex)
	REGs DE	= FCB address
On return:	REG A	= Directory Code
Comments:	Directory Code = 0,1,2,3 if file deleted successfully.	
	Directory Code = FF (hex) if file not found.	

This system call is largely self-explanatory. When executed, it modifies the directory entry of the file so that CP/M's BDOS knows that it's erased. BDOS will then release the disk space occupied by the file so that it can be used for other files when they are written.

Modifying the STORE Program

Here's an example of how this call can be used. In the STORE program, we assumed that, if a file already existed, the user would want to add the records that he typed in to the file. We could have made another assumption: that he wanted to erase whatever was in the file and start over with what he was typing in.

Let's use the Delete File system call to modify the STORE program to do this. Do the following:

1. Make a copy of STORE using PIP. Call it "STORE2".

```
A>pip store2.asm=store.asm
```

2. Add this statement to the beginning of STORE2:

```
defile  equ     13h         ;delete file
```

3. Remove the program lines from 100 to 109 and substitute the following:

```
;delete the file
            mvi     c,defile
            lxi     d,fcb
            call    bdos
```

4. Remove lines 15B through 172, including the "almess" message.

Fig. 6-2 is the flowchart for the resulting STORE2 program.

Assemble STORE2 and try running it. When you write to an existing file, everything that was in it disappears, and only your new input is left. This works because if the file wasn't there to begin with, the delete will have no effect, and if the file was there, it will be deleted. Either way, it won't be there when we get to the "Make File" system call in line 10C. Now you have two versions of the STORE program, one which will add text to a file and one which will write over the old text.

RANDOM RECORDS

If you want to read or write a file, starting at the first record and going on until you come to the end, then the "Read Sequential" and "Write Sequential" system calls which we have already described are just what you need. But suppose you want to read a record that is in the middle of a file? Or, you want to modify a record in the middle of a file? You can do it using the sequential read and write calls, but it's a little difficult. What's difficult about it? Mostly the way that the record numbers are specified in the FCB.

As you recall from the last section, there is a special byte in the file control block to indicate what record is currently being written. When 127 decimal records have been written, this byte "overflows" and is reset to 0, and another byte, the "current extent" byte, is automatically incremented. The use of two separate bytes to specify what record we're talking about makes disk access to a

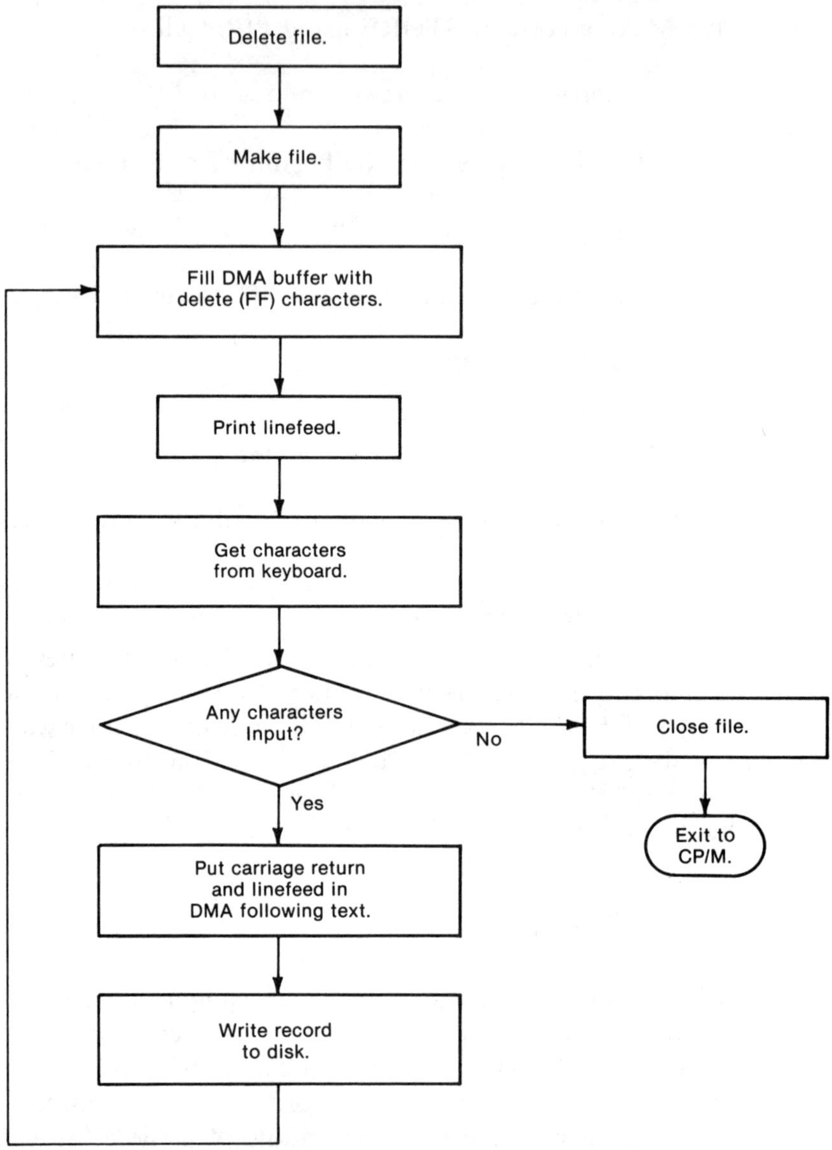

Fig. 6-2. Flowchart of the STORE2 program.

particular record somewhat more awkward than it might be. For instance, if we had a program that wanted to read the 300th record in a file, it would have to first determine what "extent" this record was on, by dividing 300 decimal by 128 decimal. Since 300 divided by 128 is 2, with a remainder of 44, our program would have to set the extent byte to 2 and the current record byte to 44 decimal

(2C hex). This isn't impossible, but it does complicate things, so Digital Research (starting with release 2.0 of CP/M) has provided a set of system calls which use a single 16-bit value to specify the record number.

Look back at the map of the FCB in the last chapter. Bytes 33, 34, and 35 (locations 7D, 7E, 7F) constitute the "random record number" and are called, respectively, r0, r1, and r2. This is shown in Fig. 6-3. The last byte, r2, is not used in CP/M systems (although it is used by MP/M). In CP/M systems, it must always be set to zero, otherwise error messages will result. The bytes r0 and r1 constitute the 16-bit record value, with the r0 byte representing the least-significant byte and r1 the most-significant byte.

However, using random reads and writes requires one more step than sequential reads and writes. The program must place the 16-bit number of the record to be accessed into bytes r0 and r1 before the read or write takes place.

We'll briefly describe the Read Random and Write Random system calls and, then, go on to show how they're used in the RANDYMOD program.

READ RANDOM SYSTEM CALL

READ RANDOM FUNCTION 33 (dec) = 21 (hex)

Enter with: REG C = 21 (hex)
REGs DE = FCB address

On return: REG A = Return Code

Comments: Return Code = 00 if read was successful.
Return Code = nonzero if error occurred.

When BDOS executes this call, it first looks at the record number in bytes r0 and r1 to see what record the program wants to read. It then figures out what "extent" the record is in, and the record number in the extent, and sets

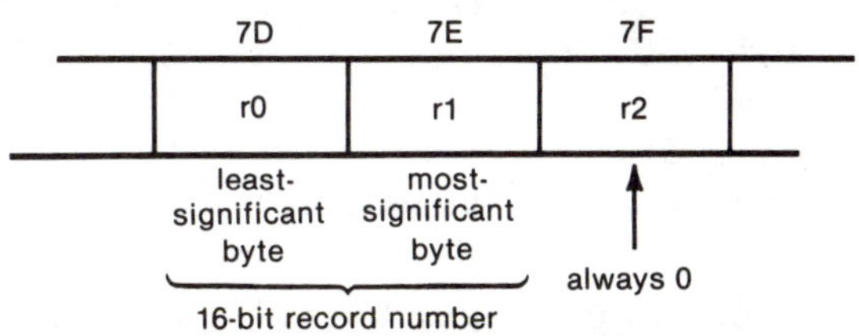

Fig. 6-3. The "random record number."

these bytes in the FCB. Then, it reads the record just as the Sequential Read system call did.

An important difference between random and sequential system calls is that the random calls do not automatically advance the record number each time they are called. So, if you do a random read and, then, do another random read, you'll be reading the same record twice unless your program has incremented the random record number in r0 and r1 before the second read.

Also note that, since Random Read has automatically set the current extent and current record bytes in the FCB, you could then do a Sequential read to read the same record again, followed by subsequent records, if you wished. This gives you the capability to plunge into the middle of a record with random access and, then, read a number of records, starting at that point, with sequential access.

The "Return Code" returned in the A-register following this call can actually have a number of nonzero values, depending on what type of error has occurred:

01 attempt to read unwritten data block.
04 attempt to read unopened extent.
06 attempt to read past end of disk (byte r2 not set to zero).

Here's a short DDT program for reading a random record:

```
-a100
0100  mvi   c,1a     Set DMA to 400.
0102  lxi   d,400
0105  call  5
0108  mvi   c,f      Open file.
010A  lxi   d,5c
010D  call  5
0110  mvi   c,21     Read random.
0112  lxi   d,5c
0115  call  5
0118  mvi   c,2      Print error code.
011A  adi   30
011C  mov   e,a
011D  call  5
0120  rst   7        Return to DDT.
```

Save this program as "test106.ddt" and then bring it back into memory with DDT. Use the "i" command to set the filename of a file that you know has a number of text records in it, such as the "sample.txt" file that we suggested you write in the section on the STORE program. Then, use the "s" command to set a record number into r0 r1 that you know is in the file. In other words, don't make the record number so large that it doesn't exist; if "sample.txt" is 12 records long, put in a number less than that.

```
A>ddt test106.ddt

-isample.txt     A file you know has more than 3 records.
-s7d
007D 00 03       Least-significant two digits.
007E 00 00       Most-significant two digits.
007F 00 00       Always zero.
0080 00 ↑
      ↑  └────── This is what you type in.
      └───────── This is junk left over.
```

Execute the program and then look at the DMA with a "d400" to see what's been read in. Now, change the r0 byte in 7D to some other record number, like a 2 or a 4. If you have file that you know is longer than 256 records, you can change both r1 and r0. For record number 350, for example, you'd convert to the hex number 015E and then put 5E into r0 (location 7D) and 01 into r1 (location 7E).

Read a number of records by changing the record number and see what happens. Ordinarily, the "return code" printed out by this program will be zero, but if you try to read a nonexistent record, you'll get one of the codes referred to above.

WRITE RANDOM SYSTEM CALL

WRITE RANDOM	FUNCTION 22 (hex) = 34 (dec)
Enter with:	REG C = 22 (hex) REGs DE = FCB address
On return:	REG A = Return Code
Comments:	Return Code = 00 if write was successful. Return Code = nonzero if error occurred.

This call is similar to the Read Random call except, of course, that the record to be written must already be in the DMA buffer. The error codes are the same except that there is a new error, 05, which indicates that a record cannot be written due to directory overflow.

As with Random Read, the current record and current extent bytes are changed to correspond to the random record number given, but none of these numbers is incremented.

Writing to a New File

Here's a short DDT program showing how this call can be used. This program assumes that we want to create a new record, so it uses the Make File system call. Note that it's necessary to close the file after writing to it.

```
-a100
0100  mvi   c,1a     Set DMA to 400.
0102  lxi   d,400
0105  call  5
0108  mvi   c,16     Make file.
010A  lxi   d,5c
010D  call  5
0110  mvi   c,22     Write random.
0112  lxi   d,5c
0115  call  5
0118  mvi   c,2      Print return code.
011A  adi   30
011C  mov   e,a
011D  call  5
0120  mvi   c,10     Close file.
0122  lxi   d,5c
0125  call  5
0128  rst   7        Return to DDT.
```

Save the program as "test107.ddt" and then load it back in with DDT. Use the "s" command to fill in the DMA buffer from 400 to 47F with whatever ASCII characters you want. Since we're starting a new file, we assume we're going to write to the first record, whose number is 0000, so use "s" again to fill in 0 values in r0, r1, and r2. Use the "i" command to set the name of the new text file (you can call it newfile2.txt) into the FCB and, then, run the program. Exit from DDT and check the dirctory to see if the new file is there.

Print it out using "TYPE." It should be the same as whatever you put in the DMA buffer.

Writing to Existing Record

If we want to write to an existing record, we need to use the Open File system call, instead of Make File, just as we did with sequential writes. Here's how we modify our program to do that:

```
-a100
0100  mvi   c,1a     Set DMA to 400.
0102  lxi   d,400
0105  call  5
0108  mvi   c,0f     Open file.
010A  lxi   d,5c
010D  call  5
0110  mvi   c,22     Write random.
0112  lxi   d,5c
0115  call  5
0118  mvi   c,2      Print return code.
011A  adi   30
011C  mov   e,a
011D  call  5
0120  mvi   c,10     Close file.
0122  lxi   d,5c
0125  call  5
0128  rst   7        Return to DDT.
```

Save this as "test108.ddt" and try it out, using the same steps as previously. As with the Read Random system call, you must be sure that the record number you put in r0 and r1 actually exists.

RANDYMOD—PROGRAM TO MODIFY A RANDOM RECORD

The following program incorporates both the Random Read and the Random Write system calls. You call it from CP/M by specifying the name of the file you want to modify:

```
A>randymod testfile.txt
```

The file name must be one which exists, or the program will print "No such filename," and return to CP/M. The program now waits for you to type in the record number, in decimal, that you wish to modify in the file. Make sure that this record exists, because the program does no checking to make sure it has been given a valid record.

You can use the "sample.txt" file that you created in the section on the STORE program for this. If "sample.txt" is 12 records long, set the record number you want to modify to a number less than that: say 3. Once the program has read the record, it prints it out on the screen, and then asks "OK to modify (y/n)?" If you answer anything other than "y", the program returns to CP/M. Otherwise, the program waits for you to type something in. As with the STORE program, you must type in a line that is less than 80 decimal characters long and terminate the line with a "return." Listing 6-2 shows the RANDYMOD program.

Next, in Fig. 6-4, we have the flowchart for the RANDYMOD program.

The listing for RANDYMOD should be fairly easy to follow since it consists mostly of routines and code fragments that have been covered before. However, there are one or two unusual items.

We can't put the DMA buffer at the usual place from 80 hex to FF hex because we want to use the Read String system call to get the input from the user. Why doesn't this work? Because Read String uses two bytes immediately preceding the actual buffer: one to store the maximum number of characters and the second to store the actual number of characters that are typed in. Unfortunately, the two bytes immediately preceding 80 hex are 7E and 7F, which are the bytes used to store r1 and r2 of the random record number. We could move the FCB, or move the DMA, or use a different way to read the characters from the keyboard, but moving the DMA seems easiest, so that's what we do in lines 100 to 105. We move it to a place that we label "dma" at the end of the program, which we specify as 128 decimal bytes using the "ds" directive.

Notice how we do arithmetic with the symbolic labels in the address field in lines 117 and 11C. We know that byte r0 is byte number 33 decimal in the FCB, so instead of figuring out what this address is and writing it in the address field, we write "fcb+33d". The assembler takes care of determining where "fcb" is, adding 33 to it, and translating the result into an address for the "shld" instruction to store in r0 and r1. A similar process takes place for the "sta" instruction in line 11C.

As we explained in the section on the STORE program, it's necessary to fill the DMA buffer with delete marks before accepting input to it from the keyboard, so that any junk remaining in the buffer between the end of the user's

Listing 6-2. The RANDYMOD Program

```
                ;*****************************************************
                ;RANDYMOD-Used to modify a record selected at random in a
                ;         file. Type filename following "randymod", and
                ;         then type record number when program loads).
                ;*****************************************************
                ;
                ;
000F =          openf   equ  0fh        ;open file
0021 =          randr   equ  21h        ;random file read
0022 =          randw   equ  22h        ;random file write
0009 =          prints  equ  9h         ;print string
0002 =          conout  equ  2h         ;console out
0001 =          conin   equ  1h         ;console in
000A =          reads   equ  0ah        ;read string
0010 =          closef  equ  10h        ;close file
005C =          fcb     equ  5ch        ;file control block
0005 =          bdos    equ  5h         ;operating system entry
00FF =          del     equ  0ffh       ;delete character
000A =          lf      equ  0ah        ;linefeed
000D =          cr      equ  0dh        ;carriage return
                ;
0100                    org  100h
                ;
                ;put dma buffer at end of program (can't be at 80h,
                ; or counts used by "prints" will
                ; overwrite r1 and r2)
0100 0E1A               mvi  c,1ah      ;set dma address
0102 11EB01             lxi  d,dma
0105 CD0500             call bdos
                ;
                ;open file (name must already be in fcb)
0108 0E0F               mvi  c,openf
010A 115C00             lxi  d,fcb
010D CD0500             call bdos
0110 3C                 inr  a          ;if a was ff, now it's 0,
0111 CA8701             jz   nofi       ; so no such file name
                ;
                ;get record number from keyboard, store in fcb
0114 CD9B01             call decibin    ;read dec number, convert it
0117 227D00             shld fcb+33d    ;store in r0, r1 of fcb
011A 3E00               mvi  a,0        ;zero out r2 of fcb
```

```
011C 327F00            sta  fcb+35d
011F CD9001            call pcrlf    ;print carriage return
                ;
                ;read random record
0122 0E21              mvi  c,randr
0124 115C00            lxi  d,fcb
0127 CD0500            call bdos
                ;
                ;display contents of dma buffer
012A 21EB01            lxi  h,dma    ;set pointer in hl
012D 0680              mvi  b,128d   ;set count in b
012F 7E         dloop  mov  a,m      ;get char from buffer
0130 CDB701            call pchar    ;display it
0133 23                inx  h        ;increment hl
0134 05                dcr  b        ;decrement b - done?
0135 C22F01            jnz  dloop    ; not yet
                ;
                ;make sure user wants to modify it
0138 0E09              mvi  c,prints ;print question
013A 11C401            lxi  d,qmess
013D CD0500            call bdos
0140 0E01              mvi  c,conin  ;get 1-char response
0142 CD0500            call bdos
0145 FE79              cpi  'y'      ;is it "y"?
0147 C0                rnz           ; no, so back to CP/M
0148 CD9001            call pcrlf    ; yes, carry on
                ;
                ;fill the dma buffer with delete marks
014B 21EB01            lxi  h,dma    ;put dma buffer address in hl
014E 0680              mvi  b,128d   ;put count in b
0150 36FF       floop  mvi  m,del    ;store delete in memory loc in hl
0152 23                inx  h        ;increment hl pointer
0153 05                dcr  b        ;decrement count
0154 C25001            jnz  floop    ;not done yet
                ;
                ;read characters into buffer from keyboard
0157 CD9001            call pcrlf    ;print linefeed
015A 3E50              mvi  a,80d    ;set max count to screen width
015C 32E901            sta  dma-2    ; (read string buffer starts two
015F 0E0A              mvi  c,reads  ; bytes before start of dma
0161 11E901            lxi  d,dma-2  ; buffer to leave room for
0164 CD0500            call bdos     ; max-count and count)
                ;
```

```
                  ;insert cr and lf in buffer following text
0167 3AEA01               lda   dma-1     ;get number of chars typed in
016A 5F                   mov   e,a       ;put it in de
016B 1600                 mvi   d,0       ;
016D 21EB01               lxi   h,dma     ;dma address in hl
0170 19                   dad   d         ;add count to addr, result in hl
0171 360D                 mvi   m,cr      ;store carriage return
0173 23                   inx   h         ;increment pointer
0174 360A                 mvi   m,lf      ;store linefeed
                  ;
                  ;write record to disk
0176 0E22                 mvi   c,randw
0178 115C00               lxi   d,fcb
017B CD0500               call bdos
                  ;
                  ;close file before exiting
017E 0E10                 mvi   c,closef
0180 115C00               lxi   d,fcb
0183 CD0500               call bdos
0186 C9                   ret             ;back to CP/M
                  ;
                  ;no such file name: print message and exit
0187 0E09         nofi    mvi   c,prints
0189 11D901               lxi   d,nfmess
018C CD0500               call bdos
018F C9                   ret             ;back to CP/M
                  ;
                  ;subroutine to print carriage return and linefeed
0190 3E0D         pcrlf   mvi   a,cr      ;print carriage return
0192 CDB701               call pchar
0195 3E0A                 mvi   a,lf      ;print linefeed
0197 CDB701               call pchar
019A C9                   ret
                  ;
                  ;decibin- subroutine to read dec number from
                  ;             keyboard, convert to binary in HL
                  ;
019B 210000       decibin lxi   h,0       ;set hl to 0
019E E5           newdig  push h          ;save hl (conin uses it)
019F 0E01                 mvi   c,conin   ;get character
01A1 CD0500               call bdos
01A4 E1                   pop   h         ;restore hl
01A5 D630                 sui   30h       ;convert from ASCII to binary
```

```
01A7 D8                         rc                ;return if it was < 0
01A8 FE0A                       cpi   10d         ;is it > 9 ?
01AA D0                         rnc               ;if so, return
                 ;
                 ;multiply contents of hl by 10 (dec), then add new digit
01AB E5                         push h            ;put hl in de
01AC D1                         pop   d
01AD 29                         dad   h           ;add hl to hl (double it)
01AE 29                         dad   h           ;double it again
01AF 19                         dad   d           ;add de (original number) to hl
01B0 29                         dad   h           ;double result
01B1 50                         mov   d,0         ;zero in d
01B2 5F                         mov   e,a         ;new digit in e
01B3 19                         dad   d           ;add digit to number (now in hl)
01B4 C39E01                     jmp   newdig      ;go look for next digit
                 ;
                 ;subroutine to print character in a-reg out on screen
01B7 E5C5D5      pchar          push h! push b! push d     ;save registers
01BA 5F                         mov   e,a         ;print ASCII character
01BB 0E02                       mvi   c,conout
01BD CD0500                     call bdos
01C0 D1C1E1                     pop d! pop b! pop h        ;restore registers
01C3 C9                         ret
                 ;
01C4 4F4B20746Fqmess  db    'OK to modify (y/n)? $'
01D9 4E6F207375nfmess db    'No such filename.$'
                 ;
01EB             dma            ds    128d        ;dma buffer
                 ;
026B                            end
```

typed-in line and the end of the buffer will not cause odd effects when it is printed out.

The DECIBIN routine at the end of the program is the same one that you saw before in the chapter on console system calls.

Trying Out the Program

Try out the program using the "sample.txt" file described in the section on the STORE program. Use TYPE2 to examine the file, and then use RANDYMOD to modify one of the records in the file. It's easy to figure out

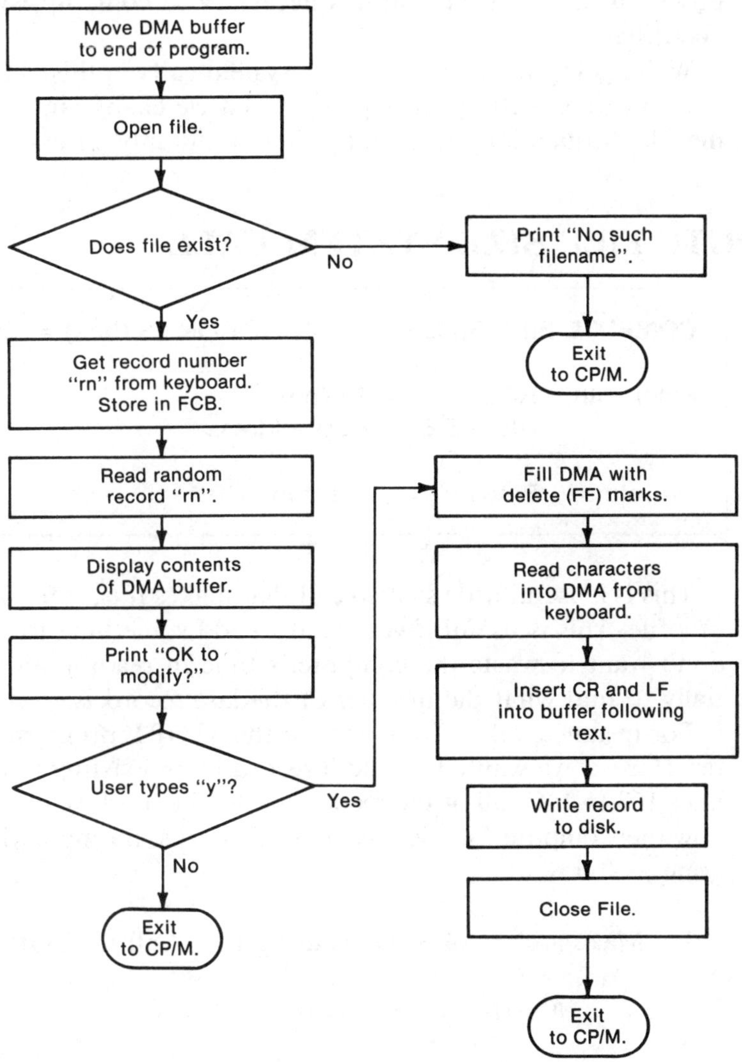

Fig. 6-4. Flowchart of the RANDYMOD program.

which record number you want to modify, since each line in the file corresponds to one record.

Not bad, is it? Using STORE, TYPE2, and RANDYMOD you can create, examine, and modify text records, just as if you were using a real word processor. Well, not really quite as well, but by now you're such a good 8080 programmer that you can probably figure out how to combine these three programs and add the features necessary to come up with a competitor for WordStar!

We're going to cover two more system calls in this chapter, both of which are concerned with what happens when we change in midstream from reading files sequentially to reading them randomly, and vice versa.

COMPUTE FILE SIZE SYSTEM CALL

COMPUTE FILE SIZE FUNCTION 23 (hex) = 35 (dec)

Enter with: REG C = 23 (hex)
REGs DE = FCB address

On return: Bytes r0, r1, r2 set in FCB

This is a useful little system call that makes it easy for you to get to the end of a file. This is useful if you want to add something to the end of a file and don't want to waste the computer's time in reading all the records sequentially to find what the number of the last record is.

For instance, take a look back at the STORE program earlier in this chapter. Here, if we wanted to add a record to an existing file, we had to read (in lines 163 to 16C) all of the records in the file until we came to the end. To see how the Compute File Size system call works, try modifying the STORE program as follows:

1. Make a copy of STORE using PIP. Call it STORE3.

```
A>pip store3.asm=store.asm
```

2. Put this statement at the beginning of STORE3:

```
cfsize  equu  23h    ;Compute file size
```

3. Change the "readr equu" statement to:

```
readr  equ  21h    ;Read random record
```

4. Delete lines 163 to 16C, and substitute the following:

```
mvi    c,cfsize      ;Compute file size.
lxi    d,fcb
call   5
mvi    c,readr       ;Read random record
lxi    d,fcb         ;  to set current record number.
call   5
```

Fig. 6-5 is a flowchart of the STORE3 program.

Instead of reading all the records until we get to the end of the file, we execute a Compute File Size system call. This sets r0 and r1 to the record number at the end of the file (r3 is set to 0). Then, in order to set the "current record" and "current extent" bytes in the FCB, we also execute a random read. This call uses the information in r0 and r1 to compute the values of the current record and byte, which is needed for sequential system calls. If we had wanted to do random writes to the file instead of sequential writes, this last step would not have been necessary because the random write call has no need for the current record and extent values.

Using the Compute File Size call will save our program a lot of time, especially on long files, when compared with reading laboriously through all the records in the file to get to the end.

SET RANDOM RECORD SYSTEM CALL

SET RANDOM RECORD FUNCTION 24 (hex) = 36 (dec)

Enter with: REG C = 24 (hex)
REGs DE = FCB address

On return: Bytes r0, r1, r2 set in FCB

This system call is similar to the Compute File Size call, except that it finds the random record number in the middle of a record rather than at the end. This is useful if you have been reading through a file using the Read Sequential system call and, suddenly, find a record whose number you want your

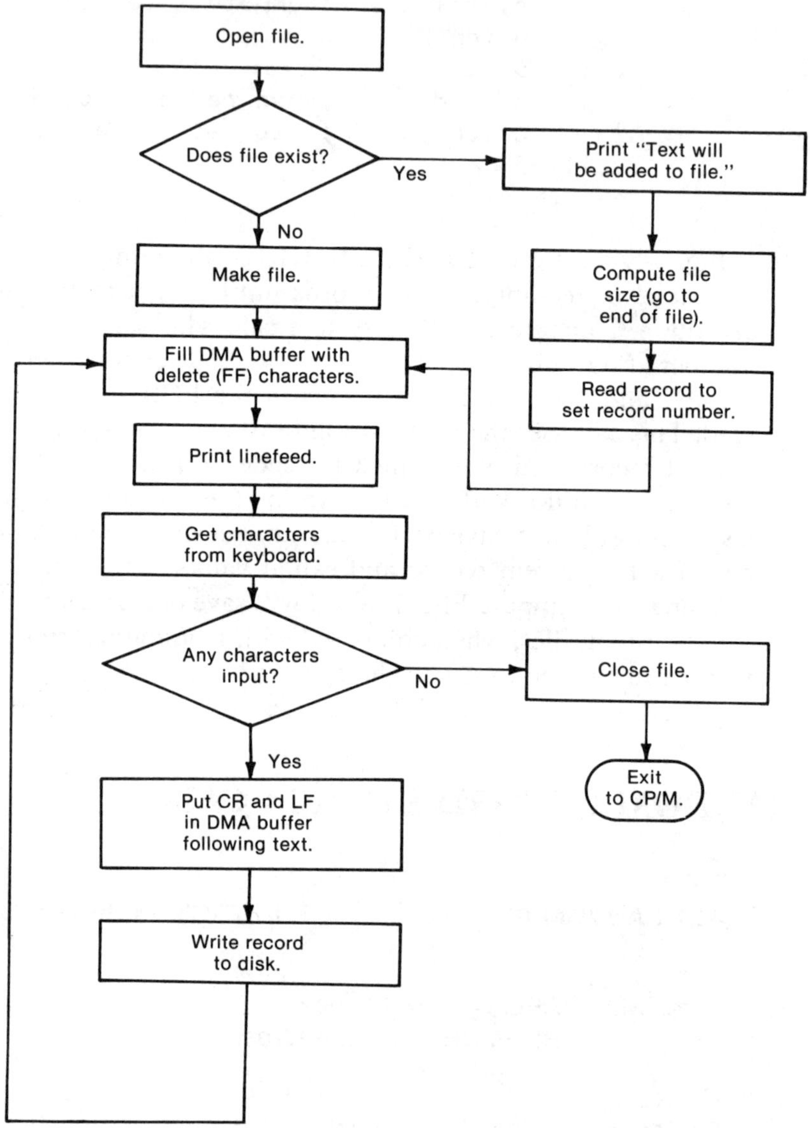

Fig. 6-5. Flowchart of the STORE3 program.

program to remember. Executing this call will put the random record number into r0 and r1, where it can be extracted and stored by your program. Or, your program can make use of the information in r0 and r1 to perform a random write operation at this point in the file.

OUT OF INK

That finishes up our description of the various system calls used to write to the disk. In the next chapter, we're going to delve deeper into the murky world of disk directories, allocation units, blocks, tracks, and sectors. We'll learn how wildcards work and how to rescue a file that has been mistakenly erased. We'll finish off the chapter with the WORDS program, which counts the words in a file, or in a whole group of files if wildcards are used in the file name. So don't go away—things are just getting interesting!

CHAPTER 7

Soul Searching

Wildcards and the Disk Directory

This chapter describes how CP/M keeps track of what programs are on a disk and where they are. We'll explain the disk directory, allocation units, extents, sectors, bit maps, and how they all fit together. We'll also explain how CP/M uses "wildcards" (the "?" and "*" characters) to refer to whole groups of files rather than single files.

Using these ideas, we'll then cover the "Search for First" and "Search for Next" system calls, whose purpose is to provide your program with information about particular files. These calls give us the tool we need for our next example: a procedure which permits you to restore a file that has been accidentally erased.

We'll finish off this chapter with WORDS, a program that counts the number of words in a text file. WORDS permits the use of wildcards in its input; that is, it will list the number of words in a whole group of files. In this program, which is somewhat more ambitious than any we've looked at so far, we'll also introduce the idea of stack management.

In addition to teaching you about the disk system, this chapter will give you the skills necessary to write a variety of such advanced utility programs as a directory program that tells you how much disk space a program occupies, a master directory program that will read all your disks one after the other and produce a file of all your programs, and a program that restores erased files. You could even write a disk utility program that would enable you to read and write to specific sectors of the disk, as is done in many "disk debugger" programs.

HOW CP/M STORES FILES ON THE DISK

In previous chapters, we've mentioned, in passing, such terms as allocation units, extents, and the disk directory. Now we're going to find out what these terms really mean and how they all work together to permit CP/M to store and retrieve a particular file on the disk.

As you recall, a standard 8-inch CP/M disk has 77 tracks, each of which contains 26 sectors. In a single-density disk, a sector is 128 bytes or the same length as a CP/M record. (In double-density disks, a sector can hold two or even four records, but let's ignore this possibility for the time being. It's the idea of how the disk is organized that's important here, not the actual numbers.) Thus, there are 77 tracks times 26 sectors for 2002 sectors on the disk. You have also learned that a file is simply a number of records. Each of these records is 128 bytes long, which is the same length as a sector. Keep in mind the *difference* between sectors and records. A sector is a physical location on the disk, while a record is 128 bytes of information that you're going to put, temporarily, in that sector. It's like a parking lot. There are a certain number of spaces (sectors) in the lot, and cars (records) come and go, leaving some spaces empty and some full.

Things would be easy if all the records in a file were just assigned to a group of sectors in order, so that a file with 100 records would simply occupy (say) sectors 450 to 550—as if all cars of the same color (representing a file) occupied one area of the parking lot. Unfortunately, things aren't that simple because of the way files actually get created. Fig. 7-1 gives a picture of how two files are probably *not* arranged.

<table><tr><td>///</td><td>///</td><td>///</td><td>///</td><td>///</td><td>///</td><td>///</td><td>///</td><td>+++</td><td>+++</td><td>+++</td><td>+++</td><td>+++</td><td>+++</td><td>+++</td></tr></table>

/ / / = file 1
+++ = file 2

Fig. 7-1. An unlikely arrangement of two files.

In the real world, however, this is what might happen. Suppose that you're using your word-processing program to write both a personal letter and an 8080 program on the same disk. You might work a little on the program and, then, a little on the personal letter, and then some more on the program. CP/M doesn't know, in advance, how long either of these documents is going to be (you probably don't either), so it doesn't try to set aside a big group of sectors for each file. As you type in parts of the program, it assigns sectors to this file, and as you type in parts of the letter, it assigns sectors to that file. As a consequence, the sectors for the two files get mixed up, like red and green cars parked randomly all over the lot. The problem then is, how is CP/M going to keep track of what sectors hold the records for a particular file? It's like asking the parking lot attendant to give you a list of the locations of every green car in the lot. The diagram given in Fig. 7-2 illustrates how the sectors of two files are randomly distributed on a disk track.

<table><tr><td>///</td><td>+++</td><td>+++</td><td>///</td><td>+++</td><td>///</td><td>///</td><td>+++</td><td>+++</td><td>+++</td><td>///</td><td>+++</td><td>///</td><td>///</td><td>///</td><td>+++</td></tr></table>

/ / / = file 1
+++ = file 2

Fig. 7-2. The random distribution of two files on a disk track.

Allocation Units

Here's a copy of the diagram of the file control block that we discussed in Chapter 5. (It is reproduced here for your convenience.)

Byte number (decimal)	Location (hex)	Contents	
0	5C	0	Drive number.
1	5D	T	File name (8 bytes).
2	5E	E	
3	5F	S	
4	60	T	
5	61	1	
6	62	0	
7	63	0	
8	64		
9	65	T	File extension (3 bytes).
10	66	X	
11	67	T	
12	68	00	Current extent.
13	69	00	Used internally by CP/M.
14	6A	00	(User should set to zero.)
15	6B	02	Number of records in current extent.
16	6C	54	Allocation units.
17	6D	00	
18	6E	00	
19	6F	00	
20	70	00	
21	71	00	
22	72	00	
23	73	00	
24	74	00	
25	75	00	
26	76	00	
27	77	00	
28	78	00	
29	79	00	
30	7A	00	
31	7B	00	
32	7C	01	Current record.
33	7D	00	Random record number.
34	7E	00	
35	7F	00	

This 36-byte file control block (FCB) is very similar to the information that CP/M keeps in a place on the disk called the "disk directory." At least one such FCB-like entry is recorded in the directory for each file. It contains all the information that CP/M needs to know about the file and where it's located on the disk.

Notice that bytes 16 to 31 of the FCB are occupied by something called "allocation units." This rather ponderous name holds the key to the way that CP/M keeps track of where the sectors are in a file.

An allocation unit is nothing more or less than a group of 8 sectors on the disk. The designers of CP/M decided it would be too complicated for the operating system to try to remember the location of every single individual record, so they grouped each eight sectors together and gave them a number, and then made up a rule: all eight sectors in a particular allocation unit must be occupied by records in the same file. It's as if each block of eight parking spaces in the lot had to be occupied by cars of the same color. This cuts down the information the operating system needs to remember about each file and speeds up disk access to the file, but it also means that there will (usually) be unused sectors at the end of each file. For example, a file 10 records long will occupy all of one allocation unit, but only two sectors of the next one, leaving 6 unused sectors which can't be used by any other file. However, this is a small price to pay for simplifying the disk directory entries.

In the FCB, there are sixteen bytes set aside to hold the allocation units. Each allocation unit is represented by a single byte. This works because there are approximately 2002 sectors, and 2002 sectors divided by 8 sectors per allocation unit gives 250 allocation units. Thus, one byte (which can have values from 0 to 255) can be used to specify any one of the 250 allocation units. Some of these sectors are used by the system, leaving 242 for the user's programs. So the sixteen bytes in the FCB (or the directory entry) can refer to 16 allocation units; this is 16 times 8, or 128 sectors, which can hold 128 records. (There can be more than 128 records in a file if different "extents" are used. We'll look at that soon.)

As we noted, the preceding description only applies if the disk system being discussed is single density. If it is a double-density system, then, instead of 16 one-byte numbers to refer to the allocation units, there are 8 two-byte numbers, with each one able to refer to any one of 256 times 256, or 65536, possible allocation units.

When you "open" a file, the operating system gets the information about which allocation units the file occupies from the disk directory and writes this information into the FCB. Let's see how this process looks in the real world.

Examining the FCB

Get into DDT and enter the following program:

```
-a100
0100  mvi   c,f      Open file.
0102  lxi   d,5c
0105  call  5
0108  rst   7        Back to DDT.
```

Now, since we want to see what happens to the FCB when we do various things to it, let's fill it with all bits (FF bytes) so we can start with a clean slate.

```
-f5c,7F,ff
```

Now dump the FCB area to see that it really is filled with FFs:

```
-d5c,7f
005C FF FF FF FF ....
0060 FF FF FF FF FF FF FF FF FF FF FF FF FF FF FF FF ................
0070 FF FF FF FF FF FF FF FF FF FF FF FF FF FF FF FF ................
```

Looks all right. Now put the name of a short program into the FCB with the "i" command. We'll use a program called "multi.txt" which is three records long. (You can create records of any length using the STORE program, since each line typed into this program is a record).

```
-imulti.txt
```

Now, dump the contents of the FCB again to see what's there. (We'll also provide some reference numbers so that you can see more easily what bytes are where.)

```
     C  D  E  F

-
d5c,7f      Drive code
                                   Current extent
005C 00 4D 55 4C .MUL
0060 54 49 20 20 20 54 58 54 00 FF FF FF FF FF FF FF TI   TXT........
0070 FF FF FF FF FF FF FF FF FF FF FF FF 00 FF FF FF ................
                                          Current record

     0  1  2  3  4  5  6  7  8  9  A  B  C  D  E  F
```

The name and file extension have been filled in from bytes 5D to 67 and, in addition, byte 5C (which is the drive code), byte 68 (which is the current extent), and byte 7C (which is the current record) have all been set to 0. The "i" command does this automatically, since this is what BDOS requires when the file is opened.

Now we'll open the file by executing our little program.

```
-g100
*0109
-
```

And now we'll dump the FCB again and see what's happened:

```
     C  D  E  F
                                                 ┌──────── Record count
-                                                │  ┌───── Allocation unit
d5c,7f                                           │  │
005C 00 4D 55 4C .MUL                            ↓  ↓
0060 54 49 20 20 20 54 58 54 00 00 80 03 61 00 00 00 TI   TXT........
0070 00 00 00 00 00 00 00 00 00 00 00 00 FF FF FF ................

     0  1  2  3  4  5  6  7  8  9  A  B  C  D  E  F
```

Lots of zeros, and a few other goodies. Byte 69 has become 0, and byte 6A is 80. (BDOS uses these bytes internally: don't worry about them.) Byte 6B (which is the "rc" or record count byte) is 03, which is the total number of records in the file. Interesting. Bytes 6C to 7B are the 16 bytes that hold the allocation units and they're all 0, except for the first one, which is 61.

Since the file is a mere 3 records long, it's only going to use one allocation unit, since each allocation unit can hold up to 8 records. And that's exactly what we see; all the allocation unit bytes are zero (meaning they're unused) except one. BDOS can look at this FCB (so can we) and know immediately that the 3 records of the file "multi.txt" are located in allocation unit number 61 (hex), which is one of the 242 (decimal) or so allocation units on the disk. So if we issued a "read record" system call, BDOS would know which sectors to read to get this file.

Extents

We've found that our 16 allocation units can hold 8 times 16, or 128 records. This is 128 times 128, or 16384 bytes, a rather large file. But what happens when a file is longer than that? Then, instead of simply assigning more allocation units to increase the size of the file, we have to do a more major operation called "opening a new extent." What's this mean? Remember that the information that we read into the FCB when we opened the file came from the disk directory. It was, in fact, an FCB-like entry in the directory, and if you looked in the directory (as we're about to do), you would see it sitting there.

Now, when a file exceeds 128 records, what we have to do is make another entry in the directory. We use the same filename and type, but we have the extent number (byte 6A) set to 1 instead of 0 (or to 2, or 3, or more, if that many extents are required). Thus, a file with 300 records would have 3 extents and, thus, 3 entries in the directory: one for the first 128 records, one for the next 128 records, and one for the 44 remaining records.

Fig. 7-3 gives a picture of how records, allocation units, sectors, extents and so on are related. Note again, that if you are using a double-density disk, these numbers will be somewhat different. In double density, a sector can hold either 256, 512, or 1024 bytes, depending on the system. The other numbers given in the diagram of Fig. 7-3 change accordingly. However, records will always consist of 128 bytes regardless of the system. This means that when you write a program, you don't need to worry about single density, double density, or whatever other peculiarities the system may have: you simply deal with 128-byte records.

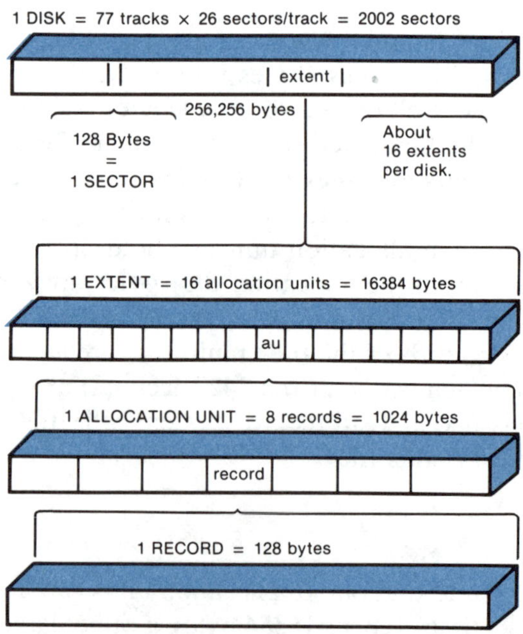

Fig. 7-3. The relationship of records, allocation units, sectors, etc.

The Disk Directory

The disk directory, itself, is stored on the disk and consists of a number of records. How many? In single density, there are 16 records, each of which can hold 4 directory entries, for a total of 64 directory slots. In double density, there are 32 records, each of which can hold 4 directory entries of 32 bytes, for a total of 128 directory slots. This means that it is impossible to put more than 64 (or 128) files on a disk, even if they are all so short that they have no trouble with disk space.

You may be wondering where the last 4 bits went, if the FCB is 36 bytes long and the directory entry only holds 32. What happens is that when a file is opened, only 32 bytes are read from the directory to the FCB. The "cr" (current record) byte and the 3 bytes which make up the random record number (r0, r1, and r2), are constructed by BDOS when they are needed, and are not a part of the permanent record of the file.

Here's what a directory entry looks like:

Byte Number (dec)	(hex)	Contents	
0	00	00	Set to 00 if file is valid; set to E5 if file is erased.
1	01	T	Filename, 8 bytes.
2	02	E	
3	03	S	
4	04	T	
5	05	F	
6	06	I	
7	07	L	
8	08	E	
9	09	C	File extension, 3 bytes.
10	0A	O	
11	0B	M	
12	0C	00	Extent.
13	0D	00	s1
14	0E	00	s2
15	0F	12	Number of records in this extent.
16	10	3C	Allocation units (unused spaces = 0).
17	11	3D	
18	12	00	
19	13	00	

20	14	00	Allocation units (unused spaces = 0).
21	15	00	
22	16	00	
23	17	00	
24	18	00	
25	19	00	
26	1A	00	
27	1B	00	
28	1C	00	
29	1D	00	
30	1E	00	
31	1F	00	

The information given in a directory slot (a slot is the position occupied by one directory entry) is not exactly the same as that in the FCB. For instance, the first byte (at location 0) is no longer the drive code. It's now called the "user number." On a single-user system, it can have either of two values: 00, meaning that the file name in this slot is in use, or E5, meaning that the file has been erased. The file name and file extension are the same as they are in the FCB and, on single-density systems, the record count is the record count. However, on double-density systems, the number in this position is not actually the record count, but is related to it by an obscure algorithm which we won't go into.

As in the FCB, bytes s1 and s2 are used for something mysterious, and are undocumented by Digital Research, and must not be asked about.

Next, we're going to discuss two systems calls that give your program the ability to read the disk directory: "Search For First" and "Search For Next."

SEARCH FOR FIRST SYSTEM CALL

SEARCH FOR FIRST		FUNCTION 17 (dec) = 11 (hex)
Enter with:	REG C	= 11 (hex)
	REGs DE	= FCB address
On Return:	REG A	= Directory Code
Comments:	Directory Code = 0, 1, 2, or 3 if file found.	
	Directory Code = FF (hex) if file not found.	

When you execute it, this system call will look at the file name in the FCB and, then, will go and read the disk directory to see if there's a file name there that matches the name in the FCB. If it finds the file, it will write the directory record that contains the name into the DMA buffer. Since there are four directory entries in each record of the directory, there will be three other entries written into the DMA besides the one you want. In order to tell your program which of these four entries is the right one, Search For First returns a number in the A-register that corresponds to the position of the desired file in the directory record:

0 means the file is the first entry in the record.
1 means the file is the second entry in the record.
2 means the file is the third entry in the record.
3 means the file is the fourth entry in the record.

This system call only looks for the *first* occurrence of a file in the directory. There are two reasons why a file whose name you have placed in the FCB may have more than one directory entry. First, it may be so large that it occupies more than one extent. Each extent that the file occupies requires an additional directory entry. Second, you may have used wildcards in the file name you placed in the FCB, in which case, a number of different file names may all fit the pattern.

WILDCARDS

As you know from using CP/M, it is possible to use the characters "?" (meaning any character) and "*" (meaning any group of characters) in a file name. When you do this, *any* filename that matches the pattern you have set up will be operated on. For instance, if you type:

```
A>dir chap????.txt
```

all the files having a name that starts with the four letters "chap" and that have an extension of "txt" will be listed, such as "chapter.txt", "chap-2.txt", and so on. Similarly,

```
A>dir *.txt
```

will list *all* files with a file type of "txt". We can use one of these two conventions in the Search For First system call: the "?" character. The "*" *cannot* be used, because it is the CCP that translates an "*" into a "?", and your program doesn't have access to the CCP.

Let's see how this call works. Type in the following program, using DDT:

```
-a100
0100  mvi   c,1a      Set DMA address to 400.
0102  lxi   d,400
0105  call  5
0108  mvi   c,11      Search For First.
010A  lxi   d,5c
010D  call  5
0110  mvi   c,02      Print out directory code.
0112  adi   30
0114  mov   e,a
0115  call  5
0118  rst   7         Back to DDT.
```

Save the program as test109.ddt, and then go back to DDT with the program:

```
A>ddt test109.ddt
```

To make the program work, all you need to do is to put the name of the "target" file (the one whose name you want to find in the directory) into the FCB. This is easily done using the "i" command. Assume you're going to look for a file called "wsibm.com":

```
-iwsibm.com
```

Now run your program:

```
-g100
2*0118
↑
└──── Position of target file in directory: 3rd.
```

Your program will print out a single digit: 0, or 1, or 2, or 3, assuming that the file you named actually exists. If there is no such file, then a "/" will be printed out, since this is the ASCII value corresponding to an "FF" code returned in the A-register. (FF plus 30 = 2F.)

And now, finally, we'll get our first look at the directory itself. Use "d" to dump the 128 bytes at location 400:

```
-d400,47f
0400 00 45 58 41 4D 50 20 20 20 43 4F 4D 00 00 00 01 .EXAMP   COM....
0410 01 00 00 00 00 00 00 00 00 00 00 00 00 00 00 00 ................
0420 00 45 58 41 4D 50 20 20 20 41 53 4D 00 00 00 01 .EXAMP   ASM....
0430 02 00 00 00 00 00 00 00 00 00 00 00 00 00 00 00 ................
0440 00 57 55 49 42 4D 20 20 20 43 4F 4D 00 00 00 0C .WSIBM   COM....
0450 03 04 00 00 00 00 00 00 00 00 00 00 00 00 00 00 ................
0460 00 42 4F 42 20 20 20 20 20 54 58 54 00 00 00 03 .BOB     TXT....
0470 21 00 00 00 00 00 00 00 00 00 00 00 00 00 00 00 ................
```

That looks like a lot of numbers, but as you can see from the ASCII printout on the right, four files are listed, and the one which we originally asked for–"wsibm.com"–is in the third position down, corresponding to the "2" that was returned as the directory code.

Let's take one of these directory listings and examine it more closely:

```
     User number (00)   Filename (45..20)   typ (43 4F 4D)   Extent   s1 s2   Record count (01)

0400 00 45 58 41 4D 50 20 20 20 43 4F 4D 00 00 00 01 .EXAMP   COM....
0410 01 00 00 00 00 00 00 00 00 00 00 00 00 00 00 00 ................

     0  1  2  3  4  5  6  7  8  9  A  B  C  D  E  F

Only one allocation unit used: number 1.
```

In the lower line, from 410 to 41F, are the allocation units, the same as they are in the FCB. These are either 16 one-byte values, if the disk is single density, or 8 two-byte values, if the disk is double density.

Now we're going to find out how to find filenames that occur more than once in the directory.

SEARCH FOR NEXT SYSTEM CALL

```
SEARCH FOR NEXT            FUNCTION 18 (dec) = 12 (hex)

Enter with:   REG C      = 12 (hex)
              REGs DE    = FCB address

On Return:    REG A      = Directory Code

Comments:     Directory Code = 0, 1, 2, or 3 if file found.
              Directory Code = FF (hex) if file not found.
```

As you can see, this system call is very similar to Search For First. The difference is that instead of starting at the beginning of the directory as Search For First does, this call starts looking for a file name at the place where either Search For First or Search For Next left off looking when it was last called. This is useful in either finding files that have more than one extent, or when the use of wildcards has made it possible for more than one file name to match the name given in the FCB.

Let's write a little program to look at a number of files. Take the program from Search For First, given earlier as "test109.ddt", and add new code as shown in the following program, starting at location 119:

```
0100  mvi  c,1a     Set DMA address to 400.
0102  lxi  d,400
0105  call 5
0108  mvi  c,11     Search For First.
010A  lxi  d,5c
010D  call 5
0110  mvi  c,02     Print out directory code.
0112  adi  30
0114  mov  e,a
0115  call 5
0118  rst  7        Back to DDT.
0119  mvi  c,12     Search For Next                  }
011B  lxi  d,5c                                      } Add new code.
011E  call 5                                         }
0121  jmp  110      Jump back to print directory.    }
```

Save it as "test110.ddt" and, then, reenter DDT with it.

You can use the program to search for a group of files, using wildcards. Here's how. First, figure out what wildcard name you want to search for. Let's say you want to look at the directory entry for every file that has a file extension of ASM. Type:

```
-i????????.asm
```

That's eight question marks, one for each character position. (As noted earlier, you can't use asterisks here because BIOS doesn't understand them; only the CCP understands asterisks.)

Now, run the program from the beginning:

```
-g100
1*0118
↑
└──────This "1" means filename found in second position.
```

Dump the contents of the DMA buffer:

```
-d400,47f
0400 00 45 58 41 4D 50 20 20 20 43 4F 4D 00 00 00 01 .EXAMP   COM....
0410 01 00 00 00 00 00 00 00 00 00 00 00 00 00 00 00 ................
0420 00 45 58 41 4D 50 20 20 20 41 53 4D 00 00 00 01 .EXAMP   ASM....
0430 02 00 00 00 00 00 00 00 00 00 00 00 00 00 00 00 ................
0440 00 57 55 49 42 4D 20 20 20 43 4F 4D 00 00 00 0C .WSIBM   COM....
0450 03 04 00 00 00 00 00 00 00 00 00 00 00 00 00 00 ................
0460 00 42 4F 42 20 20 20 20 20 54 58 54 00 00 00 03 .BOB     TXT....
0470 21 00 00 00 00 00 00 00 00 00 00 00 00 00 00 00 ................
```

Well, it's our old friend, the same directory record we saw before. Since it has an ASM file in the second position, a "1" is printed out when we run the program.

When we search for the next ASM file, we want to use the Search For Next system call, so we start our program at location 119 instead of at the beginning.

```
-g119
0*0118
↑
└──────The "0" means file found in first position.
```

Dumping the DMA buffer again shows us:

```
-d400,47f
0400 00 43 4F 55 4E 54 20 20 20 41 53 4D 00 00 00 01 .COUNT   ASM....
0410 1D 00 00 00 00 00 00 00 00 00 00 00 00 00 00 00 ................
0420 00 43 4F 55 4E 54 00 00 00 43 4F 4D 00 00 00 01 .COUNT   COM....
0430 1E 00 00 00 00 00 00 00 00 00 00 00 00 00 00 00 ................
0440 00 4D 45 4D 52 20 20 20 20 43 4F 4D 00 00 00 0C .MEMR    COM....
0450 1F 20 00 00 00 00 00 00 00 00 00 00 00 00 00 00 ................
0460 E5 54 45 53 54 31 30 30 20 43 4F 4D 00 00 00 02 .TEST100 COM....
0470 21 00 00 00 00 00 00 00 00 00 00 00 00 00 00 00 ................
```

The "0" that our program printed out shows us that the file we're looking for is in the first position, and sure enough, there it is.

We can keep doing this, executing the Search For Next system call with a -g119, and then dumping out the buffer to see what's there, until we've found every ASM file in the directory.

What good is all this? After all, you can use the regular DIR and STAT commands in CP/M to find out the same information and much more conveniently. That's true, *you* can use DIR and STAT, but your *program* can't. Everything we've shown here can be done by your program; it can set up the FCB with a program name, execute the "Search" system calls, and then examine the contents of the DMA buffer to read the directory entries. When we get to the WORDS program at the end of this chapter, we'll show you an example of just this process.

Scanning the Entire Directory

We've seen how to search the directory for all of the ASM files. If you want to look at **everything** in the directory, all you need to do is type:

```
-i????????.???
```

This will match with every file, so when you execute the program four times, it will (usually) find all four files in each record of the directory record in the FCB.

```
.cp9

-g100
  0*0118    First position.
  -g119
  1*0118    Second position.
```

```
-g119
2*0118      Third position.
-g119
3*0118      Fourth position.
```

At any time, you can dump the contents of the DMA buffer to look at this record of the directory. It will show the same page until it's found the last of the four entries; then, a new record will be loaded in:

```
-g100
0*0118      First position in next record.
```

When you see the 0, you know that a new record has been loaded in, so you can dump it to look at all four new directory entries. Continuing this process will eventually show you the entire directory and the directory entries for every program on your disk. This program will, in fact, do something a little special; it will show you not only existing files, but files that have been erased.

ERASED FILES

Look back at the dump in the Disk Directory section of this chapter that contained the file TEST100.COM. The first byte in the directory listing of this file is E5, not 00 as it is for the other files. What does the magic number E5 mean here? *It means that the file has been erased,* probably through the use of CP/M's "era" command. When you erase a file this way, CP/M doesn't actually blot out the file on the disk; it doesn't even blot out the information about the file in the directory. All it does is set this one byte in the directory entry to E5. Later, if it needs to go through the directory looking for something, it ignores all the entries whose first byte is E5, since it knows they have been erased. (E5 was apparently chosen for this purpose because it's the number that is placed in every byte of a newly formatted disk.) Of course, if BDOS, at some point, needs the space on the disk formerly occupied by the erased program, it will take it and, if it needs the space in the directory, it will take that too, but until it needs this space, the erased file is still there.

This leads to an interesting idea. Suppose you accidentally erased a file; would it be possible to get it back again, simply by changing the E5 back to 00? Sure would. Let's see how to go about it.

SAVING AN ERASED FILE

The process for saving an erased file consists basically of three steps:

1. Find the erased file in the directory and record the number of records and the allocation units it uses.
2. Set up a new FCB using the name of the erased file and the number of records and allocation units discovered in Step 1, above.
3. Write this FCB back into the directory by performing a "Close File" system call.

To make this process easier, we'll add a few lines of code to the test110.ddt program that we used above.

```
0100  mvi  c,1a     Set DMA address to 400.
0102  lxi  d,400
0105  call 5
0108  mvi  c,11     Search For First.
010A  lxi  d,5c
010D  call 5
0110  mvi  c,02     Print out directory code.
0112  adi  30
0114  mov  e,a
0115  call 5
0118  rst  7        Back to DDT.
0119  mvi  c,12     Search for Next.
011B  lxi  d,5c
011E  call 5
0121  jmp  110      Jump back to print directory.
0124  mvi  c,16     Open file      ┐
0126  lxi  d,5c                    │
0129  call 5                       │
012C  rst  7        Back to DDT.   │
012D  mvi  c,10     Close file.    ├New code
012F  lxi  5,c                     │
0132  call 5                       │
0135  rst  7        Back to DDT.   ┘
```

Save this program as test111.ddt.

You should probably practice the "rescue" procedure on a file you don't like very much, just in case something goes wrong and you can't get it back.

Use STORE to create a 3-record file; you can call it BADFILE.TXT. Check that it's there, using TYPE2 (or CP/M's "type" function). Now, erase it!

```
A>era badfile.txt
```

Use "dir" to check to see that it's really gone. Imagine your horror if this were a good file, filled with irreplaceable data, that you had–in a moment of inexcusable inattention–erased.

Step 1–Getting the Vital Information About the File

Actually, you already know how to perform this step. Load in test111.ddt with DDT. Then, type:

```
-i????????.???
```

to set up the FCB to look for all files and, then, repeatedly execute the program as shown in the last section. (The first part of the program works just the same as it did before.) Every time a new record is loaded in from the directory, dump it with "-d400,47f", and see if BADFILE.TXT is one of the four entries. (You can't just put BADFILE.TXT in the FCB and search for it because it's been erased, and BDOS can't "see" it anymore.) Eventually, you'll find the entry. Maybe it will look something like this:

```
-d400,47f
0400 00 57 53 4F 56 4C 59 31 20 4F 56 52 00 00 00 18 .WSOVLY1 OVR....
0410 29 2A 2B 00 00 00 00 00 00 00 00 00 00 00 00 00 ................
0420 E5 42 41 44 46 49 4C 45 20 54 58 54 00 00 00 03 .BADFILE TXT....
0430 2C 00 00 00 00 00 00 00 00 00 00 00 00 00 00 00 ................
0440 00 48 45 58 49 44 45 43 20 41 53 4D 00 00 00 14 .HEXIDEC ASM....
0450 1F 20 00 00 00 00 00 00 00 00 00 00 00 00 00 00 ................
0460 00 4C 4F 41 44 20 20 20 20 43 4F 4D 00 00 00 0E .LOAD    COM....
0470 21 22 00 00 00 00 00 00 00 00 00 00 00 00 00 00 ................
```

There's BADFILE.TXT, just as we hoped it would be. The E5, at the beginning of its line, signals disaster unless our rescue operation is successful. Now, what we would really like to do is simply change the E5 byte back to 00, and then write this whole record of the directory back onto the disk. Unfortunately, CP/M did not provide a system call for *writing* directory records, only for reading them–so we're going to have to work a little harder to get the information back into the directory.

Examine the directory entry carefully. The information we need to know is in two places. First, write down the number in location 42F, which contains the number of records in the file (or if you have double density, a number related to the number of records). In this case, it's 3. Then, write down all the numbers that appear in the second line of the entry—here, it's the line starting at 430. These are the numbers of the allocation units assigned to the file. There is only one allocation unit: 2C.

Step 2—Creating a New FCB With the Old Information

First, put the name of the file into the FCB:

```
-ibadfile.txt
```

Now, open the file, by executing the "open file" system call in our test111.ddt program:

```
-g124
*012C
```

The reason for opening the file is that we're going to close it, and you can't close an unopened file.

Now, put the information you found from the old directory listing into the FCB:

```
-s6a
006A 00 0  <——— This byte must be zero.
006B 00 3  <——— Number of records.
006C 00 2C <——— Allocation unit.
006D 00 .  <——— More allocation units would go here.
        ^  ^
        |  |
        |  └——— These are the values we type in.
        └—————— Junk left over in the FCB
```

The FCB now contains all the information that we need to put in the directory listing.

Step 3—Close the File

By closing the file whose name is in the FCB, we write all the information in the FCB into the directory on the disk. Execute the "close file" section of the program:

```
-g12D
*0135
```

That's it!

Is It Really Back?

Go back to CP/M and use "dir" to verify that the file has been restored. Is it back? If so, bravo! If not, you probably made a typo somewhere. Try it again.

Now, before you do any writes to the disk, *do a warm boot* (control–c). Why do we need to do this? The answer lies in a mysterious place called the "bit map."

THE BIT MAP

Ask yourself this question: when BDOS starts to write a record to the disk, how does it know which allocation units are already in use and which are available to be written in? One way it could find out is to read the directory and make a list of all the allocation units shown in the entries of active files ("active" meaning not erased). Then it would know *not* to write to these units. However, scanning the directory is a lengthy process involving a disk access, and it is not something that BDOS would want to do every single time it writes a record. So, instead of scanning the directory every time it wants to do a write, BDOS only scans it once: when the disk is first initialized (by a warm boot).

BDOS uses an area of high memory for something known as a "bit map" (sometimes called the "allocation vector"). On a single-density disk, this is simply a string of 242 bits (31 bytes). Each bit represents one of the allocation units on the disk. If the allocation unit is in use, then the bit is set to 1. If it is free, the bit is set to 0. When a warm boot is performed, BDOS scans the directory and creates a bit map based on the information it finds there. Then, every time it needs to do a "write," it looks at the bit map to see what allocation unit is free, rather than going back and looking at the directory. As it writes, it will set the bits that correspond to the allocation units it has written into to a 1, to show they have been used. When you erase a file with "era," the bits used by the file are set back to 0, to show that the allocation units, which they represent, are again available for use.

Here's how the bit map might look if most of the allocation units on the disk were in use:

```
11111111  11111111  11111111  11111111
11111111  11111111  11111111  11111111
11111111  11111111  11111111  11111111
11111111  11111111  11111111  11111100
00000000  00000000  00000000  00000000
00000000  00
```

If we erase a file, it will free whatever allocation units the file was written into, thus setting the corresponding bits to 0:

```
11111111  11111111  11111111  11111111
11000111  00110011  10001111  11111111
11111111  11111111  11111111  11111111
11111111  11111111  11111111  11111100
00000000  00000000  00000000  00000000
00000000  00
```

(Note that, as discussed above, the allocation units of a particular file aren't necessarily contiguous.)

Now it becomes clear why you need to do a warm boot after you have rescued the erased file. Suppose you rescued the erased file and, then, without doing a warm boot, caused BDOS to write something to the disk. It would look in the bit map and, finding that the allocation units of the erased file were free, it would write over them (if it needed the space). Goodbye file! To avoid this, we simply cause the bit map to be recreated, using the new information we've put in the directory with our rescue process, by doing a warm boot (or a cold one, for that matter). Our file will then be completely legitimate in all respects and will be safe from post-rescue disaster.

WORDS PROGRAM—COUNTS WORDS IN FILES AND USES WILDCARDS

The program that we're going to describe in this section is fairly lengthy, but don't let that bamboozle you. You don't really need to understand every part of the program, at least not all at once. The main point of interest is the way that the program handles "wildcards," that is, file names given to it which contain question marks and asterisks.

Here's what the program does. You type in a file name, containing wildcards if you wish. The program then finds all the files that match the name you typed in, and it counts the number of words in each one. These word counts are then printed out next to the name of each program, like this:

```
A>words *.asm

Files          Words
-------------------
SHOW     ASM = 1135
SPACE    ASM = 307
WORDS    ASM = 970
STORE    ASM = 297
```

In this example, we've counted the words in all the ASM files on the disk, but you could just as easily count all the TXT files, or all the files whose names start with "chap", or whatever.

WORDS can be a useful program for anyone doing serious writing, since managers and editors always seem to ask, "Well, how many words are there in that report, anyway?" With WORDS, it takes only a few seconds to find the length of that 50-page short story for which the *New Yorker* says it is going to pay you by the word.

How does the program count words? Essentially, by counting spaces. However, this is not quite as simple as it sounds, since a string of spaces must only be counted as one space, and carriage returns and linefeeds should also be counted as spaces, since they separate words too. Also, the program should avoid getting confused when words fall across the boundary between one record and the next.

But before we get into the actual word-counting process, let's look at how the program deals with wildcards.

A Problem With the "Search" System Calls

You learned in the last section how the Search For First and Search For Next system calls handled wildcards. If you put a file name which contains question marks in the FCB, these calls will find the directory entries for *all* the files that match the pattern. This works very well if all you're doing is looking at the directory entries, as we had to do to save the erased file. But suppose you want to actually *read* the files that you find using this process? Then there's trouble. Why? Because when you "open" a file (which you must do to read it), the Search For Next system call loses track of where it is in the directory. If you use Search For Next, and then Open File, and then Search For Next again, there will be error messages as Search For Next tries desperately to figure out why it has lost its place.

The solution to this problem is to do all the searching first and, when it's done, do all the reading. So, we first scan through the directory, looking for filenames that match the name in the FCB. When we find them, we put the names in an array called "table" in our program. Once we've found all the names that match, we go back, take them out of "table" one at a time, open the files, read them, count the words, and print out the totals.

Take a look at the program in Listing 7-1. Don't be alarmed; it may be big, but it's a pussycat. We'll take you through it section by section, until it all makes sense.

We'll need two flowcharts to describe the program in Listing 7-1. One will deal with the entire WORDS program (Fig. 7-4), and the other will cover the major subroutine called WCOUNT (Fig. 7-5), which actually counts the words in a file. Let's begin our detailed examination of the program (Listing 7-1) by thinking for a moment about the stack.

Stack Management

In the programs we have written so far, we have, in the interest of simplicity, neglected to pay proper attention to the stack. In short programs, that has not gotten us into any serious trouble, but the longer the program is, the more likely it is that improper stack management will cause us grief.

What is the stack? It's simply the area of memory where the 8080 processor stores things that are PUSHed onto it with a "push"instruction, and where the return address is stored when we do a "call" to a subroutine.

How does the 8080 know where to put the stack? That's easy; as far as the 8080 is concerned, the stack is at whatever address is in the stack pointer. The stack pointer is a 16-bit 8080 register, just like the HL- and BC-registers. It's abbreviated "sp" in assembly language. When you "push" something onto the stack, it goes to the memory address pointed to by the SP-register, and the SP-register is *decremented* two bytes so that it points to the next *lower* location in memory. Thus, if the SP-register contains 400, and you "push" a 16-bit value from some register, this value will go into locations 400 and 3FF, and the SP-register will be decremented to 3FE. Why does the stack pointer count down instead of up? Because lots of programmers like to put their program in low memory and have it (and what-

Listing 7-1. The WORDS Program

```
                ; ****************************************************
                ;WORDS-PROGRAM TO COUNT WORDS IN A FILE.
                ;       Allows wildcards in filename.
                ;
                ;       Type ''words <filename.typ>'',
                ;           (* and ? permitted).
                ; ****************************************************
                ;
0005 =          bdos      equ    05h          ;operating system
005C =          fcb       equ    5ch          ;file control block
005C =          dr        equ    fcb          ;drive code in FCB
0068 =          ext       equ    fcb+12       ;current extent in FCB
007C =          crfcb     equ    fcb+32       ;current record in FCB
0080 =          dma       equ    80h          ;DMA buffer
0011 =          sfirst    equ    11h          ;search for first
0012 =          snext     equ    12h          ;search for next
0009 =          prints    equ    09h          ;print string
0002 =          conout    equ    02h          ;console out
000F =          openf     equ    0fh          ;open file
0010 =          closef    equ    10h          ;close file
0014 =          readf     equ    14h          ;sequential read
0000 =          wflag     equ    0            ;flag value for "word"
0001 =          spflag    equ    1            ;flag value for "space"
000D =          cr        equ    0dh          ;carriage return
000A =          lf        equ    0ah          ;linefeed
001A =          ctrlz     equ    1ah          ;control-z (EOF)
                ;
                ;
0100                      org    100h
                ;
                ;set up local stack
0100 210000               lxi    h,0          ;clear HL
0103 39                   dad    sp           ;get current stack ptr
0104 22E502               shld   oldsp        ;save it
0107 310703               lxi    sp,stktop    ;put in new stack ptr
                ;
                ;set number of names in array to 0
010A AF                   xra    a            ;puts 0 in A-reg
010B 32E202               sta    nmcntr
                ;
                ;--------------------------------------------------
```

```
                 ;SCAN FOR FILENAME AND PUT IN ARRAY
                 ;
                 ;search for first occurrence of filename
                 ;
010E 0E11                  mvi     c,sfirst     ;search for first
0110 115C00                lxi     d,fcb
0113 CD0500                call    bdos
0116 B7                    ora     a            ;check directory code
0117 FEFF                  cpi     0ffh         ;if A=255, no file found
0119 CA1102                jz      error        ; so print message
011C CD3301                call    putary       ;found, put name in array
                 ;
                 ;search for next occurrence of filename
                 ;
011F 0E12        nmfnd     mvi     c,snext      ;search for next
0121 115C00                lxi     d,fcb
0124 CD0500                call    bdos
0127 B7                    ora     a            ;check directory code
0128 FEFF                  cpi     0ffh         ;if A=255 then last file found
012A CA5B01                jz      lastfile     ; so go count words
012D CD3301                call    putary       ;not last, so put in array
0130 C31F01                jmp     nmfnd        ;get another file
                 ;
                 ;-----------------------------------------------------
                 ;PUTARY-SUBROUTINE TO PUT FILENAME IN ARRAY "TABLE"
                 ;
0133 0707070707putary      rlc! rlc! rlc! rlc! rlc    ;A*32 gives 0, 32, etc.
0138 C680                  adi     dma          ;location of DMA
                 ;
                 ;         (A-reg now holds pointer to filename in dma)
                 ;
                 ;move filename from DMA to array "table", char by char
                 ;
013A 060C                  mvi     b,12         ;set up count in B-reg
013C 2A0703                lhld    pntrtab      ;set up ptr to table
013F EB                    xchg                 ; in DE-register
0140 2600                  mvi     h,0          ;set up ptr to DMA
0142 6F                    mov     l,a          ; leave in HL-reg
0143 3A5C00                lda     dr           ;get drive code
0146 77                    mov     m,a          ;put dr in new fcb
                 ;
0147 7E          repeat    mov     a,m          ;get character from FCB
0148 23                    inx     h
```

```
0149 12                 stax    d               ;put it in "table"
014A 13                 inx     d
014B 05                 dcr     b               ;done yet?
014C C24701             jnz     repeat          ; no
014F EB                 xchg                    ;save table pointer
0150 220703             shld    pntrtab
               ;
               ; increment the "number of names in array" counter
0153 3AE202             lda     nmcntr
0156 3C                 inr     a
0157 32E202             sta     nmcntr
015A C9                 ret                     ;return
               ;
               ;last file is found, so go count words in each file
               ;
015B 11B402    lastfile lxi     d,arraymess ;print "Files Words"
015E 0E09               mvi     c,prints
0160 CD0500             call    bdos
               ;
               ;-----------------------------------------------------
               ;M O V E  A  F I L E  N A M E  I N T O  F C B
               ;
               ;move filenames from array "table" into FCB
               ;
0163 210903    movnm    lxi     h,table         ;put table pointer
0166 220703             shld    pntrtab         ; in "pntrtab"
0169 215C00    movnm2   lxi     h,fcb           ;put FCB pointer
016C EB                 xchg                    ; in DE
016D 2A0703             lhld    pntrtab         ;put table ptr in HL
0170 060C               mvi     b,12            ;set count
               ;
0172 7E        spin     mov     a,m             ;get char from "table"
0173 23                 inx     h
0174 12                 stax    d               ;put it in FCB
0175 13                 inx     d
0176 05                 dcr     b               ;done yet?
0177 C27201             jnz     spin            ; no
017A 220703             shld    pntrtab         ;save table pointer
               ;
               ; clear current record number and extent in
               ; fcb before trying to open for count
               ;
017D AF                 xra     a               ;put 0 in A-reg
```

```
017E 327C00              sta     crfcb        ;clear record #
0181 326800              sta     ext          ;clear extent #
                ;
                ;-----------------------------------------------
                ;C O U N T  N U M B E R  O F  W O R D S  I N  F I L E
                ;
0184 CD9901              call    wcount       ;count words in file
0187 CD7802              call    crlf         ;do crlf
018A 3AE202              lda     nmcntr       ;done all files yet?
018D 3D                  dcr     a
018E 32E202              sta     nmcntr
0191 C26901              jnz     movnm2       ;no
                ;
0194 2AE502     alldone  lhld    oldsp        ;restore old stack ptr
0197 F9                  sphl
0198 C9                  ret                  ;return to CP/M
                ;
                ;-----------------------------------------------
                ;WCOUNT SUBROUTINE-COUNTS NUMBER OF WORDS IN FILE
                ;
0199 215C00     wcount   lxi     h,fcb        ;display filename
019C 0E0C                mvi     c,12         ; (number of char)
019E CD6202              call    ourprn
01A1 118702              lxi     d,eqmess     ;then the equal sign
01A4 0E09                mvi     c,prints
01A6 CD0500              call    bdos
                ;
                ;open file first then start counting words
01A9 AF                  xra     a            ;0 in A-register
01AA 32E102              sta     status       ;set word-continue flag
01AD 0E0F                mvi     c,openf      ;open file
01AF 115C00              lxi     d,fcb
01B2 CD0500              call    bdos
01B5 3C                  inr     a            ;check if code was ff
01B6 CA1102              jz      error        ;if so, file is gone
                ;
01B9 010100              lxi     b,1          ;start word count = 1
01BC C5         loop:    push    b            ;save word count
01BD 0E14                mvi     c,readf      ;read next record
01BF 115C00              lxi     d,fcb
01C2 CD0500              call    bdos
01C5 C1                  pop     b            ;restore word count
01C6 B7                  ora     a            ;is it end of file?
```

```
01C7 C20302              jnz     eofile      ;display it and end
01CA 218000              lxi     h,dma       ;start of record in DMA
                ;
01CD 7E         loop2:   mov     a,m         ;get character
01CE E67F                ani     7fh         ;mask off hi-bit
01D0 FE1A                cpi     ctrlz       ;is it end of file?
01D2 CA0302              jz      eofile      ;display it and end
01D5 FE20                cpi     20h         ;is it a space?
01D7 CAF501              jz      space       ;yes.
01DA FE0D                cpi     cr          ;or cr?
01DC CAF501              jz      space
01DF FE0A                cpi     lf          ;or lf?
01E1 CAF501              jz      space
                ;
                ; It's some other nonspace character.
                ;
01E4 3AE102              lda     status      ;continuation of word?
01E7 FE00                cpi     wflag
01E9 CAFA01              jz      next        ;yes, don't increment count.
01EC 03                  inx     b           ;increment word count
01ED 3E00                mvi     a,wflag     ; following chars are continuation
01EF 32E102              sta     status      ;  of word: set status
01F2 C3FA01              jmp     next
                ;
01F5 3E01       space    mvi     a,spflag    ;set status to spaces
01F7 32E102              sta     status
                ;
01FA 23         next     inx     h           ;increment DMA pointer
01FB 7C                  mov     a,h         ;at end of DMA?
01FC B7                  ora     a
01FD CACD01              jz      loop2       ;no, loop
0200 C3BC01              jmp     loop        ;yes, read next record
                ;
0203 115C00     eofile   lxi     d,fcb       ;close file
0206 C5                  push    b           ;save wordcount
0207 0E10                mvi     c,closef
0209 CD0500              call    bdos
020C C1                  pop     b           ;get it back
020D CD1C02              call    binidec     ;print it out (in dec)
0210 C9                  ret                 ;normal end of subr
                ;
0211 118B02     error    lxi     d,nofile    ;print "no file found"
0214 0E09                mvi     c,prints
```

```
0216 CD0500              call    bdos
0219 C39401              jmp     alldone        ;return to CP/M
                ;
                ;---------------------------------------------------
                ;BINIDEC subroutine-displays number in dec on screen
                ;
021C C5E1       binidec  push b! pop h!         ;get bc into hl
021E 0600                mvi     b,0            ;b holds leading 0 flag
0220 11F0D8              lxi     d,-10000       ;twos complement of 10000
0223 CD3F02              call    subcnt         ;sub 10000 and count
0226 1118FC              lxi     d,-1000
0229 CD3F02              call    subcnt         ;thousands
022C 119CFF              lxi     d,-100
022F CD3F02              call    subcnt         ;hundreds
0232 11F6FF              lxi     d,-10
0235 CD3F02              call    subcnt         ;tens
0238 11FFFF              lxi     d,-1
023B CD3F02              call    subcnt         ;ones
023E C9                  ret                    ;that's all
                ;
                ; subtract power of ten and count each time
                ;
023F 0E2F       subcnt   mvi     c,'0'-1        ;c holds ASCII count
0241 0C         sub2     inr     c              ;increment count
0242 22E302              shld    temp           ;save hl
0245 19                  dad     d              ;add neg num in de to hl
0246 DA4102              jc      sub2           ;loop till hl is neg
0249 2AE302              lhld    temp           ;get last pos value back in hl
024C 79                  mov     a,c            ;get digit back
                ;
                ; check for leading 0
                ;
024D FE31                cpi     '1'            ;less than 1?
024F D25B02              jnc     nozer          ;nope
0252 78                  mov     a,b            ;check for 0 flag
0253 B7                  ora     a              ;is it set
0254 79                  mov     a,c            ;put c back in a
0255 C8                  rz                     ;skip leading 0
0256 59                  mov     e,c
0257 CD6C02              call    condis         ;print it (zero)
025A C9                  ret
025B 06FF       nozer    mvi     b,0ffh         ;set 0 flag in b for nonzero
025D 59                  mov     e,c
```

```
025E CD6C02                  call    condis        ;print it (nonzero)
0261 C9                      ret
                ;
                ;ourprn subroutine
                ;            displays a string, using conout
                ;            HL=start address of string, C=length
                ;
0262 5E         ourprn       mov     e,m           ;get character
0263 CD6C02                  call    condis        ;print it
0266 23                      inx     h             ;increment pointer
0267 0D                      dcr     c             ;decrement count
0268 C26202                  jnz     ourprn        ;done yet?
026B C9                      ret                   ; yes
                ;
                ;condis subroutine-displays one char using conout
                ;        expects e to contain the char
                ;
026C E5D5C5     condis       push h! push d! push b
026F 0E02CD0500              mvi c,conout! call bdos
0274 C1D1E1                  pop b! pop d! pop h
0277 C9                      ret
                ;
                ;crlf subroutine-prints a return and linefeed
                ;
0278 0E021E0DCDcrlf          mvi c,conout! mvi e,cr! call bdos
027F 0E021E0ACD              mvi c,conout! mvi e,lf! call bdos
0286 C9                      ret
                ;
0287 203D2024   eqmess       db      ' = $'
028B 0D0A6E6F20nofile        db      cr,lf,'no file found',cr,lf,'$'
029D 0D0A74726Fopenerr       db      cr,lf,'trouble opening file$'
02B4 0D0A46696Carraymess     db      cr,lf,'Files          Words',cr,lf
02CB 2D2D2D2D2D              db            '-------------------',cr,lf,'$'
02E1            status       ds      1             ;last char space or not (1=sp)
02E2            nmcntr       ds      1             ;number of words
02E3            temp         ds      2             ;temporary
02E5            oldsp        ds      2             ;old stack pointer
02E7                         ds      32            ;new stack
                stktop:                            ;new stack starts here
0307 0903       pntrtab      dw      table         ;ptr to current name in table
0309            table        ds      12*30         ;table holds 30 file names
0471                         end     100h
```

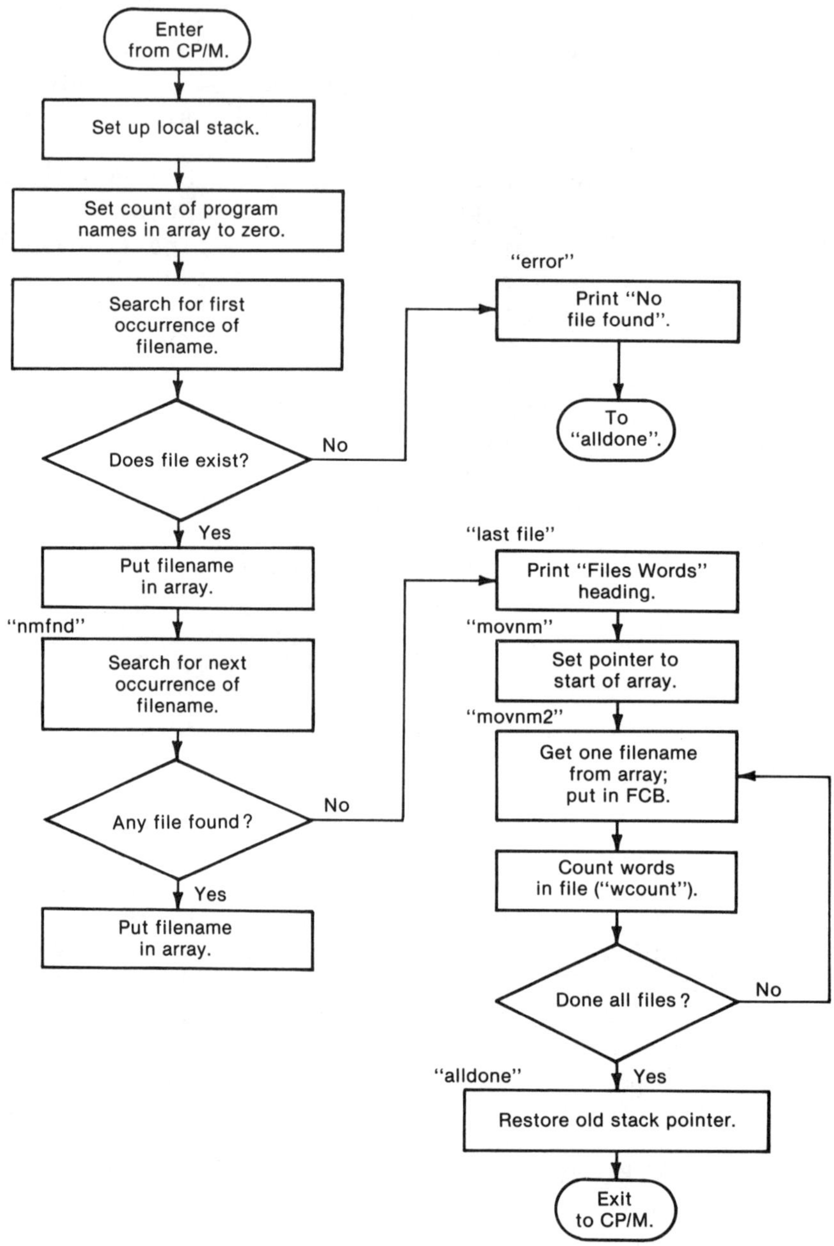

Fig. 7-4. Flowchart of the "WORDS" portion of the program in Listing 7-1.

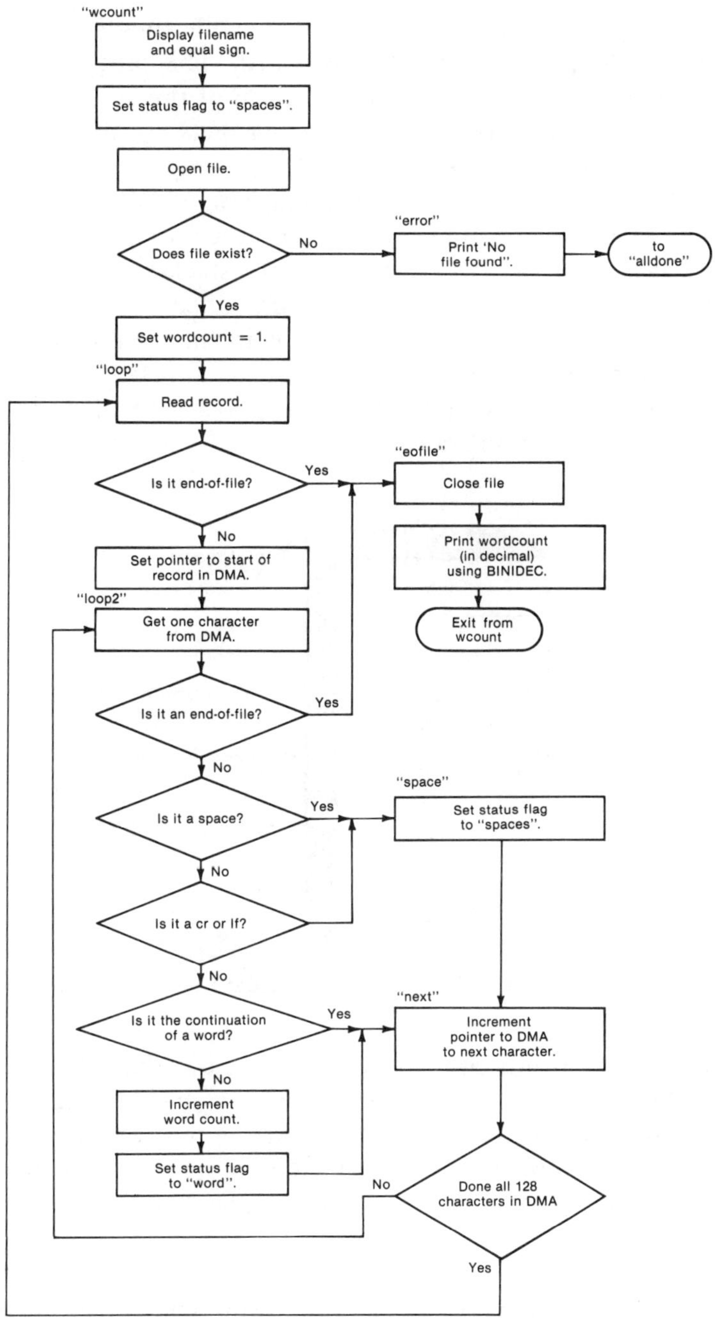

Fig. 7-5. Flowchart of the "WCOUNT" subroutine in the "WORDS program (Listing 7-1).

ever data it needs) expand upward, while they start the stack in high memory and have it expand downward. This keeps a "no-man's-land" free between the program and the bottom of the stack (until, if you're not careful, either the program or the stack gets too big, and they run into each other, and the system crashes).

What do we mean by stack management? Well, so far, whether you've been aware of it or not, we've let various other programs take care of the stack for us. When we used DDT, it started the stack at location FF (which turned out to be slightly inconvenient for us, since that's where the default DMA address is). When we ran programs in the form of COM files, we let CP/M take care of the stack.

What's wrong with that? Well, suppose we had made a mistake in our program, like putting more things on the stack than we took off (too many

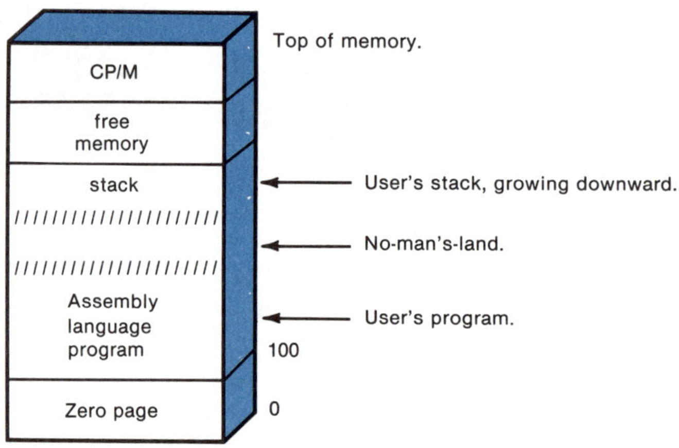

Fig. 7-6. Location ot the user's program and the stack.

PUSHes and not enough POPs). If we did that, then when we went back to DDT or CP/M, or whatever was managing the stack for us, there would be trouble because what it (DDT or CP/M) was taking off the stack wouldn't be what it thought there should be. Or, suppose we just put too many things on the stack for DDT or CP/M to handle. Then, we'd probably overwrite that part of their program just under the stack, and bad trouble would result.

So, the moral of all this is to set up your own stack in your program and make it big enough to handle everything you ever want to put in it: two bytes for every PUSH, and two bytes for every call to a subroutine. When you start your program, save the old stack pointer, and when you exit from your program, restore the stack pointer with this old value. This guarantees that CP/M or DDT will find the stack just as it was when they passed control to your program, and they'll be happy.

The SPHL Instruction

Several of the instructions that work on other 16-bit registers also work on the SP-register. For instance, "lxi sp,14ffh" will put the constant 14FF in the SP-register, and "dad sp" will add the contents of the stack pointer to the HL-register. However, to load something into the stack pointer, we need another instruction, which is "sphl". As its name implies, this instruction takes the 16-bit value from the HL-register, and puts it in the stack pointer.

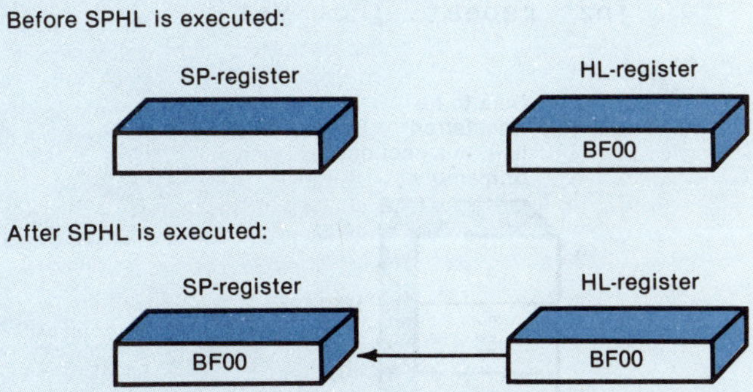

Fig. 7-7. The SPHL instruction.

Examples:

```
sphl
```

In the WORDS program, we set up the local stack at the beginning of the progam (locations 100 to 107), by adding the contents of the stack pointer and storing them in "oldstack", and then putting the address of the "top" of our own stack ("stktop") into the stack pointer with an lxi instruction. Later, when we're about to exit from our program (at location "alldone"), we restore the old stack pointer by getting it into the HL-register and transferring it into the stack pointer with an "sphl" instruction.

This is good programming practice and should be followed in all but the smallest programs. Don't say we didn't warn you.

Memory to Memory Data Transfers

It is sometimes necessary to transfer a block of data from one part of memory to another. This involves looping repeatedly through a section of code which transfers a single byte. Since this can be a comparatively time-consuming process, even in an assembly language program, it's important to make the routine that does the transfer as short and efficient as possible. There are various ways to do this, using different kinds of instructions. Here's the technique used in WORDS:

```
repeat mov  a,m      ;get byte from source block
       inx  h        ;increment source pointer
       stax d        ;put byte in destination block
       inx  d        ;increment destination pointer
       dcr  b        ;decrement count-done yet?
       jnz  repeat   ;not yet
```

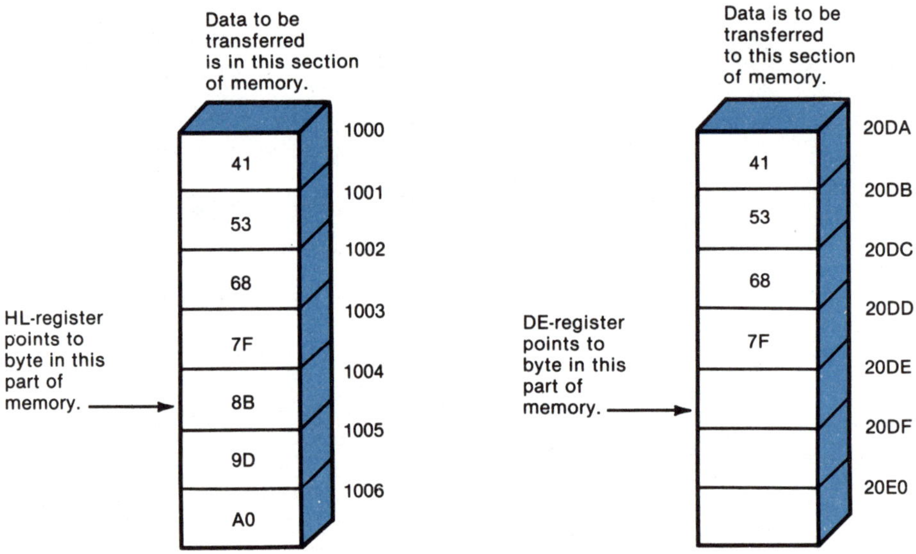

Fig. 7-8. Memory to memory data transfers.

Fig. 7-8 is a pictorial idea of how the data is arranged in memory. At the point shown in the diagram, all the data bytes down to 7F have been transferred.

Since all these instructions (except the "jnz repeat") are only one byte, the routine is short and executes quickly. Of course, the correct values of the pointers to the source and destination blocks must be placed in HL and DE, and the correct value of the count must be placed in the B-register, before the "repeat" loop is executed.

The LDAX Instruction

You're already familiar with the instructions that transfer 8-bit data to and from memory using the HL-register as a pointer. They're "mov r,m" and "mov m,r", where "r" stands for any of the 8-bit registers (a, b, c, d, and e), and "m" stands for the memory location contained in HL. Will this instruction work with other registers besides HL? No, it won't—that's not something the 8080 likes to do. In order to use the DE or BC registers as pointers to memory, we have to use several other more limited instructions: "stax" and "ldax." The limitation is that these instructions can transfer data only between memory and the A-register, rather than between memory and all the 8-bit registers as "mov" can. Otherwise, they're quite similar.

The "ldax r" instruction loads the A-register with the byte in memory at the address pointed to by register "r", where "r" stands for either the BC or the DE register, but *not* the HL register. (Of course, you will use 1-letter abbreviations for the registers: "b" for the BC-register, and "d" for the DE-register.)

Examples:

```
ldax b
ldax d
```

The STAX Instruction

Similarly, "stax r" stores the contents of the A-register into memory at the location contained in register "r", where "r" can be either the DE- or the BC-register.

Examples:

```
stax b
stax d
```

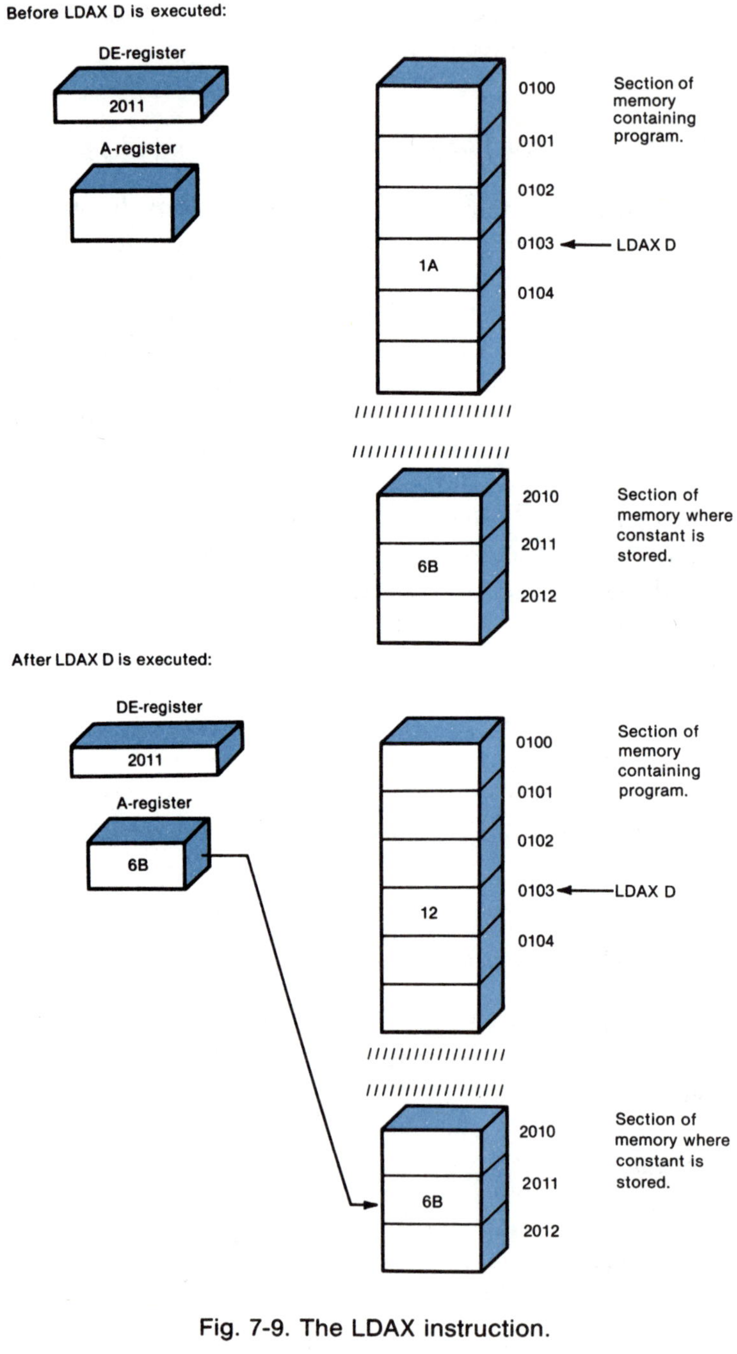

Fig. 7-9. The LDAX instruction.

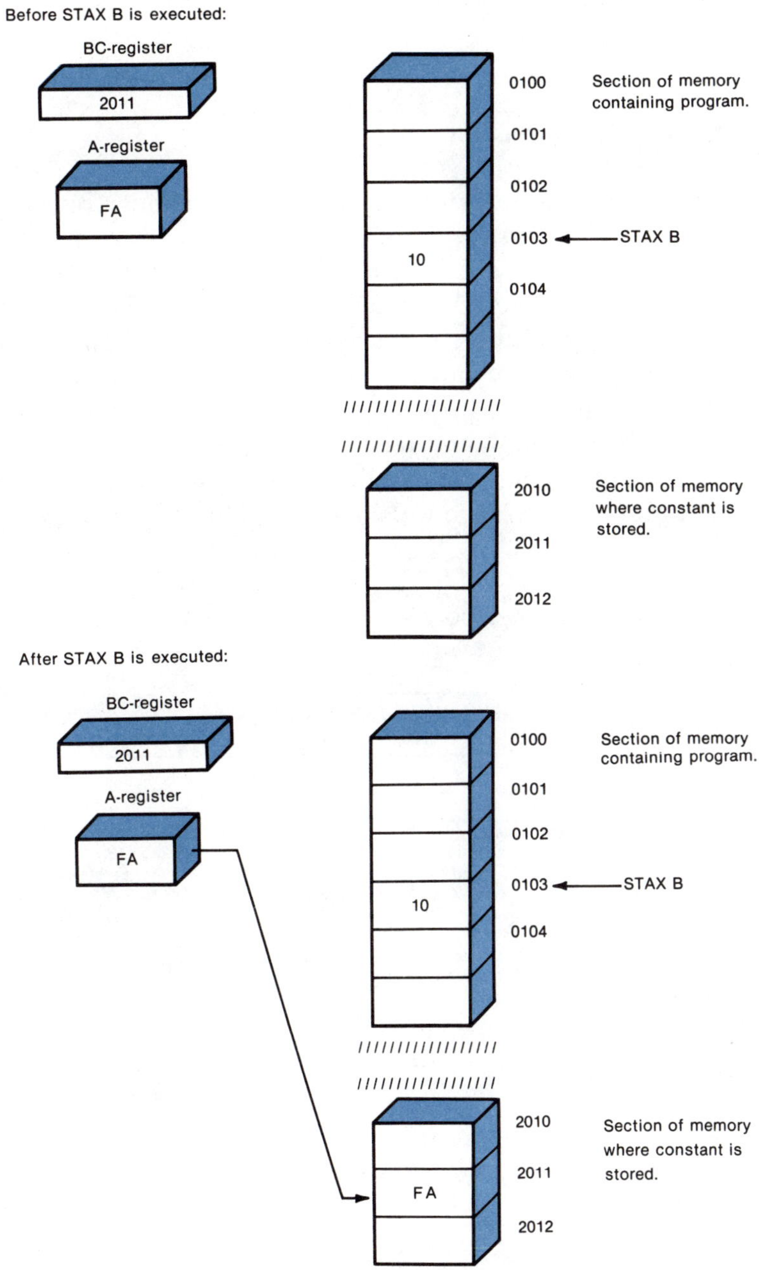

Fig. 7-10. The STAX instruction.

In setting up the DE register-pair at the beginning of the "putary" subroutine, we used another instruction that you have not yet been introduced to.

The XCHG Instruction

It's easy to take a 16-bit value from a memory register and put it in the HL-register; we use a "lhld" instruction. Unfortunately, there is no such instruction which will load a value from a memory location into the DE-register. If we knew when we were writing the program what value we wanted to load in, we could use an "lxi" instruction, but we don't, since this value changes every time we load in a new file name. So how do we get a value from memory into the DE-register? We load it into the HL-register first, with an "lhld," and then *exchange* the values of the HL and DE registers with the "xchg" instruction. This instruction is used again, just after the repeat loop, to save the contents of the DE-register in memory location "pntrtab."

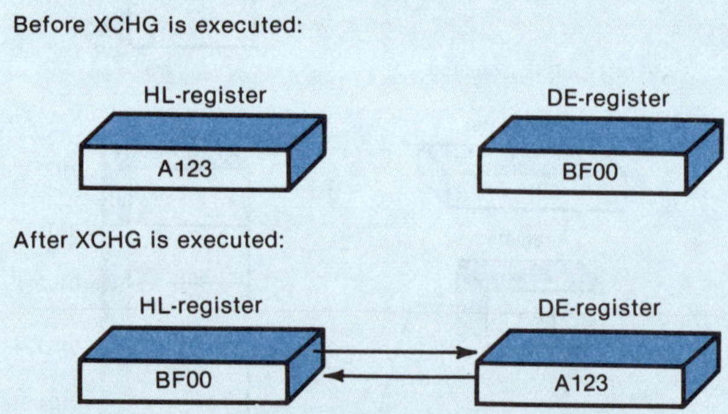

Fig. 7-11. The XCHG instruction.

Example:

xchg

How WORDS Handles Wildcards

As we described earlier, the program first looks through the disk directory for all of the program names that match the name in the FCB. These names are then stored in an array, called "table." This is accomplished in the section of the program called "Scan For File Names and Put in Array." As you can see, the code to do this doesn't look too different from the simple DDT program that we used to perform the same search "by hand" in the last section.

The actual transfer of the names to the array takes place in the subroutine "putary," and makes use of the little memory-to-memory routine described earlier. After putting the file name in "table," this part of the program then increments "nmcntr," which holds the number of file names, and, then, goes back to look for another possible match.

Once all the file names have been transferred to "table," the program then goes on to its second phase, that of reading the individual files one at a time and counting the number of words in each one. This is done in a short section of code called "Count Number of Words in File." All this section does is keep track of how many files have been counted, using the "nmcntr" variable. Once they've all been counted, it restores the old stack pointer and returns to CP/M in "alldone."

The real work of counting the number of words in each file is performed by the subroutine "wcount." This subroutine starts by displaying the file name and opening the file. The rest of the routine consists mostly of two nested loops: (1) the outer one, "loop," reads a new record every time it is entered, while (2) the inner one, "loop2," examines a new character each time it is entered.

We use a 1-byte variable called "status" to keep track of whether we're in the middle of a word, in which case "status" is set to 0, or in the middle of a group of spaces, in which case "status" is set to 1.

Depending on what the character is that we've read, and what "status" is set to, we do different things. If the character is a space, or a carriage return, or a linefeed, then "status" is set to a 1. If the character is not any of these things, then we assume it's part of a word and either one of two things may happen. If "status" is a 0 (meaning that the last character was a nonspace character and, thus, we're already in the middle of a word), no action is taken. If, on the other hand, "status" is set to a 1 (meaning that the last character was a space), then, first, the word count is incremented, and second, "status" is set back to 0. Thus, every time we change from a space to a nonspace character, we count one word.

Subroutines in WORDS

If you played with the BINIDEC routine earlier in the book, you'll notice that it's somewhat different here. We've added a refinement; it no longer prints out leading zeros. It accomplishes this by using the B-register as a status flag to keep track of whether or not a nonzero character has been encountered in the process of printing the decimal number. If so, then the B-register is set to 1, otherwise it's 0. If the routine is about to print a zero, it first checks to see if the B-register is 0. If so, it doesn't print anything, but goes on to calculate the next digit.

The "ourprn" subroutine simply prints out a string of characters on the string, starting with the character at the address in the HL-register. This is useful for printing out the names of the files; they aren't terminated with dollar signs, so we can't use the Print String system call.

The "condis" and "crlf" subroutines should be self-explanatory; in the interest of making them look more compact, they have been written with a lot of ! signs.

It's All Over but the Cheering

That about takes care of our description of the WORDS program, which is the longest we're going to try to cover in this book. If it isn't all clear to you right away, keep working on small sections of the program. One of the best ways to try to understand a long program is to sit down and imagine how you would try to write a particular section of it yourself. Then, compare your code with the program. They may be surprisingly similar, in which case, you'll immediately understand what that part of the program is supposed to do. And, if they don't look the same, then, at least you'll have defined the problem to yourself and, in comparing the differences, you'll learn something new about programming.

In the next chapter, we're going to turn to something different: how to interface assembly language routines with higher-level language programs.

CHAPTER 8

Teamwork

Using Systems Calls From BASIC

Besides being called from assembly language routines, the system calls that we've described in the preceding chapters can also be called from higher-level languages such as BASIC, Pascal, and FORTRAN. (They can even be called from programs such as dBASE II™, a data-base program with a built-in procedure for interfacing with machine-language routines.) When called in this way from higher-level languages, the system calls are usually part of a short assembly language routine which performs a specific function that is difficult or time-consuming to accomplish in the higher-level language.

This chapter describes how to to call assembly-language routines from within a BASIC program. Although BASIC is used in the examples, many of the techniques described are applicable to other high-level languages as well.

There are four main questions that must be answered in order to connect an assembly language routine to a BASIC program.

These are:

1. Where do we put the assembly language program in memory?
2. How do we get it there?
3. How do we transfer control between BASIC and the assembly language routine?
4. How do we pass arguments (data) between BASIC and the assembly language routine?

---

dBASE II is a trademark of Ashton-Tate, Inc.

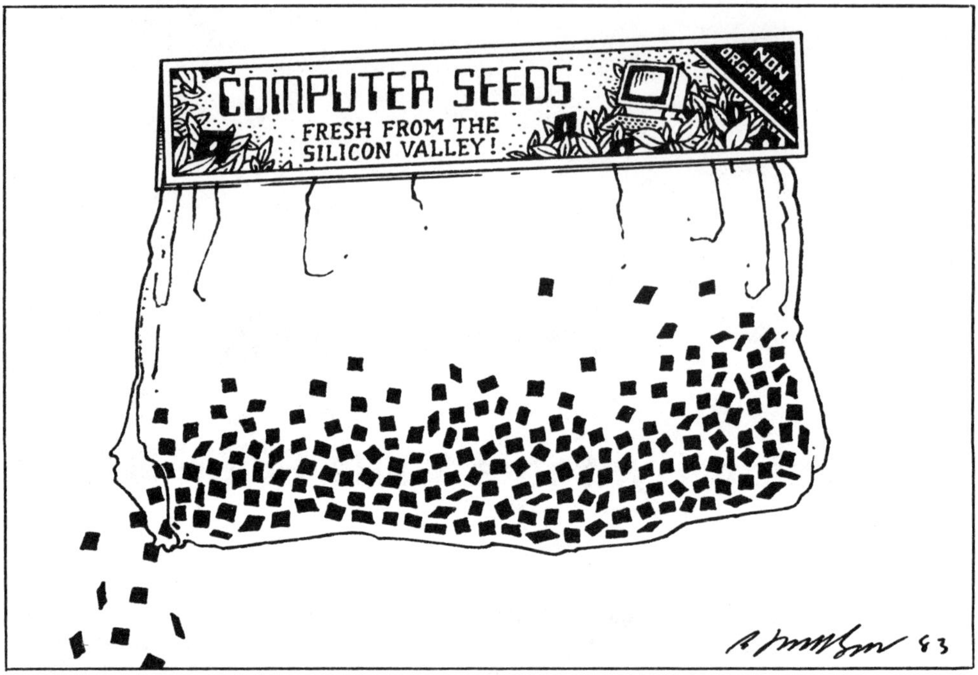

We're going to start off by describing the four questions that are raised above and, then, we will use an example program to illustrate one possible set of answers (the simplest one). Don't worry if all the details don't seem completely clear while you're reading about the four problems. Things will straighten themselves out when we get to the example. In fact, you might want to glance forward at the example program (which is called BINIHEX2) from time to time as you're reading about the four problems–just to keep yourself grounded in reality.

Once we've everything working in the simplest possible way, we'll go back and, using different approaches and examples, explore some of the more complicated alternative solutions to the problems. Before we start, let's agree on a convention: "assembly language" will be abbreviated to "A-L" in the rest of this chapter. This will save a lot of writing for us, and a lot of eyestrain for you.

WHERE DO WE PUT THE A-L PROGRAM IN MEMORY?

When there's only one program in memory, there's usually no problem about where to put it. A-L programs always go at 100 hex, and BASIC programs go wherever the BASIC interpreter puts them, growing upward from itself. Fig. 8-1 shows what that looks like with an A-L program.

The CCP need not be in memory when a program is running, so it can be overwritten. That is, A-L programs may extend all the way up to the bottom of BDOS, an address called FBASE. We'll say more about FBASE later.

The BASIC interpreter always uses the CCP area. Fig. 8-2 shows how memory looks when BASIC is loaded.

Notice how the user's program grows upward into free memory, while the BASIC stack grows downward to meet it. This means that we never know exactly where the space in between the two is going to be. It can get gobbled up by the program or by the stack and only the BASIC interpreter knows when that's going to happen. So this area doesn't look like a good place to try to put an A-L routine. Where else could it go?

The way BASIC handles this is by providing a way to "protect" a section of memory above the stack. This is usually accomplished when BASIC is first loaded, by specifying a memory address in the load command string. For instance, if we loaded our particular BASIC interpreter, MBASIC5, with the following command,

```
A>mbasic5 /m:a000
```

then, mbasic would start its stack at A000 hex, and would let it grow downward from there. Thus, the memory between A000 and FBASE (the bottom of BDOS) would be available for our A-L program.

Let's see how this "protected" memory looks. It is illustrated by the diagram in Fig. 8-3. So if we put our A-L program at A000 hex, we know it will be safe and happy, provided, of course, that there is enough room for it between A000 and the bottom of BDOS (FBASE).

Anyway, that is the way things *should* be. The way they really are, however, is more complicated. This is because (at least, in this first and simplest approach) we have to load our A-L routine using DDT and, thus, *it must fit below DDT.*

Why do we have to load it using DDT? That's a long story and we'll get to it in the next section. For the time being, let's see what memory looks like with DDT loaded. This is shown in Fig. 8-4.

The question, then, is, where is the bottom of DDT? If we know this address, which we'll call DBASE, then we can assemble our A-L program so that it lies just below it.

Finding out exactly where DBASE is may not be easy. However, the following table shows the approximate addresses for various sized systems.

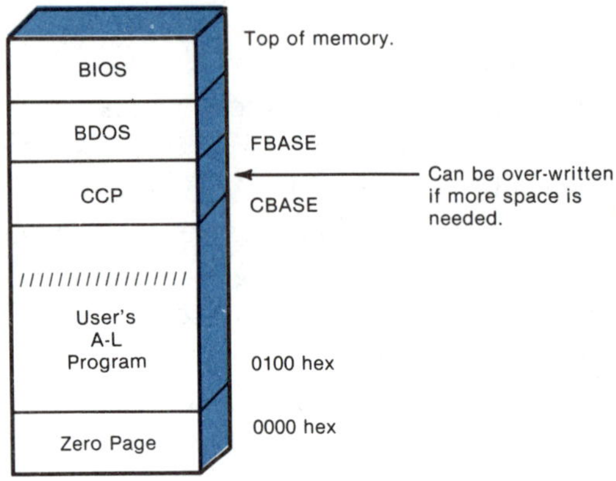

Fig. 8-1. Location of assembly language program in memory.

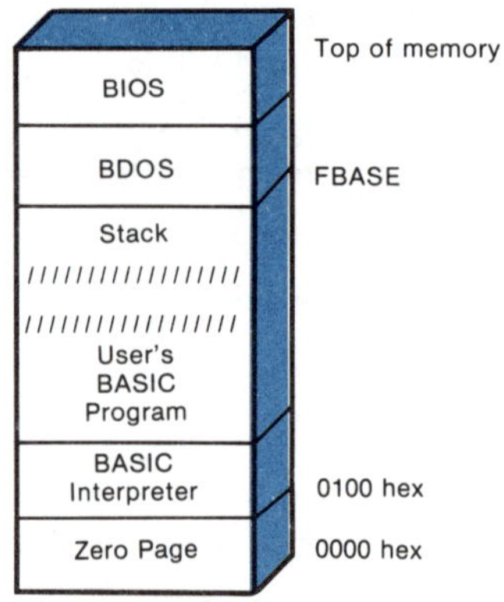

Fig. 8-2. Location of BASIC interpreter in memory.

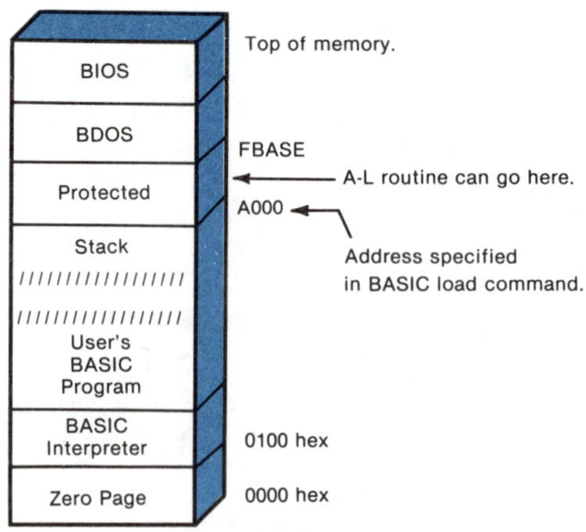

Fig. 8-3. A "protected" memory area for the assembly language subroutine.

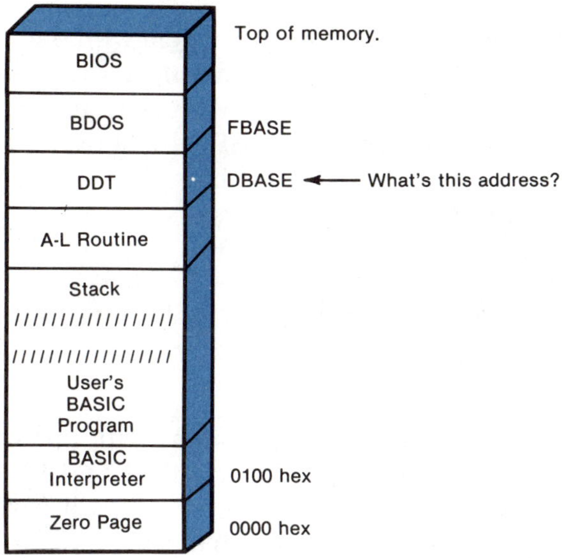

Fig. 8-4. Memory with DDT loaded in.

Although these addresses may vary somewhat from one version of CP/M to another, they will be good enough if you make sure that your A-L routines leave some space as a fudge-factor between themselves and DBASE.

32K	48K	56K	64K	System Size
5400	9400	B400	D400	DBASE (bottom of DDT)

There's another way to figure out where DBASE is. Load DDT, and use it to look at itself! You should begin by turning off your system and then powering it up again, to ensure that all unused memory is filled with zeros. Then, load DDT and use the "d" command to look in high memory, somewhere around the addresses given in the preceding table. Below a certain point, memory will be filled with all zeros (or sometimes FFs, depending on your system). Above that point, it will be filled with the hex code of the DDT program. You should be able to find this point by trial and error. When you do, you've found DBASE.

So now, you know where to put your A-L routine in memory: just below the address that you've found for DBASE. Or even a good bit below, if memory space is not critical. (It won't be in our short demonstration programs.)

There is, of course, a problem with this approach. Since we are using DDT to load the A-L program, we have to put it lower in memory than we want to. Although this isn't a problem with our example programs, it could certainly become an inconvenience if we were using a very long BASIC program that needed all the space it could get. Normally, we can load programs all the way up to FBASE (the bottom of BDOS), but now, we can only load as far as DBASE, the bottom of DDT. Later, we'll look at ways to avoid this problem.

HOW TO GET THE A-L PROGRAM WHERE WE WANT IT TO GO

Suppose we write our A-L routine with our word processor in the usual way, assemble it with ASM, create the COM file with LOAD, and then put the routine into memory simply by calling it from CP/M as with any other COM-file program. What will happen? Well, it turns out that the LOAD program only wants to create COM files for programs that start at 100 hex. This is an unfortunate limitation, but that's the way it is. So if we specify ORG to be someplace in high memory, say A000, the routine will assemble properly, but LOAD will not be able to digest it and error messages will ensue.

What to do? This is where DDT comes in. It turns out that DDT, bless its little heart, *will* load a HEX file anywhere that we want, in either high memory or low. All we have to do is say:

```
A>asm testprog           Assemble the program.
A>ddt testprog.hex       Load resulting HEX file with DDT.
-g0                      Back to CP/M.
A>
```

Now, we can go on and load BASIC, with the proper memory limit, and we're on our way. We'll see exactly how this is done when we get to our example program.

HOW DO WE TRANSFER CONTROL BETWEEN BASIC AND THE A-L ROUTINE?

There are two parts to this question: getting from BASIC to the A-L routine, and getting back.

Getting From BASIC to the A-L Routine

We tell BASIC where the A-L routine is located in memory with the DEFUSR statement:

```
20 DEF USR1 = &HA000
```

This statement appears only once, at the beginning of the program. From it, BASIC knows that every time the routine "USR1" is called, BASIC should transfer control to location A000. (The "&H" specifies that the address which follows will be in hexadecimal.)

To actually go to this routine, we execute a BASIC statement like:

```
50 D=USR1(A)
```

This statement could take a wide variety of forms. In fact, whenever "USR1" appears in the program, BASIC will transfer control to the A-L routine at A000.

Getting Back to BASIC From the A-L Routine.

Going this way is much easier. All we have to do in the A-L routine is a "ret" and, presto, we're back in BASIC.

HOW DO WE PASS ARGUMENTS BETWEEN BASIC AND THE A-L ROUTINE?

One of the unfortunate limitations of BASIC is that only one argument can be passed from BASIC to the A-L routine, and only one argument can be returned. (There are ways around this problem, but they can be somewhat complicated.) Take the BASIC statement:

```
B = USR1(A)
```

The variable A is the argument that is passed *from* BASIC to the A-L routine. From the viewpoint of the BASIC program, passing the value of the variable A is automatic. When this statement is executed, the BASIC interpreter makes sure that this value is passed to the A-L routine.

The variable B is the argument that is returned *to* BASIC from the A-L routine. Again, from the viewpoint of the BASIC program, the procedure is automatic. Once the statement has been executed, B will have whatever value was returned by the A-L routine, and BASIC can make use of the value in subsequent statements. So it's fairly straightforward to deal with these arguments in the BASIC program. But what does the A-L routine have to do first, to find out what the value of A is and, second, to pass the value of B back to BASIC?

BASIC keeps a set of memory locations deep in its innards that are called the "Floating Point Accumulator," or FAC. These locations are used to pass arguments back and forth between BASIC and the A-L routine. Either 2, 4, or 8 of these locations are used to hold the argument, depending on its variable type. For integer variables, which are two bytes long in BASIC, two of the locations are used, as shown in Fig. 8-5:

If we assume that the BASIC variable "A" is an integer, then, when the statement "USR1(A)" is executed in the BASIC program, BASIC will automatically put the the value of A into the FAC. When control passes from BASIC to the A-L routine, BASIC makes sure that the HL-register contains the address of FAC-3. Thus, at the beginning of the A-L routine, all you have to do is get the variables out of the FAC using the address of FAC-3 in the HL-register.

An added nuance here, which we won't make use of but which could come in handy in some situations, is that the A-register holds a number which tells you what kind of variable is in the FAC:

2 = integer
3 = string
4 = single-precision floating point
8 = double-precision floating point

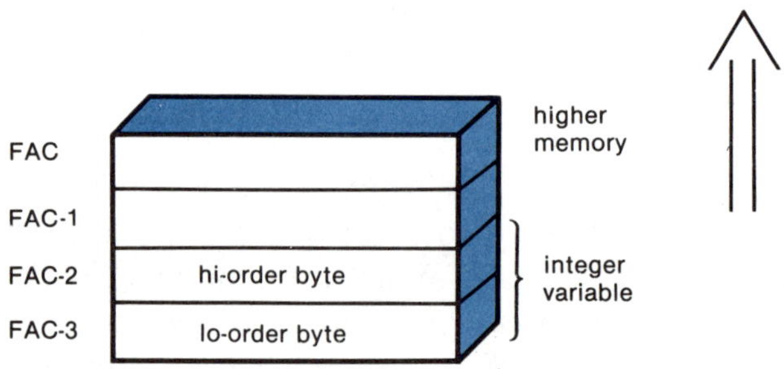

Fig. 8-5. The Floating Pointer Accumulator.

So, if your A-L routine doesn't know what kind of variable to expect, it can find out by looking at the A-register. (Note that these numbers also tell the number of bytes in the variable.)

In the example that follows, we're going to describe how integers are passed to the A-L routine and, later in the chapter, we'll show how strings are communicated. We won't cover floating point variables since these can vary from one version of BASIC to another, but the principles involved are much the same.

How do we pass a variable to BASIC when we *return* from the A-L routine? The same way: we put it into the FAC. There's no need to put anything in the HL-register since BASIC already knows where the FAC is. The value returned by the A-L routine should be of the same type (integer, string, etc.) as the value that was passed to it.

BINIHEX2—A-L ROUTINE CALLED FROM BASIC

You should recognize the name of this program; you've seen it before in the chapter on console system calls. We're going to take this same program and modify it to work with BASIC. That is, we'll give BASIC the responsibility for getting the decimal number from the user and converting it to binary (it does this automatically). All that our A-L routine will have to do is print out the binary number in hex digits.

This is actually a handy little routine since many versions of BASIC don't have a way to print out variables in hex format. Here's the BASIC program:

```
10 DEFINT A-Z
20 DEF USR1=&HA000
30 INPUT"decimal number"; A
40 PRINT"hex equivalent is: ";
50 D=USR1(A)
60 PRINT:PRINT
70 GOTO 30
```

We'll assume that you're familiar enough with BASIC to follow what's happening here.

We define the entry address of our USR1 routine to be A000 because we know this is well below the bottom of DDT (DBASE), which is at B400 in our 56K system. (This will be different on different-sized systems. See the preceding discussion on where to put the A-L routine.) We could have placed it closer to DBASE, but there's plenty of room in memory for these short example programs, so we don't have to be too precise. With larger programs, it would be wise to assemble the A-L routine first, examine the PRN file to see how long it is, and then ORG it so that the end of the A-L routine fits just below DBASE.

For simplicity, we define all variables in the BASIC program to be integers, using the DEFINT statement. The integer variable A is passed to the USR1 routine, which is the BINIHEX2 program (Listing 8-1).

Listing 8-1. The BINIHEX2 Program

```
               ; ****************************************************
               ;BINIHEX2-Converts binary to hex, prints it out
               ;         (to be called from BASIC program)
               ;
0001 =         conin   equ  1h
0002 =         conout  equ  2h
0005 =         bdos    equ  5h
000A =         lf      equ  0ah
               ;
A000                   org  0a000h
               ;
               ;transfer integer from FAC to hl register
               ;  (on entry hl holds pointer to lo-order byte in FAC)
A000 5E                mov  e,m       ;put lo-byte in e
A001 23                inx  h         ;bump the pointer
A002 56                mov  d,m       ;put hi-byte in d
A003 EB                xchg           ;put de in hl
               ;
               ;convert binary to hex and print it out
               ;  (on entry hl holds the binary integer)
A004 7C                mov  a,h       ;put h in a (first digit)
A005 CD15A0            call print1    ;  print left-hand digit
A008 7C                mov  a,h       ;put h in a (second digit)
A009 CD19A0            call print2    ;  print right-hand digit
A00C 7D                mov  a,l       ;put l in a (third digit)
A00D CD15A0            call print1    ;  print left-hand digit
A010 7D                mov  a,l       ;put l in a (fourth digit)
A011 CD19A0            call print2    ;  print right-hand digit
A014 C9                ret            ;exit binihex
               ;
               ;print contents of a
               ;
```

```
A015 07070707 print1 rlc ! rlc ! rlc ! rlc  ;move high 4 bits to low
A019 E60F     print2 ani  0fh       ;get rid of high 4 bits
A01B C630            adi  30h       ;change hex to ASCII
A01D FE3A            cpi  3ah       ;if more than 9
A01F DA24A0          jc   notbig    ;  (it's not)
A022 C607            adi  7h        ;  then add bias (10=A, etc.)
A024 CD28A0   notbig call pchar     ;print digit
A027 C9              ret
              ;
              ;subroutine to print character in a-reg out on screen
              ;
A028 E5       pchar  push h         ;save hl (conout uses it)
A029 5F              mov  e,a       ;print hex digit
A02A 0E02            mvi  c,conout
A02C CD0500          call bdos
A02F E1              pop  h         ;get hl back
A030 C9              ret
              ;
A031                 end
```

We ORG the program just where we want it to go, at A000. The first thing that the program does is get the value of the integer A out of the FAC. Since HL is pointing to FAC-3, the "mov e,m" instruction will put the low-order (least significant) byte of A into the E-register. Incrementing HL causes it to point next to FAC-2, so "mov d,m" will put the high-order byte of A into the D-register. The complete integer is now in DE, and we swap it into HL with the "xchg" instruction so that we can process it in the way we did before in BINIHEX.

After printing out the four hex digits from HL, we return to BASIC with a "ret" instruction. In this case, there is no argument passed back to BASIC. The "D" in the expression D=USR1(A) in line 50 is a "dummy" argument, meaning that it's not used but must be there for the sake of form.

Want to try all this out? Here's how to do it. You should have a disk that contains the BASIC interpreter, the ASM assembler, your text editor, and DDT.

1. Type in the BASIC program and save it on your disk as "BINTEST.BAS". (Remember not to use lowercase letters in the names of BASIC programs.)
2. Type in BINIHEX2 using your word-processing program and save it on your disk as "binihex2.asm".

3. Assemble it by typing:

    A>asm binihex2

4. Use DDT to load the HEX version of the program by typing:

    A>ddt binihex2.hex

5. Return from DDT with a "-g0".
6. Load the BASIC interpreter and, at the same time, protect the necessary space in high memory by typing:

    A>mbasic5 /m:&ha000

   (Of course, the "a000" will vary, depending on your system.)
7. In BASIC, load your program back from the disk by typing:

```
    Ok                          (BASIC prompt)
load "BINTEST"          (or "BINTEST.BAS")
```

8. Type "run" and see if it works!

You should be able convert from decimal to hex just as you did in the DECIHEX program.

The BINIHEX2 routine can be used in any BASIC program you like. You'll probably be able to think of all sorts of situations where it might come in handy. You could, for instance, explore some of the inner workings of BASIC by using BINIHEX2 to print out the addresses of variables, and then using PEEKs and BINIHEX2 to print out their contents in hex. (For more on this, see the VARPTR function in your BASIC book.)

Now that you have an idea of what's involved in linking an assembly language routine to BASIC, we're going to go back and explore some alternative ways of doing things.

OTHER WAYS TO PUT THE A-L ROUTINE INTO MEMORY

Maybe you think it's not elegant to use DDT to load the A-L routine, or maybe you don't want to keep DDT on your disk just to load a small A-L routine to work with BASIC. Is there a way to get the A-L routine into memory without using DDT? Yes, more than one. They each have their drawbacks.

Using LOAD in High Memory

Here's a way that *doesn't* work very well, although it sounds reasonable enough at first.

The idea is this. Since LOAD only works with programs that start at 100 hex, why not simply ORG our routine at 100h and then start the program off with "filler"—a "ds" directive that will insert enough bytes to move the program up to where we want it to be. For instance, if we have to ORG it at 100h, but we really want it to be at a000, we can change the program like this:

```
        ;*****************************************************
        ;BINIHEX2-Converts binary to hex, prints it out
        ;          (to be called from BASIC program)
        ;
0001 =  conin   equ  1h
0002 =  conout  equ  2h
0005 =  bdos    equ  5h
000A =  lf      equ  0ah
        ;
0100            org  0100h
        ;
0100            ds   9f00h ;100h + 9f00h = a000h
        ;
        ;transfer integer from FAC to hl register
        ; (on entry hl holds pointer to lo-order byte in FAC)
A000 5E         mov  e,m   ;put lo-byte in e
A001 23         inx  h     ;bump the pointer
A002 56         mov  d,m   ;put hi-byte in d
A003 EB         xchg       ;put de in hl
       .        .            .
       .        .            .
       .        .            .
```

Well, that looks just fine. We can assemble the program with ASM, and that's fine too. However, when we use LOAD, we get our first clue that all is not well.

```
A>load binihex2

FIRST ADDRESS A000
LAST  ADDRESS A030
BYTES READ    0031
RECORDS WRITTEN 3F
```

"Records written 3F"? That's an awful lot of records! If we use STAT on "binihex2.com", we see that it's occupying 40K bytes on the disk. Terrific. LOAD has actually stored all the meaningless bytes between 100h and a000h in the file.

So this scheme doesn't seem so good. It works, but even a few such small routines will quickly fill up our disk. There must be a better way.

Moving the A-L Routine After Loading

Let's think about another way to get the A-L routine where we want it. Why can't we assemble it at 100 hex, like any other program, and then just take all the bytes of the program and move them up to high memory where we want them? We could use the code segment, which we discussed in the last chapter, for moving the contents of a block of memory to another location.

Sounds good. The trouble is that if you move a program to a different place in memory, all of the "memory reference" instructions in the program will be wrong. Memory reference instructions are those that refer to particular addresses (like "jmp" and "call") which jump *to* a specific memory location. For instance, in BINIHEX2, the instruction at location A005 which is "call print1") should be CD15A0, since it wants to jump to a subroutine at location A015. But, if we assemble BINIHEX2 at 100h, this instruction will become CD1501, which is a "call" to a subroutine at location 0115, not A015.

What we need, then, is a way to fool the assembler into thinking that things are up in high memory when, in fact, they're just down in the program, which starts at 100h. This way, when we move the program up to high memory, the instructions will say the right thing ("call print1" will be CD15A0, and so on).

So, how do we fool the assembler? Very cleverly! But to understand it, you need to know what the dollar-sign symbol means to the assembler.

The "$" Label

When the "$" symbol is used in the address field of an instruction, it takes on the value of the current program line. For example, suppose you have the following section of code:

```
               .           .
               .           .
               .           .
                    ;end of main part of program
                    ;
 0111 CD1501                call       print
 0114 C9                    ret
                    ;
                    ;start of subroutine print
                    ;
 0115 7C            print   mov        a,h
               .           .
               .           .
               .           .
```

All this shows is a program fragment that calls a subroutine and the beginning of the subroutine, "print". Nothing unusual here. Now, let's write it slightly differently.

```
               .           .
               .           .
               .           .
                    ;end of main part of program
                    ;
 0111 CD1501                call       print
 0114 C9                    ret
                    ;
                    ;start of subroutine print
                    ;
 0115               print   equ        $
 0115 7C                    mov        a,h
               .           .
               .           .
               .           .
```

By using the $ symbol and an EQU directive, we've given "print" the value 0015, because that is the memory location at this point in the program. Subsequent "CALLs" to print will go to location 0015, just as they would have if it were simply used to label the line as in the first code fragment.

So how can we use the dollar sign? Well, we can now *modify* the value that the assembler gives to a label; whereas before, it could only have the value of the line it was on. And this suggests a solution to our problem; that is, a way to have instructions occupy one place in memory while they refer to some place else. Since the label "print" is given its value with an EQU directive, we can change that value by doing arithmetic on the operand field that contains the "$". For instance, we could change the "equ" line in the above example to:

```
          .                .
          .                .
          .                .
                ;end of main part of program
                ;
0111 CD1503             call      print
0114 C9                 ret
                ;
                ;start of subroutine print
                ;
0315            print   equ       $ + 200h
0115 7C                 mov       a,h
          .                .
          .                .
          .                .
```

This would give "print" the value of 0315h, or $ + 200h. And look at this: the "call print" instruction changes so as to refer to address 0315, even though the the "print" subroutine is still *located* at 0115. (Remember that the high and low bytes appear in reverse order in 8080 language, so that CD1503 means a "jmp" to 0315.)

In our situation, we need to move our routine from some place around 100h, in low memory, to some place up around A000h (or whatever address is appropriate to your system) in high memory. To do this, we need to come up with a number that's the difference between 100h and A000h. Actually, we don't need to do the calculation. We can let the assembler do it for us.

```
                 .            .
                 .            .
                 .            .
                   ;end of main part of program
                   ;
0111 CD15A0                   call      print
0114 C9                       ret
                   ;
                   ;start of subroutine print
                   ;
A015               print      equ       $ + (0a000h - 100h)
0115 7C                       mov       a,h
                 .            .
                 .            .
                 .            .
```

A000h minus 100h is 9F00, and adding 115 gives A015h, which is just where we want "print" to go when we move the program to high memory.

To summarize: we're going to do two things. First, we will assemble and load our program at 100h, but move all its bytes up to where we want them in high memory, after the program has been loaded. Second, we will change all the labels in the program so that they will have the correct values for their new locations in high memory.

Let's see how BINIHEX2 looks when we make these changes. We'll call the result BINIHEX3 (Listing 8-2).

Listing 8-2. BINIHEX3 Program

```
            ; ******************************************************
            ;BINIHEX3-Converts binary to hex and prints it out
            ;         (to be called from BASIC program).
            ;
0001 =      conin  equ  1h
0002 =      conout equ  2h
0005 =      bdos   equ  5h
000A =      lf     equ  0ah
            ;
A000 =      destin equu 0a000h                ;where the routine will go
            ;
0100               org  100h
            ;
            ;routine to move rest of program to high memory
            ;
```

```
0100 013200          lxi  b,ending-start+1  ;nbr of bytes to move
0103 111401          lxi  d,start           ;where they come from
0106 2100A0          lxi  h,destin          ;where they're going
0109 1A        movem ldax d                 ;get byte
010A 13              inx  d                 ;increment pointer
010B 77              mov  m,a               ;store byte
010C 23              inx  h                 ;increment pointer
010D 0B              dcx  b                 ;decrement count
010E 78              mov  a,b               ;both B and C must be 0
010F B1              ora  c                 ;  so OR them to see
0110 C20901          jnz  movem             ;otherwise not done
0113 C9              ret                    ;return to CP/M after move
               ;
0114 =         start equ  $
               ;
9EEC =         offset equ destin-start
               ;
               ;transfer integer from FAC to hl register
               ; (on entry hl holds pointer to lo-order byte in FAC)
0114 5E              mov  e,m               ;put lo-byte in e
0115 23              inx  h                 ;bump the pointer
0116 56              mov  d,m               ;put hi-byte in d
0117 EB              xchg                   ;put de in hl
               ;
               ;convert binary to hex and print it out
               ; (on entry hl holds the binary integer)
0118 7C              mov  a,h               ;put h in a (first digit)
0119 CD15A0          call print1            ; print left-hand digit
011C 7C              mov  a,h               ;put h in a (second digit)
011D CD19A0          call print2            ; print right-hand digit
0120 7D              mov  a,l               ;put l in a (third digit)
0121 CD15A0          call print1            ; print left-hand digit
0124 7D              mov  a,l               ;put l in a (fourth digit)
0125 CD19A0          call print2            ; print right-hand digit
0128 C9              ret                    ;exit binihex
               ;
               ;shift if necessary, and change to ASCII
               ;
A015 =         print1 equ $+offset
0128 7070707         rlc! rlc! rlc! rlc     ;move high 4 bits to low
A019 =         print2 equ $+offset
012D E60F            ani  0fh               ;get rid of high 4 bits
012F C630            adi  30h               ;change hex to ASCII
```

```
0131 FE3A             cpi   3ah              ;if more than 9
0133 DA24A0           jc    notbig           ; (it's not)
0136 C607             adi   7h               ; then add bias (10=A, etc.)
A024 =        notbig  equ   $+offset
0138 CD28A0           call  pchar            ;print digit
013B C9               ret
              ;
              ;subroutine to print character in a-reg out on screen
              ;
A028 =        pchar   equ   $+offset
013C E5               push  h                ;save hl (conout uses it)
013D 5F               mov   e,a              ;print hex digit
013E 0E02             mvi   c,conout
0140 CD0500           call  bdos
0143 E1               pop   h                ;get hl back
0144 C9               ret
              ;
0145 =        ending  equ   $
              ;
0145                  end   100h             ;starting address
```

The program now has two parts. The first part is the transfer routine, whose sole job is to move the rest of the program up to high memory. This is a fairly straightforward loop, which moves all the bytes between "start" and "ending" to the block in high memory that starts with the location "destin" (for "destination"). When we're done with the transfer, we go back to CP/M with a "ret".

Notice how all the labels in the main part of the program have been given new values with the "equ $+offset" statement. If you look at the assembled hex code, you'll see that all the jumps and calls go to the appropriate locations in high memory.

Here's how we use this version of the program:

1. Type in BINIHEX3, assemble it with ASM, and create a COM file version with LOAD. LOAD will not generate an enormous file because the program doesn't occupy any space in high memory–yet.
2. From CP/M, simply type:

   A>binihex3

   This will load the program into memory, where it will then move itself up to high memory. (The "move" part of the program will be left behind, but we don't care.)

3. Load BASIC the same way as before:

   A>mbasic5 /m:&ha000

4. From BASIC, load the BINTEST program:

   Ok
   load "BINTEST"

5. Type "run," and watch it go!

Unfortunately, as you will have noticed, this approach also has a glaring defect. Because we need to use the CCP part of CP/M to load BASIC *after* we have loaded the A-L routine, we can't locate the A-L routine just under FBASE (the bottom of BDOS) where we would like to. We must put it below CBASE, the bottom of the CCP. This loses us about 800 hex bytes of memory. Too bad.

POKEing the A-L Routine Into Memory From BASIC

Our next attempt to put the A-L routine in memory is time-consuming to set up, but it has a major advantage. We can overwrite the part of the memory used by the CCP. Since the CCP occupies about 800 hex (2048 decimal) bytes, this can offer a substantial saving in memory space.

But where is FBASE? Let's summarize where the major parts of the CP/M system are stored in various sized systems:

System Size	32K	48K	56K	64K
FBASE (BDOS)	6400	A400	C400	E400
CBASE (CCP)	5C00	9C00	BC00	DC00
DBASE (DDT)	5400	9400	B400	D400

Again, remember that these values are approximate. Any modifications made to the CP/M system will cause the locations to change. For instance, if your BIOS has been modified, it may be larger than standard—sometimes, as much as several-K larger. Treat this table with skepticism.

There is, however, a very exact way to find out where FBASE (the starting address of BDOS) is on your system. It's the address stored in locations 6 and 7 of memory. Remember how, when you do a "call bdos", you're doing a "call 5"? Well, the instruction at location 5 is a jump to the beginning of BDOS, so the two bytes following the C3 in location 5 are the address to be jumped to. The problem is, how do you examine these bytes?

The first idea that probably occurs to you is to look at them with the "d" instruction of DDT. Sorry, no cigar. When DDT is loaded, it changes the address in this location so that it can intercept calls to BDOS and, thus, keep control of the calling program. So, looking with DDT won't help.

But, listen! The distant sound of trumpets! It's HEXDUMP to the rescue! The name may not sound too romantic, but the program is really somewhat dashing. You'll find it in Appendix B, and what it does is to let you do a DDT-like dump on any 128-byte section of memory, without using DDT. Type it in, assemble and load it, and fool around with it a little. It's a useful little program.

Now, use it to dump page 0. That is, after the program loads, type 0 and a carriage return:

```
A>hexdump
0
```

You'll see something like this:

This is a "jmp" instruction.

This is the start of BDOS address C406.

```
0000 C3 03 D2 94 00 C3 06 C4 23 AF 23 36 40 23 77 23
0010 36 01 11 80 BB D5 C1 F1 AF 32 81 00 CD 06 E0 F5
```

(and so on)

The contents of locations 6 and 7 contain 06 and C4, so we know our BDOS starts at C406, and we know that we can locate our A-L program any place below this address. Note that this address differs by almost 100 hex bytes from the one given in the table. (Again, these addresses may be different on your system.)

So, how do we go about POKEing an A-L routine in from BASIC? Let's summarize the steps involved:

1. Assemble the A-L routine at the desired location in high memory (just below BDOS).

2. Using the PRN file, write down the hex values of all the bytes in the routine.
3. Translate these hex values into decimal values. This is necessary because most BASIC languages only understand decimal. (If your language understands hex values that are preceded by "&h", then you can skip this step.)
4. Add these decimal values to your BASIC program in the form of DATA statements and, also, add a few lines to read the data statements and POKE them into memory, at the same address where you assembled the routine.

Of course, the tedious part of this is in translating the hex values to decimal and typing them into your BASIC program by hand. However, it's not so bad for short routines.

Now, we have the PRN listing (Listing 8-3) for our BINIHEX program, assembled at location C000 hex. We've chosen this location because, on our 56K system, FBASE (the bottom of BDOS) is at C406. We thus have more than 400 hex bytes to put our program in, which is plenty. Actually we could have used an ORG of C3D5, since the routine is only 30 hex bytes long (C3D5 + 30 = C405), but that would be cutting it a little close if we ever wanted to add a line or two to the routine.

Listing 8-3. PRN Listing for the BINIHEX Program

```
               ; ************************************************
               ;BINIHEX4-Converts binary to hex, prints it out.
               ;           To be called from BASIC program.
               ;           Version to be POKEd in from BASIC.
               ;
0001 =         conin  equ  1h
0002 =         conout equ  2h
0005 =         bdos   equ  5h
000A =         lf     equ  0ah
               ;
C000                  org  0c000h    ;goes on top of CCP
               ;
               ;transfer integer from FAC to hl register
               ; (on entry hl holds pointer to lo-order byte in FAC)
C000 5E               mov  e,m       ;put lo-byte in e
C001 23               inx  h         ;bump the pointer
C002 56               mov  d,m       ;put hi-byte in d
```

```
C003 EB                 xchg            ;put de in hl
                ;
                ;convert binary to hex and print it out
                ; (on entry hl holds the binary integer)
C004 7C                 mov  a,h        ;put h in a (first digit)
C005 CD15C0             call print1     ; print left-hand digit
C008 7C                 mov  a,h        ;put h in a (second digit)
C009 CD19C0             call print2     ; print right-hand digit
C00C 7D                 mov  a,l        ;put l in a (third digit)
C00D CD15C0             call print1     ; print left-hand digit
C010 7D                 mov  a,l        ;put l in a (fourth digit)
C011 CD19C0             call print2     ; print right-hand digit
C014 C9                 ret             ;exit binihex
                ;
                ;print contents of a
                ;
C015 07070707   print1  rlc ! rlc ! rlc ! rlc     ;move high 4 bits to low
C019 E60F       print2  ani  0fh        ;get rid of high 4 bits
C01B C630               adi  30h        ;change hex to ASCII
C01D FE3A               cpi  3ah        ;if more than 9
C01F DA24C0             jc   notbig     ; (it's not)
C022 C607               adi  7h         ; then add bias (10=A, etc.)
C024 CD28C0     notbig  call pchar      ;print digit
C027 C9                 ret
                ;
                ;subroutine to print character in a-reg out onto screen
                ;
C028 E5         pchar   push h          ;save hl (conout uses it)
C029 5F                 mov  e,a        ;print hex digit
C02A 0E02               mvi  c,conout
C02C CD0500             call bdos
C02F E1                 pop  h          ;get hl back
C030 C9                 ret
                ;
C031                    end
```

Look at the hex values given in the second column of the PRN listing of this routine: 5E, 23, 56, EB, and so on, down to C9 at the end. Write down these values and, next to each one, write its decimal equivalent:

Hex	Decimal
5E	94
23	35
56	86
EB	235
.	.
.	.
C9	201

Double check your work; it's easy to make a mistake.

Here's the listing of the revised BASIC program needed to make use of these values. We've placed them in DATA statements and added a subroutine (lines 100 to 140) to poke them into memory starting at location C000.

```
10 DEFINT A-Z
15 GOSUB 100
20 DEF USR1=&HC000
30 INPUT"decimal number"; A
40 PRINT"hex equivalent is: ";
50 D=USR1(A)
60 PRINT:PRINT
70 GOTO 30
100 FOR I=&HC000 TO &HC030
110 READ D
120 POKE I,D
130 NEXT I
140 RETURN
200 DATA 94,35,86,235,124,205,21,192,124,205,25,192,125,205,21,192
210 DATA 125,205,25,192,201,7,7,7,7,230,15,198,48,254,58,218,36,192
220 DATA 198,7,205,40,192,201,229,95,14,2,205,5,0,225,201
```

Type all this in, and SAVE it as BINTEST2.

After all this work, we should reap some sort of reward, and we do. It's easy to load the routine. First, we load BASIC, being careful to protect the memory space where our program goes.

```
A>mbasic5 /m:&hc000
```

Then, when BASIC is loaded, we load the program:

```
Ok
load "BINTEST2"
```

That's all there is to it. Now we can type "run," and we'll be airborne immediately, since the BASIC program will POKE BINIHEX4 into memory and then jump to it as soon as it gets to the USR1 statement.

HEX Files, and Using a BASIC Program to Load the A-L Routine

As our last method of loading an A-L routine into memory, we'll make use of a special BASIC program that can directly load a HEX file: "HEXLOAD.BAS".

In order to understand what the program does, you need to know something about the format of HEX files. HEX files are rather strange beasts. They're translations of a COM file (which as you know consists simply of the bytes that make up a program, the same bytes you will find in the left-hand columns of a PRN listing). These translations are in another format consisting of all ASCII characters. For instance, if you had a "mov e,m" instruction in your assembly listing, it would be assembled as the 8-bit (one-byte) number 5E, which is 01011110 in binary.

In a hex file, the 5 is translated into an ASCII "5", which is represented by the one-byte number 35 hex, or 00110101 binary. Then, the E is translated into an ASCII "E", which is 45 hex, or 01000101 binary. Thus, every byte of a COM file becomes two bytes of a HEX file.

There's more. The entire file is broken down into groups of 16 one-byte digits (which is 32 ASCII characters). Each such group is given a separate load address (the place where the group is supposed to be loaded in memory) and a count (which shows how many of the characters in the 16-character group have actually been used). Usually they're all used, except for the last group in the file. In addition, there's a checksum for each group, which neither our program nor you need to worry about.

If we take a look at an actual HEX file, we'll see something like this:

```
:10C000005E2356EB7CCD15C07CCD19C07DCD15C00F0D0A
:10C010007DCD19C0C907070707E60FC630FE3ADA1B0D0A
:10C0200024C0C607CD28C0C9E55F0E02CD0500E1DA0D0A
:01C03000C9460D0A
:0000000000000D0A
```

Each of these lines is read into our BASIC program as a separate string variable, since they are separated by carriage-return and linefeed ASCII characters. Let's take a look at the first line to see how it's constructed.

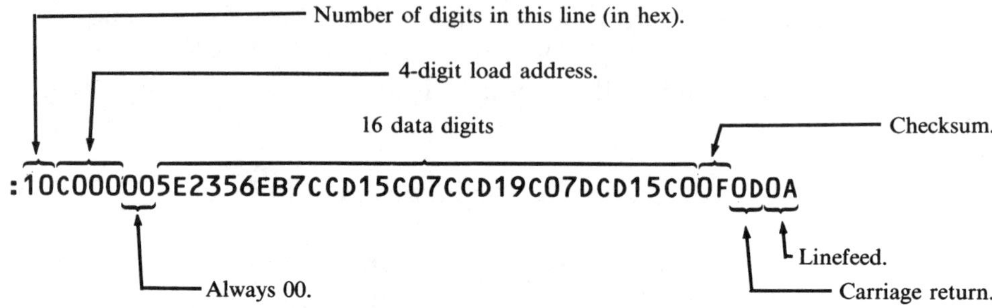

The 10 (hex) at the beginning of the line shows that all 16 (decimal) positions in the group are filled. The load address for the group is at C000. Then come two zeros and, finally, the 16 data bytes, in the form of 32 ASCII characters. This is followed by the checksum and the carriage return/linefeed characters. In the next to the last line, only one data byte is to be loaded, at address C030. It's C9 (which is a "ret" instruction). Finally, in the last line, the count is 00, which is the signal for end-of-file.

This particular HEX file happens to be for BINIHEX4, which you may remember from the last section. You might like to compare the values in this HEX file with those in the PRN listing shown earlier. We'll be using this program again in a minute as an example.

First, however, take a look at the BASIC program HEXLOAD.BAS:

```
100 DEFINT A-Z : CLEAR 1000
110 F$="BINIHEX4.HEX"                          'name of file to be loaded
120 OPEN "I",#1,F$                             'open file, "input" mode
130 INPUT #1,XX$                               'read one string
140 IF MID$(XX$,2,2)="00" THEN END
150 AD$ = MID$(XX$,4,4)                        'address to be loaded into
160 ST$=MID$(XX$,10,LEN(XX$)-11)               'data string (hex characters)
170 PRINT CHR$(10);CHR$(13);AD$;" ";           'print address
180 H$=AD$ : IH=3                              'convert address to decimal
190 GOSUB 1000
200 AD=H
210 FOR J=1 TO LEN(ST$) STEP 2                 'get data from string and store
220 DA$=MID$(ST$,J,2)                          'data byte
230 PRINT DA$;" ";                             'print data byte
240 H$=DA$ : IH=1                              'convert data byte to decimal
250 GOSUB 1000
260 DA=H
```

```
270 POKE AD,DA : AD=AD+1                    'store data and increment address
280 NEXT J                                  'go get next data byte
290 GOTO 130                                'go get next string
980 '
990 'subroutine to convert ASCII string to decimal number
1000 H=0
1010 FOR I=0 TO IH
1020 X=ASC(MID$(H$,IH+1-I,1))-48 : IF X>9 THEN X=X-7
1030 H=H+(X*16^I)
1040 NEXT I
1050 RETURN
```

This program reads in one line of the hex file at a time. Which HEX file? The one put into the program at line 120. (You could also change it so it asks you to type it in from the keyboard.) An INPUT statement then reads one string of 16 data bytes (with its load address, checksum, etc., as shown in the preceding program.) This is assigned to the variable XX$. The program then uses string functions to break up the line into the various components: the load address AD$, the string of data, ST$, and each individual data byte DA$. It doesn't bother with the count number, preferring instead to derive this directly from the length of the data string. Both the 4-digit address and the 2-digit data have to be translated into decimal, since BASIC speaks only decimal. This is done in the subroutine at line 1000. The subroutine looks, in order, at the characters in the string H$ and then translates them into decimal numbers, using either two or four digits, depending on the value of IH. If IH is 3, then four digits are used, if it's 1, then two digits are used. The conversion is done by adding the first (rightmost) digit to the second digit multiplied by 16, then adding the result to the third digit multiplied by 256, and adding this result to the fourth digit multiplied by 4096. These numbers are derived by raising 16 to the IA power. (See the program HEXIDEC that is described earlier in the book for an example of a similar approach.)

Once each data byte is found, it's POKEd into the appropriate address. When the line is finished, the program INPUTs a new line. When it sees a count of 00, it quits.

The program prints the load address of each line of bytes and then prints each byte as it's decyphered and POKEd into memory. This way, you can be assured that the program is doing what it's supposed to do. And, it's enjoyably hypnotic to watch the little bytes marching across the screen and into your computer's memory. However, if you're going to load really large A-L programs, you may want to remove the statements that do the printing (lines

170 and 230) so the program will run faster. Once you've typed this program into memory and stored it as a BAS file, using it is really rather simple.

Let's use the same BASIC program that we used in the preceding examples to test BINIHEX4. We'll change it slightly so that the DEFUSR1 statement sets up the entry address of the A-L routine at C000:

```
10 DEFINT A-Z
20 DEF USR1=&HC000 ←———— Change this to C000.
30 INPUT"decimal number"; A
40 PRINT"hex equivalent is: ";
50 D=USR1(A)
60 PRINT:PRINT
70 GOTO 30
```

We're going to use three programs: the BASIC program BINTEST.BAS which will call the A-L routine, the A-L routine BINIHEX4.HEX, and the BASIC program used to load the A-L routine, HEXLOAD.BAS.

Here's how to do it:

1. Call up BASIC, at the same time protecting the appropriate memory address:

   A>mbasic5 /m:&hc000

2. Load and run HEXLOAD.BAS from BASIC:

   run "HEXLOAD"

   It will execute, loading in the A-L routine whose name appears in line 120.
3. Still in BASIC, load in the BASIC program that you want to use:

   run "BINTEST"

That's all there is to it. If you try it out you should get the same results that you got using the last approach. To simplify the loading procedure, you could merge your own BASIC program and HEXLOAD into a single program, which would execute HEXLOAD first, and then go on to whatever it's supposed to do. Or, you could chain them together, making the following line the last statement of HEXLOAD to be executed:

```
140 IF MID$(XX$,2,2)="00" THEN RUN "BINTEST"
```

Don't forget to make all the load addresses the same. The number you type in when you load BASIC must be the same as the number in the DEFUSR statement which, in turn, must be the same as the ORG of the A-L routine.

HEXIBIN2—PASSING ARGUMENTS TO BASIC FROM AN A-L ROUTINE

Our next example shows how an argument is passed back to BASIC from the A-L routine. This program, as you have no doubt gathered from the name, takes a hex number typed on the keyboard and converts it to decimal on the video screen. It is the complement of BINIHEX—with these two programs, you have a complete set of utilities for handling hex conversions. (There's another version of this program, called HEXIDEC, in Appendix B. It operates as a COM file directly from CP/M, without BASIC.)

We'll assume that this program will be loaded from DDT, although it could be modified to be self-relocating or to be POKEd in from BASIC, as in the preceding examples. Here's the listing of the BASIC program:

```
10 DEFINT A-Z
20 DEF USR2=&HA000
30 PRINT"hex number? ";
40 A=USR2(D)
50 PRINT"decimal equivalent is "; A
60 STOP
```

That's pretty simple. After printing "hex number?", we go to the HEXIBIN2 routine to get the input from the keyboard. HEXIBIN2 converts these typed hex digits to a binary number, which is returned to the BASIC program as the variable A. The BASIC program then (as it always does) converts this number to decimal for printout. (Note that we can't input hex numbers into our BASIC program directly from the keyboard, since BASIC has no function to do this.)

The important part of this example is how the A-L routine passes a value back to BASIC. Listing 8-4 shows HEXIBIN2.

Listing 8-4. The HEXIBIN2 Program

```
                ; ****************************************************
                ;HEXIBIN2-Converts hex typed on keyboard to
                ;          binary (to be called from BASIC program).
                ;
0001 =          conin   equ  1h
0002 =          conout  equ  2h
0005 =          bdos    equ  5h
                ;
A000                    org  0a000h
                ;
                ;save the address of FAC (actually FAC-3)
A000 2244A0             shld temp
                ;get the number from keyboard, put in hl
A003 CD15A0             call hexibin
                ;put value in hl back in FAC
A006 EB                 xchg            ;put number in de
A007 2A44A0             lhld temp       ;put FAC address in hl
A00A 73                 mov  m,e        ;put lo-byte in FAC-3
A00B 23                 inx  h          ;bump pointer
A00C 72                 mov  m,d        ;put hi-byte in FAC-2
                ;print linefeed
A00D 0E02               mvi  c,conout
A00F 1E0A               mvi  e,0ah      ;ASCII for linefeed
A011 CD0500             call bdos
                ;back to basic
A014 C9                 ret
                ;
                ;
                ;hexibin-subroutine to read hex number from
                ; keyboard, store result in binary in hl
                ;
A015 210000 hexibin lxi  h,0            ;clear hl
A018 E5     newch   push h              ;save hl
A019 0E01               mvi  c,conin    ;get character
A01B CD0500             call bdos
A01E E1                 pop  h          ;restore hl
A01F D630               sui  30h        ;convert ASCII digit to binary
A021 F8                 rm              ;return if < 0
A022 FE0A               cpi  10d        ;is it > 9 ?
A024 FA2FA0             jm   addto      ; yes, so it's digit (0 to 9)
                ;not digit, maybe it's letter (a to f)
```

```
A027 D627          sui   27h        ;convert ASCII letter to binary
A029 FE0A          cpi   0ah        ;is it less than a (hex)
A02B F8            rm               ; yes, return
A02C FE10          cpi   10h        ;is it greater than f ?
A02E F0            rp               ; yes, return
            ;
            ;rotate hl register four bits left and
            ; add new digit to right-hand side
A02F 57     addto  mov   d,a        ;save new hex digit in d
A030 0E04          mvi   c,4        ;set up loop to count 4 bits
A032 7D     shift  mov   a,l        ;shift l
A033 17            ral
A034 6F            mov   l,a
A035 7C            mov   a,h        ;shift h
A036 17            ral
A037 67            mov   h,a
A038 0D            dcr   c          ;are we done yet?
A039 C232A0        jnz   shift      ; not yet
A03C 7D            mov   a,l        ;mask off lower 4 bits of l
A03D E6F0          ani   0f0h
A03F B2            ora   d          ;"or" the new digit on to l
A040 6F            mov   l,a
A041 C318A0        jmp   newch      ;go back for next character
            ;
A044        temp   ds    2
            ;
A046               end
```

The trick here is that the routine must save the contents of the HL-register before it does anything else. That's because, when we first go from BASIC to our A-L routine, the HL-register contains a pointer to FAC-3, as described before, and our program needs to remember where the FAC is for later use. This is easily taken care of with a "shld temp" instruction at the beginning of the program, where "temp" is a two-byte location.

Having done this, we call the subroutine "hexibin" which actually gets the value from the keyboard, and returns with it in the HL-register. Now the problem is to get this value back into the FAC before we return to BASIC, so that BASIC will know what value to assign to the variable A. We "xchg" the number into the DE register, get the pointer to FAC-3 back from "temp", and then move the two bytes out of DE, and store them one at a time into the location in HL and in the following location (FAC-3 and FAC-2). This is just where BASIC expects them to be, so our job is done and we "ret" back to BASIC.

Something to notice here is that you can't break into the routine from BASIC by using control–c or the "break" key. Thus, if you changed the BASIC program so that it continuously asked for the hex number (by adding line "55 GOTO 30", for example), there would be no way to get back to the BASIC program. One way to avoid this problem is to have BASIC check for a 0 being returned by the A-L routine. If it finds one, it knows that the user is done with the routine and jumps out of the loop.

OPERATING ON STRINGS WITH AN A-L ROUTINE

There are many situations where you might want to use an A-L routine to do something to a string variable, rather than a numeric variable, as in the previous examples. For instance, if your BASIC doesn't have an INSTR function to search one string for another, you could add this feature with an A-L routine. Or, you could add the LINE INPUT or PRINT USING functions.

In our example, we'll try something a little less ambitious. We'll write a routine to convert any lowercase letters in a string to uppercase. This might be useful if, for example, you wanted to search the string for a name, and didn't want to worry about whether the word was capitalized in the string.

BASIC handles the transferring of string variables somewhat differently than it does numeric variables. The FAC is not used at all. Instead, the DE-register is used to point to a three-byte "descripter" which contains the address and the length of the string. Fig. 8-6 illustrates how it's arranged.

So, getting to the string itself becomes a two-step process. First, we find the address of the descripter and from that we get the address of the string. The BASIC program for our example looks like this.

```
10 DEF USR1=&HA000
20 INPUT A$
30 B$=USR1(A$+" ")
40 PRINT A$
50 PRINT B$
60 STOP
```

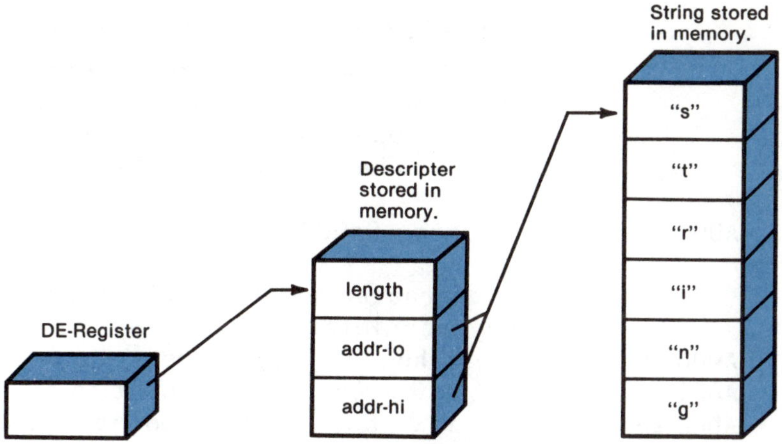

Fig. 8-6. Using a three-byte descripter.

You type in any string you like, and the program will change any lowercase letters that it finds to uppercase. Then, it prints out both the original version, A$, and the modified all-uppercase version, B$.

Notice the plus sign and the space following the A$ in line 30. What's all that about? It's a subtlety that has to do with the way BASIC handles string variables. If we had written:

```
30 B$=USR1(A$)
```

BASIC would have actually converted the lowercase letters in A$ to uppercase and would have then set B$ equal to this same string. By including the space (or doing any other sort of operation on the string A$) in line 30, we cause BASIC to create a whole new string (A$+" ") in a temporary work area. It is this temporary string that is then modified by our UCASE routine. A$, itself, remains unchanged, with its lowercase letters intact, while the temporary string is made permanent and assigned the name B$.

Listing 8-5 shows the program for the A-L routine UCASE, which actually does the conversion.

When we first enter the routine, we get the address of the descripter from the DE-register and "xchg" it into HL, where we use it to get first the length of the string (which we put in the C-register), and, then, the two bytes of the

Listing 8-5. The A-L Routine UCASE

```
                ; ***********************************************
                ;UCASE-Routine to convert lowercase letters
                ;       to uppercase in a BASIC string
                ;       (to be called from BASIC).
                ;
A000                   org   0a000h
                ;
                ;get character count and address of string
                ;from descripter
A000 EB                xchg            ;put descripter ptr in hl
A001 4E                mov   c,m       ;put count in c
A002 23                inx   h         ;move pointer to address
A003 5E                mov   e,m       ;lo-byte of address in e
A004 23                inx   h
A005 56                mov   d,m       ;hi-byte in d
A006 EB                xchg            ;de (address of string) in hl
                ;
                ;change lowercase letters in string to uppercase
A007 7E         newch  mov   a,m       ;get character from string
A008 FE61              cpi   'a'       ;is it less than "a" ?
A00A FA15A0            jm    nolow     ; yes, so not lowercase
A00D FE7A              cpi   'z'       ;is it more than "z" ?
A00F F215A0            jp    nolow     ; yes, so not lowercase
A012 D620              sui   20h       ;convert to uppercase
A014 77                mov   m,a       ;put back in string
A015 23         nolow  inx   h         ;increment address
A016 0D                dcr   c         ;done yet?
A017 C207A0            jnz   newch     ; no, get next character
                ;
                ;back to BASIC
A01A C9                ret
                ;
A01B                   end
```

address of the string (which goes back in the DE-register). Once we've got this address, we "xchg" it into HL, and we're ready to start changing lowercase letters to uppercase letters.

We don't have to pass anything back to BASIC when we return, since BASIC already knows where the string is that we modified.

BACK TO BASICS

Now that you know how to add assembly language routines to BASIC, you may not have so much free time anymore. All of the BASIC programmers, who can't get the computer to do what they want in that language, will come to you asking, "Please, just a little routine to do a fast bubble-sort of my data?", "Please, just a little routine put my output in columns on the screen?", and so on. You may have to get an unlisted number.

CHAPTER 9

The Innermost Soul of CP/M

How to Modify CP/M for Different Peripherals

WHY YOU'RE READING THIS CHAPTER

Scene I: You have a nice CP/M system that runs with a dot-matrix printer. The printer is fast but the print quality leaves something to be desired. So one day, after saving your pennies for a year or two, you decide to upgrade your printer to a letter-quality daisy-wheel model. You buy the new printer, bring it home, plug it in, and–it doesn't work! The dealer says he can modify your CP/M system to handle the new printer, but it will take three weeks and cost more than you want to spend.

Scene II: You have just purchased, by mail order, a brand new CP/M system, along with a printer. But, when you unpack the boxes and set everything up, you find that the printer doesn't work. What's more, you find that the system won't work with any other printer either. Someone suggests that the printer driver has not yet been installed in the CP/M version supplied with the machine.

Scene III: You have a printer with extra features that can be selected under software control, like compressed or expanded print or different pitches for the type face. Unfortunately, the control

characters that should activate these features are already being used by your word-processing program for something else. What you need is for your printer to respond to a different set of control characters, but you don't want to rewire the printer.

Given any of the above situations, and assuming that you don't have a resident programmer on your staff, what should you do? Stay tuned; you'll find the answers in this chapter.

While our discussion is mostly about printers, the techniques used are applicable to other input/output devices as well, such as modems, tape transports, different video terminals, or whatever.

WHAT IS THE BIOS ANYWAY?

In the preceding chapters, we've been working our way deeper and deeper into what we call the "soul" of CP/M; that is, the hidden part of the operating system which isn't visible to the casual user of CP/M. In this chapter, we're going to penetrate to the most hidden part of CP/M: the BIOS (or Basic Input/Output System). You could call the BIOS the innermost soul of CP/M.

As you may recall, the external part of CP/M is the CCP (Console Command Processor), which looks at what you type on the keyboard and takes action accordingly. The CCP is the outward facade that CP/M presents to the world. To perform I/O, the CCP then calls the BDOS, or Basic Disk Operating System. Applications programs do the same thing, using a "call bdos" instruction, as you know from writing your own programs as described in the previous chapters. The BDOS is a section of code that is the same for all versions of CP/M, no matter what machine it is running on. The main purpose of BDOS is to handle disk files, but it also channels I/O requests for other peripherals.

In order for BDOS to actually carry out its duties, it must at some point communicate with the actual physical devices connected to the machine: the disk drives, video screen, keyboard, printer, and so forth. Since these peripherals can come from a variety of manufacturers and can operate in a variety of different ways, the subroutines which drive them must be different for each piece of equipment. This collection of subroutines is what constitutes the BIOS. These subroutines are called "driver" routines, meaning that they "drive" a particular peripheral device. When you change from one kind of printer to another, it's this driver in the BIOS that must be modified to "speak" to the new printer.

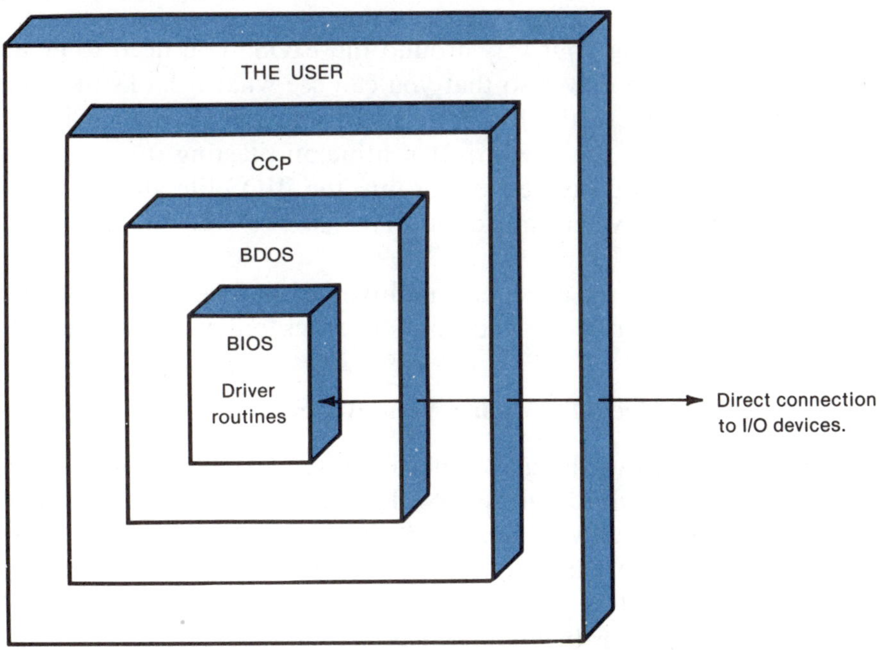

Fig. 9-1. BIOS communicates with I/O devices.

Notice that although the BIOS is at the innermost position in CP/M, it has (as do many innermost souls) a direct connection with the outside world. In fact, it is the *only* part of CP/M that can actually communicate with physical devices.

Outline of This Chapter

What we're going to do in this chapter is teach you how to modify a driver routine so that your CP/M system can operate with a different printer. The techniques involved will also work for adding or changing other peripherals (such as your video display or the addition of a modem). Changes to the disk drives are considerably more complicated and should probably be left to the dealer unless you are a very ambitious programmer.

Because every system uses different hardware, every BIOS will be different. We can't, therefore, tell you *exactly* how to modify your own BIOS. What we can do, however, is show you an example: how to modify a particular BIOS. Once you understand our example, you should be able to apply the same techniques to your own situation.

There are three steps involved in writing a new driver for your BIOS, and we've given each of them a separate section in this chapter. The three steps are:

1. Learning your way around the BIOS. You need to be able to find the existing driver so that you can see what it looks like, how it relates to the rest of the BIOS, and where to put the new driver.
2. Writing the new driver routine and testing it.
3. Inserting the new driver into the BIOS file and writing the new BIOS to the system tracks of your disk.

These steps are all somewhat involved but we'll cover them slow and easy, and when we're done and you look back on everything, it'll seem easy!

What You Need To Modify Your BIOS

There are two things you need before you can modify your BIOS. The first is the ASM file of the BIOS. This is supplied (or can be) by the friendly people who put your system together for you. It contains the actual 8080 code that communicates with I/O devices. This file is usually called something with "BIOS" in it, like IOBIOS.ASM or GBBIOS.ASM. If the file contains the I/O for the disk system, then it will be very long, like 20 or 30 pages or so when printed out. But, often, the supplier will leave out the part of the

BIOS that deals with the disk system and then it will be fairly short, on the order of a half-a-dozen pages. You need this file because it's what you're going to modify. That is, you're actually going to use your word-processor program to alter parts of a section of this file. Then, you'll reassemble it with ASM and write it back onto the "system tracks" of your disk.

The second thing that you'll need is the specifications for your UART or serial board. "UART" stands for "Universal Asynchronous Receiver/Transmitter." The UART is a "chip" or integrated circuit that is installed on one of the boards in your computer, namely the "serial board," which allows the computer to communicate in serial mode with external devices. We'll talk more about what all this means in the next section. Until then, just get your hands on the spec sheet. It will tell you what numbers to output to what "port" in the UART in order to send signals to various I/O devices.

Some versions of the BIOS.ASM file include information on the UART at the beginning of the listing. Thus it is possible to modify your BIOS without the actual spec sheet, provided that the UART is already installed and operating and your listing has this information. It's also easier if you have a device already operating that is similar to the one you plan to install. That is, if you already have a printer running and want to change to another printer, you may not need the spec sheet or the comments in the listing. This is because you can use the existing driver as a model for what to do. But, if you don't have any printer at all, then you really need the spec sheet. In any case, it will make your life a little easier.

LEARNING YOUR WAY AROUND THE BIOS

Writing a new driver routine for your CP/M system is a little like being a building contractor who lands a job in a strange city. Suppose you're given the job of tearing down the old office building at the corner of Main and North Street in a city that you've never before visited (called Bioston) and, then, are to build a new high-rise on the site.

You drive your pickup into town, and the first problem that you're faced with is finding out where the intersection of Main and North Street is. Right away you need to scare up a map so you can get to the job site.

The ASM file of your BIOS (called BIOSIO.ASM, NSBIOS.ASM, or whatever) is the map you need to get to the job site, which is the printer driver routine. In this section, we're going to give you a little course in map-reading; that is, how to get where you want to go in the BIOS. The BIOS is a long listing, but remember that you don't need to understand all of it. Like someone navigating in an unfamiliar city, you only need to recognize a few intersections and landmarks along a particular route in order to get to your destination.

We'll show you some of these important features first, and then introduce you to the complete BIOS. Remember that the particular BIOS we will be describing is only one example of the hundreds of possible versions of BIOS out there in CP/M land. Yours will be somewhat different, but it should be similar enough so that you can follow on your own BIOS the steps that we describe here. Reading your own BIOS listing will make the most sense if you assemble it with ASM and, then, refer to the PRN listing as, often, the hex values of things are important.

The BIOS Introduces Itself

Here's the first part of our example BIOS:

```
                ;TITLE ++ BIOS FOR DIO WITH CP/M 2.2 REV 2.7 ++
                ;                 W. W. COMPONENTS
                ;**************************************************
                ;       BIOS FOR IMSAI DIO-C CONTROLLER WITH CP/M 2.2
                ;**************************************************
                ;       BIOS VERSION 2.7:    SINGLE DENSITY, 128 B/S
                ;                            DOUBLE DENSITY, 256 B/S
                ;                            DOUBLE DENSITY, 1024 B/S
                ;**************************************************

0000 =          FALSE   EQU 0
FFFF =          TRUE    EQU NOT FALSE

0038 =          MSIZE   EQU 56                  ;MEMORY SIZE IN K-BYTES
0036 =          SSIZE   EQU MSIZE-2             ;2K FOR CP/M,BIOS AND BUFF
001B =          REVNUM  EQU 27                  ;BIOS REV #
0016 =          CPMREV  EQU 22                  ;CP/M REV #

                ;       "BIAS" IS ADDRESS OFFSET FROM 3400H FOR
                ;       MEMORY SYSTEMS OTHER THAN 16K (REFERRED TO
                ;       AS "B" THROUGHOUT THE TEXT).
8800 =          BIAS    EQU (SSIZE-20)*1024 ;ADDR OFFSET FROM 3400
                ;                           (20K SYSTEM)
BC00 =          CCP     EQU 3400H+BIAS          ;BASE OF CCP
C406 =          BDOS    EQU CCP+806H            ;BASE OF BDOS
D200 =          BIOS    EQU CCP+1600H           ;BASE OF BIOS
```

This BIOS starts out describing itself, where it comes from, and what it's for. It comes from "WW Components," is for the Imsai 8080, and is version 2.7 of the BIOS.

Address Location Arithmetic

Next, we come to a very important part of the BIOS. All BIOS listings contain some calculations in the beginning that define and then set up the beginning address of the BIOS, itself, in memory. The addresses are usually calculated according to a set of rules laid down by Digital Research (the developers of CP/M). They start out by specifying the memory size that the BIOS is working with. In the present example, we're looking at a BIOS that's set up for a 56K memory size. (If your BIOS has other weird statements in it at this point, such as various options that must be set to true or false, ignore them. They won't influence this discussion.)

In the first line, we see that the size of the computer's memory, MSIZE, is set to 56 (38 hex). All BIOS.ASM files should have such an equate. If we want to change our BIOS to work on a machine with a different memory size, the first thing that we will do is change this number to the appropriate value.

The next important number looks a bit strange; it's called BIAS. (In other listings, it may have other names, like IOBIAS.) It's the distance, in memory, between where the CPM system is on your system and where it is on a "virgin" CP/M as it comes from the factory. Brand new systems are configured for 20K memories, and are then moved up to the top of memory where they will reside in a particular machine. BIAS is related to a certain magic number—yes, a genuinely magic number called N—which we will be discussing in the last section of this chapter: how to insert your driver into the BIOS. We'll have a lot more to say about this later.

BIAS is used to define the starting locations of the major parts of the CP/M system: CCP, BDOS, and BIOS. The "standard" starting location for the bottom of the CCP is 3400 in a 20K system. As you can see, the CCP is 806 hex bytes long in this listing, since BDOS starts at CCP+806H. The CCP and the BDOS, together, are 1600 hex bytes long so, in our 56K system at least, BIOS ends up starting at D200 hex.

I/O Equates and Other Goodies

In the next section of code, shown in Listing 9-1, the BIOS very kindly tells us something about the UART: namely, the meaning of each bit when we read the "status" of an I/O device. Thus, bit 1 is "receiver ready," and so forth. This will be useful information later. Following this is a series of "equates," which are places where certain variables and addresses in the BIOS are given values. We see that the CRT status port "CRTST" is at 03 hex, the keyboard data port is at 14 hex, the variable RXRDY is given a value of 2, and so on.

Listing 9-1. The Bits in an I/O Device

```
          ; *****************************************************
          ;       I/O DEFINITION EQUATES
          ; *****************************************************
          ;       USEFUL THINGS TO KNOW
          ;       MPU-B STATUS PORT
          ;            (TERMINAL/TRANSMITTER REFERENCE)

          ;       0 = TxRDY       TRANSMITTER READY
          ;       1 = RxRDY       RECEIVER READY
          ;       2 = TxE         TRANSMITTER EMPTY
          ;       3 = PE          PARITY ERROR
          ;       4 = OE          OVERRUN ERROR
          ;       5 = FE          FRAMING ERROR
          ;       6 = SYNDET      SYCN DETECT
          ;       7 = DSR         DATA SET READY

          ;CONSOLE STATUS PORT (IN HEX) - 15 = PARALLEL
          ;                              13 OR 4 = SERIAL
          ;                              3 = SYSTEM
          ;CONSOLE DATA PORT (IN HEX) -   14 = PARALLEL
          ;                              12 OR 4 = SERIAL
          ;                              2 = SYSTEM

0003 =    CRTST    EQU  3H              ;CRT STATUS PORT
0002 =    CRTDATA  EQU  2H              ;CRT DATA PORT
0015 =    IKBST    EQU  15H             ;IKB1 STATUS PORT
0014 =    IKBDATA  EQU  14H             ;IKB1 DATA PORT
F803 =    VIODATA  EQU  0F803H          ;VIO DATA PORT
0002 =    RXRDY    EQU  02H             ;CONSOLE STATUS
          ;                              READY BIT (RxRDY)
0003 =    IOBYTE   EQU  0003H           ;INTEL I/O BYTE
F800 =    VIOINIT  EQU  0F800H          ;VIO INIT ENTRY POINT
FFFD =    VIOID    EQU  0FFFDH          ;POINTER TO VIO ID
0023 =    PRTS     EQU  23H             ;PRINTER STATUS PORT
0022 =    PRT      EQU  22H             ;PRINTER DATA PORT
```

Notice especially PRTS and PRT, the printer status port and the printer data port, respectively. We'll be using the numbers that they're equated to, 23 hex and 22 hex, when we write our printer driver.

The ORG Statement and the Jump Table

In the next section of code, we finally get to the actual beginning of our program: the ORG statement. Usually, this location is defined in terms of various other locations which, in turn, are defined in terms of the memory size of your computer, among other things. In this case, the ORG is at the start of BIOS plus 0C70 hex. The listing doesn't start at the beginning of BIOS because all the drivers for the disk system are located there, between D200 and D200+0C70. Our listing is really only a small part of the BIOS: the nondisk part.

But think about this. How is BDOS, which wants to call some driver routine in the BIOS, going to find it? If we fool around—as we're going to do in this chapter—adding instructions to the BIOS and reassembling it so we can insert our driver in it, the starting addresses of all the drivers following the one we changed will be different. How will BDOS find them? The answer is that it makes use of a clever programming idea called a "jump table."

A jump table is merely a bunch of jumps at the beginning of the listing. Each jump goes to one of the driver routines, like LIST, and CONST, and so on. Since these jumps are part of the listing we're going to reassemble, the values in their address fields will change when we reassemble the file. Thus,

Listing 9-2. Jump Table

```
                ; *********************************************
                ;          USER CUSTOMIZED I/O DEVICES.       *
                ;           DO NOT REARRANGE JMP TABLE.       *
                ; *********************************************

DE70                      ORG     BIOS+0C70H

DE70 C3F8DE     INITIO:   JMP     INITVC
DE73 C3BFDE     LIST:     JMP     LISTIO
DE76 C3B3DE     LISTST:   JMP     LISTSTIO
DE79 C388DE     CONST:    JMP     CONSTIO
DE7C C39BDE     CONIN:    JMP     CONINIO
DE7F C3A7DE     CONOUT:   JMP     CONOUTIO
DE82 C3CBDE     PUNCH:    JMP     PUNCHIO
DE85 C3D7DE     READER:   JMP     READERIO
```

BIOS doesn't care where the driver routines themselves are, it just cares where the jump table is, and the jump table is always in the same place: at the beginning of the listing. BIOS "calls" one of the locations in the jump table, and the jump takes BDOS to the proper driver.

Notice, however, that BDOS assumes the jumps in the jump table (Listing 9-2) will always be in the same order. When it calls on the second jump in the table, it expects to find a jump to LISTIO, not PUNCHIO. That's why the listing says "DO NOT REARRANGE JUMP TABLE."

The Dreaded IOBYTE and the Trouble It Causes

Now we can actually start to follow a trail through the listing to our destination. Look at the jump table; the second jump is to LISTIO. This is to the LIST device. As you recall, CP/M permits different physical devices to be assigned to different logical devices. There are four logical devices:

CON:
RDR:
PUN:
LST:

which stand for console, reader, punch, and list. There are also various physical devices, like TTY:, and CRT:, and LPT:. You can change the assignments of physical to logical devices by using STAT. When you do this, STAT changes something called the IOBYTE, which is location 3 in memory.

Now, when BIOS gets a call to the LIST routine, it doesn't know what physical device it's intended for until it checks the IOBYTE. Based on what it finds there, it will either go to the driver for the printer, or to some other driver. That's why LISTIO and LISTSTIO (for "list status I/O") aren't really driver routines but, instead, are a different form of jump table. Here's what they look like:

```
               ;      LIST OUT - LST:
               LISTIO:
DEBF CDE3DE           CALL DISPATCH
DEC2 03               DB    3         ;USE IOBYTE BITS 7-6
DEC3 55DF             DW  CRTOUT      ;00 - TTY: (CRT OUTPUT)
DEC5 55DF             DW  CRTOUT      ;01 - CRT: (CRT OUTPUT)
DEC7 35DF             DW  LPTOUT      ;10 - LPT: (LINE PTR OUTPUT)
DEC9 6FDF             DW  VIOOUT      ;11 - UL1: (VIDEO OUTPUT)
```

This section works by first calling a routine named DISPATCH which looks at the IOBYTE and decides which of the four routines for the four possible physical I/O devices it should go to. Usually, the line printer is assigned to the LST: device, so DISPATCH will figure this out from the IOBYTE and jump to the address in the third DW statement in this routine, which is called LPTOUT for "line printer output."

In some versions of BIOS, the IOBYTE is not used and this whole section of code is nonexistent. This is true of the example BIOS provided in Digital Research's *CP/M Alteration Guide*. In other versions, it's implemented in a different way. Let's follow along to LPTOUT (Listing 9-3) and see what that looks like.

Listing 9-3. Line Printer Output Subroutine

```
                  ; ************************************************
                  ;         LIST CHARACTER IN C
                  ; ************************************************
DF35 DB23         LPTOUT: IN   PRTS    ;CHECK STATUS PORT
DF37 E685                 ANI 85H      ;MASK OFF BITS
DF39 EE85                 XRI 85H      ;ALL BITS SET?
DF3B C235DF               JNZ LPTOUT   ;NO-NOT READY
DF3E 79                   MOV A,C      ;YES, CHARACTER TO A-REGISTER
DF3F D322                 OUT PRT      ;SEND TO PRINTER
DF41 C9                   RET          ;RETURN
```

Well, would you look at that! It's the actual instructions to tell the UART to accept a character and send it on to the printer. We've reached the end of our journey; this is the very routine that we're going to modify. For a change, it doesn't call another routine–it's the end of the line.

The PRTS (printer status) and PRT (printer) constants were defined earlier to be 23 hex and 22 hex. These are the "ports" that are accessed by the IN and OUT instructions.

The IN Instruction

IN and OUT instructions are the chief way that the 8080 microprocessor communicates with the outside world. As their names imply, IN gets data from a data port and puts it in the A-register, while OUT sends data from the A-register to a data port. There are 256 possible data ports: the appropriate

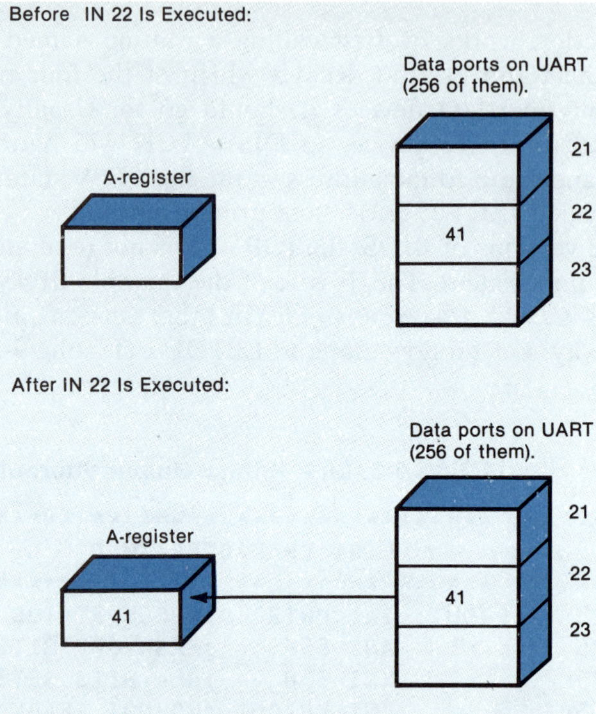

Fig. 9-2. The IN instruction.

one is specified by a 2-digit hex number (or a label equated to it) in the address field.

Note that the data ports and their addresses are not the same as memory and its addresses. The data ports are a separate group of registers and, since there are only 256 of them, they are addressed with 2-digit hex numbers. This is illustrated in Fig. 9-2. Thus, the 5A in the instruction "IN 5A" refers to a data port, *not* to memory address 5A.

The byte that is read into the A-register can either be data, such as a 41 hex "A" character read from the keyboard, or it can be a "status byte," whose purpose is to inform your program about the status of a UART or an input/output device. The values of a status byte must be known from the operation manuals for the UART or input/output device.

The OUT Instruction

As noted above, OUT takes an 8-bit byte *from* the A-register and puts it into the data port specified in the operand field of the instruction. This byte can either be data that is to be transferred to an output device (such as a 41

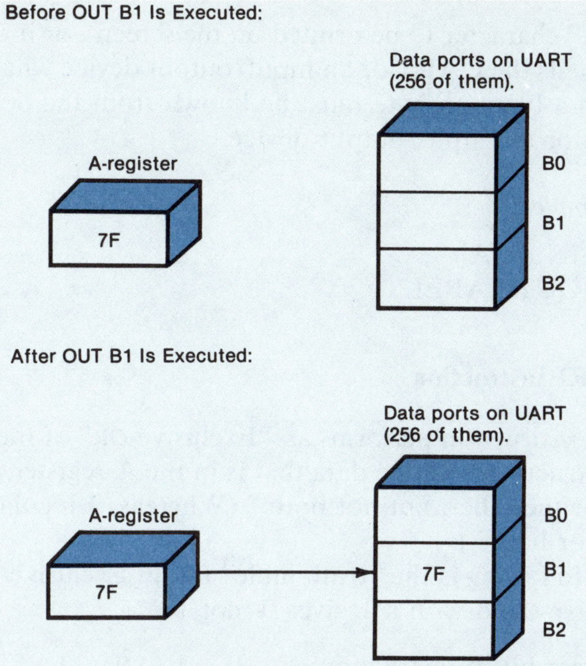

Fig. 9-3. The OUT instruction.

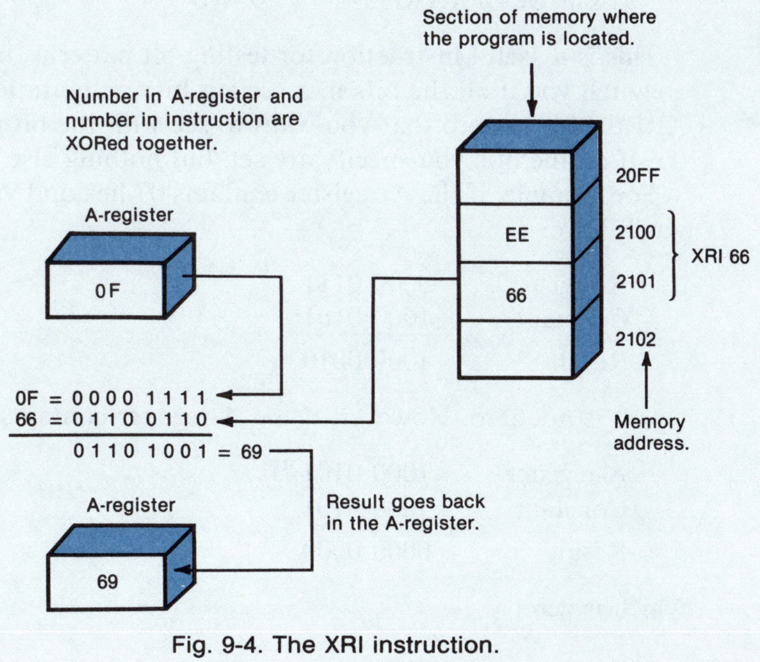

Fig. 9-4. The XRI instruction.

hex "A" character to be printed on the screen), or it can be a "function byte" which tells the UART or an input/output device what to do. The values to be used in a function byte must be known from the operation manuals for the UART or the input/output device.

Examples:

```
IN   5Ah
OUT LABEL
```

The XRI Instruction

This instruction performs an "Exclusive-OR" of the one-byte data that is in the instruction with the data that is in the A-register. An Exclusive-OR means "one or the other, but not both." (Whereas, a regular OR means "one or the other, or both.")

The following is the "truth table" for an Exclusive-OR. Note that a 1 that is Exclusive-ORed with a 1 gives 0, not 1.

Data bit in instruction:	0	1	0	1
Data bit in A-register:	0	0	1	1
Exclusive-OR (XRI)	0	1	1	0

This is a useful instruction for testing bit patterns, because it will immediately tell you if all the bits in a certain bit configuration are set to 1. Simply XRI the bit pattern that you want to see with the bit pattern in the A-register. If all the bits you specify are set, but nothing else is, the result will be 0.

For example, if the A-register contains 07 hex and you XRI it with 85 hex, you'll have:

A-register	0000 0111
Constant	1000 0101
Result	1000 0010

which is not zero. However, if the A-register contains 85 hex, you'll get:

A-register	1000 0101
Constant	1000 0101
Result	0000 0000

which is zero.

The first thing we do in LPTOUT is read the status of the printer port to see if the printer is ready to receive data. We do this with an IN instruction to the port that holds the printer status: number 23 hex. This will return a byte that looks like this:

DSR	SYNDET	FE	OE	PE	TxE	RxRDY	TxRDY
7	6	5	4	3	2	1	0

Now, what we want to see when the printer is ready to receive a character is this: the DSR, TxE, and TxRDY bits must be set. The other bits can be anything they like. So we first mask off the other bits with an ANI (AND immediate) instruction, using an 85 hex, which is a 10000101 binary. As a result, only bits 7, 2, and 0 can have a value other than zero. They *may* be zero, but they may also be a one. All the other bits are definitely a zero.

Now, we want to make sure that bits 7, 2, and 0 are set to zero, so we XRI the A-register with 85 again. If not, we go back to check again with the JNZ instruction.

Once all the bits are set properly in the status word, we're ready to receive data. The data byte has been in the C-register all along. (Remember how you put it there yourself before doing a call to BDOS?) So we move it to the A-register, and then OUT it to the printer output port, which is 22 hex. Then we return.

What could be simpler?

I/O Initialization

Usually, the particular UART you're using needs to be initialized before it can function properly. Thus, there is a section of code in the BIOS that is activated every time you do a warm boot (or a cold one). Listing 9-4 shows what this routine looks like.

Different UARTs need different kinds of initialization. (You can find out what yours needs from its spec sheet.) In our example, our UART is a strange little fellow that wants to be told "0, 0, 0, 40, AE, 27" before he can do anything. Look at the listing. Every time an "OUT CRTST" is executed, the value in the A-register is sent to the crt status register (3 hex). And, every time an "OUT PRTS" is executed, the value is sent to the printer status register (23 hex). Thus, the sequence of numbers referred to in Listing 9-4 is sent to both the crt port and the printer port of the UART.

Listing 9-4. I/O Initialization Code

```
                ; ******************************************************
                ;       INIT USER I/O; I.E., CONSOLE, PUNCH, AND LIST DEV.
                ******************************************************

                INITVC:
                ;       INIT UART (RECOMMENDED CMDS BY IMSAI)
DEF8 AF                 XRA A
DEF9 D303               OUT CRTST
DEFB D303               OUT CRTST
DEFD D303               OUT CRTST
DEFF D323               OUT PRTS
DF01 D323               OUT PRTS
DF03 D323               OUT PRTS
DF05 3E40               MVI A,40H  ;RST 8251
DF07 D303               OUT CRTST
DF09 D323               OUT PRTS
DF0B 3EAE               MVI A,0AEH ;MODE
DF0D D303               OUT CRTST
DF0F D323               OUT PRTS
DF11 3E27               MVI A,27H  ;CMD
DF13 D303               OUT CRTST
DF15 D323               OUT PRTS
```

If you're changing from one printer to another, you probably won't have to add anything to this initialization process, but if you add a driver that wasn't there before, then you'll have to add code in this section to initialize the new ports on your UART.

THE COMPLETE BIOS LISTING

In Listing 9-5, we show the complete BIOS listing from which the various sections used previously were extracted. Look it over and see if you can locate them. To return to our analogy of finding your way around in a strange city, glancing over this listing is like getting a view of the city from an airplane. You'll see how the various far-flung locations lie in relation to each other. Remember that even this is not the entire BIOS, since all the disk I/O has been (mercifully) left out by the firm that sold us the system.

Listing 9-5. The Complete BIOS Listing

```
                ;TITLE ++ BIOS FOR DIO WITH CP/M 2.2 REV 2.7 ++
                ; ******************************************************
                ;       BIOS FOR IMSAI DIO-C CONTROLLER WITH CP/M 2.2
                ; ******************************************************
                ;       BIOS VERSION 2.7: SINGLE DENSITY, 128 B/S
                ;                         DOUBLE DENSITY, 256 B/S
                ;                         DOUBLE DENSITY, 1024 B/S
                ; ******************************************************

0000 =          FALSE   EQU  0
FFFF =          TRUE    EQU  NOT FALSE

0038 =          MSIZE   EQU  56              ;MEMORY SIZE IN K-BYTES
0036 =          SSIZE   EQU  MSIZE-2         ;2K FOR CP/M, BIOS, AND BUFF
001B =          REVNUM  EQU  27              ;BIOS REV #
0016 =          CPMREV  EQU  22              ;CP/M REV #

                ;       "BIAS" IS ADDRESS OFFSET FROM 3400H FOR
                ;       MEMORY SYSTEMS OTHER THAN 16K (REFERRED TO
                ;       AS "B" THROUGHOUT THE TEXT).

8800 =          BIAS    EQU  (SSIZE-20)*1024 ;ADDR OFFSET FROM 3400
                ;                             (20K SYSTEM)
BC00 =          CCP     EQU  3400H+BIAS      ;BASE OF CCP
C406 =          BDOS    EQU  CCP+806H        ;BASE OF BDOS
D200 =          BIOS    EQU  CCP+1600H       ;BASE OF BIOS

                ; ******************************************************
                ;       I/O DEFINITION EQUATES
                ; ******************************************************
                ;       USEFUL THINGS TO KNOW
                ;       MPU-B STATUS PORT
                ;           (TERMINAL/TRANSMITTER REFERENCE)

                ;       0 = TxRDY            TRANSMITTER READY
                ;       1 = RxRDY            RECEIVER READY
                ;       2 = TxE              TRANSMITTER EMPTY
                ;       3 = PE               PARITY ERROR
                ;       4 = OE               OVERRUN ERROR
                ;       5 = FE               FRAMING ERROR
                ;       6 = SYNDET           SYCN DETECT
```

```
                ;       7 = DSR                    DATA SET READY

                ;CONSOLE STATUS PORT (IN HEX) - 15 = PARALLEL
                ;                              13 OR 4 = SERIAL
                ;                              3 = SYSTEM
                ;CONSOLE DATA PORT (IN HEX) -  14 = PARALLEL
                ;                              12 OR 4 = SERIAL
                ;                              2 = SYSTEM
0003 =          CRTST   EQU  3H                ;CRT STATUS PORT
0002 =          CRTDATA EQU  2H                ;CRT DATA PORT
0015 =          IKBST   EQU  15H               ;IKB1 STATUS PORT
0014 =          IKBDATA EQU  14H               ;IKB1 DATA PORT
F803 =          VIODATA EQU  0F803H            ;VIO DATA PORT
0002 =          RXRDY   EQU  02H               ;CONSOLE STATUS
                ;                                READY BIT (RxRDY)
0003 =          IOBYTE  EQU  0003H             ;INTEL I/O BYTE
F800 =          VIOINIT EQU  0F800H            ;VIO INIT ENTRY POINT
FFFD =          VIOID   EQU  0FFFDH            ;POINTER TO VIO ID
0023 =          PRTS    EQU  23H               ;PRINTER STATUS PORT
0022 =          PRT     EQU  22H               ;PRINTER DATA PORT

                ; ********************************************************
                ;       USER CUSTOMIZED I/O DEVICES.                     *
                ;       DO NOT REARRANGE JMP TABLE.                      *
                ; ********************************************************

DE70                    ORG  BIOS+0C70H

DE70 C3F8DE INITIO:     JMP  INITVC
DE73 C3BFDE LIST:       JMP  LISTIO
DE76 C3B3DE LISTST:     JMP  LISTSTIO
DE79 C388DE CONST:      JMP  CONSTIO
DE7C C39BDE CONIN:      JMP  CONINIO
DE7F C3A7DE CONOUT:     JMP  CONOUTIO
DE82 C3CBDE PUNCH:      JMP  PUNCHIO
DE85 C3D7DE READER:     JMP  READERIO

                ;       CONSOLE STATUS - CON:
                CONSTIO:
DE88 CD8FDE             CALL CONS              ;GETS STAT OF SPECIFIC DEVICE
DE8B C8                 RZ                     ;IF NOT READY RETURN 0 IN A
DE8C 3EFF               MVI  A,0FFH            ;ELSE RETURN FF
DE8E C9                 RET                    ;Z FLAG SET CORRESPONDINGLY
```

```
DE8F CDE3DE CONS:    CALL DISPATCH
DE92 01              DB   1            ;USE IOBYTE BITS 1-0
DE93 45DF            DW   CRTSTAT      ;00 - TTY: (CRT STATUS)
DE95 45DF            DW   CRTSTAT      ;01 - CRT: (CRT STATUS)
DE97 45DF            DW   CRTSTAT      ;10 - BAT: (CRT STATUS)
DE99 5FDF            DW   IKBSTAT      ;11 - UC1: (IKB1 STATUS)
            ;        CONSOLE IN - CON:
            CONINIO:
DE9B CDE3DE          CALL DISPATCH
DE9E 01              DB     1          ;USE IOBYTE BITS 1-0
DE9F 4ADF            DW   CRTIN        ;00 - TTY: (CRT INPUT)
DEA1 4ADF            DW   CRTIN        ;01 - CRT: (CRT INPUT)
DEA3 4ADF            DW   CRTIN        ;10 - BAT: (CRT INPUT)
DEA5 64DF            DW   IKBIN        ;11 - UC1: (IKB1 INPUT)

            ;        CONSOLE OUT - CON:
            CONOUTIO:
DEA7 CDE3DE          CALL DISPATCH
DEAA 01              DB     1          ;USE IOBYTE BITS 1-0
DEAB 55DF            DW   CRTOUT       ;00 - TTY: (CRT OUTPUT)
DEAD 55DF            DW   CRTOUT       ;01 - CRT: (CRT OUTPUT)
DEAF 55DF            DW   CRTOUT       ;10 - BAT: (CRT OUTPUT)
DEB1 6FDF            DW   VIOOUT       ;11 - UC1: (VIO OUTPUT)

            ;        LIST STATUS - LST:
            LISTSTIO:
DEB3 CDE3DE          CALL DISPATCH
DEB6 03              DB     3          ;USE IOBYTE BITS 7-6
DEB7 42DF            DW   LISTSTC      ;00 - TTY: (CRT OUTPUT)
DEB9 42DF            DW   LISTSTC      ;01 - CRT: (CRT OUTPUT)
DEBB 42DF            DW   LISTSTC      ;10 - LPT: (LINE PTR OUTPUT)
DEBD 42DF            DW   LISTSTC      ;11 - UL1: (VIO OUTPUT)

            ;        LIST OUT - LST:
            LISTIO:
DEBF CDE3DE          CALL DISPATCH
DEC2 03              DB     3          ;USE IOBYTE BITS 7-6
DEC3 55DF            DW   CRTOUT       ;00 - TTY: (CRT OUTPUT)
DEC5 55DF            DW   CRTOUT       ;01 - CRT: (CRT OUTPUT)
DEC7 35DF            DW   LPTOUT       ;10 - LPT: (LINE PTR OUTPUT)
DEC9 6FDF            DW   VIOOUT       ;11 - UL1: (VIDEO OUTPUT)
```

```
              ;        PUNCH OUT - PUN:
              PUNCHIO:
DECB CDE3DE            CALL DISPATCH
DECE 05                DB      5          ;USE IOBYTE BITS 5-4
DECF 55DF              DW   CRTOUT        ;00 - TTY: (CRT OUTPUT)
DED1 73DF              DW   PUNOUT        ;01 - PTP: (H. S. PUNCH OUTPUT)
DED3 6FDF              DW   VIOOUT        ;10 - UP1: (VIO OUTPUT)
DED5 55DF              DW   CRTOUT        ;11 - UP2: (CRT OUTPUT)

              ;        READER IN - RDR:
              READERIO:
DED7 CDE3DE            CALL DISPATCH
DEDA 07                DB      7          ;USE IOBYTE BITS 3-2
DEDB 4ADF              DW   CRTIN         ;00 - TTY: (CRT INPUT)
DEDD 74DF              DW   RDRIN         ;01 - PTR: (H.S. READER INPUT)
DEDF 4ADF              DW   CRTIN         ;10 - UR1: (CRT INPUT)
DEE1 4ADF              DW   CRTIN         ;11 - UR2: (CRT INPUT)
              DISPATCH:
DEE3 E3                XTHL               ;SAVE CALLER'S H, GET TABLE ADD
DEE4 56                MOV  D,M           ;SHIFT COUNT
DEE5 23                INX  H             ;POINT TABLE
DEE6 3A0300            LDA  IOBYTE        ;GET IO ASSIGNMENTS BYTE
DEE9 07       DSHFT:   RLC
DEEA 15                DCR  D
DEEB C2E9DE            JNZ  DSHFT         ;SHIFT TO POSITION BITS
DEEE E606              ANI  06H           ;MASK BITS
DEF0 5F                MOV  E,A           ;D ALREADY CLEAR
DEF1 19                DAD  D             ;INDEX INTO TABLE
DEF2 7E                MOV  A,M
DEF3 23                INX  H             ;TABLE WORD TO HL
DEF4 66                MOV  H,M
DEF5 6F                MOV  L,A
DEF6 E3                XTHL               ;PUT ADDR OF ROUTINE, GET CALLER'S H
DEF7 C9                RET                ;GO TO ROUTINE

              ; *********************************************************
              ;        ;INIT USER I/O; I.E. CONSOLE, PUNCH, AND LIST DEV.
              ; *********************************************************
              INITVC:
              ;        INIT UART (RECOMMENDED CMDS BY IMSAI)
DEF8 AF                XRA  A
DEF9 D303              OUT  CRTST
DEFB D303              OUT  CRTST
```

```
DEFD D303             OUT  CRTST
DEFF D323             OUT  PRTS
DF01 D323             OUT  PRTS
DF03 D323             OUT  PRTS
DF05 3E40             MVI  A,40H        ;RST 8251
DF07 D303             OUT  CRTST
DF09 D323             OUT  PRTS
DF0B 3EAE             MVI  A,0AEH       ;MODE
DF0D D303             OUT  CRTST
DF0F D323             OUT  PRTS
DF11 3E27             MVI  A,27H        ;CMD
DF13 D303             OUT  CRTST
DF15 D323             OUT  PRTS

DF17 21FDFF           LXI  H,VIOID      ;VIO ID 1 ADDRESS
DF1A 3E56             MVI  A, 'V'       ;1ST ID
DF1C BE               CMP  M            ;SAME?
DF1D C22FDF           JNZ  NOVIO
DF20 23               INX  H            ;VIO ID 2 ADDRESS
DF21 3E49             MVI  A,'I'        ;2ND ID
DF23 BE               CMP  M            ;SAME?
DF24 C22FDF           JNZ  NOVIO
DF27 CD00F8           CALL VIOINIT      ;INIT VIO
DF2A 3E97             MVI  A,97H        ;VIO AS OUTPUT
DF2C C331DF           JMP  INITIO1
DF2F 3E94    NOVIO:   MVI  A,94H        ;CRT AS OUTPUT
             INITIO1:
DF31 320300           STA  IOBYTE
DF34 C9               RET

             ; ***********************************************************
             ;        LIST CHARACTER IN C
             ; ***********************************************************
DF35 DB23    LPTOUT:  IN   PRTS         ;CHECK STATUS PORT
DF37 E685             ANI  85H          ;CHECK BOTH READY BITS
DF39 EE85             XRI  85H
DF3B C235DF           JNZ  LPTOUT
DF3E 79               MOV  A,C
DF3F D322             OUT  PRT
DF41 C9               RET               ;USER PRINTER IO
```

```
              ; ********************************************************
              ;       RETURN LIST STATUS (FF IF READY, ELSE 0)
              ; ********************************************************
DF42 3EFF     LISTSTC:MVI  A,0FFH
DF44 C9               RET

              ; ********************************************************
              ;       CONSOLE STATUS RETURNED IN A.
              ; ********************************************************
              CRTSTAT:
DF45 DB03             IN   CRTST        ;STATUS PORT
DF47 E602             ANI  RXRDY        ;TEST RxRDY
DF49 C9               RET               ;Z=1, CHAR NOT READY

              ; ********************************************************
              ;       CONSOLE IN RETURNS THE CHARACTER IN A
              ; ********************************************************
              CRTIN:
DF4A CD45DF           CALL CRTSTAT
DF4D CA4ADF           JZ   CRTIN        ;GET RxRDY
DF50 DB02             IN   CRTDATA      ;GET CHARACTER
DF52 E67F             ANI  7FH          ;STRIP PARITY
DF54 C9               RET

              ; ********************************************************
              ;       CRTOUT SENDS THE CHARACTER IN C TO OUTPUT
              ; ********************************************************
              CRTOUT:
DF55 DB03             IN   CRTST        ;GET STATUS
DF57 0F               RRC               ;TxRDY?
DF58 D255DF           JNC  CRTOUT       ;REPEAT, NOT READY
DF5B 79               MOV  A,C          ;CHAR TO ACCUM
DF5C D302             OUT  CRTDATA      ;CHARACTER TO PORT
DF5E C9               RET

              ; ********************************************************
              ;       IKB1 STATUS RETURNED IN A.
              ; ********************************************************
              IKBSTAT:
DF5F DB15             IN   IKBST        ;STATUS PORT
DF61 E602             ANI  RXRDY        ;TEST RxRDY
DF63 C9               RET               ;Z=1, CHAR NOT READY
```

```
              ; *******************************************************
              ;       IKB1 IN RETURNS THE CHARACTER IN A
              ; *******************************************************
              IKBIN:
DF64 CD5FDF           CALL IKBSTAT
DF67 CA64DF           JZ   IKBIN        ;GET RxRDY
DF6A DB14             IN   IKBDATA      ;GET CHARACTER
DF6C E67F             ANI  7FH          ;STRIP PARITY
DF6E C9               RET

              ; *******************************************************
              ;       VIOOUT SENDS THE CHARACTER IN C TO VIO
              ; *******************************************************
              VIOOUT:
DF6F 79               MOV  A,C
DF70 C303F8           JMP  VIODATA      ;VIO RETURNS TO CALLER

              ; *******************************************************
              ;       PUNCH CHARACTER IN REGISTER C
              ; *******************************************************
              PUNOUT:
DF73 C9               RET               ;NULL ROUTINE

              ; *******************************************************
              ;       READ CHARACTER INTO A FROM READER DEVICE
              ; *******************************************************
              RDRIN:
DF74 3E1A             MVI  A,1AH        ;ENTER END OF FILE
              ;                          (REPLACE LATER)
DF76 E67F             ANI  7FH          ;REMEMBER TO
              ;                          STRIP PARITY BIT
DF78 C9               RET
DF79                  END
```

HOW TO MODIFY YOUR PRINTER DRIVER

In order to create a new driver for our BIOS, you first must determine the kind of driver program you need to write. You must know what kind of printer you have and which communications "protocol" it uses. "Protocol" is just a fancy word for "procedure." In this case, it means the procedure by which the the printer tells the computer that it is ready to accept data.

Protocols and Other Diplomatic Niceties

With some printers, you can simply wait for it to be ready, throw a character at it, wait for it to be ready, throw a character at it, and so on, until you're done, and it will print the characters just fine. Such a printer is called a "standard serial printer," or a "teletype-like printer." The Epson is such a beast. Other more complex printers, such as the "daisy-wheel" printers, require one of two possible advanced protocols, either "xon/xoff" or "etx/ack." For instance, the NEC printer needs etx/ack while the Diablo 630 likes xon/xoff. These protocols are designed to allow the printer to work with a bunch of characters at a time rather than with single characters.

XON/XOFF Protocol

You have probably already used xon/xoff and not known it. Xon/xoff is the same thing as the "control–s/control–q" that CP/M uses to freeze and unfreeze the scrolling of the display on the screen. In CP/M, control–s will freeze the display. Striking any key, thereafter, generates a control–q which will unfreeze the display. Control–s means xoff, i.e., "turn off transmission" while control–q means xon, i.e., "turn on transmission."

A printer uses this technique of xon/xoff when it has a built-in "character buffer" that can hold a certain number of characters for printing. The buffer may be, for example, 1024 bytes long. What the buffer does is allow the computer to send characters to the printer at a fairly fast rate (say, 1200 baud, or about 120 characters per second) and then hold them while the slower printer mechanism prints them out (which may occur at roughly 30 characters per second). This way, while the buffer in the printer is emptying, the computer can go on its merry way and do more processing. Provided the computer is set up properly, you could then be editing a file while the printer was spitting characters out on the paper, and your text editor would not be slowed down by the 30 character/second printer. You would only notice a delay when the printer needed its buffer filled again, and this would occur at a rate of 1200 or more baud, so it wouldn't take long.

Normally, the way all this happens is that after your printer driver sends each character, it reads a status word from the printer and looks to see if the printer is sending back a control–s, which means "Stop! my buffer is full. Don't send any more characters until it's empty." If there is no control–s being sent back, the computer sends the next character, and so on, until it receives a control–s. At that point, it goes into a wait loop searching for a control–q to come from the printer. The control–q means the printer buffer is once again empty. ("Hello, I'm empty; you can send more data.") Fig. 9–5 shows how this looks in flowchart form.

The point of all this protocol is that the computer only waits for the printer after every 1024 characters, instead of after every character, and is, therefore, free to do other tasks while printing is taking place.

ETX/ACK Protocol

Etx/ack protocol is similar to that of the xon/xoff procedure, but it is implemented differently. In this case, a block of characters (often 128) is sent to the printer followed by an "etx" character (03 hex = control–c). "Etx" means "end of text." Then, after the printer has printed out the entire block of characters, it sends an "ack" (06 hex = control–f) back to the computer. "Ack" means "Acknowledge. I have received your last transmission."

Writing a Sample Driver

In the last section, where we explored the BIOS listing, we found a driver for the simplest kind of printer–a "teletype-like" device with no advanced protocol. What we're going to do in this section is write a driver for a printer that uses xon/xoff protocol. Then, in the next section, we'll show you how to insert this driver into your BIOS so your entire CP/M system can use the new printer.

Specifically, our printer will be a Diablo 630 daisy wheel. We are using it for word processing and it is hooked to our CP/M system through a serial board running at 1200 baud. The serial board uses an Intel 8251 UART, which is what our driver must talk to.

Look back at the driver in the last section. When it wants to know if it can send a character, it checks to see if 3 bits are set: number 7 for "Data Set Ready," number 2 for "Transmitter Empty," and number 0 for "Transmitter Ready." Here's how the status word looks with these bits set:

Signal	DSR	SYNDET	FE	OE	PE	TxE	RxRDY	TxRDY
	1	0	0	0	0	1	0	1
Bit number	7	6	5	4	3	2	1	0

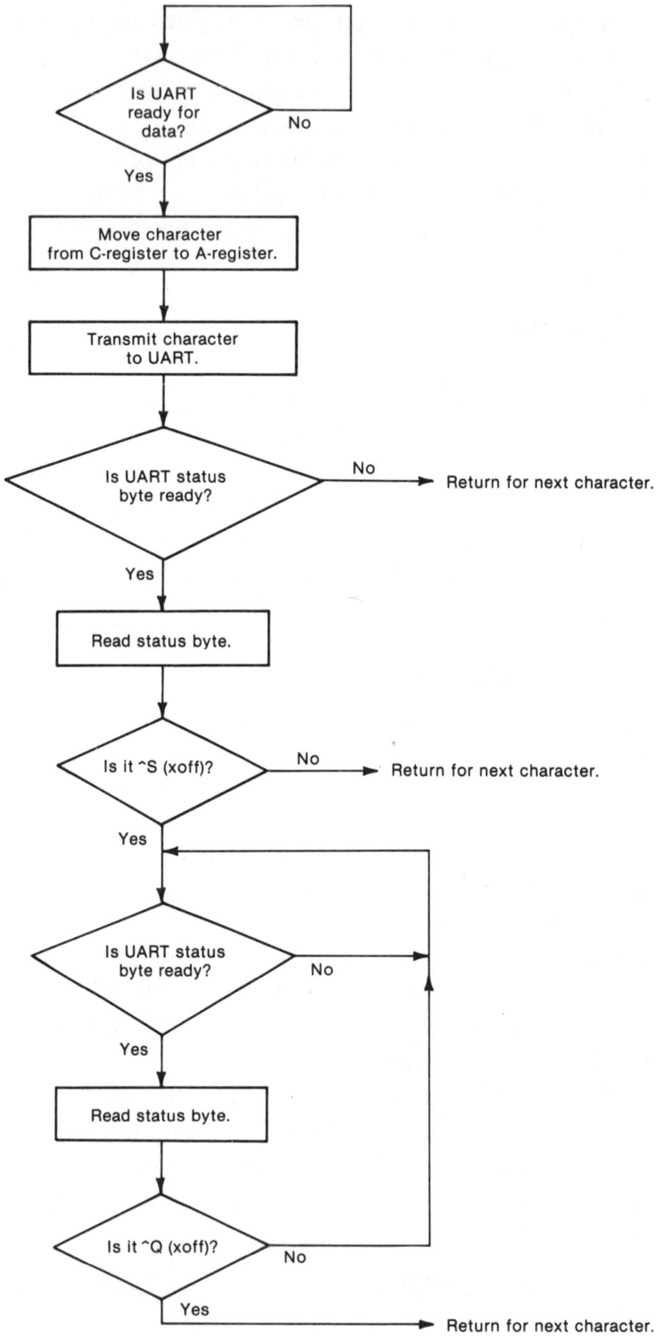

Fig. 9-5. Flowchart of the XON/XOFF protocol program.

Using the xon/xoff protocol is somewhat more complicated. We need to ask the UART two different kinds of questions: first, whether the UART is ready to receive a character *from* the BIOS, and second, whether the UART has a character ready to give *to* the BIOS. In the first case, we ask the UART whether bits 0 and 2, for "transmitter ready" and "transmitter empty" are set. In the second case, we want to know whether bit 1, for "receiver ready," is set.

When a program CALLed the driver for the simple "teletype-like" printer driver in the last section, there was only one possible outcome. The driver would wait until the UART said the printer was free and then send the character.

With "xon/xoff," there are two things that can happen when a program calls the driver to send a character to the printer. In either case, a character gets sent to the UART to be transmitted to the printer. Then, either (1) the UART will *not* have sent an "xoff" (in which case, control will return to the calling program so that it can get another character) or (2) the UART *will* have sent an "xoff" (in which case, the driver will not return to the calling program, but will wait until the "xon" is received before it goes on). Listing 9–6 is the listing for the new driver.

We're assuming here that we don't need to do anything further to initialize the UART. If we did, we'd need to add the appropriate instructions to the initialization part of the program. From the preceding descriptions, you shouldn't have any trouble following the operation of the driver.

Testing the Driver

If you're very confident about your programming, you may want to go right ahead and assemble your new driver right into the BIOS without testing it out. If so, you can skip the next few paragraphs.

Inserting the new driver into the BIOS and writing it on the system tracks of a diskette (as we'll describe in the next section) is somewhat involved, and not something you want to do too many times. It would be nice if there was an easier way to test out your new driver to see if it works. Then, you could debug it without going through the whole procedure of assemblying a new BIOS every time you change a single instruction in your code. Here's how we do it:

1. We put the driver routine at 100 hex, just like any other program. We can use either the DDT "a" command, or assemble it with ASM.
2. We put a "jmp 100" instruction at the start of the printer driver routine in the BIOS.

Listing 9-6. New Driver Program

```
; ***********************************************************
;       LIST CHARACTER IN C                                 *
; ***********************************************************

; New xon/xoff printer driver.
; (was just a RET return instruction.)

LPTOUT: in   prts    ;Input 8251 status
        ani  05h     ;AND 8251 for ready to send
        xri  05h     ;Exclusive-OR to get zero flag
        jnz  lptout  ;Loop till UART register ready
        mov  a,c     ;Get list character from C to A
        out  prt     ;Output to UART data register and send
        in   prts    ;Is UART ready with a character
        ani  02h     ;Does receiver have a character ready
        xri  02h     ;Mask
        rnz          ;If not zero, then continue normally
        in   prt     ;Yes-get the character
        cpi  13h     ;Is it a ^S freeze (xoff)
        rnz          ;Nope-so skip it
lpt1:   in   prts    ;It was a ^S so now we must wait for
                     ;a ^Q to return
        ani  02h
        xri  02h
        jnz  lpt1
        in   prs     ;Character is ready
        cpi  11h     ;Is it a ^Q (xon)
        jnz  lpt1    ;No, so loop till it is, i.e., let ptr
                     ;buffer empty
        ret          ;Finally, a ^Q so return for next char
```

We'll assume at this point that you've written an appropriate driver routine of your own. It may not be perfect, but it's ready for a preliminary test. Thus, as we describe how to test our routine, you can—if you're ready—follow the same steps with your own routine.

First, you have to know where to put the "jump 100" instruction. This isn't hard if you've assembled your existing BIOS into a PRN file. Simply look through the listing for the printer driver routine and write down the address where it starts. In our 56K system, this address is DF35 hex, as you can see from the BIOS listing that was described in the last section.

So, either write your driver with your word-processing program (call it NEWDRIVE.ASM), assemble it to get a HEX file, and call it in with DDT:

```
A>ddt newdrive.hex
```

or, type it in directly from DDT using the "a" command. In either case, ORG it at 100 hex.

At this point, your printer should not be operating (you have not toggled it on with control–p). Use the "a" command to insert a "jmp 100" at the start of the driver routine in BIOS. For our particular BIOS, we'd say:

```
-aDF35
DF35   jmp 100
DF38   .
-
```

Note that you are modifying the very BIOS that you're operating with. If you do something wrong, the system may die, so save your files before you get in too deep.

Now comes the moment of truth. Toggle on the printer by typing control–p. Hit "return" a few times. The printer should respond. Type something, and then hit return. It should be printed out. If the wrong thing, or nothing, happens, either your driver is defective or your "jmp 100" instruction is in the wrong place. Back to the old drawing board.

INSTALLING THE NEW DRIVER INTO YOUR BIOS

Once you have the driver working in this nonstandard location, you can install it into your CP/M system. That's the subject of this section.

Before we can complete this process, you'll need to learn about two new CP/M utility programs, MOVCPM and SYSGEN, and about the magic number N that we mentioned earlier. We'll cover these topics first, and then summarize the complete procedure at the end of the section.

The MOVCPM Program—What's It Hiding?

MOVCPM is an amazing program. It actually contains within it most of the CP/M operating system. That is, it contains the CCP and BDOS. It may also have part of the BIOS in it. If the people who configured your system did not put the disk part of BIOS in your BIOS.ASM file, then they put it in the MOVCPM program. What MOVCPM may not have in it are the drivers for the other I/O peripherals: the console, the printer, and so on. They're probably in the BIOS.ASM file. MOVCPM may have these routines in it, but they may not work on your equipment, or they may be merely skeletal drivers that don't work on any equipment.

Here's how MOVCPM works. When you call it, it loads three things into memory: (1) the MOVCPM program itself, (2) the CCP, BDOS, and maybe part of BIOS in the form of a COM file, and (3) a bit map, which tells it which bytes of the COM file need to be "relocated" and which don't.

One question that should immediately occur to you is, "where in memory does the MOVCPM *put* this COM file?" It can't put it in high memory where CP/M normally goes, since the actual system we're operating with is already there, and you can't make major changes in the very same sections of code that constitute your operating system, without getting into big trouble. So MOVCPM keeps this version of CP/M in low memory, starting at location 900 hex, which just leaves room for the program and the bit map below it. This version of CP/M is called the system "image," a name that means that the instructions of code look just like the actual operating version of CP/M in high memory, but are in the wrong place to actually execute.

Fig. 9-6 illustrates what memory looks like when MOVCPM is at work. When you call MOVCPM from CP/M, you need to specify two parameters. The first is the size memory that your machine has, 64K or whatever. Second, you need to tell it whether you want the image of CP/M to be moved to high memory and executed. This is something you almost never want, since the CP/M image is probably incomplete and won't work, and will result in a crashed system if you try to execute it. If you *don't* want this to happen, you type an asterisk after the size:

```
A>movcpm 56 *
         ↑  ↑
         |  └──This means "leave the image in low memory; don't relocate or execute it."
         └─────This means "we want to generate CP/M for a 56K system."
```

You can also use an asterisk in the memory field if you want to simply use all the available memory.

```
A>movcpm * *      (Takes 64K in a 64K system, etc.)
```

In our particular case, we can't do that because the upper 8K of our machine, although present, is used for special video drivers. (The routine figures out how much memory you have by testing higher and higher addresses to see if it can put something into each location and then read it out. When it can't, that's the top of memory.)

How does MOVCPM go about moving this "image" of CP/M to high memory? It starts off with all the individual 8080 instructions written as if they were in a 20K system. Next, it figures out the difference or "bias" between a 20K system and the size that we specified, like 56K. Then it uses the bit map to change only those bytes which represent addressees in the code (the last two bytes of a "jmp" instruction, for instance). That's it. The resulting new "image" sits in low memory waiting for the next thing that we want to do with it. Even though the addresses are changed *as if* the BIOS were in high memory, it is not actually moved there.

What we do now is save this image using the SAVE utility. MOVCPM is very helpful here because it tells us just what to type:

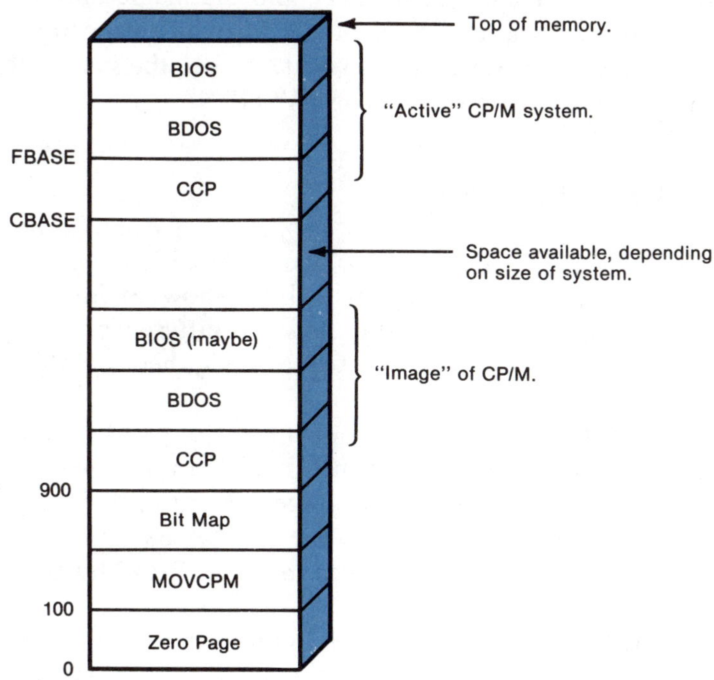

Fig. 9-6. Memory when MOVCPM program is operating.

```
A>movcpm 56 *

CONSTRUCTING 56K CP/M vers 2.2
READY FOR "SYSGEN" OR
"SAVE 45 CPM56.COM"
A>
```

So we type "save 45 cpm56.com". The image is 45 separate 256-byte "pages" long, and MOVCPM suggests we call the file "CPM56.COM", which we're happy to do.

The Urge to Merge

Once we have the file of the CP/M image, CPM56.COM, safely stored on our disk, what then? Well, we're going to merge the BIOS.ASM file, which we've modified by putting our new driver into it, into CPM56.COM, using both a special technique in DDT and the magic number N. Then we'll take the resulting complete image of CP/M (which we can call "CPM56n.COM", where "n" stands for new) and write it onto the system tracks of a formatted but otherwise virgin disk, using SYSGEN.

The Magic Number "N"

Now that you know how to use MOVCPM, you can be admitted to the small and privileged group who know how to find the magic number N. What is this number? Really, it is the difference, or offset, between where MOVCPM puts the image of CP/M and where CP/M actually goes in high memory.

In Figure 9–7, notice how the "image" of CPM that is placed in low memory by the MOVCPM program is related to the image of CP/M that will be placed on the system tracks of the new disk. This new image will occupy exactly the same addresses as the CP/M that is currently running in high memory, except for the changes made to BIOS by the addition of the new driver.

The CCP is located at 980 hex in the system image, but will be at BC00 hex (in our 56K system) when actually installed and running. BDOS is located at 1186 in the image, but will be at C406 when running, and so forth. You can see that all these pairs of numbers are related by the same constant, which we can find by subtracting any two of them.

How Do We Find Out All These Addresses, Anyway?

In order to find the magic number N, we need to know at least one pair of addresses: the one in the MOVCPM image in low memory and the one that is in the running CP/M in high memory. A good "pair" to work on is CBASE, the bottom of the CCP. The first half of this is easy because, in the system image, the CCP is always at 980 hex, no matter what size system you have. CBASE for high memory, as we discussed before in the chapter on BASIC, is not quite so easy to find. However, if you look at locations 6 and 7 hex in memory while CP/M is running (not DDT), you'll find an address that is close to the start of BDOS. The CCP is usually about 800 hex bytes long, so if you subtract 800 from this address, you'll get CBASE. In our case, C406 – 800 = BC06. But we know that the CCP is going to start on a page boundary, so we figure that it's probably at BC00.

Another way to find CBASE is to look at the BIOS.PRN (not the ASM) listing. As we described earlier in the chapter, CBASE and several other fas-

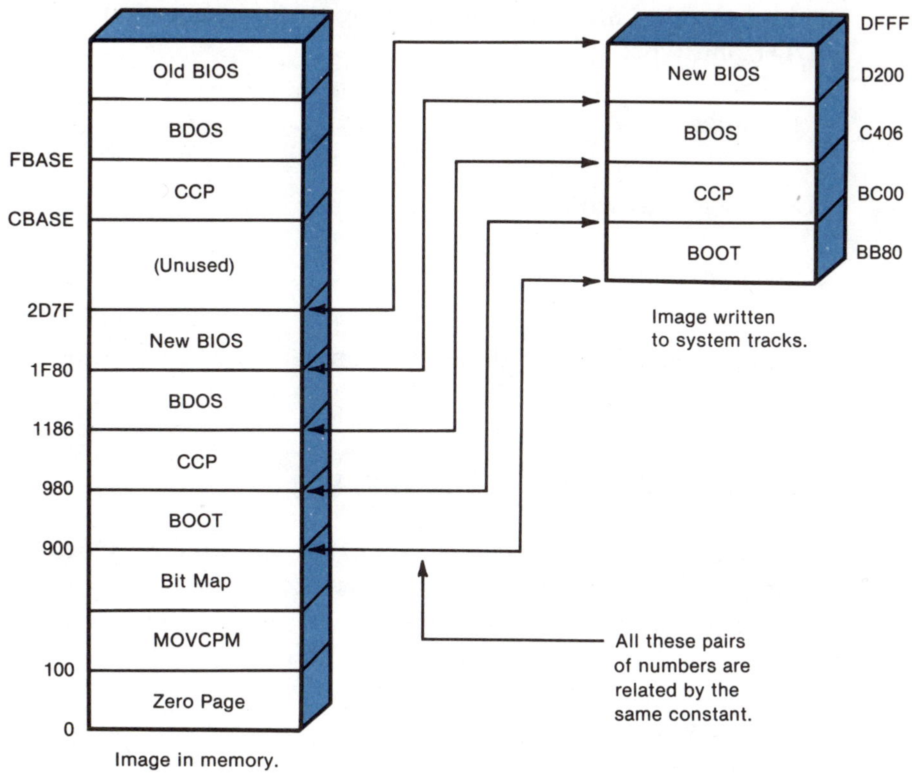

Fig. 9-7. Location of CP/M "image" in memory.

cinating addresses are often part of the address location arithmetic in the beginning of the file. Checking this file, we find that BC00 is, in fact, the start of the CCP.

DDT's Hex Arithmetic Function

Did you know that DDT had a handy function that will perform arithmetic on hexadecimal numbers? Of course you did. If we type:

```
-hx,y
```

where x and y are 4-digit hex numbers, DDT will print out x + y and x–y in hex, for our gratification and amusement.

In this case, we want to know the difference between, say, 980 and BC00. It would also be nice if we got a negative number, so that we could simply add it to other numbers later to perform the conversions. Thus, we get into DDT and type:

```
-h980,bc00
```

DDT responds with:

```
C580,4D80
```

The difference between these two numbers is what we want: 4D80. It is, in fact, our magic number N.

Finding the Magic Number the D.R. Way

In the *CP/M Alteration Guide,* Digital Research provides a table of these magic numbers for different memory sizes. This table will work for some CP/M systems but not for others (such as the one in our examples). The problem is that the table assumes a certain size BIOS. If your BIOS has been enlarged, either by you or by the vendor who configured the system, the table will give you the wrong value.

These are the values of N that are shown in the *CP/M Alteration Guide:*

Memory Size	Offset N
20K	D580
24K	C580
32K	A580
40K	8580
48K	6580
56K	4580
62K	2D80
64K	2580

Note that for our 56K system, it gives a value of 4580 instead of the 4D80 that we know is correct. The difference between these two values is 800 hex, which is just how much additional space our modified BIOS takes up.

If you have the standard-size BIOS, then the table will be useful to you, but you should verify the actual location of your CP/M system by one of the methods previously described before you accept the figures in the table at face value.

What Good Is This Magic Number?

We need to know this number for two reasons. First, we want to be able to look at certain sections of code in the MOVCPM image in low memory and know what we're looking at. We know where things are in BIOS in high memory from the BIOS.ASM listing, and we need to be able to translate this into equivalent locations in low memory. The magic number N does this, as we shall see.

Secondly, we're going to use another one of DDT's useful features—the ability to load a HEX file with a "bias" or offset, instead of at the ORG address of the file. Thus, if we have a HEX file that is ORGed at, say, D200, and we want to load it into memory somewhere else, say at 1F80, we simply figure out the magic number that is the difference of these two numbers and type it into DDT following the "r" (for "read") command. As you can see, this is the same old magic number, 4D80. If, for example, we want to load a HEX file called NEWBIOS.HEX (which is ORGed at D200) using this bias, we type:

```
-inewbios.hex
-r4d80
```

and the file will be placed in memory at 1F80.

INSERTING THE NEW DRIVER INTO THE CP/M SYSTEM

At this point, you should have a working driver routine that you're ready to insert into your CP/M operating system. In the procedure that we're going to describe, we'll make use of the knowledge you've acquired in the previous sections.

Merging Your New Driver Into the BIOS.ASM File

The first thing that we want to do is create a new version of the BIOS.ASM file: one which incorporates your new driver. (Remember that this file will have different names depending on your system: BIOSIO.ASM, GBBIOS.ASM, or whatnot.)

Start by making a copy of the old BIOS.ASM file. Call it NEWBIOS.ASM:

```
A>pip newbios.asm=biosio.asm
```

Bring NEWBIOS.ASM into your word-processing or text-editing program. Delete the program lines for the existing driver. Then, either type in the assembly code for the new driver, or (if your word processer will let you) copy the file containing the new driver into the right place in NEWBIOS.ASM.

Also, if you need to add anything to the initialization part of BIOS to get the UART off on the right foot, now is the time to do it.

Reassemble the new BIOS:

```
A>asm newbios
```

You now have NEWBIOS.HEX and NEWBIOS.PRN.

Create the CP/M Image

You can now use MOVCPM to create the CP/M image, as described in the last section. If you already have the system image (CPM56.COM or whatever) stored as a file, you can skip this step. Refer to the last section to see how MOVCPM is used.

```
A>movcpm 56 *
A>save 45 cpm56.com
```

Of course, the numbers here will be different, depending on your system.

Read in the CP/M Image Using DDT

We're going to use DDT to do the actual merging of the new driver into the system image. Load the system image as you call DDT:

```
A>ddt cpm56.com
```

To make sure that everything is where you think it is, use DDT to explore this image. Here's the beginning of the CCP in the system image:

```
-d980
0980 C3 5C BF C3 58 BF 7F 00 20 20 20 20 20 20 20 20 .\..X...
0990 20 20 20 20 20 20 20 20 43 4F 50 59 52 49 47 48         COPYRIGH
09A0 54 20 28 43 29 20 31 39 37 39 2C 20 44 49 47 49 T (C) 1979, DIGI
          (etc.)
```

It should be just the same as the running CCP in high memory, so look at that:

```
-dbc00
BC00 C3 5C BF C3 58 BF 7F 00 20 20 20 20 20 20 20 20 .\..X...
BC10 20 20 20 20 20 20 20 20 43 4F 50 59 52 49 47 48         COPYRIGH
BC20 54 20 28 43 29 20 31 39 37 39 2C 20 44 49 47 49 T (C) 1979, DIGI
          (etc.)
```

Using the "d" command lets us see that the sign-on message is really there. Check the beginning of BIOS. It should be a jump table:

```
-l1f80
1F80  JMP  D3D3
1F83  JMP  D334
1F86  JMP  DE79
1F89  JMP  DE7C

      (etc.)
```

Now look in the running BIOS. It should be the same thing:

```
-ld200
D200  JMP  D3D3
D203  JMP  D334
D206  JMP  DE79
D209  JMP  DE7C

      (etc.)
```

Find the old driver routine (if there is one) in the system image and in the running BIOS. They may not be the same.

Merge in the New BIOS File

We're going to use DDT to merge the NEWBIOS.HEX file into the image of CP/M in low memory. This is where the magic offset number N comes in. Although NEWBIOS.HEX is ORGed in high memory (at DE70 in our case), we want to lay it down on top of the BIOS part of the system image in low memory (at 2BF0 in our case).

```
-inewbios.hex
```

That puts the file name in the FCB.

```
-r4d80
```

That reads in the file with an offset of 4d80. You should now look at the image with the "l" command to make sure that the new driver is where you want it to be. If so, you're ready to save the image as a file back onto the disk.

```
-g0
A>save 45 cpm56n.com
```

cpm56n.com — The "n" means "new."

45 — This is the same number of 256-byte pages that MOVCPM told you to save originally (unless your modification has expanded BIOS past a page boundary).

Writing the New Image to the System Tracks

Now, we're ready to actually create a new system disk. Take a formatted disk and put it in drive B.

SYSGEN is often used, as you no doubt know, to simply copy the current CP/M system from the system tracks of the working disk to those of a formatted disk. In that case, no file name is specified when we call it. However, we want to use the CPM56n.COM file when we generate our new system, so we type:

```
                    ┌──────── Don't forget the "n".
                    ↓
A>sysgen cpm56n.com
```

SYSGEN will reply with:

```
                                                    ┌──── Type this "b."
                                                    ↓
SYSGEN VER 2.0
DESTINATION DRIVE NAME (OR RETURN TO REBOOT)b
DESTINATION ON B, THEN TYPE RETURN ←──────────────────┐
FUNCTION COMPLETE                                      │
DESTINATION DRIVE NAME (OR RETURN TO REBOOT) ←─────────┤
                                                       └Type returns here.
```

SYSGEN will write the new version of the operating system onto the system tracks of the new disk.

That's it! You're done! You have a new custom-configured operating system that you made yourself. There are a lot of people out there who will pay good money for this sort of talent. Test it out using DIR and TYPE to see if it will really print out when you toggle on the printer with control-p. If you're testing an xon/xoff or an etx/ack printer, you'll need to send enough characters at once to fill up the printer buffer.

If it doesn't work, go back to the beginning of this section and follow the steps very carefully. Check that you know where everything is in memory, both in the system image in low memory and in the running CP/M in high memory. If your driver worked when you tested it with DDT at location 100, it should work when installed in the driver.

Good luck!

Quick Summary of Driver Installation Steps

Once you are able to perform this installation process quickly, this is what you'll be typing on the screen. (We'll assume that you aren't going to check memory with DDT.) Of course, the memory size and the number of pages to SAVE will be different depending on your system.

```
A>pip newbios.asm=biosio.asm

(Add driver to newbios.asm with word processor, store
revision as NEWBIOS.ASM)

A>asm newbios

A>movcpm 56 *         }
A>save 45 cpm56.com   }——►(These steps won't be necessary each time.)

A>ddt cpm56.com

-inewbios.hex
-r4d80
-g0

A>save 45 cpm56n.com

A>sysgen
```

A SHORTCUT

Under some special circumstances, you don't even need to use the assembler to modify your BIOS. You can do it directly with DDT, using a process similar to that previously described, but somewhat shorter. Essentially what this involves is using the "a" command of DDT to put the code for the new driver into BIOS, rather than reassemblying the BIOS.ASM file. This could be useful if the driver you want to install is not too complex, or if you're making minor changes in an existing driver, or debugging it.

The limitation of this process is that the new driver must fit into the space occupied by the old one. Otherwise, when you type in the instructions using the "a" command, you may be overwriting something important. Actually, you might be able to expand the driver a little, depending on what routine follows the driver. If it's the routine that returns the status of the list device, it may never be used, so you can overwrite it. Check your BIOS.ASM listing to see what's there.

As described in the last section, get your new driver working at 100 hex by placing a "jmp 100" at the start of printer driver in the running BIOS. Once it's working at 100 hex, move it up to high memory with the "m" command of DDT. For instance, if your routine is 44 hex bytes long and is going to be installed in location F209, you'd type:

```
-m100,44,f209
```

Note that you're directly modifying the operating system that you're using, so if you make a mistake, things could die a quick death. You don't (obviously!) want to use this system to modify the drivers of any peripherals that are currently in use.

The instructions for your driver are now at the right place in the running BIOS, but they have the wrong addresses, having been assembled at 100 hex. Go through the code with the DDT "a" command and change the memory reference instructions to the correct values. For instance, if there's a "jmp 100" instruction in the program, you'll need to change it to "jmp f209".

Now, turn on your printer. (It should work since it's running with the new driver, right?) Use DDT's "l" command to dump the code for the driver routine to the printer:

```
-lf209
```

You're going to need this printout in a minute.

If you don't already have it, create a file containing your current system image, using MOVCPM:

```
A>movcpm 64 *
A>save 43 cpm64.com
```

This assumes that your MOVCPM contains a working version of BIOS. If it doesn't (some MOVCPM's have only a skeletal BIOS), then you'll have to make up a current version of CPM64.COM (or whatever) by assemblying BIOS.ASM and merging it into CPM64.COM with DDT as described in the last section. This may make the process seem like not much of a shortcut, but if you're debugging, you'll only have to create this CPM64.COM file once.

After that, you can skip this step entirely. Bring this image into memory with:

```
A>ddt cpm64.com
```

Now you have to find the old driver in the image in low memory. You can either use the magic number N as described earlier or you can simply search through the code with DDT, looking for the instructions that you know are in the driver.

Once you find the old driver, you type the new one over the top of it, using the "a" command. Type it in exactly as it appears on the printout that you made above. The memory reference instructions will be wrong for their current locations in low memory, but they'll be right later when loaded from the disk system tracks into high memory.

Save this modified image as CPM64N.COM:

```
-g0
A>save 43 cpm64n.com
```

Use SYSGEN to write this new image to the system tracks of a formatted disk:

```
A>sysgen cpm64n.com
```

There you are again! A complete working CP/M system with your own custom modification. Boot up the new disk and test the driver by using it to TYPE some long files.

MODIFYING BIOS FOR DIFFERENT CONTROL CHARACTERS

It may happen that you have a printer with special functions like compressed or elongated print fonts, different color ribbons, or the like. It may also be the case that there's no convenient way to send these control codes to the printer from your program, so these special functions are difficult to use. One solution to this problem is to modify the printer driver in your BIOS to reinterpret certain characters.

Listing 9-7. Print Driver Program

```
                ; **************************************************
                ;
                ;new printer driver for Epson MX-80
                ;
                ;incorporates compressed-mode facility
                ;   control-w toggles between compressed and normal
                ;
                ; **************************************************
                ;
0100                    org 100h
                ;
0100 DB23       test    in  23h     ;get printer status
0102 E685               ani 85h     ;mask off test bits
0104 EE85               xri 85h     ;are they all on
0106 C20001             jnz test    ;no-wait
0109 79                 mov a,c     ;get character in A-reg
010A FE17               cpi 17h     ;is it a control-w ?
010C CA1201             jz  control ;yes
010F C32801             jmp exit    ;no
                ;
                ;it's a control-w
                ;
0112 3A2B01     control lda toggle  ;is toggle set to 0 ?
0115 B7                 ora a
0116 CA2201             jz  comp    ;yes
                ;toggle set to nonzero, so turn OFF compressed print
0119 2F                 cma         ;change A-register to 0
011A 322B01             sta toggle  ; set toggle
011D 3E92               mvi a,92h   ;get code to turn OFF c.p.
011F C32801             jmp exit
                ;toggle set to zero, so turn ON compressed print
0122 2F         comp    cma         ;change A-register to non-0
0123 322B01             sta toggle  ; set toggle
0126 3E0F               mvi a,0fh   ;get code to turn ON c.p.
                ;print the character and return
0128 D322       exit    out 22h     ;send to printer
012A C9                 ret         ;return
                ;
012B 00         toggle  db  0       ;if 0, normal mode
                ;                   ;if non-0, compressed mode
                ;
012C                    end
```

As an example, let's take the Epson MX-80. If you send it a control–o (0F hex), it will start printing in compressed mode. If you send it a control–r (12 hex) it will go back to the normal mode. However, our word-processing program lets us use only a few control characters for user-defined functions and neither control–o or control–r are among them. However, control–w is. We'd like to set things up so that when the driver sees one control–w, it sends a control–o to turn on the compressed mode, and when it sees the *second* control–w, it turns off the compressed mode with a control–r.

Listing 9–7 is a new driver program that will do exactly that.

As shown here, it's ORGed at 100, ready to be checked out by DDT. Once you know it works, it can then be assembled into BIOS and merged into CPM64.COM with DDT, as previously described.

THE SKY'S THE LIMIT

There are, of course, dozens of things you can do along these lines once you know how to get in and modify your BIOS. The only limit is your imagination. Have fun!

APPENDIX A

Hexadecimal Notation

WHY USE HEXADECIMAL NOTATION?

Why don't computers just use decimal notation like everyone else? Wouldn't that be a lot simpler for everyone involved? Yes, it would be simpler for humans, no question about it. We're used to counting by tens. However, it would be much more difficult for the computer. Computers, as everyone knows, are full of transistors, and transistors are really just very small switches that can be turned on and off by other transistors. And these switches, like the light switches on your wall at home, have only two positions: on and off. No one has yet figured out how to make a transistor that has ten positions (at least one that will work reliably in a computer). So humans must think of a digit as having ten possible values (from 0 to 9), while computers think in terms of a binary digit that has only two possible values: either 0 or 1. This binary digit (binary means "two") is called a "bit."

BINARY NOTATION

When a computer counts, it starts with 0, like everyone else. It then goes to one. So far, we can identify with that. But what happens next? The poor thing has run out of all possible values for this digit! There *are* only 0 and 1! So it does just what we do in the decimal system when we run out of digits. It adds a new column to the left of the one's column, which gives it 10.

Of course, this 10 isn't 10 decimal but 10 binary, which is the same as 2 decimal. The column next to the one's column isn't the ten's column, as it is in decimal notation, it's the two's column. (The third column over is the

four's column, the fourth column is the eight's column, and so on.) Thus, 11 binary is the same as 3 decimal, and 100 binary is the same as 4 decimal. Here is a list of the first 16 binary numbers:

Binary	Decimal	Binary	Decimal
0	0	1000	8
1	1	1001	9
10	2	1010	10
11	3	1011	11
100	4	1100	12
101	5	1101	13
110	6	1110	14
111	7	1111	15

So four columns in the binary system lets us count from 0 to 15 (decimal). A piece of information that is 4 bits long is sometimes called a "nybble" and a piece of information that is 8 bits long is called a "byte." Since there are 16 possible numbers (counting 0) in a nybble, there are 16 times 16, or 256, possible numbers in a byte. For instance, the binary number 11111111 is 255 decimal, the binary number 1000000 is 128 decimal, and the binary number 10000 is 16 decimal. (See the list of binary to decimal equivalents given later in this appendix.)

DECIMAL NOTATION

All right, now we know something about binary notation and why computers like to use it. But, what does binary have to do with hexadecimal? The problem is that while computers are happy thinking in binary, the binary system turns out to be very difficult for humans to read. For example, here's the decimal number 48458 expressed in binary: 1011110101001010. Who can handle this long a string of ones and zeros? How would you like to do arithmetic on such a number, or try to remember it, or write it down accurately? Not so easy. Well then, why not just translate each binary number into its decimal equivalent, and talk about that? The computer can then think in binary and convert to decimal when it wants to communicate with humans. Good idea, and one that's used very often in the computer business. Most applications programs communicate with the user in decimal notation, and even whole languages, like BASIC and FORTRAN, are made to speak in decimal to the user.

However, when we really want to talk about what is going on in the computer on a detailed level (as we often do when we write assembly language programs), the decimal system has certain glaring disadvantages. For one thing, the decimal number doesn't tell us anything about how the bits look in the binary number and, in many programming applications, we need to deal with patterns of bits. It's not instantly obvious, for example, that 240 decimal is 11110000 in binary. Another related problem is that the *number* of digits used for a particular binary number has no easy relationship to the number of digits used in a decimal number. Thus, 1001 and 1010 both have four digits, but 1001 is 9 decimal (which has one digit), and 1010 is 10 decimal (which has two digits). This is awkward for printouts and for visualizing what's going on.

HEXADECIMAL NOTATION

Fortunately, in the dim and distant past of computer development, someone came up with a compromise between binary (which is easy for the computer to read) and decimal (which is easy for the human to read). This compromise is called "hexadecimal" notation (or "hex" for short). Where binary is a number system based on two, and decimal is based on ten, hexadecimal is based on sixteen. Hexadecimal works by grouping together 4 bits (a nybble) and assigning a symbol to each value that those 4 bits can represent. Since 4 bits can have any of 16 possible values, we need 16 symbols. It seems natural to assign 0 (hexadecimal) to the value 0 (decimal), and to assign 1 (hex) to 1 (decimal), and so on, up to 9. But what happens then? We've run out of decimal digits, and we still have six more values to represent. We need more symbols and they shouldn't be too obscure, or it will be hard to find hardware to print them out. Why not use letters of the alphabet? "A" through "F" will handle it nicely. This is illustrated in Table A-1.

Table A-1. Binary, Decimal, and Hex Equivalents

Binary	Decimal	Hexadecimal
0	0	0
1	1	1
10	2	2
11	3	3
100	4	4
101	5	5
110	6	6
111	7	7
1000	8	8
1001	9	9
1010	10	A
1011	11	B
1100	12	C
1101	13	D
1110	14	E
1111	15	F

Now every possible value of a nybble (4 bits) has a unique symbol. Also, every possible value of a byte (8 bits) can be represented by two of these symbols: FF (hex), for example, represents 11111111 binary, or 255 decimal. Also 44 (hex) represents 10001000 binary, or 68 decimal, and so on. Remember the number 11110000 that we referred to above and which is 240 decimal? It's represented by F0 in hex, where the F represents the 1111, and the 0 represents the 0000. Notice how easy it is to recognize the bit-pattern 11110000 when you look at "F0." The hex number lets you "see" the binary number, whereas, the decimal number doesn't. Each byte can be uniquely specified by two hexadecimal symbols, and each symbol represents exactly 4 bits.

Learning to Think in Hex

Now we have a whole new numbering system: hexadecimal, or base 16. How hard is it to learn to get around in hex? If it were necessary to learn, for instance, how to multiply two 4-digit hex numbers together using pencil and paper, then it might take a long time to become proficient in hex. Fortunately, we don't have to learn that much about the hex system to deal with computers. If you need to do arithmetic on hex numbers, it is usually a simple addition or subtraction. You can either do this in your head (after a little practice), or you can convert the hex numbers to decimal, do the arithmetic on the decimal equivalents, and then convert the answer back to hex. We'll show how these conversions are done in the next section.

Hexadecimal Arithmetic

Let's try a little arithmetic in hexadecimal just to see what it's like. For simplicity at this point, we'll adopt the convention used in many assemblers and other programs; an "h" immediately following a number means it's a hex number and a "d" immediately following a number means it's a decimal number. Thus, 22h is 22 hex, which is 34 decimal, while 22d is 22 decimal, which is 16 hex.

What's 2h plus 2h? Since both these numbers are the same as their decimal equivalents and the answer is also the same as its hex equivalent, there's no problem. The answer is 4h. Similarly, 4h plus 3h is 7h. What about 5h plus 5h? Let's count on our fingers. While we count out loud, "six, seven, eight, nine," we put up one, two, three, and four fingers. Now what? We don't count "ten." Because we're in hexadecimal, the next digit after nine is "A." So, as we put up the fifth finger, we count "A," and that's the answer.

What about Ah plus 4h? Let's count on our fingers again. Starting with "A," we'll count until we have four fingers in the air: "B, C, D, E." E is the answer. To add 7h to Bh, we'd start at "B" and count until we had seven fingers in the air: "C, D, E, F, 10, 11, 12." So the answer is 12h. (Notice how "F" in hex is similar to 9 in decimal, in that the next number after it is 10.)

Let's try adding some 2-digit hex numbers. We'll write them down in columns just as we do when doing arithmetic in decimal notation.

```
  4 B h
+ 1 9 h
-------
  6 4 h
```

Starting with B, we can count 9 more: "C, D, E, F, 10, 11, 12, 13, 14." So, Bh plus 9h is 14h. We write down the 4 and carry the 1 to the next column (the sixteen's column), where we add 4h and 1h and, then, the 1h we carried, giving us 6h. Thus, the answer is 64h.

What about larger hex numbers? Try this:

```
  B C 9 0 h
+   2 A 2 h
-----------
  B F 3 2 h
```

The addition of 2h and 0h is 2h (in the one's column). Then, 9h and Ah is 13h (in the sixteen's column), so we write down the 3 and carry 1 to the next column (the 256's column). Here, we add Ch and 2h and the 1 we carried, giving us Fh (with nothing to carry). Bh and nothing is Bh, so that's the answer: BF32h.

Subtraction is easy too:

```
  C F 3 4 h
-   A 1 6 h
-----------
  C 5 1 E h
```

We start by trying to take 6h from 4h, but we can't, since it's smaller, so, just as in decimal subtraction, we borrow one from the next column over. (This is the sixteen's column, so we're really borrowing 16d, which is 10h.) We add the 10h to the 4h, giving 14h, and 14h less 6h is Eh, as you can prove by counting backwards on six fingers: "13, 12, 11, 10, F, E." Since we borrowed 1 from it, the 3 at the top of the sixteen's column has been reduced to 2, so when we take 1 from it again, only 1 is left. In the 256's column, we take Ah away from Fh, which leaves 5h (counting on five fingers: "E, D, C, B, A"). And, finally, in the 4096's column, nothing taken away from Ch leaves Ch. And that's our answer: C51Eh.

That's not so bad, is it? It took you years to learn decimal arithmetic, and here you are, learning a whole new numbering system in just a few minutes!

Hexadecimal Bit Patterns

Another thing that it is useful to do in hex is being able to recognize the bit patterns of the sixteen hex digits. A good approach to this is to copy down

Table A-1 on a filing card and tape it up near your computer. If you do a lot of assembly language programming, you will find that you will refer to it so much that eventually the bit patterns will become second nature.

The most useful bit patterns to recognize are 0000 binary which, of course, is 0h, and 1111 binary, which is Fh. Often, a routine will set all the bits in a section of the computer's memory to 1 and, then, if you look into memory with DDT or a similar program, you'll find it filled with F's. Another useful bit pattern is 7Fh, which is all the bits in a byte being set except the leftmost one (01111111). This can be used to "mask off" an extraneous upper bit to obtain the ASCII code for a character. The ASCII character codes for letters run from 41h to 7Ah, so if you see memory filled with these values, you know you're looking at text.

CONVERTING HEX TO DECIMAL

Finding the decimal equivalent of a hex number is mostly a matter of remembering that the digit in each column of a hex number is sixteen times larger than the same digit would be in the column to the right. (Just as in a decimal number, each digit is ten times bigger than the same digit in the column to the right.)

Let's find the decimal equivalent of BF3Ch. (For clarity, we'll show decimal numbers without the "d".) The one's column is easy. Just look up the value of Ch on your little card (Table A-1). Ch is 12, so write that down. Now, take the 3 in the sixteen's column and multiply it by 16: that's 48. In the 256's column, we first need to convert the Fh to 15, and then we can multiply it by 256 to arrive at 3840, which we also write down. Finally, in the 4096's column, we convert Bh to 11, which we multiply by 4096, obtaining 45056. Now we can add 12, 48, 3840, and 45056. This gives us 48956, and that's the answer. The following entry shows how this looks.

```
B F 3 C

     Ch = 12, 12 * 1    =    12
     3h =  3,  3 * 16   =    48
     Fh = 15, 15 * 256  =  3840
     Bh = 11, 11 * 4096 = 45056
                          -----
                          48956
```

CONVERTING DECIMAL TO HEX

It's not quite so easy to extract a hex number from a decimal number since, instead of multiplication, we must now use division. The idea is this. To convert a 4-digit hex number to decimal, we first see how many 4096's there are in it. Then, we convert that number to hex and write it down; it's the digit in the 4096 column. Then, we work with the *remainder* of this division. We see how many 256's there are in the remainder, convert this number to hex, and write it down in the 256's column. The remainder of this division we then divide by 16, obtaining a value which we convert to hex and write down in the sixteen's column. The remainder of *this* division is the number of one's, which we convert to hex and write down in the one's column. Let's try it with a number that may look strangely familiar (it's the result of the previous section's conversion): 48956.

First, we find that 4096 goes into 48956 exactly 11 times, with a remainder of 3900. Decimal 11 is Bh, so we write down B in the 4096's column. We divide the remainder of 3900 by 256 (the next column), which gives 15 with a remainder of 60. Decimal 15 is Fh, so we write down F in the 256's column. Next, we divide 60 by 16, which gives us 3 with a remainder of 12. We know that 3d is 3h, so we write down 3 in the sixteen's column. And, finally, we convert 12 (the remainder) to Ch, and write that down in the one's column. And, amazing as it may seem, we get what we started with in the last section: BF3Ch. Let's illustrate this.

48956 / 4096 = 11, remainder = 3900.	11d = Bh	B F 3 C h
3900 / 256 = 15, remainder = 60.	15d = Fh	
60 / 16 = 3, remainder = 12.	3d = 3h	
12 / 1 = 12, no remainder.	12d = Ch	

As with most things, it takes practice to become comfortable with hexadecimal. Practice doing some conversions and some arithmetic and, before long, you'll be able to work with hex almost as well as your computer!

APPENDIX B

Utility Programs

In this appendix, we've collected several programs that may prove to be useful or amusing, but which did not fit into the rest of the book.

HEXDUMP

This program will dump—that is, print out the contents in hex numbers—any 128-byte section of memory. It is very similar to the "d" command of DDT, except that it doesn't print the ASCII representations of each byte alongside the hex. This would be easy to add to the program, however, if you want it.

This program is useful for looking at parts of memory when you don't want to use DDT. For example, DDT modifies the page zero addresses when it's loaded, so if you want to see what they are in their normal state, HEXDUMP is just what you want.

Listing B-1. The HEXDUMP Program

```
                ;**************************************************
                ;HEXDUMP-Program to dump 128 bytes of memory.
                ;          Requires starting address in hex.
                ;
                ;
0002 =          conout  equ  2h         ;console out
0001 =          conin   equ  1h         ;console in
0005 =          bdos    equ  5h         ;operating system
                ;
0100                    org  100h
```

```
                ;
                ;get address from user and initialize counts
0100 CD7101             call hexibin   ;get address in hex
0103 7D                 mov  a,l       ;mask off right-hand digit
0104 E6F0               ani  0f0h
0106 6F                 mov  l,a
0107 0E08               mvi  c,8       ;set number of lines
0109 CD2E01             call pcrlf     ;print linefeed
                ;
                ;print address and start new line
010C 0610       nuline  mvi  b,16d     ;set nbr of bytes per line
010E CD2E01             call pcrlf     ;print linefeed
0111 CD3F01             call phex      ;print address
0114 CD3901             call pspac     ;print two spaces
0117 CD3901             call pspac
                ;
                ;print the bytes for this line
011A 56         nubyte  mov  d,m       ;get byte into d
011B CD4801             call pbyte     ;print it
011E CD3901             call pspac     ;print space
0121 23                 inx  h         ;increment hl
0122 05                 dcr  b         ;done with this line?
0123 C21A01             jnz  nubyte    ; not yet
                ;
                ;done this line
0126 0D                 dcr  c         ;done all lines?
0127 C20C01             jnz  nuline    ; not yet
012A CD2E01             call pcrlf     ;yes-print linefeed
012D C9                 ret            ;back to CP/M
                ;
                ;subroutine to print a return and linefeed
012E 3E0D       pcrlf   mvi  a,0dh     ;print carriage return
0130 CD6401             call pchar
0133 3E0A               mvi  a,0ah     ;print linefeed
0135 CD6401             call pchar
0138 C9                 ret
                ;
                ;subroutine to print a space
0139 3E20       pspac   mvi  a,20h     ;print space
013B CD6401             call pchar
013E C9                 ret
                ;
```

```
                ;*************************************************
                ;phex-routine to print binary number in hl
                ;       out on screen in hex
                ;
013F 54         phex    mov   d,h        ;print 2 digits from H
0140 CD4801             call  pbyte
0143 55                 mov   d,l        ;print 2 digits from L
0144 CD4801             call  pbyte
0147 C9                 ret
                ;
                ;subroutine to print 2-digit hex number (in d)
0148 7A         pbyte   mov   a,d        ;print left-hand digit
0149 CD5101             call  print1
014C 7A                 mov   a,d        ;print right-hand digit
014D CD5501             call  print2
0150 C9                 ret
                ;
                ;subroutine to print one hex digit (in a)
0151 07070707   print1  rlc! rlc! rlc! rlc!    ;move hi 4 bits to lo
0155 E60F       print2  ani   0fh        ;get rid of high 4 bits
0157 C630               adi   30h        ;change hex to ASCII
0159 FE3A               cpi   3ah        ;if it's more than 9
015B DA6001             jc    pdig       ; (it's not)
015E C607               adi   7h         ; add bias (A=10, etc.)
0160 CD6401     pdig    call  pchar      ;print digit
0163 C9                 ret
                ;
                ;subroutine to print character in a-register
0164 E5C5D5     pchar   push h! push b! push d!    ;save registers
0167 0E02               mvi   c,conout ;print character
0169 5F                 mov   e,a
016A CD0500             call  bdos
016D D1C1E1             pop d! pop b! pop h!    ;get register back
0170 C9                 ret
                ;
                ;*************************************************
                ;hexibin-reads hex number from keyboard,
                ;          stores result in binary in hl
                ;
0171 210000     hexibin lxi   h,0        ;clear hl
0174 E5         newch   push  h          ;save hl
0175 0E01               mvi   c,conin    ;get character
0177 CD0500             call  bdos
```

```
017A E1                pop  h          ;restore hl
017B D630              sui  30h        ;ASCII digit to binary
017D F8                rm              ;return if < 0
017E FE0A              cpi  10d        ;is it > 9 ?
0180 FA8B01            jm   addto      ;no, so it's 0 to 9
            ;not digit, maybe it's letter (a to f)
0183 D627              sui  27h        ;convert ASCII to binary
0185 FE0A              cpi  0ah        ;is it < a (hex)
0187 F8                rm              ; yes, return
0188 FE10              cpi  10h        ;is it > f (hex)
018A F0                rp              ; yes, return
            ;rotate HL 4 bits left and add digit to left side
018B 57     addto      mov  d,a        ;save new hex digit in d
018C 0E04              mvi  c,4        ;set C to count 4 bits
018E 7D     shift      mov  a,l        ;shift l
018F 17                ral
0190 6F                mov  l,a
0191 7C                mov  a,h        ;shift h
0192 17                ral
0193 67                mov  h,a
0194 0D                dcr  c          ;done 4 bits yet?
0195 C28E01            jnz  shift      ; not yet
0198 7D                mov  a,l        ;mask off lo 4 bits of L
0199 E6F0              ani  0f0h
019B B2                ora  d          ;"or" new digit onto L
019C 6F                mov  l,a
019D C37401            jmp  newch      ;go get next character
            ;
01A0                   end
```

MICRO SPACE INVADERS

This program (Listing B-2) is just about the smallest possible space game that you can have on a CP/M system.

You're in charge of a battery of four phasers, each of which is aimed at a different quadrant of the galaxy. Your mission is to shoot down the invading Klipson battle cruisers. They may appear in any of the four sectors and you must respond by firing the phaser in the appropriate sector. However, you don't have much time as the Klipsons will be approaching at warp-factor 11. Keep your fingers poised over the number keys 1, 2, 3, and 4. When the Klipson appears (symbolized on your screen by an evil-looking asterisk), press the key corresponding to the sector that he's appeared in. If you get the wrong sector, you lose a point. And, if you're not fast enough and he gets through and destroys the earth, you also lose a point. It is only when you're fast and accurate that you gain a point. The program keeps score for you.

Listing B-2. Game Program

```
                ; ***************************************************
                ;MICRO SPACE INVADERS
                ;
                ; ***************************************************
                ;
0005 =          bdos    equ   5h
0001 =          conin   equ   1h
0002 =          conout  equ   2h
0009 =          printf  equ   9h
000B =          chkcon  equ   0bh
0020 =          space   equ   20h
002A =          aster   equ   2ah
000A =          lf      equ   0ah
000D =          cr      equ   0dh
F800 =          time    equ   0f800h
0003 =          mask    equ   3h
                ;
0100                    org   100h
                ;
                ;print header
                ;
0100 0E09       start   mvi   c,printf
0102 118301             lxi   d,header
0105 CD0500             call  bdos
                ;
                ;get random number, use it to print spaces
                ;
0108 3A8101             lda   random    ;get random number
010B 07                 rlc             ;shift left twice
010C 07                 rlc             ; to multiply by 4
010D 47                 mov   b,a       ;put in b as counter
010E 04                 inr   b         ;add 1 to ensure it's not 0
010F C5         newsp   push  b         ;save it
0110 0E02               mvi   c,conout  ;print space
0112 1E20               mvi   e,space
```

```
0114 CD0500          call bdos
0117 C1              pop  b          ;get it back
0118 05              dcr  b          ;is count 0 yet?
0119 C20F01          jnz  newsp      ;no, so print another space
                ;
                ;print asterisk
                ;
011C 0E02            mvi  c,conout
011E 1E2A            mvi  e,aster
0120 CD0500          call bdos
                ;
                ;run timer while checking keyboard
                ;
0123 0100F8          lxi  b,time     ;set time in bc
0126 C5         loop push b          ;save bc
0127 0E0B            mvi  c,chkcon   ;check keyboard for char
0129 CD0500          call bdos
012C B7              ora  a          ;anything yet?
012D C23F01          jnz  quick      ;yes, character typed
0130 C1              pop  b          ;no, get bc back
                ;
0131 0C              inr  c          ;increment c
0132 C22601          jnz  loop       ;loop if not 0 yet
0135 04              inr  b          ;increment b
0136 C22601          jnz  loop       ;loop if not 0 yet
                ;
                ;timer out-not quick enough
                ;
0139 119801          lxi  d,messnq   ;set up "not quick" message
013C C35A01          jmp  print      ;go print it
                ;
                ;character hit before time out-quick enough
                ;
013F C1         quick pop b          ;get bc back
0140 79              mov  a,c        ;save c for later
0141 328201          sta  hold
                ;
                ;read character
                ;
0144 0E01            mvi  c,conin    ;read character
0146 CD0500          call bdos
0149 0631            mvi  b,'0'+1    ;ASCII 0 plus 1
```

```
pb014B 90                 sub   b          ;subtract from char in a
014C 47                   mov   b,a        ;save in b
                  ;
                  ;see if character typed matches random number
                  ;
014D 3A8101               lda   random     ;random number in a
0150 B8                   cmp   b          ;compare with character
0151 11AD01               lxi   d,messw    ;set up "wrong" message
0154 C25A01               jnz   print      ;go print if not match
0157 11BE01               lxi   d,messr    ;match-use "right" message
                  ;
015A 0E09         print   mvi   c,printf   ;print message
015C CD0500               call  bdos
                  ;
                  ;make up new random number
                  ;
015F 3A8201       setran  lda   hold       ;get last value of count
0162 47                   mov   b,a        ;save in b
0163 3A8101               lda   random     ;get last random number
0166 80                   add   b          ;add old count
0167 E603                 ani   mask       ;mask off upper six bits
0169 328101               sta   random     ;save result
                  ;
                  ;wait for user to signal ready
                  ;
016C 0E09                 mvi   c,printf   ;ask if user ready
016E 11CA01               lxi   d,messj
0171 CD0500               call  bdos
0174 0E01         wait    mvi   c,conin    ;wait for key press
0176 CD0500               call  bdos
0179 FE20                 cpi   space      ;is it the space-bar?
017B C27401               jnz   wait       ;not yet
                  ;
017E C30001               jmp   start      ;begin again
                  ;
                  ;
0181 02           random  db    2
0182              hold    ds    1
                  ;
0183 0D0A0A0A20header db    cr,lf,lf,lf,' 1---2---3---4',cr,lf,'$'
0198 0D0A0A4E4Fmessnq db    cr,lf,lf,'NOT QUICK ENOUGH.$'
01AD 0D0A0A5752messw  db    cr,lf,lf,'WRONG TARGET.$'
```

```
01BE 0D0A0A4120messr   db    cr,lf,lf,'A HIT!!!$'
                  ;
01CA 0D0A0A5072messj   db    cr,lf,lf,'Press space-bar to start again.
                  ;
                  ;
```

HEXIDEC

This program will print out the decimal equivalent to any positive 4-digit hex number that you type in from the keyboard. It is called directly from CP/M.

Listing B-3. Hex-to-Decimal Conversion Program

```
              ;*******************************************************
              ;hexidec-Converts number typed in hex on keyboard
              ;        into decimal, and prints it out on screen.
              ;
000A =        lf      equ  0ah        ;linefeed
              ;
0100                  org  100h
              ;
0100 CD0C01           call hexibin    ;get hex character
0103 3E0A             mvi  a,lf       ;print linefeed
0105 CD6C01           call pchar
0108 CD3B01           call binidec    ;print decimal number
010B C9               ret             ;that's all
              ;
              ;*******************************************************
              ;hexibin-reads hex number from keyboard,
              ;        stores result in binary in hl
              ;
0001 =        conin   equ  1h
0005 =        bdos    equ  5h
0030 =        asc0    equ  30h
000A =        dec10   equ  10d
0027 =        bias    equ  27h
00F0 =        mask    equ  0f0h
              ;
010C 210000 hexibin lxi  h,0          ;clear hl
010F E5     newch   push h            ;save hl
```

```
0110 0E01              mvi   c,conin    ;get character
0112 CD0500            call  bdos
0115 E1                pop   h          ;restore hl
0116 D630              sui   asc0       ;convert ASCII digit to binary
0118 F8                rm               ;return if < 0
0119 FE0A              cpi   dec10      ;is it > 9 ?
011B FA2601            jm    addto      ; yes, so it's digit (0 to 9)
                ;not digit, maybe it's letter (a to f)
011E D627              sui   bias       ;convert ASCII letter to binary
0120 FE0A              cpi   0ah        ;is it less than a (hex)
0122 F8                rm               ; yes, return
0123 FE10              cpi   10h        ;is it greater than f ?
0125 F0                rp               ; yes, return
                ;rotate hl register four bits left and
                ; add new digit to right-hand side
0126 57         addto  mov   d,a        ;save new hex digit in d
0127 0E04              mvi   c,4        ;set up loop to count 4 bits
0129 7D         shift  mov   a,l        ;shift l
012A 17                ral
012B 6F                mov   l,a
012C 7C                mov   a,h        ;shift h
012D 17                ral
012E 67                mov   h,a
012F 0D                dcr   c          ;are we done yet?
0130 C22901            jnz   shift      ; not yet
0133 7D                mov   a,l        ;mask off lower 4 bits of l
0134 E6F0              ani   mask
0136 B2                ora   d          ;"or" the new digit on to l
0137 6F                mov   l,a
0138 C30F01            jmp   newch      ;go back for next character
                ;
                ;*********************************************************
                ;binidec-converts binary number in hl to
                ;          decimal, prints result on screen
                ;
0002 =          conout equ   2          ;console output
0005 =          bdos   equ   5          ;BDOS entry point
                ;
013B 11F0D8     binidec lxi  d,-10000   ;print number of 10,000s
013E CD5A01            call  subcnt
0141 1118FC            lxi   d,-1000    ;print number of thousands
0144 CD5A01            call  subcnt
```

```
0147 119CFF          lxi  d,-100    ;print number of hundreds
014A CD5A01          call subcnt
014D 11F6FF          lxi  d,-10     ;print number of tens
0150 CD5A01          call subcnt
0153 11FFFF          lxi  d,-1      ;print number of ones
0156 CD5A01          call subcnt
0159 C9              ret            ;that's all
             ;
015A 0E2F    subcnt  mvi  c,'0'-1   ;c holds ASCII version of count
015C 0C      sub2    inr  c         ;increment count
015D 227901          shld temp      ;save hl
0160 19              dad  d         ;add neg const from de to hl
0161 DA5C01          jc   sub2      ;loop until result in hl goes neg
0164 2A7901          lhld temp      ;get last positive value back in hl
0167 79              mov  a,c
0168 CD6C01          call pchar     ;print digit
016B C9              ret
             ;print character in a-register on screen
016C D5C5E5  pchar   push d ! push b ! push h !    ;save registers
016F 5F              mov  e,a       ;character in e
0170 0E02            mvi  c,conout
0172 CD0500          call bdos      ;call conout routine
0175 E1C1D1          pop h ! pop b ! pop d !    ;get registers back
0178 C9              ret
             ;
0179 0100    temp    dw   1
             ;
017B                 end
```

FILEDUMP

This program (Listing B-4) takes any *file* and prints out the contents in a hex format similar to the "d" function of DDT (except that ASCII equivalents aren't printed out). Each 128-byte record is shown separately. Scrolling can be stopped and started with control–s.

This is a useful program for investigating how the records of a particular file are actually stored on the disk. It is a more convenient version of the technique that is shown in Chapter 5 for examining the contents of files in hex, where each record had to be read in separately and examined using DDT.

Listing B-4. Program for Outputting a File in Hex

```
; ***********************************************************
;FILEDUMP-Program to dump a file to the screen or printer
;          in hex format.
; ***********************************************************
;
;
bdos    equ   5h          ;operating system
conout  equ   2h          ;console output
fcb     equ   5ch         ;file control block
dma     equ   80h         ;record buffer
openf   equ   0fh         ;open file
readr   equ   14h         ;read record
prints  equ   9h          ;print string
;
        org   100h
;
;set up local stack
        lxi   h,0         ;save old stack pointer
        dad   sp
        shld  oldsp
        lxi   sp,stktop   ;load new stackpointer
;
;open file, read records
        mvi   c,openf     ;open file
        lxi   d,fcb
        call  bdos
        inr   a           ;add 1 to A-register. If it was ff,
        jz    nofile      ; now it's 00, so no such file
;
newrec  call  pcrlf       ;print return & linefeed
        mvi   c,prints    ;print header
        lxi   d,hmess
        call  bdos
;
        mvi   c,readr     ;read record
        lxi   d,fcb
        call  bdos
        ora   a           ;check A-register to see if EOF
        jnz   done        ; non-0 is EOF
;
;print out contents of DMA in hex format
        call  pbuff
        jmp   newrec
;
```

```
;end-of-file, or no file, so print message and return to CP/M
nofile lxi  d,nfmess  ;print "no file" message
       mvi  c,prints
       call bdos
done   lhld oldsp     ;restore old stack pointer
       sphl
       ret            ;return to CP/M
;
; *********************************************************
;pbuff-subroutine to print contents of DMA in hex
;
;set address and initialize counts
pbuff  lxi  h,dma     ;put addr of record in HL-reg
       mvi  c,8       ;set number of lines
       call pcrlf     ;print linefeed
;
;print address and start new line
nuline mvi  b,16d     ;set number of bytes per line
       call pcrlf     ;print linefeed
;
;print the bytes for this line
nubyte mov  d,m       ;get byte pointed to by hl into d
       call pbyte     ;print it
       call pspac     ;print space
       inx  h         ;increment hl
       dcr  b         ;done all bytes on this line?
       jnz  nubyte    ; not yet
;
;done this line
       dcr  c         ;done all lines?
       jnz  nuline    ;  not yet
       call pcrlf     ;yes - print return & linefeed
       ret            ;back to main program
;
;subroutine to print a carriage return and linefeed
pcrlf  mvi  a,0dh     ;print carriage return
       call pchar
       mvi  a,0ah     ;print linefeed
       call pchar
       ret
;
;subroutine to print a space
pspac  mvi  a,20h     ;print space
       call pchar
       ret
```

```
;
; ***********************************************************
;phex - routine to print binary number in hl
;       out on screen in hex
;
phex    mov  d,h        ;print two digits from h
        call pbyte
        mov  d,l        ;print two digits from l
        call pbyte
        ret
;
;subroutine to print 2-digit hex number (in d)
pbyte   mov  a,d        ;print left-hand digit
        call print1
        mov  a,d        ;print right-hand digit
        call print2
        ret
;subroutine to print one hex digit (in a)
print1 rlc! rlc! rlc! rlc    ;move high 4 bits to low
print2 ani  0fh         ;get rid of high 4 bits
        adi  30h        ;change hex to ASCII
        cpi  3ah        ;if it's more than 9
        jc   pdig       ; (it's not)
        adi  7h         ;then add bias (A=10, etc.)
pdig    call pchar      ;print digit
        ret
;
;subroutine to print character in a-register out on screen
pchar   push h! push b! push d   ;save registers
        mvi  c,conout  ;print character
        mov  e,a
        call bdos
        pop d! pop b! pop h    ;get registers back
        ret
;
nfmess db   'No such filename.$'
hmess  db   '0 1 2 3 4 5 6 7 8 9 A B C D E F$'
oldsp  ds   2
       ds   32
stktop:
;
       end
;
```

APPENDIX C

Summary of 8080 Instructions

This appendix summarizes the architecture of the 8080 and the 8080 instruction set. Most of the instructions are explained in detail in the main part of the book. If you don't have any assembly language programming experience, don't read this appendix until you've read the first part of this book. This will avoid the possibility of your being blown away by seeing so many instructions all at once.

8080 ARCHITECTURE

The diagram shown in Fig. C-1 illustrates the principal 8080 registers.

Registers

Registers B and C can be accessed either as separate 8-bit registers, or together as a single 16-bit register called the BC-register. Similarly, the D- and E-registers can be combined into the 16-bit DE-register, and the H- and L-registers can be combined into the 16-bit HL-register.

The 8-bit A-register (sometimes called the "Accumulator") is the principal arithmetic register on the 8080 microprocessor. The term "arithmetic" used in this section includes the Boolean (logical) operations of "AND," "OR," and "Exclusive-OR." The A-register is almost always used alone as an 8-bit register, but it can be combined with the Program Status Word (PSW) to form a 16-bit entity that can be stored on the stack.

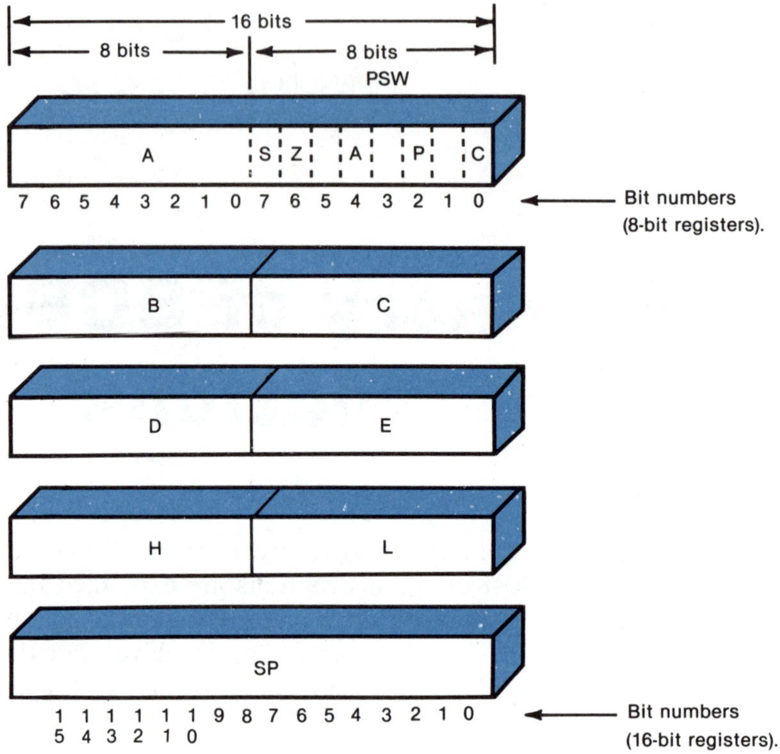

Fig. C-1. Registers of the 8080 microprocessor.

The 16-bit HL-register is often used as a pointer to a particular address in memory. When this is done, the 8-bit data in the address pointed to by HL can be called "M" (for "memory") in some 8080 instructions. In this case, "M" is referred to as if it were another register. For example,

```
mov c,m
```

means, move the contents of the memory location pointed to by the HL-register into the C-register. There is no "M" register–it is simply the memory location pointed to by HL.

The BC- and DE-registers can be used for temporary storage and for a few arithmetic operations on 16-bit numbers. They can also be used as pointers to memory, using the LDAX and STAX instructions, although this is not quite as easy as using the HL-register.

All of the 8-bit registers (A, B, C, D, E, H, and L) can be used for temporary storage of 8-bit data.

The Stack Pointer (SP) holds the 16-bit address that is the current top of the stack. If you PUSH something onto the stack, it will be placed in memory at the address in the SP, and if you CALL a subroutine, the address to which you will RETurn is placed in memory at this address. When something is placed on the stack (by a PUSH or a CALL) the SP is automatically *decremented* two locations (since two bytes hold a 16-bit address), and when something is taken off the stack (by a POP or a RET), the SP is *incremented.* This is the opposite of what you might expect because the stack grows *downward* in memory.

In addition to the registers shown in Fig. C-1, there is also a 16-bit Program Counter (PC) (which holds the address of the instruction currently being executed) and an 8-bit Instruction register (I) (which holds the instruction being executed). These registers are seldom accessed in normal 8080 programming.

Program Status Word

The Program Status Word contains the five "flags" used in the 8080 processor. These flags are set, following the completion of some instructions (mostly 8-bit arithmetic instructions), to indicate the outcome of different operations. They can have either of two values, 1 or 0. Jumps, calls, and returns can sample these values automatically to decide what to do. (For example, JZ will cause a jump if the zero flag is set, but not if it isn't.)

The flag bits, and the mnemonic associated with each value, is shown in Table C-1. The sign flag is used to indicate whether the result of an arithmetic instruction is plus or minus (positive or negative). The Zero flag indicates whether the result of an operation is zero or nonzero. The Auxiliary Carry flag indicates whether there has been a carry from Bit 3 to Bit 4 in an arithmetic operation. Its primary use is in BCD (binary-coded decimal) arithmetic.

Table C-1. Flags of the PSW

FLAG	BIT NAME (In PSW)	MNEMOMIC	
		Bit=0	Bit=1
Sign	S	P (plus)	M (minus)
Zero	Z	NZ (nonzero)	Z (zero)
Auxiliary carry	A	(No Mnemonics)	
Parity	P	PO (parity odd)	PE (parity even)
Carry	C	NC (no carry)	C (carry)

The Parity flag is set to 1 whenever the result of an arithmetic operation contains an even number of bits, and set to zero when it contains an odd number of bits. This is useful for running parity checks on data to see if a bit has been lost. (Neither the parity flag nor the Auxiliary Carry flag is used in this book.) The Carry flag is used to indicate when the result of an arithmetic or shift operation results in a bit being carried or shifted out of the A-register.

8080 INSTRUCTIONS

Most summaries of assembly language instructions list them either in alphabetical order or in order of numerical op codes. Neither of these approaches is ideal, since when you want to look something up, you usually don't know the instruction yet. You start with an idea of what you want to accomplish in the program and you want to know what instruction will do it for you. Accordingly, we've arranged the instructions in seven functional groups:

1. 8-bit Transfers.
2. 16-bit Transfers.
3. 8-bit Arithmetic.
4. 16-bit Arithmetic.
5. Jumps, Calls, and Returns.
6. Rotates.
7. Other instructions.

"Transfers" means moving data from one register to another, or between a register and memory. In a transfer, the data are not altered.

In general, instructions that have an X in them, like LXI, operate on register pairs and 16-bit values. Also, an I at the end of an instruction stands for "immediate," which means that the data referred to in the instruction are stored immediately next to the instruction in the program, and not someplace else in memory.

We've made no attempt in this summary to show such niceties as how many bytes each instruction takes, how long it takes to execute, or exactly what flags are set. For this, you should consult the 8080 or 8085 reference manuals available from the Intel Corporation.

Remember: when "M" and "m" are referred to in the following descriptions, they stand for the memory location contained in the HL-register. Of course, for this to work, you must put the appropriate address in the HL-register before executing an instruction with an "m" as an operand.

Also remember: numbers used in an ASM listing are *assumed to be in decimal* unless otherwise specified. If a number is meant as a hex number, it must be followed by an "h," as in 0ffh. Also, hex numbers starting with a letter must be preceded by a zero, or ASM will think they're a name. For clarity, it's probaby best to put a "d" after decimal numbers as well, although this is optional. Numbers followed by "b" are assumed to be in binary notation, as in 11110000b.

8-Bit Transfers

MOV R1,R2 Moves data from register R2 to register R1, where R1 and R2 can be any one of the registers A, B, C, D, E, H, L, or M.

Examples:

```
mov a,b
mov h,d
```

MVI R,data Puts an 8-bit data byte into R, where R can be any one of the registers A, B, C, D, E, H, L, and M. (The data are stored in the byte immediately following the MVI instruction.)

Examples:

```
mvi d,31
mvi b,const (where "const" is given a numerical value
  in an EQU statement)
```

LDA Addr Puts an 8-bit byte, located in memory address Addr, into the A-register.

Examples:

```
lda 3c00h
lda const
```

STA Addr Stores an 8-bit byte from the A-register into memory address Addr.

Examples:

```
sta e010h
sta temp
```

LDAX RR Loads the A-register with 8-bit data contained in memory location that is pointed to by register RR, where RR is either "b" or "d," meaning the BC- or DE-register.

Example:
ldax b

STAX RR Stores an 8-bit value from the A-register into memory location that is pointed to by register RR, where RR is either "b" or "d," meaning the BC- or DE-register.
Example:
stax d

16-Bit Transfers

LHLD Addr Loads the HL-register with a 16-bit value that is stored in memory addresses Addr and Addr + 1.
Example:
lhld pointr

SHLD Addr Stores a 16-bit value from the HL-register into memory locations Addr and Addr + 1.
Example:
shld 0bd80h

LXI RR,data Loads a 16-bit data word into register RR, where RR can be "b," "d," "h," or "sp," meaning BC, DE, HL, or SP. The data are in the two bytes immediately following the instruction.
Examples:
lxi d,0005h
lxi h,ptr1

PUSH RR Puts the 16-bit contents of register RR onto the top of the stack, where RR can be "b," "d," "h," or "psw," meaning BC, DE, HL, or the register-pair formed by the A-register and the PSW. It decrements the stack pointer twice.
Example:
push h

POP RR Takes the 16-bit value from the top of stack and puts it in register RR (where RR is defined as in PUSH). It increments the stack pointer twice.
Example:
pop b

XTHL Exchanges the two 16-bit values in the HL-register and the top of the stack.

Example:
```
xthl
```

SPHL Loads the 16-bit contents of the HL-register into the stack pointer (SP) register.

Example:
```
sphl
```

PCHL Loads the 16-bit contents of the HL-register (usually an address) into the program counter (PC) register. This has the effect of causing a JMP to that address.

Example:
```
pchl
```

XCHG Exchanges the two 16-bit values in the HL-register and the DE-register.

Example:
```
xchg
```

8-Bit Arithmetic

In the instructions that follow, R stands for any of the registers A, B, C, D, E, H, L, or M (written as "a," "b," "c," "d," "e," "h," "l," or "m").

Examples:
```
add b
cmp c
```

In those instructions involving two operands, the first operand is always in the A-register and the second is in register R. The result is always left in the A-register. (Register R is unchanged.) Thus, in the first example given above, the contents of the B-register are added to the contents of the A-register, and the result is left on the A-register.

Note that all these 8-bit arithmetic instructions set the various flags to the appropriate values: zero or nonzero, plus or minus, and so on.

ADD R Adds contents of register R to the A-register.
SUB R Subtracts contents of register R from A-register.
INR R Increments the contents of register R.
DCR R Decrements the contents of register R.

CMP R Compares the contents of register R with the contents of the A-register. (This causes the flags to be set as if a subtraction had taken place, although the contents of register A are unchanged.)

ANA R Logically ANDs the contents of register R with the contents of the A-register.

ORA R Logically ORs the contents of register R with the contents of the A-register.

XRA R Logically Exclusive-ORs the contents of register R with the contents of the A-register.

In the instructions that follow, "data" means a numerical or a symbolic representation of an 8-bit data item.

Examples:

adi 0ffh

ori mask (where "mask" is defined in an "equ" statement)

ADI data Adds 8-bit data to contents of A-register.

SUI data Subtracts 8-bit data from contents of A-register.

CPI data Compares 8-bit data with contents of A-register.

ANI data Logically ANDs 8-bit data with contents of A-register.

ORI data Logically ORs 8-bit data with contents of A-register.

XRI data Logically Exclusive-ORs 8-bit data with contents of A-register.

16-Bit Arithmetic

In the following instructions, RR stands for registers BC, DE, HL, or SP (written as "b," "d," "h," or "sp"). Note that these instructions *do not* set the flags!

DAD RR Adds contents of register RR to contents of HL-register.

INX RR Increments register RR.

DCX RR Decrements register RR.

Jumps, Calls, and Returns

JMP Addr Transfers control of the program to memory location Addr, where Addr can be either a number or a symbolic label.

Examples:

jmp 100h

jmp start

CALL Addr Transfers control of the program to memory location Addr, and also puts the return address (the location of the next instruction following the CALL) on the stack. Decrements the stack pointer twice.

RET Transfers control of the program to the memory location pointed to by the contents of the top of the stack. Increments the stack pointer twice.

The JMP, CALL, and RET instructions all have variants that only execute when a particular condition is true. Thus,

```
jz start
```

will only transfer control of the program to "start" if the results of a previous arithmetic operation left the zero flag set to 1. If the condition is not met, control simply passes to the next instruction in line. Rather than list all of these instructions separately, we've arranged them in a table (Table C-2). The most-used of these instructions are probably JNZ, JZ, JNC, JC, JP, and JM.

Table C-2. Variants of the JMP, CALL, and RET Instructions

Instruction executes if flag set to	JUMP	CALL	RETURN
Nonzero	JNZ	CNZ	RNZ
Zero	JZ	CZ	RZ
No Carry	JNC	CNC	RNC
Carry	JC	CC	RC
Parity Odd	JPO	CPO	RPO
Parity Even	JPE	CPE	RPE
Plus	JP	CP	RP
Minus	JM	CM	RM

Rotations

All rotations are done on the contents of the A-register. The A-register can be rotated either right or left, and the bits pushed off the end can either circle round and appear on the other end of the A-register, or they can go to the carry bit of the program status word. The diagrams shown in Fig. C-2 illustrate the various possibilities.

RAL "Rotate Accumulator Left."

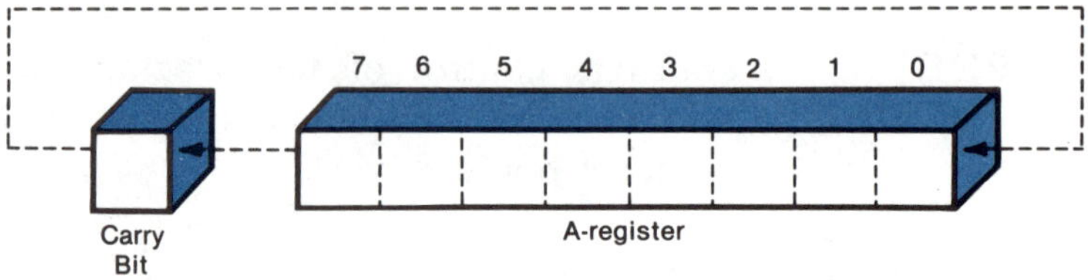

Example: ral

RAR "Rotate Accumulator Right"

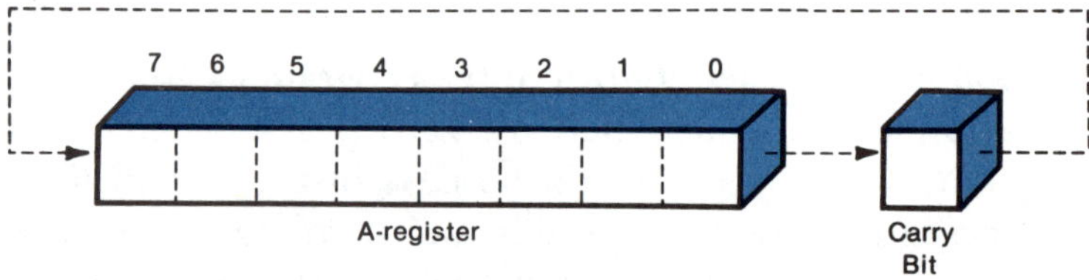

Example: rar

RLC "Rotate Accumulator Left Through Carry"

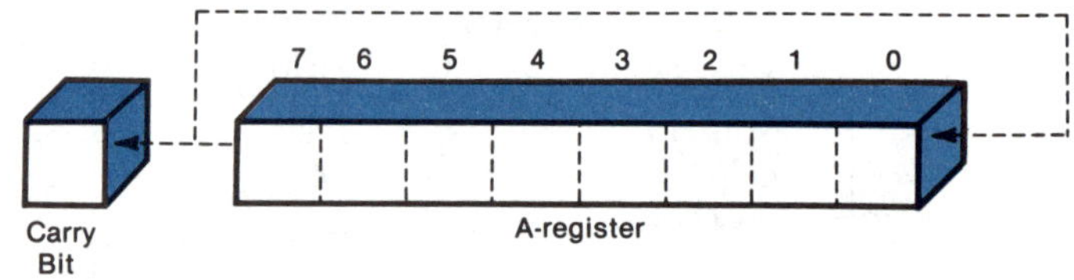

Example: rlc

RRC "Rotate Accumulator Right Through Carry"

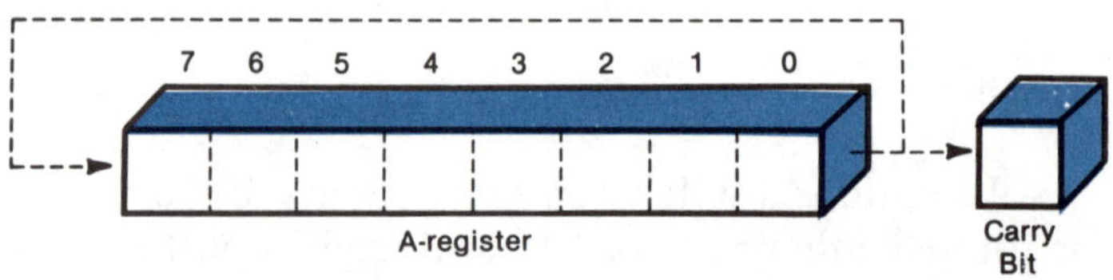

Example: rrc

Fig. C-2. Rotations.

Other Instructions

The 8080 microprocessor communicates with the outside world by using only two instructions:

IN Inputs an 8-bit byte of data into the accumulator from the data port specified in the instruction. The data ports are numbered from 1 to FF (hex).

Example:

```
in 23h
```

OUT Outputs an 8-bit byte of data from the A-register to the data port specified in the instruction.

Example:

```
out ptr      (where "ptr" is defined elsewhere).
```

There are several instructions that you can use to alter the bit in the carry flag:

CMC Complements the carry flag. That is, it changes it to 0 if it was 1, and vice versa.

Example:

```
cmc
```

STC Sets the carry flag to 1, no matter what it was before.

Example:

```
stc
```

You can also complement the A-register; that is, change every bit that's a 1 to a 0, and vice versa.

CMA Compliments the A-register.

Example:

```
cma
```

There are a number of instructions that are designed to operate on BCD (binary-coded decimal) format numbers. This is a way of using 4 bits to represent the 10 decimal digits and it is popular on mainframe computers that are used for business. We aren't going to describe BCD here, so these instructions will go unexplained. The "auxiliary carry" bit in the program status word is used with BCD calculations.

DAA Means "Decimal Adjust Accumulator."
ADC Means "Add to Accumulator with Carry."
ACI Means "Add with Carry Immediate to Accumulator."
SBB Means "Subtract from A-register with Borrow."
SBI Means "Subtract Immediate from A-register with Borrow."

You can halt the operation of the computer and you can also have an instruction which does nothing.

HLT Halts the computer, which is then paralyzed, unless there's an interrupt. Not to be used frivolously.
Example:
hlt

NOP Means "No Operation." It can be used as a "filler" in a program.
Example:
nop

And, finally, there are several instructions connected with the use of the interrupt system. Since we are not concerned with the use of interrupts in this book, we won't attempt to explain them. However, they are:

DI Means "Disable Interrupts."
EI Means "Enable Interrupts."
RIM Means "Read Interrupt Mask."
SIM Means "Set Interrupt Mask."

The instruction RST (which we use when returning from a program we've written in DDT) was designed for use in the interrupt system. However, it can be executed by any program. There are 8 such instructions: RST 0 through RST 7. They are each the equivalent of a CALL instruction, but they transfer control only to certain predefined locations in memory.

RST 0 is a CALL to location 0000 hex
RST 1 is a CALL to location 0008 hex
RST 2 is a CALL to location 0010 hex
RST 3 is a CALL to location 0018 hex
RST 4 is a CALL to location 0020 hex
RST 5 is a CALL to location 0028 hex
RST 6 is a CALL to location 0030 hex

RST 7 is a CALL to location 0040 hex

Since these are one-byte instructions, instead of a three-byte instruction as CALL is, you might find a use for them if you're writing a very short or very fast code. DDT uses them because it uses the interrupt system. Of course, you have to be very careful, since the addresses are located in CP/M's semi-sacred zero page. You don't want to overwrite or jump to an area that CP/M is using for something important.

RST n Causes a CALL to a location indicated by "n", as shown in the preceding list.

Example:

rst 3

ASSEMBLER DIRECTIVES

Assembler directives are placed in the instruction field of an ASM listing as if they were 8080 instructions, but they're not. They're instructions to the ASM program itself. For this reason, they're sometimes called "pseudo-ops."

ORG Causes ASM to start assemblying at the memory location given in the address field.

Example:

org 100h (causes assembly to start at location 100 hex)

END Causes the assembly to end. Any subsequent statements will not be processed. If followed by an address, this address will be the starting address used in HEX files.

Example:

finish end 100h

EQU Defines a symbolic label as having a specific value. Note that this directive does not set aside any memory to hold the value, it simply causes ASM to remember what value is associated with a label.

Example:

bdos equ 5h (defines the label bdos to have the value of 5 hex)

Example:

lnfeed equ 0ah (defines the label lnfeed to have the value of 0a hex)

DB Means "define bytes." This directive is used to set a single 8-bit byte or strings of bytes in memory to a specific value. A number of bytes can be placed in the same db directive by separating them with commas. A string of ASCII characters can be used if it starts and ends with single quotes ('). Symbolic values (labels) can be used to represent bytes if they are defined elsewhere.

Examples:

```
decten db 10d
crlf   db 0dh, 0ah
mess1  db 'Type your name ',0dh,0ah
mess2  db 'What?',cr,lf
```

DW This directive is similar to DB, except that it defines 16-bit words. A number of words can be used if they are set off with commas, and ASCII characters can be used if they are delimited by single quotes. However, strings must be limited to 2 characters.

Examples:

```
mask dw 0ff00h
data dw 0d4h, 63h, 7dh, 0c9h
crlf dw 0d0ah
abee dw 'ab'
```

DS This directive is used to set aside an area of memory for storage of bytes or groups of bytes. The number given in the address field is the number of bytes to be set aside. The memory locations thus reserved are filled with zeros by the assembler.

Examples:

```
temp   ds 2    (sets aside two-byte word)
stemp  ds 1    (sets aside 1 byte)
buffer ds 400d (sets aside 400 bytes)
```

APPENDIX D

Tables

This appendix contains the following charts and tables:

1. ASCII character set with hexadecimal equivalents.
2. Hexadecimal-to-Decimal conversion (one-byte values).
3. Multiples of 1K (1024), in decimal and hexadecimal.
4. Decimal, Hex, and Binary conversion (4-bit values).

ASCII CHARACTER SET WITH HEXADECIMAL EQUIVALENTS

First, we give you the hexadecimal values for some common needs, like the linefeed or carriage return, and then we furnish the complete ASCII Code and show the hexadecimal values for each ASCII character.

Hex	ASCII
07	bell (or beep)
09	tab
0A	linefeed
0D	carriage return

Hex	ASCII	Hex	ASCII	Hex	ASCII	Hex	ASCII	Hex	ASCII	Hex	ASCII
20	Space	30	0	40	@	50	P	60	`	70	p
21	!	31	1	41	A	51	Q	61	a	71	q
22	"	32	2	42	B	52	R	62	b	72	r
23	#	33	3	43	C	53	S	63	c	73	s
24	$	34	4	44	D	54	T	64	d	74	t
25	%	35	5	45	E	55	U	65	e	75	u
26	&	36	6	46	F	56	V	66	f	76	v
27	'	37	7	47	G	57	W	67	g	77	w
28	(	38	8	48	H	58	X	68	h	78	x
29	)	39	9	49	I	59	Y	69	i	79	y
2A	*	3A	:	4A	J	5A	Z	6A	j	7A	z
2B	+	3B	;	4B	K	5B	[	6B	k	7B	{
2C	,	3C	<	4C	L	5C	\	6C	l	7C	¦
2D	-	3D	=	4D	M	5D	}	6D	m	7D	}
2E	.	3E	>	4E	N	5E	^	6E	n	7E	~
2F	/	3F	?	4F	O	5F	_	6F	o	7F	rubout

HEXADECIMAL-TO-DECIMAL CONVERSION

On the next page, we furnish an easy-to-use listing that will permit you to make fast and accurate conversions between hex and decimal notations, and vice versa.

Hex	Dec	Hex	Dec	Hex	Dec	Hex	Dec	Hex	Dec	Hex	Dec
00	0	2B	43	56	86	81	129	AC	172	D7	215
01	1	2C	44	57	87	82	130	AD	173	D8	216
02	2	2D	45	58	88	83	131	AE	174	D9	217
03	3	2E	46	59	89	84	132	AF	175	DA	218
04	4	2F	47	5A	90	85	133	B0	176	DB	219
05	5	30	48	5B	91	86	134	B1	177	DC	220
06	6	31	49	5C	92	87	135	B2	178	DD	221
07	7	32	50	5D	93	88	136	B3	179	DE	222
08	8	33	51	5E	94	89	137	B4	180	DF	223
09	9	34	52	5F	95	8A	138	B5	181	E0	224
0A	10	35	53	60	96	8B	139	B6	182	E1	225
0B	11	36	54	61	97	8C	140	B7	183	E2	226
0C	12	37	55	62	98	8D	141	B8	184	E3	227
0D	13	38	56	63	99	8E	142	B9	185	E4	228
0E	14	39	57	64	100	8F	143	BA	186	E5	229
0F	15	3A	58	65	101	90	144	BB	187	E6	230
10	16	3B	59	66	102	91	145	BC	188	E7	231
11	17	3C	60	67	103	92	146	BD	189	E8	232
12	18	3D	61	68	104	93	147	BE	190	E9	233
13	19	3E	62	69	105	94	148	BF	191	EA	234
14	20	3F	63	6A	106	95	149	C0	192	EB	235
15	21	40	64	6B	107	96	150	C1	193	EC	236
16	22	41	65	6C	108	97	151	C2	194	ED	237
17	23	42	66	6D	109	98	152	C3	195	EE	238
18	24	43	67	6E	110	99	153	C4	196	EF	239
19	25	44	68	6F	111	9A	154	C5	197	F0	240
1A	26	45	69	70	112	9B	155	C6	198	F1	241
1B	27	46	70	71	113	9C	156	C7	199	F2	242
1C	28	47	71	72	114	9D	157	C8	200	F3	243
1D	29	48	72	73	115	9E	158	C9	201	F4	244
1E	30	49	73	74	116	9F	159	CA	202	F5	245
1F	31	4A	74	75	117	A0	160	CB	203	F6	246
20	32	4B	75	76	118	A1	161	CC	204	F7	247
21	33	4C	76	77	119	A2	162	CD	205	F8	248
22	34	4D	77	78	120	A3	163	CE	206	F9	249
23	35	4E	78	79	121	A4	164	CF	207	FA	250
24	36	4F	79	7A	122	A5	165	D0	208	FB	251
25	37	50	80	7B	123	A6	166	D1	209	FC	252
26	38	51	81	7C	124	A7	167	D2	210	FD	253
27	39	52	82	7D	125	A8	168	D3	211	FE	254
28	40	53	83	7E	126	A9	169	D4	212	FF	255
29	41	54	84	7F	127	AA	170	D5	213		
2A	42	55	85	80	128	AB	171	D6	214		

MULTIPLES OF 1K (1024), IN DECIMAL AND HEXADECIMAL

A "K" is simply a number that is equal to 1024 (decimal). It's a convenient number to use in the computer world since it's almost 1000 (decimal) and, at the same time, is exactly equal to 400 hex, both of which are nice round numbers. The numbers shown in the table listing are common memory sizes for 8-bit computers (which, in general, use a 16-bit address bus), thus limiting them to addresses smaller than FFFF (hex). Note: The "Hex − 1" column in the table shows the highest memory location in a computer with the given K-bytes of memory.

K	Decimal	Hex	Hex − 1
1K	1024	400	3FF
2K	2048	800	7FF
4K	4096	1000	FFF
8K	8192	2000	1FFF
16K	16384	4000	3FFF
20K	20480	5000	4FFF
32K	32768	8000	7FFF
48K	49152	C000	BFFF
56K	57344	E000	DFFF
64K	65536	10000	FFFF

DECIMAL, HEX, AND BINARY CONVERSION

In this section, we have a chart that will allow a fast and easy conversion between the three numerical value systems of decimal notation, hexadecimal notation, and binary notation.

Decimal	Hex	Binary
0	0	0 0 0 0
1	1	0 0 0 1
2	2	0 0 1 0
3	3	0 0 1 1
4	4	0 1 0 0
5	5	0 1 0 1
6	6	0 1 1 0
7	7	0 1 1 1
8	8	1 0 0 0
9	9	1 0 0 1
10	A	1 0 1 0
11	B	1 0 1 1
12	C	1 1 0 0
13	D	1 1 0 1
14	E	1 1 1 0
15	F	1 1 1 1

Summary of BDOS System Calls (For CP/M 2.2)

This appendix lists all of the 36 system calls used in CP/M 2.2. The typical calling sequences are written in DDT format for brevity. This means that all numbers in this column are in hexadecimal notation. No attempt is made to show how a returned value is dealt with following the call to BDOS "call 5." For more information on system calls, check the program examples in the text.

Function Number in C-register		Function	Value passed to function	Value returned by function	Typical calling sequence	Refer to page number
Dec	Hex					
0	00	System Reset	None	None	mvi c,0 call 5	68
1	01	Console Input	None	A = ASCII character	mvi c,1 call 5	63
2	02	Console Output	E = ASCII character	None	mvi c,2 mvi e,65 call 5	32
3	03	Reader Input	None	A = ASCII character	mvi c,3 call 5	96
4	04	Punch Output	E = ASCII character	None	mvi c,4 mvi e,65 call 5	98

Function Number in C-register		Function	Value passed to function	Value returned by function	Typical calling sequence	Refer to page number
Dec	Hex					
5	05	List Output (Printer)	E = ASCII character	None	mvi c,5 mvi e,65 call 5	93
6	06	Direct Console I/O (Input)	E = ff (hex)	A = 00 or A = ASCII character (note 1)	mvi c,6 mvi e,ff call 5	87
		Direct Console I/O (Output)	E = ASCII character	None	mvi c,6 mvi e,65 call 5	
7	07	Get I/O Byte	None	A = I/O byte value	mvi c,7 call 5	98
8	08	Set I/O Byte	E = I/O byte value	None	mvi c,8 mvi e,D2 call 5	105
9	09	Print String (see note 2)	DE = string address	None	mvi c,9 lxi d,200 call 5	72
10	0A	Read Console Buffer	DE = buffer address	Characters in buffer	mvi c,a lxi e,300 call 5	76
11	0B	Get Console Status	None	A = FF (hex) or A = 00	mvi c,b call 5	45
12	0C	Return Version Number	None	HL = version number	mvi c,c call 5	*
13	0D	Reset Disk System	None	None	mvi c,d call 5	*
14	0E	Select Disk	E = disk drive number	None	mvi c,e mvi e,2 call 5	*
15	0F	Open File	DE = FCB address	A = directory code (note 3)	mvi c,f lxi d,5c call 5	142
16	10	Close File	DE = FCB address	A = directory code (note 3)	mvi c,10 lxi d,5c call 5	173
17	11	Search For First	DE = FCB address	A = directory code (note 3)	mvi c,11 lxi d,5c call 5	210

Function Number in C-register Dec	Hex	Function	Value passed to function	Value returned by function	Typical calling sequence	Refer to page number
18	12	Search For Next	DE = FCB address	A = directory code (note 3)	mvi c,12 lxi d,5c call 5	214
19	13	Delete File (note 5)	DE = FCB address	A = directory code (note 3)	mvi c,13 lxi d,5c call 5	182
20	14	Read Sequential Record	DE = FCB address	A = directory code (note 4)	mvi c,14 lxi d,5c call 5	147
21	15	Write Sequential Record	DE = FCB address	A = directory code (note 4)	mvi c,15 lxi d,5c call 5	171
22	16	Make File	DE = FCB address	A = directory code (note 4)	mvi c,16 lxi d,5c call 5	170
23	17	Rename File	DE = FCB address	A = directory code (note 3)	mvi c,17 lxi d,5c call 5	*
24	18	Return Login Vector	None	HL = login vector	mvi c,18 call 18	*
25	19	Return Current Disk	None	A = current disk drive	mvi c,19 call 5	*
26	1A	Set DMA Address	DE = new DMA address	None	mvi c,1a lxi d,80 call 5	149
27	1B	Get Allocation Address	None	HL = allocation address	mvi c,1b call 5	*
28	1C	Write Protect Disk	None	None	mvi c,1c call 5	*
29	1D	Get Read/Only Vector	None	HL = read/only vector	mvi c,1d call 5	*
30	1E	Set File Attributes	DE = FCB address	A = directory code (note 3)	mvi c,1e lxi d,5c call 5	*
31	1F	Get Disk Parameters Address	None	HL = disk parameters address	mvi c,1f call 5	*

Function Number in C-register		Function	Value passed to function	Value returned by function	Typical calling sequence	Refer to page number
Dec	Hex					
32	20	Set User Code	E = user code (0 to 31)	None	mvi c,20 mvi e,1 call 5	*
		Get User Code	E = FF	A = user code	mvi c,20 call 5	
33	21	Read Random Record	DE = FCB address	A = error code (note 6)	mvi c,21 lxi d,5c call 5	185
34	22	Write Random Record	DE = FCB address	A = error code (note 6)	mvi c,22 lxi d,5c call 5	187
35	23	Compute File Size	DE = FCB address	bits r0, r1, r2 in FCB set to file size	mvi c,23 lxi d,5c call 5	196
36	24	Set Random	DE = FCB address	bits r0, r1, r2 in FCB set to record number	mvi c,24 lxi d,5c call 5	197

NOTES:

1. On Input, AA = 0 means no character is ready yet. Direct console I/O does not recognize the normal control codes (^P, ^S, etc.)
2. The string must terminate with a "$" character.
3. Directory Code (I)
   = FF if file cannot be found.
   = 0, 1, 2, or 3 if file found. Number corresponds to position of file entry in directory page.
4. Directory Code (II)
   = 00 if operation was successful.
   = nonzero if end-of-file (reading), disk full (writing), or directory full (make file).
5. Wildcards ("?" characters) can be used in the program name.
6. Error codes returned in random record operations:
   00 Operation successful.
   01 Reading unwritten data (read only).
   02 (Unused).
   03 Cannot close current extent.
   04 Seek to unwritten extent (read only).
   05 Directory overflow opening new extent (write only).
   06 Seek past physical end of disk.
7. The descriptions of the Functions marked with an asterisk (*) are not included in this book.

APPENDIX F

Summary of DDT Commands

This appendix summarizes the commands used in DDT. Except for the first section, which is about loading DDT, they are arranged in alphabetical order: A, D, F, G, H, I, L, M, R, S, T, U, and X.

LOADING DDT

From CP/M, type:

```
A>ddt
```

A COM or HEX program can be loaded into memory from the disk at the same time that DDT is loaded, by appending the program name to "ddt". (Different file extensions can be used for COM files, like "ddt".)

```
A>ddt testprog.com
A>ddt test110.ddt
```

DDT loads itself into the CCP area of high memory and also uses various parts of page zero. It loads the COM or HEX program into the TPA, starting at address 100 hex for COM files, and, at the starting address specified by the program, for HEX files.

"A" FOR ASSEMBLE

This command lets you type in programs in a symbolic format; that is, instructions mnemonics may be used, but not labels.

From DDT, type "a" followed by the address (in hex) where you want to start the assembly:

```
-a100
```

or

```
-a20B0
```

DDT responds with the address in memory of the next instruction:

You type symbolic instructions in this column.

```
-a100
100 mvi c,0
102 call 5
105 ret
106
```

Type a "return" when you're done.

DDT tells you the address of the next instruction.

"D" FOR DUMP MEMORY

"Dump" means to display a portion of memory in hexadecimal format. From DDT, type "d" followed by the starting address of the memory block you want to look at.

```
-d400
0400 41 0A 00 00 00 DE D0 00 01 B7 D8 AC 7E E9 42 43 A...........~.BC
```

(16 lines will be displayed)

ASCII equivalents to the hex values are printed on the right, with periods used for nonprintable values.

If no ending address is specified, 16 lines of 16 bytes each are displayed. An ending address can also be used, following the starting address:

```
-d400,42f
```

This will cause the dump to stop when the ending address is reached (in this case, after 3 lines).

If neither a starting nor an ending address is typed, 16 lines will be dumped starting at the last address used (initially 100, when DDT is loaded).

"F" FOR FILL

This command is used to fill an area of memory with a constant hex value. After "f", type the starting address, the ending address, and the constant that is to be filled in (all in hex):

```
-f400,500,ff
```

will fill the block of memory from 400 to 500 with the value ff. The constant must be a one-byte value–in the range 0 to ff hex.

"G" FOR GO

This command is used to transfer control to a program at a particular address in memory–in other words, to execute the program. The usual form is "g" followed by the starting address:

```
-g100
```

which will cause the program that starts at 100 hex to be executed. It is similar to a jump instruction in assembly language, or a GOTO in BASIC. A "g" to location 0 brings you back to CP/M (with a cold boot):

```
-g0
A>
```

Note that the only way to get back to DDT once you've used "g" is is to have your program end with an "RST 7" instruction (or you can use breakpoints).

You can also use the "g" command to set "breakpoints," which are temporary jumps back to DDT that are inserted automatically in your program and then deleted once they've been used. Breakpoints are useful if you want to execute only a portion of a program that you're debugging. You insert a breakpoint at the end of the section you want to execute, and DDT will regain control from your program at that point, leaving your program unchanged in memory. Thus, only the section of your program between the starting address (the first address specified in the "g" command) and the breakpoint (the second address specified) will be executed.

Either one or two breakpoint addresses can be typed following the starting address:

```
-g100,124         Sets a breakpoint at 124.
-g100,127,13d     Sets breakpoints at 127 and 13d.
```

"H" FOR HEXADECIMAL ARITHMETIC

DDT can be used to perform addition and subtraction of hexadecimal numbers, using the "H" command. After "h", type the two numbers separated by a comma:

```
-h980,bc00 <------ You type this.
C580,4D80  <------ DDT types this.
 ^    ^
 |    |
 |    +----------- Difference of 980 and BC00.
 +---------------- Sum of 980 and BC00.
```

"I" COMMAND

See the "R" Command.

"L" FOR LIST

This command is used to list a program in disassembled symbolic form (as opposed to dumping it in hex numbers with "d"). It can be thought of as the inverse operation of the "A" command.

If you type a "l" followed by an address, 12 lines of instructions will be displayed:

```
-l100 <---------- You type this.
100 MVI A,50 }
102 STA 01FE } DDT displays this.
105 MVI C,A  }
etc.
```

You can also specify an ending address, in which case, the last address displayed will be the one you specify:

```
-l100,116
```

If no address is specified, disassembly will start at the current line, which is initially 100 when DDT is loaded, but which is set to the last line displayed whenever "l" is used.

```
-l
```

"M" FOR MOVE

"M" allows the contents of one block of memory to be moved to another part of memory. After "b", type the starting address of the block to be moved, the ending address of the block to be moved, and the address that the block is to be moved to.

```
-m100,124,200
   ^   ^   ^
   |   |   |___ Starting address of destination block.
   |   |_______ Ending address of source block.
   |___________ Starting address of source block.
```

"R" FOR READ

This command is used in conjunction with the "I" command to permit DDT to read a program from the disk into the Transient Program area (TPA) of memory. Once in memory, the program can either be executed by DDT, or debugged using any of DDT's various commands. Either COM or HEX files may be loaded, although COM files can be given different file types, like "DDT."

Before this command is used, the "I" command is used to insert the name of the COM or HEX program into the File Control Block at 5C hex. To do this, simply type the name of the program, along with its file type, following "i":

```
-itestprog.hex
```

Now to actually read the program into the TPA, type "r":

```
-r
```

COM files will be loaded at 100 hex and HEX files will be loaded at the address that you specified in the "end" statement of the ASM file when you created the program. Make sure the program does not overwrite the zero page (0 to ff hex), since DDT uses this area.

Note that using "i" and "r" together like this has the same effect as loading in the COM or HEX program when you first load DDT:

```
A>ddt testprog.hex
```

is the same as

```
A>ddt
-itestprog.hex
-r
```

An optional offset can also be used with the "R" command. This causes the program to be loaded into a different address than the one that it normally would be; that is, 100 hex for COM files and the address specified in the ASM file's "end" statement for HEX files. The new address is found by adding the offset to the normal address–that is, the offset is the difference between the new address and the normal one. To use this option, type the offset after the "r":

```
-r40
```

If, in this case, a COM file had already been specified by the "I" command, the program would be loaded at 140, since 100 (the normal loading address of COM files) plus 40 equals 140.

"S" FOR SET MEMORY

This command lets you insert hexadecimal values into memory. It is invoked by typing "s" followed by the address at which you want to start inserting values. It responds by typing a line number and the current contents of the line:

```
-s110
110 B5
```

You can now type in a new value or, if you want to leave this address unchanged, you can simply press "return" to go on to the next address. A period is used to terminate the function.

```
            ┌──── You type numbers in this column.
            │
-s110       ↓
110 B5 c0
111 00 b6
112 00     ←──── Nothing is inserted here; "return" leaves current value unchanged.
113 2D c9
114 76 0
114 7F .   ←──── Type period to terminate function.
-
```

"T" FOR TRACE

Tracing is a very clever function whereby DDT can execute the instructions of your program and at the same time keep control of the computer itself, so that it can print out all sorts of useful information about what your program is doing.

The information printed out consists of the contents of the various 8080 registers. To use this command, you must first have your program in memory ready to be executed. You then type a "t" followed by the number of instructions you want to see executed, in hexadecimal.

For example, we show in Listing F-1 what happens when you load and then use "t" to trace the first 8 instructions of the program "barber.ddt" from Chapter 2 in this book.

Listing F-1. Using "T" for Trace

```
A>ddt barber.ddt
DDT VERS 2.2
NEXT  PC
0200 0100
-t8
COZOMOEOIO A=00 B=0000 D=0000 H=0000 S=0100 P=0100 MVI E,20
COZOMOEOIO A=00 B=0000 D=0020 H=0000 S=0100 P=0102 MVI C,02
COZOMOEOIO A=00 B=0002 D=0020 H=0000 S=0100 P=0104 PUSH D
COZOMOEOIO A=00 B=0002 D=0020 H=0000 S=00FE P=0105 CALL 0005
COZOMOEOIO A=00 B=0002 D=0020 H=0000 S=00FC P=0005 JMP A800
COZOMOEOIO A=00 B=0002 D=0020 H=0000 S=00FC P=A800 JMP AEA2
COZOMOEOIO A=00 B=0002 D=0020 H=0000 S=00FC P=AEA2 XTHL
COZOMOEOIO A=00 B=0002 D=0020 H=0108 S=00FC P=AEA3 SHLD B74A
```

Contents of flags.

C = carry
Z = zero
M = minus
E = even parity
I = interdigit carry

Contents of A-register.

Contents of BC register.

Contents of DE register.

Contents of HL register.

Contents of stack pointer.

Contents of program counter.

Instruction executed.

"U" FOR UNTRACE

This command is very similar to trace, except that nothing is printed out. You simply type "u" and the number (in hex) of the instructions you want DDT to execute:

```
-u10
```

This is useful if you want to trace a particular segment of your program using "t," but this part isn't at the start of the program. Using "u," you can skip over the first part of your program without the printout (which can be time-consuming for even a few hundred instructions), but, at the same time, let DDT keep control of the program so that it will stop at the point you want it to. Once these initial instructions have been "untraced," that is, traced without printing, you can trace the next, defective, group of instructions using "t."

Thus, if you know, for example, that your program executes a loop of say, 10 instructions correctly five times, but does something incorrect on the sixth iteration of the loop, you can say:

```
-u50 ←—— Skips over 50 good instructions.
-t10 ←—— Traces 10 bad instructions.
```

"X" FOR EXAMINE REGISTERS

It's often helpful to be able to look at—and alter—the contents of the various 8080 registers when you're trying to debug a program. The "x" command lets you do both these things. You can also examine and change the contents of the flags. To do this, you type "x" followed by a one-letter mnemonic for the register that you want to look at or modify. For instance,

```
-xp          ←—— If you type this,
P=1024 100 ←—— DDT will respond with "P=1024", the contents of the program
-                 counter.
       └——— You change it to 100 hex by typing the number in this column. If
              you only type a carriage return, the number is unchanged.
```

Sometimes you have to type a 4-digit hex number, as in the case of the registers BC, DE, HL, the program counter P, and the stack pointer S. For the A-register, you must type a 2-digit number and, for the flags, you must type a single binary digit: 0 or 1.

Here's a list of the mnemonics used for the various registers, together with the range of values that can be put into them:

A	A-register	0 to FF
B	BC-register	0 to FFFF
D	DE-register	0 to FFFF
H	HL-register	0 to FFFF
S	Stack Pointer	0 to FFFF
P	Program Counter	0 to FFFF
M	Minus Flag	0 to 1
C	Carry Flag	0 to 1
Z	Zero Flag	0 to 1
E	Even Parity Flag	0 to 1
I	Interdigit (Auxiliary) Carry Flag	0 to 1

Notice that if you want to put just a 2-digit (8 bit) number into, say, the B-register, you must put an entire 4-digit (16 bit) number into the BC-register. With the "x" command, there is no way to work with the B, C, D, E, H, or L registers as separate 8-bit registers.

APPENDIX G

Summaries of Programs Used and Locations of Instruction Descriptions

This appendix provides an itemized listing of the programs used in this book and the instruction descriptions given in the book. They are arranged by chapter for your convenience.

PROGRAMS USED

Alongside each program name is a short description of what it does.

Chapter 2

test.ddt	Prints "HI" returns to DDT.
test1.ddt	Prints series of "HLs".
test2.ddt	Prints "HIs" with Check Console Status.
barber.ddt	Prints ASCII characters.
test3.ddt	Beeps keyboard.
test4.ddt	Beep with ^C escape.
test4.com	Beep with RET instead of RST.

Chapter 3

test5.ddt	Print string.
test6.ddt	Read console buffer.
test7.ddt	Read console and print string.
namedisp.ddt	Parabola name display.
test8.ddt	Direct console I/O.
test9.ddt	Password.
test10.ddt	Type to printer.
test11.ddt	Get I/O byte.

Chapter 4

test1.asm	Assembled version of test1.ddt.
decibin.hex	Decimal to binary routine.
binihex.asm	Binary to hex routine.
decihex.asm	Decimal to hex conversion.

Chapter 5

test100.ddt	Open file.
test101.ddt	Open file, return directory code.
test102.ddt	Read record.
test103.ddt	Read record with DMA at 400.
test104.ddt	Read record, DMA at 400, print directory code.
type2.com	Imitates CP/M TYPE function.
lines.com	Counts lines in a file.

Chapter 6

test105.ddt	Write sequential record.
store.asm	Store text in file (add to existing file).
store2.asm	Store text in file (delete existing file).
test106.ddt	Read random record.
test107.ddt	Write random record (new file).
test108.ddt	Write random record (old file).
randymod.asm	Modify a random record.
store3.asm	Version of store using compute file size.

Chapter 7

test109.ddt	Search For First (in disk directory).
test110.ddt	Search For First and next.
test111.ddt	Save erased file.
words.asm	Counts words in file, uses wildcards.

Chapter 8

binihex2	Decimal to hex converter.
binihex3	Version to be relocated in memory.
binihex4	Version to be POKEd in from BASIC.
LOADHEX.BAS	BASIC program to load HEX files.
hexibin2	Hex to decimal converter (runs from BASIC).
ucase	Convert lowercase letters to uppercase.

DESCRIPTIONS OF INSTRUCTIONS

Alongside each instruction is listed the specific section in the chapter where the instruction is described.

Chapter 2

MVI	Console Out
CALL	Console Out
RST	Console Out
JMP	Console Out
ORA	Get Console Status
JZ	Get Console Status
PUSH	Get Console Status
POP	Get Console Status
INR	Get Console Status
MOV	Get Console Status
CPI	Get Console Status
JNZ	Get Console Status
RET	Console Input
INR	Get Console Status

Chapter 3

LXI	Print String
STA	Read Console Buffer
DCR	Name Display Program
INX	Direct Console I/O
LDA	List Output
RLC	Get I/O Byte
ANI	Get I/O Byte
ADI	Get I/O Byte

Chapter 4

RM	Decibin Routine
RP	Decibin Routine
SUI	Decibin Routine
DAD	Decibin Routine

Chapter 5

SHLD	Lines Program
LHLD	Lines Program

Chapter 7

SPHL	Words Program
LDAX	Words Program
STAX	Words Program
XCHG	Words Program

Chapter 9

IN	Printer Driver
OUT	Printer Driver
XRI	Printer Driver

Index

C

D

T

U

W

X

Y

Z

TO THE READER

Sams Computer books cover Fundamentals — Programming — Interfacing — Technology written to meet the needs of computer engineers, professionals, scientists, technicians, students, educators, business owners, personal computerists and home hobbyists.

Our Tradition is to meet your needs and in so doing we invite you to tell us what your needs and interests are by completing the following:

1. I need books on the following topics:

____
____
____
____
____
____
____
____

2. I have the following Sams titles:

____
____
____
____
____
____
____
____

3. My occupation is:

_____ Scientist, Engineer
_____ Personal computerist
_____ Technician, Serviceman
_____ Educator
_____ Student
_____ D P Professional
_____ Business owner
_____ Computer store owner
_____ Home hobbyist
Other ______________________________
____

Name (print)____
Address____
City ______________________State ____________Zip ____________

Mail to: **Howard W. Sams & Co., Inc.**
Marketing Dept. #CBS1/80
4300 W. 62nd St., P.O. Box 7092
Indianapolis, Indiana 46206

22030

Need Other Books in the Sams/Waite Primer Series?

YOUR OWN COMPUTER (2nd Edition)
Shows how to choose a computer for your own uses and explores applications, buzzwords, programs, hardware, and peripherals for 30 different models.
Waite and Pardee
No. 21860 . . . . **$8.95**

BASIC PROGRAMMING PRIMER (2nd Edition)
Gives you fundamental BASIC keywords, statements, and functions usable with the IBM® PC, Apple® II, or any other computer running a variation of Microsoft BASIC. Also covers advanced BASIC, new game program listings, more.
Waite and Pardee
No. 22014 . . . . **$17.95**

MICROCOMPUTER PRIMER (2nd Edition)
Shows you basic computer concepts, the electronics behind the logic, what happens inside the computer as a program runs, and a little about languages and operating systems.
Waite and Pardee
No. 21653 . . . . **$14.50**

COMPUTER GRAPHICS PRIMER
A classic Sams best seller that helps you learn all types of graphics programming, including animation. Many program examples written in Applesoft.
Mitchell Waite
No. 21650 . . . . **$15.95**

C™ PRIMER PLUS
A clear, complete introduction to the C language that guides you in the fundamentals, covers use of Microcomputer C with assembly language, and contains many sample programs usable with any standard C compiler.
Waite, Prata, and Martin
No. 22090 . . . . **$17.95**

SuperCalc® PRIMER
Makes it much easier for you to find your way out of a sticky calculation, hit the right keys to get a given answer, or otherwise get the most out of your SuperCalc spreadsheet program. Fully illustrated.
Waite, Burns, and Venit
No. 22087 . . . . **$9.95**

TIMEX SINCLAIR BASIC PRIMER, WITH GRAPHICS
Easiest, most effective introduction ever to computers and programming. Graphics let you "see" your commands work as your own programs gradually develop into realities.
Waite and Chapnick
No. 22077 . . . . **$9.95**

UNIX™ PRIMER PLUS
Presents the elements of UNIX clearly, simply, and accurately, for ready understanding by anyone in any field who needs to learn, use, or work with UNIX in some way. Fully illustrated.
Waite, Martin, and Prata
No. 22028 . . . . **$19.95**

SOUL OF CP/M® : HOW TO USE THE HIDDEN POWER OF YOUR CP/M SYSTEM
Teaches you how to use and modify CP/M's internal features, use CP/M system calls, and more. You'll need to read *CP/M PRIMER,* or be otherwise familiar with CP/M's outer-layer utilities.
Waite and Lafore
No. 22030 . . . . **$18.95**

CP/M BIBLE: THE AUTHORITATIVE REFERENCE GUIDE TO CP/M
Gives you instant, one-stop access to all CP/M keywords, commands, utilities, conventions, and more. A must for any computerist using any version of CP/M.
Waite and Angermeyer
No. 22015 . . . . **$19.95**

CP/M PRIMER (2nd Edition)
Completely updated to give you the know-how to begin working with new or old CP/M versions immediately. Includes CP/M terminology, operation, capabilities, internal structure, and more.
Waite and Murtha
No. 22170 . . . . **$16.95**

PASCAL PRIMER
Guides you swiftly through Pascal program structure, procedures, variables, decision making statements, and numeric functions. Contains many useful examples and eight appendices.
Waite and Fox
No. 21793 . . . . **$17.95**

SAMS BOOK & SOFTWARE ORDER CARD

Catalog No.	Qty.	Price	Total	Catalog No.	Qty.	Price	Total

☐ Check ☐ Money Order
☐ MasterCard ☐ Visa

Subtotal	
Add local tax where applicable	
Add Handling Charge	2.00
Total Amount Enclosed	

Account Number ______________ Expires ______________

Name (print ______________

Signature ______________

Address ______________

City ______________ State ______________ Zip ______________

Offer good in USA only. Prices subject to change without notice. Full payment must accompany your order. **X0438**

Call 1-800-428-3696 for the name of your nearest Sams retailer or distributor (residents in IN, AK, HI call 317-298-5566).

If your retailer or distributor doesn't stock the Sams publication you need, you can order it through him or directly from us. Orders placed directly with us are subject to a $2.00 additional handling charge per order.

PHONE ORDERS

Depending on where you live, call either number listed above and charge your Sams publication to your VISA or MASTERCARD.

MAIL ORDERS

Use the order form below, or if it's missing, send your order on a plain piece of paper.

(1) Include your name, street or RD address, city, state, and zip.

(2) Tell us the titles of the books you need, the product numbers (see other side of this card) and the quantity of each one you'd like.

(3) Add up the total cost for the books, add your state's sales tax if applicable, and then add $2.00 for handling.

(4) Include your check or money order for the full amount due, or

(5) Charge it to your VISA or MASTER CARD. To charge it, list your account number and the card expiration date. Shipping charges will be added to credit card orders.

(6) Mail your order to:
Howard W. Sams & Co., Inc.
Dept. No. X0438
4300 West 62nd St., P.O. Box 7092
Indianapolis, Indiana 46206

In Canada, contact Lenbrook Electronics, Markham, Ontario L3R 1H2

All books available from Sams Distributors, Bookstores, and Computer Stores. Offer good in U.S. only. Note: Distributor, Computer Store and Dealer inquiries are welcome.

See other side for list of Sams/Waite Primers and their prices.

Place
Stamp
Here

HOWARD W. SAMS & CO., INC.

4300 WEST 62ND STREET P.O.BOX 7092
INDIANAPOLIS, INDIANA 46206